Teaching Management

How can every management class be a dynamic, unforgettable experience? This much-needed book distills over half a century of the authors' combined experience as university professors, consultants, and advisors to corporate training departments. In a lively, hands-on fashion, it describes the fundamental elements in every learning situation, allowing readers to adapt the suggestions to their particular teaching context. It sparks reflection on what we do in the classroom, why we do it, and how it might be done more effectively. The chapters are broadly organized according to things done before class, during class, and in between and after class, so that every instructor, whether newly minted Ph.D.s facing their first classroom experience, experienced faculty looking to polish their teaching techniques, consultants who want to have more impact, or corporate trainers wishing to develop in-house teaching skills, can benefit from the invaluable advice given.

James G. S. Clawson and Mark E. Haskins are Professors of Business Administration at the Darden Graduate School of Business Administration, University of Virginia.

Advance praise for *Teaching Management*

"I have never understood why the academic world does so little to prepare new faculty members for the most important work they do – teaching. Now that Jim Clawson and Mark Haskins have created this thoughtful field guide to the complex issues and problems inherent in teaching any subject matter, omitting this work as preparation would be like sending soldiers to battle without ammunition or armor. The many insights in this book are gleaned from a career in education and from imparting it to new faculty at the Darden School – known for outstanding educators – and we should all be grateful that so much wisdom has at last been codified."
Allan R. Cohen, *Edward A. Madden Professor and Director of Corporate Entrepreneurship, Babson College*

"Bravo! Finally a book that acknowledges academia's best-kept secret – no one's been teaching the professor how to teach. Clawson and Haskins have created a practical guide that explores both the magic and mechanics of good teaching and learning. The mix of theory and practice, accessible writing style, and structured opportunities for readers to think about their own teaching make this a wonderful resource for young educators and seasoned veterans alike."
Joan V. Gallos, *Professor of Leadership, Henry W. Bloch School of Business and Public Administration and former Dean of the School of Education, University of Missouri-Kansas City*

"At our Leadership Learning Center in Eastern Kazakhstan, working with Darden, KIMEP and KAFU, we have been lacking the essential tool for ensuring that we can confidently and consistently bring first-class instruction to our leaders in-country, in their native tongue. We have been searching for the appropriate 'train-the-trainer tool' and Clawson's and Haskin's book has fulfilled this need by helping us to transform our instruction style successfully."
Dale Perry, *President, AES Kazakhstan*

"In one well-organized volume, Clawson and Haskins have created a comprehensive, engaging, and useful handbook for new and experienced management educators. Students of business administration,

degree and nondegree, will be the real beneficiaries of this extraordinary work by two master teachers."
John W. Rosenblum, *Dean Emeritus, Darden Graduate School of Business Administration, University of Virginia*

"Clawson and Haskins have made an outstanding contribution to the teaching field! This is an excellent resource for experienced teachers, and should be required reading for all new doctoral students in the management disciplines."
Roy J. Lewicki, *Fisher College of Business, The Ohio State University*

"The best sales person often gets promoted to be head of sales. The most brilliant engineer is frequently elevated to run the engineering department. And, an impressive background in management research and theory is often enough to qualify for a position with a consulting firm or a professorship at a business school. But, there is no intrinsic correlation between expertise in sales, engineering or management research/theory and the ability to teach or lead others. This brilliant book will show you how to bridge the gap! And, if you are already a skilled teacher, you will find this book to be an inspiration and guide to even greater effectiveness."
Michael J. Gelb, author of *How to Think Like Leonardo DaVinci* and *Discover Your Genius*

"Wondering why your MBAs or executives seem uninterested in or resistant to what you teach? Want to know how to plan a course and class, choose the right method, develop new materials, employ technology effectively and evaluate students in a way that develops them? Grounded soundly in the precepts of adult learning, this book is an excellent A to Z guide to making you an inspiring and effective teacher of management."
Michael Beer, *Professor Emeritus, Harvard Business School and Chairman, Center for Organizational Fitness*

"*Teaching Management* is a unique and valuable resource for those who want their teaching to be relevant to the knowledge, motivating to the student, and effective in achieving lasting learning. Firmly grounded in learning theory, it shows how to prepare and present in ways that

are based upon a lifetime of success in teaching. Jim Clawson and Mark Haskins have done a wonderful service to those who aspire to be successful in the classroom."
Nicholas Fritz, *President, Knowledge Implementation Corporation*

"In *Teaching Management*, Jim Clawson and Mark Haskins have done an excellent job of detailing the preparation necessary to make a class appear spontaneous. I am glad they took the time to share their principles, which they have used so capably in the classroom."
Jay Kloosterboer, *Executive Vice President – Business Excellence, AES Corporation*

"Reading this book is like getting a teaching certificate in management education. Two master teachers themselves, Clawson and Haskins have achieved an amazing balance between learning theory and practical, engaging approaches, between the rigor of academia and the interactive demands of corporate learners. Their encyclopedic survey of teaching methods ranges from valuable insights on classical approaches such as the case method all the way to action learning and simulations. This is the most comprehensive book on teaching business management that has ever been written. Both corporate trainers and management professors will return to it again and again for more insights and value."
David Giber, Ph.D., *Senior Vice President, Linkage, Inc., 25 years of experience in developing managers*

"For the first time in my professional career I have found a rare gem – a book that in a clear, structured, conceptually sound and yet engaging way distils the wisdom of the teaching profession. Most management teachers at the best business schools in the world have received a formidable academic education, but are self-trained in terms of their teaching skills. This excellent book provides valuable support for novices, and allows more experienced teachers to discover that what they have been doing for years fits into a 'greater design' and that there are more tricks of the trade to learn."
Nenad Filipović, Ph.D., *Professor of General Management, IEDC – Bled School of Management, Slovenia*

"Clawson and Haskins do an exceptional job of reminding management professors of the theoretical aspects of teaching and the practical challenges of executing the vision of the chief executive. The text reminds the reader (and professors) of the breadth of knowledge and skills that are necessary to successfully manage and lead businesses of virtually any size. They succinctly discuss the range of topics that business students deserve to understand before graduating and the power of learning through the case study approach. Although perhaps intended for professors, I found this a motivating and instructive text for helping me identify opportunities for making my firm more successful."

Dennis J. Paustenbach, *President and CEO, ChemRisk*

Teaching Management

A Field Guide for Professors, Corporate Trainers, and Consultants

James G. S. Clawson
AND
Mark E. Haskins

CAMBRIDGE
UNIVERSITY PRESS

CAMBRIDGE UNIVERSITY PRESS
Cambridge, New York, Melbourne, Madrid, Cape Town, Singapore, São Paulo

Cambridge University Press
The Edinburgh Building, Cambridge CB2 2RU, UK

Published in the United States of America by Cambridge University Press, New York

www.cambridge.org
Information on this title: www.cambridge.org/9780521689861

First published 2006

Printed in the United Kingdom at the University Press, Cambridge

A catalogue record for this publication is available from the British Library

ISBN-13 978-0-521-86975-1 hardback
ISBN-10 0-521-86975-7 hardback

ISBN-13 978-0-521-68986-1 paperback
ISBN-10 0-521-68986-4 paperback

Contents

Figures

Sources to chapter quotations

The opening chapter quotations have been obtained from the following sources: Ch. 2: E. Schein, *Organizational Culture and Leadership*, Jossey-Bass, 1985; ch. 3: T. Szasz, *Second Sin*, Doubleday, 1973 and J. Keats, in a letter to George and Georgiana Keats dated March 19, 1819; ch. 4: M. Thatcher, "Let Our Children Grow Tall," a speech to the Institute of Socio-Economic Studies, September 15, 1975; ch. 5: from an anonymous article, "Teacher's Task Defined by President of Harvard," *New York Times*, March 22, 1959; ch. 6 from an article by J. Kaufman, "A New Species of Instruction," *Wall Street Journal*, May 8, 2002; ch. 7: a twist on the common proverb, "A picture is worth a thousand words"; ch. 8: "Sophist," translated by B. Jowett, in M. Adler (ed.), *Great Books of the Western World: Plato*, Encyclopedia Britannica, Inc. 1992; ch. 9: J. Locke, *An Essay Concerning Human Understanding*, Prometheus, 1994; ch. 10: in J. Griffith, *Speaker's Library of Business Stories, Anecdotes, and Humor*, Prentice-Hall, 1990; ch. 11: G. Pool at www.quotationspage.com/quote/31298.html; ch. 12: "Nicomachean Ethics," translated by W. D. Ross, in M. Adler (ed.), *Great Books of the Western World: Aristotle II*, Encyclopedia Britannica, Inc. 1992 and R. Revans, *The Origins and Growth of Action Learning*, Chartwell-Bratt, 1982; chs. 13 and 14: common proverbs; ch. 15: O. Wilde at www.quotationsbook.com/quotes/22286/view; ch. 16: T. Carlyle, *Sartor Resartus* (Oxford World's Classics), Oxford University Press, 2000; ch. 17: T. Masson at www.quotationsbook.com/quotes/1295/view and M. S. Peck, *The Road Less Traveled*, Simon & Schuster, 1978; ch. 18: T. Groneberg, *The Secret Life of Cowboys*, Scribner, 2003; ch. 19: G. Highet, *The Art of Teaching*, Alfred A. Knopf, 1950; ch. 20: P. Frost and R. Stablein, *Doing Exemplary Research*, Sage Publications, 1992; ch. 21: from an anonymously written news item titled, "View from the Bridge," *Time*, November 17, 1958; ch. 22: in J. Griffith, *Speaker's Library of Business Stories, Anecdotes, and*

Humor, Prentice-Hall, 1990; ch. 23: C. Baudelaire, *My Heart Laid Bare & Other Essays*, Haskell House, 1974; ch. 24: B. Berenson at www.quotationsbook.com/quotes/41122/view; ch. 25: G. Greene, *The Power and the Glory*, Penguin, 1982; ch. 26: a popular version of a similar quote from M. Twain, *Tom Sawyer Abroad*, Tor Books, 1993; ch. 27: J. Fogarty, from his song *Centerfield*, Concord Music Group, 1985.

Why this book on teaching management?

JAMES G. S. CLAWSON AND
MARK E. HASKINS

I (Jim) remember my first calculus course. It was at a school recognized by many as one of the top two or three schools in the world. The instructor was a graduate student, a gentleman working on his Ph.D. in mathematics. He was a nice enough man, soft-spoken and relatively congenial before and after class. He even seemed mildly interested in the various nonmathematical events happening around him – Watergate, Vietnam, and the pollution of the environment. Yet when class began, he turned into a creature from another planet: he turned his back on the class and began lecturing (speaking into the board rather), bouncing his words off the board in a spray pattern that drifted over us and settled ever so lightly on our young heads. He wrote fast, and we wrote fast. Sometimes we'd stop writing and raise our hands, but the instructor, his eyes somewhat glazed over by the beauty of the equations and mathematical connections he was painting, often did not see us, or ignored us, and continued until his cognitive cantata was completely composed and the final chord sounded. Then, holding the chalk lightly like a baton between his thumb and index finger, and characteristically giving an ebullient wave of his writing hand, he would turn and face us with a thin, satiated smile and ask, "Any questions?" the true meaning of which was, "True mathematicians (musicians) will have understood and felt the beauty of this development and will appreciate its elegance. Let's not disrupt the effect of the whole by dissecting its parts for the less-educated or -sophisticated."

I've lost count of how many times I've sat in such classes at a business school or a corporate university or talked with others who have. Although good people and good scholars, instructors of this kind are ill-prepared to initiate others into their fields. One wonders how they were able to grasp the subject and become enamored of it, assuming they met similar initiations.

I (Mark) remember my first year as a faculty member at the Darden School. If imitation is the greatest form of flattery, Ray Smith, a veteran

1

Darden School professor whose fifty-eight accounting classes I sat in on and tried to emulate later that day in my own, was flattered probably more than he ever had been in his life. I will admit it now, some 20 years later, that I was clueless. I had never taught MBA students before. I had never taught case method before. I had never taught a class with 60 students in it before. I had never taught such bright and gifted students before. Not only was I clueless, but I was also willing to try almost anything I saw Ray do. Alas, that was not a good idea. Not because Ray was not a great teacher – he was. Rather, it was because I was not Ray. I did not have his personality, his manner, his unique experiences, or even his opinions and views on the subject matter.

Fortunately, I survived that first semester and learned an important lesson – there are indeed certain teaching fundamentals, nuances, and "tricks of the trade" that can be learned, *and* I had to have the courage, the professional dedication, and the willingness to work at operationalizing those fundamentals in ways that fit who I was. To this day, it continues to be a process of exploration and experimentation. Classroom ideas get tested; some are discarded, some are kept. I wish I had had this volume when I first started teaching, if for no other reason than to have accelerated and enhanced the development of my teaching. My one hope for this book is that it does that, in some small way, for those who read it. I believe, like Jim, that we have a sacred trust as teachers to foster our students' learning of subject matter but also their interest in learning itself. Therefore, I invite you to dedicate yourself to the teaching craft – to envisioning the classroom as if it were full of your own children (or full of your best friends) for whom you want to deliver your very best. I invite you to use this volume as both a call to arms to invest in your teaching and as a modest collection of ideas to spark your own discovery of how to be a bit better at teaching than you already are.

This volume is intended for several audiences. As we have written the chapters and distilled some of the teaching insights we wanted to share, we had business school doctoral students and newly appointed business school instructors in mind. Also prominent in our thinking were business school faculty who were not necessarily new to the teaching profession but who were still (or newly) interested in raising their game, so to speak. We also have spent many years working with corporate trainers and consultants who are regularly called on to instruct others to design instructional experiences and/or materials and who face the challenge of creating memorable, powerful learning experiences. To all of them, we offer some insights we've developed over the years to increase teaching effectiveness. Each of the groups faces some interesting challenges.

Doctoral students

Stories like the ones we shared, even though they are our own, worry us. They worry us in light of emerging data on the relative academic preparation of American students compared with students of other countries. They worry us in light of the number of Ph.D.s who are produced and annually enter the ranks of university faculty. They worry us when we see students in class who are unable to demonstrate ability with subjects they've taken before. They worry us when we leave a classroom and walk back to our office wondering how many came away from our classes with a similar experience. They worry us because we do not believe we have had atypical educational experiences.

The widespread lack of attention in the United States to university teacher training is unfortunate and, we would even assert, unethical. Roughly 600 colleges and universities in North America offer doctoral programs in business. Some of those schools have a practical teaching requirement – that is, one that requires students to teach courses before they leave. But even those schools leave learning about teaching to onthejob training. Only a small number of business school doctoral programs require formal education in adult learning theory, teaching theory, and teaching techniques. In the end, graduate business schools certify to the world that their doctoral graduates are two things – researchers and teachers – yet virtually all of those graduates' formal training is focused on research methodology and technique.

One argument says that Ph.D.s are primarily researchers and therefore don't need instructor training. We believe that presents a falsely narrow view of the careers they will lead. Yes, they will (we hope) conduct research and add to the body of knowledge in their fields. They will also, however, be put in the classroom almost immediately, often by administrators who don't understand their field, and be confronted with a room full of students, sometimes as many as 700 at a time. That is not a formula for a world-class learning experience. If instructors are not interested in, or well prepared for, facilitating their students' learning, is not sensitive to variations in learning styles, and is not committed to student learning more than instructor professing, the all too frequent and deplorable consequences are that students merely endure the class, cram for the exam, pass by the skin of their teeth, and leave the course unchanged, perhaps even jaded, by the experience. That experience may significantly shape their interest in the subject matter, their ability to build on basic concepts for higher level training, and eventually impact the shape of their careers. Rather than turning students onto a field, we are, in many cases, turning students off because we ignore, or at best, marginalize, the teaching craft.

Graduate business schools, we believe, have a responsibility to teach their graduates not only how to do research, but also how to teach. For some schools that responsibility is manifest in nothing more than cheap labor to staff introductory courses. In others, courses on teaching are offered only in the related school of education for those students who choose to swim upstream across departmental boundaries. Few graduate business schools require course work on adult learning and pedagogy for the doctoral degree – despite the fact that most of those graduates will soon be teaching.

The underlying philosophy seems to be that if a doctoral student is bright, experienced in attending classes, and – by virtue of his or her research and academic training – has something to say, that person will be an acceptable teacher. The related underlying assumption is that learning about teaching is not worthwhile, that teaching is simple and easy. In some schools, that philosophy is taught explicitly. Doctoral students and new professors alike are told that they should focus their time on research and not worry about the quality of their teaching above some sadly minimal level. Indeed, the message is often sent that time and energy spent on teaching is not merely a non-career-enhancing endeavor, but actually a negative effort since it diverts time from research. In such a milieu, learning about teaching, talking about teaching, practicing teaching, and developing skill at teaching are posited as a waste of time.

One thesis of this volume is simply that newly minted Ph.D.s in business should be taught how to teach. We ought to require all Ph.D. candidates to receive formal training in teaching. We ought to grade them on how well they can teach, and we ought to encourage them, as we do in regard to their research, to plan on continuing to learn about teaching throughout their careers. We ought to hold conferences and circulate published insights about how to teach more effectively.

Teaching should not be isolated to the purview of the schools of education. Biologists, chemists, physicists, accountants, mathematicians, historians, language instructors, and management scholars should all have teacher training including an emphasis on the value of excellent teaching as part of their doctoral-level certification.

There are others who feel that way. Ph.D. program teaching requirements at the Harvard Business School, the University of Virginia, Babson College, Georgia Tech, and Texas A&M, among others, demonstrate the growing awareness of the need for such training. This book was written in part as an effort to provide doctoral program administrators and instructors elsewhere a readily available resource for initiating teacher training in their programs. It is an attempt to provide doctoral level instructors with some practical materials for classroom use. It is an attempt to bring a rigorous concern about the quality of teaching to doctoral programs worldwide. It is, in summary, an attempt to provide a little balance between the heavily research-oriented focus of most doctoral programs and their common lack of attention to quality teaching.

University instructors

For instructors who have some years in the saddle, to use an old cowboy expression, this book is also germane. Who among us cannot benefit from some reflection on our teaching after having been at it for 5, 10, 15, or even 30 years? The contents of this book are intended to serve as a stimulus for reflecting on what we do in the classroom, why we do it, and how it might be done more effectively. It is not uncommon, especially if our teaching has met with a modicum of success over the years, to keep on doing what we have always done. Why change? Why do anything different? Well, subject matter changes, students change, the business environment changes, and perhaps more significantly, we change. Maybe the youthful connection we had with our students when we first began teaching is gone as we have aged and they have not. Perhaps the unbridled enthusiasm we could hardly mask when we simply anticipated standing in front of the classroom in our early years has morphed into a comfortable, mildly taken-for-granted routine. And is it possible that when we hear the same question, in the same course, at the same juncture in the topical flow, we might seem a little less patient in our demeanor and a little more terse in our explanation than when we first bumped up against such a question from a student 19 years earlier? And who hasn't experienced the moment in a discussion when you pose an example or make a reference to something that you realize pertains to a world that existed before the students in your class were even born? Ah, yes, a bit of reflection and personal evaluation can be a good thing in order to put the full measure of our early years' joy of teaching back into our experienced years. Writing this book was certainly such an experience for us. We hope that reading it can be for you, too.

Corporate trainers and consultants

This volume is also intended to serve others who teach managers – not just those who address them in business school, degree-program classrooms. Consultants and corporate trainers work almost daily with practicing managers in the field. They hold seminars, retreats, conferences, training sessions, coaching sessions, and a myriad of other events designed to educate people about how to better run their businesses.

There are hundreds of consulting firms whose primary focus is teaching practicing managers how to do their jobs more effectively. Many of those instructors do not hold Ph.D.s, nor have they been trained in learning or teaching theory. As consultants, perhaps they were once corporate trainers and have set out on their own to bring their services to a wider range of clients. Perhaps they have access to some proprietary assessment tool or perhaps they have developed a model that makes sense to them and have been able to convince others of its worth. However they began, many of those consultants, even ones we've observed who have been conducting training sessions for decades, seem to need some insight on how adults learn and how they might best be taught. One does not have to travel far in interviewing employees who bemoan how sleepy their last consultant-based corporate training experience was. We see it often in our work – and though it is sad, there's a certain relief that it won't take much to delight those customers – their level of expectation has been so lowered, they no longer expect "education" to be fun, exciting, or even productive.

In many ways, corporate trainers face a more difficult challenge than consultants. At least consultants have the opportunity to see a variety of corporate cultures and propensities to learning and extract from those lessons about how adults best learn. Except for conferences, corporate trainers typically live in the same environment most of their professional lives. Their values, assumptions, beliefs, and expectations about how to teach, what to teach, and how to develop people tend to be reinforced, both negatively and positively, from their day-by-day experiences with the same management, the same guidance, the same participants, and the same imperatives. They swim in a cultural sea that may not, often does not, understand nor reinforce the principles of effective adult learning.

Perhaps you think we're being a bit hypercritical – taking on universities, consultants, and corporate learning environments. Yet to us, it seems ironic that the very channels that purport to teach others often seem so unimaginative and uninspiring in their approach to teaching. Regardless of the quality of teaching that you've personally seen and experienced and perhaps done, we hope that the ideas and approaches introduced here will help you become a better teacher. If you're just beginning, perhaps it will save you some time in the school of hard knocks. If you're an experienced teacher, perhaps you'll see some familiar themes and maybe some new ones that will help you continue to refine your craft. We intend that the concepts included here will be useful to doctoral students in all business related fields who will one day be teaching future managers. We also hope they'll be useful consultants who present to, strive to persuade, try to motivate, and ultimately teach practicing managers all over the world. We hope these ideas will be helpful to corporate trainers who toil in the bowels of the bureaucratic beast to educate their fellow employees how they all can do better.

Do not mistake our point. We are not saying that anyone who didn't have formal training is not a good teacher. We know many teachers who have never had formal training in teaching yet who are excellent teachers, take it seriously, and have a significant positive impact on their students. Nor are we saying that process supersedes content. Of course process without content is worthless; we do not advocate a focus on the teaching of something at the expense of having something to offer. And we conclude there is little danger that the constituencies mentioned above will err in that direction. Our interest in writing and compiling this volume is to say simply that: (1) doctoral students will be teachers as well as researchers and they ought to be required to learn something about teaching and learning so they will be better prepared to fulfill the demands made of them by their profession; (2) current business school faculty can benefit from reflecting on their craft and considering new and different approaches; (3) consultants are teaching their clients almost every day and they would be more effective if they understood how to teach more powerfully; and (4) corporate trainers could have a bigger impact if they studied and learned how to teach more effectively.

To that end, the schools we have mentioned and perhaps others, as well as consultancies and corporate training departments, have begun to work hard to develop programs or courses that explore how people learn, how best to teach, and how to develop graduates with skills as teachers as well as researchers. We are aware of several consulting firms, for example, that offer seminars and training devoted just to the process of instruction, not to any specific content. In most cases, perhaps, that has not yet become an institutional value, but is being developed by highly motivated individuals. In other cases, the schools have developed broad acceptance of the idea that doctoral students should be trained in teaching as well as in research, and companies have determined that their corporate trainers and consultants should become better teachers.

Teaching and learning

Because this book is about teaching, it is also necessarily about learning. Teaching as professing is often thought of unilaterally: you teach (profess "knowledge") and your responsibility ends there. If the students get it, well, good. If they don't, something must be wrong with them, not you – after all, you are the subject-matter expert.

But teaching by itself isn't worth much. You can "teach" all day long and cover an extensive amount of material, but if your student hasn't learned the material, the exercise is an enormous waste of time and energy for both of you. This volume takes the view that instructors have multiple responsibilities, and key among them is the facilitation of learning. For many readers, this will not be a new concept, but for others, it is. Those who teach should understand that learning is their "bottom line," not how much material they have covered, or how good a show they put on, or even how well their students like them.

Although the topics addressed here relate to instructors in all disciplines, this book will focus more particularly on business examples and disciplines. Many of the references and most of our experiences come from that setting. Yet the principles outlined here apply to a variety of disciplines and colleges. If you are a graduate program administrator or instructor whose interest is piqued by the prospect of teaching doctoral candidates about teaching or the thought of developing incoming new faculty, or of working with more experienced teachers, this book may provide a set of materials that you could use to initiate a doctoral candidate course or a teacher development seminar.

Structure of the book

This book has four areas of emphasis: things that happen before class, things that happen during class, a brief after-class section dealing with grading and counseling students, and finally a section on managing professional teachers. The first section explores issues related to planning for teaching: adult learning theory, planning a course, planning single class sessions, and developing syllabi. The second section addresses the major methods and channels of teaching including lecturing, discussion, and case method. Chapters on the techniques of using audiovisual materials and various kinds of tactical teaching tips (e.g. role playing and experiential methods) also appear here. The third section has a chapter each on grading students and counseling them. Although those chapters are focused on academic environments, many of the principles appear in the private sector as well: force curve evaluations and guiding participants on career and related issues. The last section steps back from the classroom and explores a challenge that most teachers eventually find themselves dealing with: administration. One either gets promoted from the corporate training classroom to the management office or the assistant professor finds him- or herself suddenly in charge of a department or executive education program.

This lineup is clearly not exhaustive. We could think of several topics that also would bear careful attention, but we just did not have the space to deal with them here – perhaps in a later edition. Further, we mix theory and practice so that readers will see the frameworks and research beneath our approaches. Nevertheless, our primary interest is more in helping instructors understand and teach better than in presenting an arm's length, detached, purely conceptual perspective.

We don't believe there is a single recipe for becoming a world-class teacher. Rather, we include here some research, some ideas, what we think are "fundamentals," some habits or tendencies, a few admonitions, some recurring dangers to be aware of, and a ton of lessons learned from 50 years of collective experience that we want to share with readers. While these ideas have helped us, the real key for you is to take these ingredients and adapt them to your personality, to your students, to your institution, and to your subject matter. We invite you to customize. We hope the contents will be thought-provoking and stimulating. We suggest that as instructors (or soon-to-be instructors), you might consider that there is an unwritten classroom covenant linking instructors, students, students' future employers, and the institutional sponsor of the educational experience: namely that all parties involved should do their best to ensure that the learning is efficient, powerful, and long-lasting. Whatever the nuances of your particular situation may be, and however it may differ from ours, the common element is undeniable: the people in our classrooms ask us to be the best instructors we can possibly be. We view that challenge as hugely important, a professional privilege, even a sacred stewardship.

We have been colleagues at the same institution for over 21 years. That in itself is special and all the more so when we recount all the conversations we have had with one another, and with other colleagues, over the years on the subject of teaching. We have shared teaching stories of disappointment and pure excitement. We have pushed one another on how to be better on this or that dimension. We have collaborated on and debated instructional designs and celebrated instructional successes. Indeed, we have been the beneficiaries of a culture and an environment where that is supported. To that end, we are grateful for the support of the Darden Graduate School of Business Administration and the Darden Graduate Business School Foundation, whose generous support over the years has made this book possible. We're grateful to many people who have read and edited many versions of this book, including Barbara Richards, Karen Harper, Gerry Yemen, Amy Lemley, and others. Kathie Amato, director of Darden Business Publishing, has been a wonderful support. We're thankful, too, to Katy Plowright and Chris Harrison at Cambridge University Press for their guidance, support, and encouragement through the publishing process.

Lastly, I (Jim) am grateful to Tony Athos, formerly of the Harvard Business School and since passed away, and to Sherwood Frey, of the Darden School, for their examples and instruction. Their examples and direct coaching have been very powerful in my life and in the development of my teaching philosophy. I (Mark) am grateful to Bill Rotch, also deceased, and Ed Freeman, both of the Darden School, for their encouragement to expand my teaching comfort zone. We wish to dedicate this volume to our wives, Susan Clawson and Leslie Haskins, for their undying support and encouragement throughout the writing process, and to our students, who have challenged us to be better teachers and who have appreciated our honest efforts in that regard.

1 | Fundamental elements in teaching

JAMES G. S. CLAWSON

Students in the back row of a class in Japan are reading the newspaper while the instructor up front drones on about his subject. Across the Pacific at one of the world's most renowned universities, a physics professor spends his entire time talking to the chalkboard while writing formulae. Three thousand miles away in England, another professor reads to his students from the textbook for most of the hour. In South Africa, a college professor cannot get the overhead projector to work and spends fifteen minutes of a sixty-minute class wrestling with his audiovisual aids. At a high-level executive program in Germany, the room is filled with round tables and medieval columns so that participants cannot speak to each other. At a New Jersey corporate training facility, the participants file in, weary to have to sit through another mind-numbing experience – as the renovation crew on the floor above begins its drilling and hammering. And at a meeting of the Southeastern United States-Japan Society, the former chairman of Nissan Motors declares that the reason more Japanese firms don't build plants in the United States is that they can't find candidates who are well-educated enough.

These situations demonstrate organizations' worldwide tendency to squander prime learning opportunities. Universities, consulting firms, and corporate training departments all too often subject their students, clients, and participants to poor teaching technique and poor learning experiences that undermine their very purposes. This phenomenon is a global tragedy, a tragedy of opportunity that turns aspiring students off to a variety of disciplines, and more than that, to learning in general. The costs to students, whose investment in education and potential for future accomplishment are compromised, are significant. The costs to business and the economy – witness the former Nissan executive's comment – can be huge. All too often, bright, energetic students feel discouraged and dissuaded from pursuing further studies by the stultifying nature of many learning environments. Often that is because

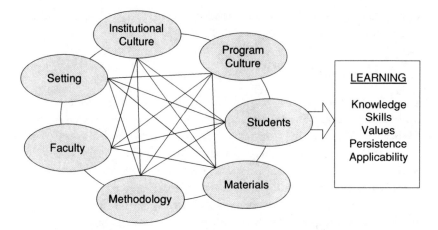

Figure 1.1 Fundamental elements in teaching

teachers have learned to focus on their subject matter at the expense of devoting attention to the learners.

In many cases, the fault lies with instructors – they get bogged down in their subject matter and ignore their students or they mindlessly perpetuate the instructional methods that their teachers used. We often talk and write about how effective this or that teacher's style was and remember the teachers who taught us well. But effective teaching – teaching that results in long-term, usable learning – is a function of much more than just a teacher's attributes.

If we take a systems view of teaching for a moment, we see quickly that there are at least seven elements that contribute to learning: institutional culture, program culture, students, teacher, pedagogical approach, materials, and facilities. Each element in Figure 1.1 links with the others. The students are in the physical facilities. The materials interact with the teaching methodology. The institutional culture affects how the instructor behaves. And so on. All those elements are closely linked. The sum of their collective effects determines the quality of learning that results.

Harmony among those elements facilitates learning. If one or more elements contradict one or more of the other elements, learning will be diminished. All seven elements will probably not be perfectly aligned in any one teaching situation, yet an awareness of how each interacts with others helps instructors plan for and improve their alignment and hence the learning. This seven-element framework provides the conceptual spine of this chapter and previews much of what will be developed in the book. Consider each element separately.

Institutional culture

Every instructor operates within an institutional culture. Every school and virtually every business has written and oral histories, rich in their ability to convey an institution's established norms and attitudes. The reputation that a school or a corporate training department has and the view it has of itself influence the way members of its community function. For example, an institution with a reputation of honesty among its students may expect the faculty to set relatively few controls on cheating and to develop and support an honor system; a school steeped in empirical research expects its faculty to behave in ways consistent with that tradition, emphasizing research and deemphasizing the student experience; a training department within a practically oriented organization will expect its members to teach and learn principles that students immediately apply. These historical realities shape and often define an institution.

All organizations also develop subcultures; what constitutes an acceptable mode of instruction can vary from department to department. The challenge for instructors, experienced as well as novice, is to understand the historical culture in which they are teaching and make adjustments to match that context. One way of assessing an institution's culture is to examine its emphasis on teaching versus research. Most universities focus heavily on the research end of the scale shown in Figure 1.2, while most businesses focus on the teaching/application end of the scale. Consulting firms often subscribe to a mixed model that tries to balance research with teaching process. We believe a blend is possible in all three settings.

The cultural focus of an institution along this teaching-research continuum will affect how its instructors behave. Those that emphasize teaching will likely attract and develop teachers with good classroom skills. Those that emphasize research will probably have teachers with less effective classroom skills. Those that take a middle road will build a reputation for mixed quality in the classroom setting. Students, of course, usually prefer the classroom focus; their instructor's published output means little to them. Yet we must remember that the university scholar's audience is a broad one and does not end at the door to the classroom. Likewise, the consultant is always looking for new

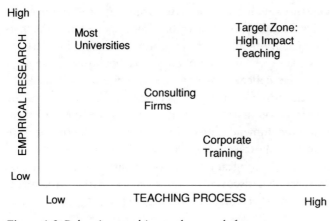

Figure 1.2 Balancing teaching and research focus

insights, models, methods, and solutions to offer existing and prospective clients. Corporate trainers too must understand and synthesize effective business practices so as to enhance their company's talent.

Instructors' promotions and salary levels are usually good indicators of an institution's culture. Other indicators of an institution's teaching subculture include how classes have been taught in the past, how many students are in the majority of classes, who teaches those classes, how often and in what forums the instructors engage in discussions of teaching activity, the level of support the institution offers for teaching activities (comfortable, up-to-date classroom space, audiovisual support, and general attitude toward innovative teaching techniques). Each of those indicators provides a view of what is valued in the institution's culture.

As a springboard for reflection, you might simply rate your present organization on the grid in Figure 1.2 and then check with your colleagues to see if they share a similar view. Talk about what indicators informed your assessment. Then note the kinds of indicators you've seen at other institutions or that you might expect to see at organizations representing both ends of the spectrum.

Institutional culture

An individual department's culture may vary significantly from the rest of the organization. The university, for instance, may have a lecture-dominated culture while the graduate school of business may have a case-oriented culture. Such differences are important to note because they can tell you something about how the larger organization, such as the university, may view members of the subunit or college in question. If, for instance, you are a faculty member of a particular program (e.g., MBA) in a particular college that balances its criteria for excellence (teaching, research, administrative service, etc.) differently from the rest of the university, you may have greater uncertainty about ratification of promotion recommendations. Similarly, a manufacturing company focused on ever-shorter cycle times may be unsympathetic to a corporate training staff's program design time request. Such disparities should be acknowledged, discussed, and reconciled before investments of time and money have been made and before expectations have taken root.

The size of the subunit and its number of instructors surely affect the nature of its subculture. Smaller subunits may tend to have a stronger esprit de corps than larger ones. And a subunit's demographics, years in residence, and prior work experience all influence its culture.

Here is a series of questions that may help you begin to assess your unit's distinctive subculture:

1. What do the unit's instructors value?
2. How does this compare with the values of the larger organization?
3. Does the unit's preferred pedagogical approach sit at odds with the tendencies and desires of the larger institution?
4. Do the instructors tend to be promoted?
5. Are the unit's instructors included on important committees and task forces of the larger organization?
6. Are instructors seen as mavericks or part of the organization's mainstream?
7. What is a normal teaching load for an instructor?
8. What are the current and desired relationships between students and instructors?

Cultural alignment, or at least blended fit, is not a trivial issue for both learning outcomes and instructor careers. Consider, for example, that in the late 1980s, deep, protracted, and severe differences between the organizational behavior department within Yale's School of Public Management and the rest of the faculty and administration of the school led to the unprecedented dismissal of that department's untenured faculty and the canceling of the classes taught by its tenured faculty. Similarly, the sociology department at Washington University was disbanded in the 1990s because of differences with the rest of the school. We have heard of corporate training departments being closed, and all educational programs outsourced because of a need for a better, more effective curriculum.

Students

Learning begins and ends with the students. The characteristics they bring to the classroom affect what they learn and how they learn. People have different learning styles, different educational and professional backgrounds, and different interests, each of which will shape their learning. Students' levels of education should influence your selection of instructional materials. Varying levels of student experience and maturity call for different methods of instruction and evaluation. Students' general level of motivation and their motivation toward particular subjects may also influence the selection of teaching methods. And the students' motivation for study will be in part a reflection of the other demands (social life and athletics, for instance) on their time, energy, and curiosity.

You can heighten your students' motivation to study by demonstrating the course's relevance to their goals, interests, and daily problems. Part of a course's relevance depends on what other courses students are taking and have taken. If the course fits into an integrated program, you can manage that more carefully; if it is part of a wide range of courses offered that they can select from, you may have to work harder to point out how the course's material fits with the rest of the students' experience.

Collectively, students are capable of creating a "student culture," depending on their number and diversity and the expectations that they have as well as expectations placed on them. That student subculture may or may not support the teaching objectives of the institution. Demonstrations at many universities during the late 1960s and early 1970s clearly showed the impact a student body can have on schools' learning objectives and the operating goals of society.

Individually, students vary widely in how they learn. They have, for instance, different cognitive styles. Students learn in different and characteristic ways. Further, given their past experience with educational programs, they have come to expect certain patterns in their educational encounters. A program that uses a markedly different pedagogical pattern, from the one individuals or groups of students are used to, will put them off balance. The effective teacher will be aware of this and will work to lessen the effect. For example, if you wish to teach cases and your students' past experience has been predominately lecture, the students are likely to be confused when you first introduce cases to them. Similarly, some students used to learning in one way – say, deductive sequential memorization – may have difficulty when suddenly confronted with an inductive, holistic creative learning exercise or class.

Again, people have different learning styles. Neurolinguistic programming (NLP) is a theory of psychological development that suggests that people process information in one of three dominant ways: some preferring to hear it, some preferring to see it, and some preferring to experience it. Effective instructors will recognize that there are probably all three types in any one classroom and will work to include audio, visual, and emotional components in their classes. Though humankind is touted as being the most flexible of mammals, we as instructors reduce the effectiveness of our teaching when we do not allow for variations in our students' cognitive styles.

Faculty

As this book emphasizes, your personal characteristics as an instructor will clearly mold your students' learning experience. Those characteristics extend beyond your teaching style to include your mannerisms, personality, values, techniques of punishment and praise, ability to explain or to ask questions, and a host of other factors. Instructors have habitual ways of behaving and communicating (just as students do) that set a tone for the class that permeates its learning. Though I don't believe that instructors can be all things to all people, I do think we can modify our habits and approaches so as to reach the broadest range of learners. If we aren't ready and able to do this, how can we expect our students to alter their characteristic ways of thinking and learning to accommodate *our* styles? The willingness of each to accommodate the other enhances the effectiveness of a learning situation.

Instructors *learn* how to teach. They watch their parents, their elementary, middle, and high school teachers, and their university professors. Often they draw conclusions about what they don't want to do from these observations, but that is a very inefficient method of learning since the array of options left to choose from remains enormous. Instructors learning on the job how to teach may, by trial-and-error, grow and develop into excellent teachers.

Yet experience alone will not ensure the development of a good instructor. For some, as Samuel Coleridge pointed out, experience is like the stern light on a passing ship, illuminating only the wake where one has gone but offering no help in guiding one's direction. It is useful, therefore, to have some kind of teacher development activity. That may be informal peer coaching, teaching meetings, or a more formalized teacher development program.

I also believe that people teach and can only teach what they *are*. Our attitudes toward our subject matter, toward our students, toward learning, toward life are all communicated daily, moment by moment in the classroom. An instructor who thinks he can separate who he is from what he teaches is fooling himself, even in working with impersonal subject matter. If you are interested in the students, it shows. If you cannot wait to get out of the classroom, it shows. If you discount the questions students ask, it shows. Students pick up on the little signals, your voice tone, your facial expressions, the way you press students, the attitude you bring to class. These and a myriad of other signals convey our attitude to our subject and in turn influence the students' attitude and approach to it also. If we are enthusiastic, they are enthusiastic. If we are dismissive of them, they may be dismissive of us and our subject matter. In part, your attitude will determine whether or not your students will get close enough to the subject matter to "catch the bug." It is in that sense that we teach what we are.

Materials

Teaching is in part an art. A significant portion of that art is the selection of materials – lecture notes, chapters, books, magazines, reprints, cases, films, documentaries, exercises, and so on. A course's subject matter is not always self-evident. Even the selection of subject matter for the same course will often differ for different instructors. Introduction to finance can start in a number of ways, develop in a number of ways, and end in a number of ways.

The selection of materials for a course sets you on one of several paths. By selecting certain items and not others, you begin to answer certain questions: Which aspects of the subject will we emphasize?

Which teaching and learning techniques will we favor? Which theories are most useful? How fast will we go? What level of entry knowledge will we assume? How much skill development will we incorporate? And even (increasingly an issue) what language will we work in?

Many instructors leave the choice of materials up to the institution or to an unknown textbook author. When an institution prescribes a text, the assumption many new instructors may make is that "they," the wise old department seniors, have reviewed the alternatives and selected the best one, the one that has the most truth and best fits the need. If the text is a given, as it may be for some new instructors, you have to determine if your personal style and approach to the field is consistent with the text's and decide whether or not to push for a change. Accepting the book, you have to then sort out how to fit your view of the field with the author's and then how you can best present that view to the students.

Some instructors voluntarily choose a text even when one is not pre-scribed and in so doing, yield much of their creative opportunities to the text's author. Publishing companies demand teaching notes, over-head slides, diagrams, discussion questions, charts, exam questions, and even class outlines in their teaching manuals. It is easy to see how that is helpful to instructors and helps them see how another might teach some concepts, but I worry that some instructors become little more than conduits through which the ideas of others flow. If you use a text, remember that you can only teach what you are, and that you should feel free to examine the teacher's manual with a critical eye. Be ready to develop your own exercises, your own overheads, your own test items, your own way of evaluating.

The choices of how to teach and what materials to use extend over the course of a term. If you use the same kind of material throughout the program, students are likely to get bored with its predictability. Use your freedom and creativity in selecting materials to vary the medium through which the students engage your subject. Variety in materials adds some spice and interest to a classroom. Experiment with the use of films, tapes, props, cases, and other kinds of materials.

Methodology (pedagogical approach)

Instructors choose the method by which they teach. For some, it is not an explicit choice, but rather one that they make matter-of-factly by virtue of their training and coaching. You can choose from among at least four main popular teaching methods: lecturing, case method, discussion, and experiential exercises. The more you become familiar with each of them and the ways in which they can be employed – either over a course or in short bursts amidst each other within a class – the better prepared you will be to respond to the learning needs of the moment.

Each method has its strengths and weaknesses. *Lecturing* to students gives instructors the opportunity to convey important information relatively quickly. The instructor is also able to maintain virtually complete control over the teaching side of the learning equation. On the down side, since lecturing is primarily a one-way communication pattern, it is difficult to know how students are responding to your efforts. Thoughtful lecturers wrestle with how well their messages are getting across. Are my lectures relevant to the students' interests and focus in life? Are the lectures overly difficult? Are my students understanding what I'm presenting?

The case method relies on learning by analysis and discussion of descriptions of actual events involving the area of study. Case method helps students develop their analytic and decision-making skills and to learn to present their ideas articulately. It presents the opportunity to teach many social skills pertinent to professional relationships while simultaneously presenting the content of the subject area. On the other hand, instructors of case method have less control over what happens in the learning situation than the lecturer. Case method also requires a certain level of experience among the students; novices in a field are likely to be unable to participate in deep discussions of complex, real situations. Perhaps the case method's greatest drawback is that it is less efficient in presenting what is already known to be a valid analysis, principle, or concept. On the other hand, presenting is not equivalent to learning. Yet even here, the case method gives the instructor important insight into what the *students* know and therefore what can be effectively (though perhaps much less efficiently) introduced to them.

Discussion or seminar techniques mix aspects of the lecture and case methods. Here, students are involved in a dialogue with the instructor. The instructor can maintain control over most of what happens and can gain insight into the thinking and understanding of the students. Discussions can become abstract and theoretical, though, and leave students searching for links to the practical world.

Experiential learning exercises are fun, popular, and creative. More-over, these small simulations or parodies of real world circumstances produce a personal experience that can either provide fodder for learning itself or cement learning more solidly and render it more available to the students in the future. Experiential exercises can be difficult to orchestrate, though, and can leave students wondering what the connections to their real world applications might be.

Setting (facilities)

Learning occurs in physical settings and it is a function of the relationship between the senses and the brain's processing. If the five senses are diverted from the subject matter by irrelevant sounds, sights, and experiences (such as temperatures too hot or too cold or lighting too bright or too dim), learning is inhibited. The classroom's size, shape, color, and accommodations can have a tremendous impact on learning. Students are almost always peripherally aware of the size of the room, the comfort and condition of the furnishings, the temperature, the lighting, the noise of the chalk, the squeak of the movable blackboards, the echo off the bare walls, and even the dreariness or vibrancy of the paint color.

The ideal learning setting is transparent. The ultimate, if unachievable, objective is that the setting disappears from everyone's attention because it is so conducive to learning that instructor and students alike can focus on the topic at hand and engage with it. If the instructor is using different media, it should be in a seamless, noninterruptive way. Tripping over cords, trying to figure out the sound system or the lighting, or scratching the chalkboard with poor-quality chalk filled with rock pits, or any of hundreds of other distractions can divert students' attention from the subject matter, can break the learning mood, and may even erode students' confidence in the instructor and his or her material altogether.

Many instructors take the room, the arrangement of the chairs, the positioning of the overhead and computer projector, even the room assignment itself as a given. But these are all manageable teaching-effectiveness variables, and the instructor desirous of improving his or her skills will observe and manage these factors as well. Pay attention to the setting. Look at all the features of the setting you'll be using to teach in. Go early to practice in the room. Pace around it, practice your voice in it, view your writing and overheads from the back row. Imagine the conversations that can occur in this setting. Can people talk easily with each other or do they have to crane their necks to observe and address other classmates? Where are you most likely to make a fool of yourself? Are all of the steps the same height? (There is nothing quite so embarrassing as holding forth in front of thirty to ninety students in an intense instructional moment and then catching your heel on a step and falling to the floor!) How do the lights work? How does the audiovisual equipment work? How do the chalkboards work (if electrically controlled)? Do you have room to spread out all of your materials? What distractions are there? What will students think of this room?

If you take the time and interest to check things out, you will likely discover several little details that, corrected and managed, will make your class go more smoothly. A case in point is the handing out of papers. How many times have you seen an instructor divide a large sheaf of papers in half, hand one batch to the left and one to the right and then try to talk while some are passing papers, others are holding on to the stack trying to follow the instructor's comments on the handout, and others fidgeting nervously because they don't have the handout in front of them. Handouts are a common and often mismanaged part of a classroom setting. A simple but powerful fix that takes very little time was given me by my mentor and coach at Harvard, Tony Athos. Simply count the number of chairs in your room from one of the aisles and count out your handouts in advance of the class, stacking them at 90-degree angles. Then, when the moment comes to give the handouts, you take the top stack and give it to the first row, the next stack to the second row, and so on. Further, if you begin with the longer rows (usually in the back of amphitheater-style rooms), by the time you have reached the front of the room and turned around to refer to the handout, everyone in the room has one in front of them and the place is quiet again.

Interrelatedness of the basic elements

These seven elements of a basic teaching situation are not independent balls to juggle concurrently; rather, each is connected to and will affect the other(s). If you change your teaching materials it may have an effect on how well the room serves your learning purposes. If you admit a different kind of student, he or she may affect your choice of teaching technique. If you teach in a different program, your style may affect the students differently from how it did in your previous program. The lines in Figure 1.1 portray these various relationships. It is important to note that the elements and their connections form a whole that collectively determines the quality of the learning output. The elements are somewhat like chemical elements that can be combined to form a compound. Some elements work better with one element than another. Different mixes can be used to create new compounds. The chemist must be careful how he mixes the elements lest he create something dangerous. An appropriate mix will produce a compound that is both stable and highly useful. Well planned and carefully executed, the combination of particular elements in particular ways creates valuable and powerful compounds.

The learning that comes out of the combination of these seven elements forms an eighth element in the model. Effective learning is learning that the students can use either in discussion or in practical affairs throughout their lives. Effective learning occurs on at least three levels – behavioral skills, knowledge, and values – and in a way that is lasting. Effective learning is that which allows a student to draw on it throughout her life to think more wisely, to behave more expertly, and to choose more appropriately. Learning that is intellectually regurgitated for an exam and then promptly forgotten and not available to the student is hardly effective and will be of minimal impact. In fact, courses of this nature may even be counterproductive in that they distance students from the thrill of education and effective learning.

Conclusion

Institutional culture. Program culture. Students. Teacher. Pedagogical approach. Materials. Facilities. Effective teaching, teaching that results in learning, is a function of at least those seven elements. As you prepare to teach, develop your own teaching tools and skills, and then as you begin to collect years of experience as a teacher, I encourage you to consider each of these areas that influence the learning of your students and manage them well. Most businesses talk about the importance of the bottom line. In their case, it's profits. Here, the bottom line is the effectiveness of your students' learning. Unfortunately, and unlike the business world, that is not something that you can measure when they leave your class, and you may not ever be able to get an inkling of how much your students learned. But it is that learning result that counts, not the quality of your teaching. If you understand how each of those seven elements contributes to learning and are willing to manage them, you will surely improve the quality of their learning. And if you can improve the quality of their learning, you will have been a quality teacher.

2 | *Levels of learning: one, two, and three*

JAMES G. S. CLAWSON AND
MARK E. HASKINS

> The human mind needs cognitive stability.
> Therefore, any challenge to or questioning
> of a basic assumption will release anxiety
> and defensiveness. In this sense, the shared
> basic assumptions that make up the culture
> of a group can be thought of at both the
> individual and group levels as psychological
> cognitive defense mechanisms that permit
> the group to continue to function.
> Recognizing this connection is important
> when one thinks about changing aspects of
> a group's culture, for it is no easier to do
> that than to change an individual's pattern
> of defense mechanisms. In either case the
> key is the management of the large amounts
> of anxiety that accompany any relearning at
> this level.
>
> – Edgar Schein,
> *Organizational Culture and Leadership*

Human learning occurs on at least three levels. At Level One is Visible Behavior, the things that people say and do that can be captured on film. At Level Two is Conscious Thought, the things that people are aware they're thinking but that they do not choose to reveal at Level One. At Level Three are the Values, Assumptions, Beliefs, and Expectations (VABEs) that people hold about the way the world should be. VABEs are often "preconscious" or "semiconscious," yet they often reveal themselves at Level One. (See Figure 2.1, in which only that above the underline is visible.)

A major question for educators is where to begin with instructional intent. Do we target Level One (L1), Level Two (L2), or Level Three

26

1. Visible Behavior
2. Conscious Thought
3. Values, Assumptions, Beliefs, and
   Expectations (VABEs)

Figure 2.1 Levels of learning

(L3)? Most learning seems to begin at L2. Consider large undergraduate lecture courses or consulting discussions or any classroom in any setting – the primary input is at L2, Conscious Thought. The question is whether that cognitive input will ever manifest itself at L1 (regurgitation in conversation or on an exam) or seep down into L3; that is sufficiently becoming a part of the person's view of the world that it becomes a part of their "normal" habitual behavior at L1.

Some would argue that the learning that begins at L1, with *doing*, is more likely to seep down to L3 than learning that begins at L2. That may be the case – especially in young children. Educational ropes courses, experiential exercises, and day-to-day experience are all L1 learning opportunities where the premise is if you *do* something, and it works, the "principle" in the doing will seep down to L3 and become a part of your core VABEs.

That premise raises the issue of the connections between and among these levels. If a person has a habit of behaving in one way at L1, does this mean that it is "conscious" to him or her at L2? Not necessarily. A significant portion of people's behavior at L1 seems to jump directly there from L3 and may not become "conscious" at L2. That is why many people seem to espouse one principle and live another.

Habits play an important role at all three levels. Indeed, when you ask corporate executive groups about the level of habitual behavior at L1, L2, and L3, the common answers are very powerful. Most groups will say 80 percent, 90 percent, and 99 percent respectively. Think about it. If 80 percent of what people do is habitual, and 90 percent of the way they think is habitual, and 99 percent of the things they believe and value are habitual, any kind of instructional effort must overcome huge obstacles. Habitual behavior is routine and not easily changed. Those who teach undergraduates may hypothesize lower levels of habitual behavior; however, as time goes by, in our experience, the common perception is that most human behavior is habitual – and the deeper you go, the more habitual it becomes.

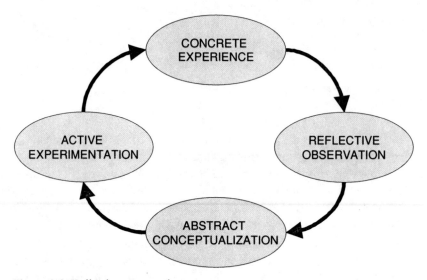

Figure 2.2 Kolb's learning cycle

So a key question becomes, "When you teach, what level are you targeting?" If you only want students to be able to repeat a formula, a principle, a framework, or a concept later on, you may be targeting L1 and L2. There's a lingering question as to whether the person's "learning" actually becomes a part of his or her regular behavior thereafter, that is, whether the "insight" at L2 ever seeps into L3 in any kind of permanent way.

David Kolb's learning cycle is closely related to that multilevel perspective; you may be familiar with it. Kolb (1984) posited that every human being goes through a learning cycle many times a day. That cycle is composed of four elements: Concrete Experience, Reflective Observation, Abstract Conceptualization, and Active Experimentation. Arrayed in a circle (see Figure 2.2), Concrete Experience is the polar opposite of Abstract Conceptualization and Reflective Observation is the polar opposite of Active Experimentation. The theory goes that people, beginning in infancy, have experiences (our L1). They reflect on those experiences to varying degrees (our L2). They may or may not incorporate their reflective conclusions ("What happened there?") into their world view (Abstract Conceptualization or our L3) and then actively use the newly formed "principle" in the future. Variations in emphasis on any of these four steps and in the connections between and among them lead to characteristic learning or cognitive styles.

We assert that L3 learning is the most powerful. That is, if you can get a person to incorporate what you're teaching at their L3, the odds are that it will become a part of them and be included in their regular, habitual repertoire of behaviors. How can you impact or influence another's core values, assumptions, beliefs, and expectations? First, try to engage people at the level of their VABEs. There are a number of techniques for doing so; but you must decide whether you are comfortable seeking to influence your students on that level. Many instructors are not.

We have heard teachers say, "It's not my place or purpose to try to influence people's values and beliefs." If that sounds like you, we invite you to rethink that conclusion. Consider, for example, trying to teach financial concepts. Perhaps you want to get the point across that a company's debt-to-equity ratio is an important thing to consider in assessing its health. You might include that element on a list of things the students "should" memorize. And you might get them to regurgitate it on an exam – or if you're teaching in a corporate program, to acknowledge it at the end of the hour or program. But the question, really, will linger: "Will they actually use the debt-to-equity ratio in their future assessments of companies?" If they don't, you could conclude that the concept has not really filtered down into their core VABEs. They may be able to "regurgitate" from L2 at a meeting or cocktail party the "importance" of debt-to-equity ratios, but unless they use it, unless they *believe* that it's important to use, they will not really have *learned* the concept – not at L3.

So, first, do you believe that you can, should, and as an instructor have the right to attempt to influence people at the level of their core VABEs? If not, you'll spend the rest of your instructing career dabbling at the relatively superficial L1 and L2 levels (mostly at L2). And while that may be satisfying in terms of seeing your students progress on an exam, whether they value the subject matter, are turned on by it, or even want to continue using the concepts you taught them after the class is over, remains to be seen.

One way to begin to engage people at L3 is to come right out and ask them about their core beliefs and values on a topic. Surprised? You're not alone. Most instructors don't do that. That is, most instructors assume (based on their own L3 reactions) that they're dealing with people at L2, within their cognitive awareness. If you were to begin your financial debt-to-equity class, for example, with the question, "What are the most important things to consider when thinking about the health of a company?" and write down on the board what you got from students, you, as an instructor, would have a much better understanding of where your class was starting from, and further, what their semiconscious beliefs actually were about the important issues. Debt-to-equity ratio may or may not come up.

People have countless values, assumptions, beliefs, and expectations at L3, many of which they would be unable to clearly articulate. Yet, working backward from their behavior, regardless of what they *say* they believe, their behavior at L1 will reveal their underlying VABEs. In other words, people vote with their feet – they behave what they believe *even if* they try to convince themselves and others differently at L1.

Typical Instructional Content for Each Level

Teaching that targets L1 is targeting specific behaviors. Usually that occurs in skill-building classes, but if your experience is like ours, it's often difficult to distinguish between cognitive skills and behavioral skills. If you intend to teach a person to value a company, for example, there are a lot of cognitive analytical skills that go into being able to lay out the analysis on paper – the L1 behavioral skill.

Experiential programs, so-called "ropes courses" or "challenge learning," are often targeted at L1. Participants go into the woods or a large open space and strive together to complete a physical task. Though the experience is largely L1, a wide variety of assessments have explored the impact of experiential learning at L2 and L3. If the post-exercise debriefs are weak or seem unrelated to the working environment, the L2 and L3 impact is minimal. On the other hand, for someone with self-confidence issues, climbing a 35-foot pole and jumping into space can be a life-changing event, mostly at L3 and around the "simple" realization that a person can do more than he or she thought possible. Even when no clear L2 "principle" seems to emerge from this experience, the L3 insight might in fact color and shape all the person's other activities.

In-class skill development exercises, for example, learning to "listen actively" in the Rogers (1995) sense, also target L1. An instructor can identify at the end of an exercise or module whether or not a student can demonstrate reflective listening. If the student can do so at L1, the odds are they can discuss it at L2. That is, they could describe what the theory is and what the pitfalls are and why, Rogers would argue, that reflective listening is a powerful tool for relationship and personal development. Whether or not that capacity was translated into a deep-seated belief and whether that student will employ reflective listening over time is another question.

Level Two Teaching

Targeting L2 means attempting to change the way people think. Indeed, that seems to be where most educational effort is expended. Vast lecture halls, textbooks, problem sets, and presentation preparation are largely about augmenting or refining the students' thought processes. Yet if somewhere around 90 percent of the way people think is habitual, changing a person's thinking patterns is likely to be an uphill battle. We know it happens, though, especially at the analytical level. If you introduce weighted cost of capital techniques to people interested in valuing a company, they are likely going to incorporate that way of thinking into their consciousness. But this is not a sure thing. Thomas Kuhn, for example, in his book *The Structure of Scientific Revolutions* (1996) demonstrated that even among the scientific community, of all people on the earth most likely to be responsive to empirical data, it sometimes takes literally a generation before new paradigms (solar centricity in the fourteenth century, or in the twentieth century, relativity) are generally accepted *among the scientific community*. So, there's no guarantee that your students will "learn" a thing at L2 and still translate it into a habit of thinking or of believing at L3.

The intent to influence people at L3 consists of the belief that you as an instructor have a right to help people modify their basic belief systems – and that you can learn how to do so well. University and corporate educators sometimes shrink from this prospect, but politicians and clergy accept it readily. L3 impact is a deeper impact. If you influence a person's basic values, assumptions, beliefs and expectations about the way the world is or should be, you will influence that person's life for decades, maybe even for the rest of his or her life.

Bill Glasser (1999) eloquently makes the point. He notes for example that newborn infants begin immediately to "learn," to draw conclusions from which they form some basic assumptions about the way the world is and the role their parents are playing in it. In what Glasser calls "control theory," the first three assumptions the parents convey are

1. I know what's right for you.
2. I have a right to tell you what's right for you.
3. I have a right to punish you if you don't do what I think is right for you.

What child in what country does not learn these three "realities" of life long before it can speak or even walk? And most people, although they challenge those assumptions sometime in their teens, never really reject them, they simply cross over from being recipients of those principles to being promulgators – as adults and then as parents. In executive education seminars, we often ask participants, "How many of you have worked for people who still subscribe to the principles of control theory?" Virtually every hand goes up, every time.

Csikszentmihalyi (1993) asks a key question about life: "Will you ever be anything more that a vessel transmitting the memes and genes of previous generations on to the next?" Sadly, for most people, the answer is no. Csikszentmihalyi argues that the truly mature person is one who has "transcended" his dual legacy (memes and genes) by pausing, examining the two components, and then consciously choosing which to perpetuate and which to let go of. That is the most profound kind of learning available in this life. And it is, essentially, L3 learning.

Finally, McGill and Slocum (1993) suggest that different kinds of learning exist based on a person's openness to new ideas: "knowing," "understanding," and "learning." The trained scientists in Kuhn's study "knew" things that made it difficult for them to "learn" new things. Indeed, we all "know" things that may or may not serve a function in our modern world. Our capacity to reexamine that "knowledge" and revise it is an L3 kind of activity and one that, in essence, underpins all of the other kinds of learning.

Conclusion

People learn at different levels. People in essence "know" a lot of things that inhibit their learning of other things. Teachers may or may not be aware that when they interact with students in any way, they are teaching them something. Whether it's what they want to teach or not, and whether it's targeting a long-lasting level or not, is another question. Our hope is that, as an instructor, your awareness of the levels of learning – visible behavior, conscious thought, and underlying values, assumptions, beliefs, and expectations – will help you plan for and execute your instructional efforts with greater effect.

Further reading

Csikszentmihalyi, Mihalyi, *The Evolving Self: a Psychology for the Third Millennium*. New York: HarperCollins, 1993.

Glasser, William, *Choice Theory*. New York: Perennial, 1999.

Kolb, David, *Experiential Learning: Experience as the Source of Learning and Development*. New York: Financial Times Prentice Hall, 1983.

Kuhn, Thomas S., *The Structure of Scientific Revolutions*, 2nd edn, Chicago: University of Chicago Press, 1996 [1970].

McGill, Michael E., and John W. Slocum, Jr., "Unlearning the Organization," *Organizational Dynamics* (Autumn 1993), 67ff.

Rogers, Carl, *On Becoming a Person*, New York: Mariner, 1995.

Schein, Edgar, *Organizational Culture and Leadership*, San Francisco: Jossey-Bass, 1985.

3 | Adult learning theory: it matters

JAMES G. S. CLAWSON

> Every act of conscious learning requires the
> willingness to suffer an injury to one's
> self-esteem. That is why young children,
> before they are aware of their own
> self-importance, learn so easily.
>
> — Thomas Szasz

> Nothing ever becomes real till it is
> experienced.
>
> — John Keats

If teaching is about helping others learn, then we as teachers ought to understand the learning process of adults – people who, like us, have spent many years in schools, many years in society, and in some cases, many years working in business.

Adults don't learn like children. Adults are more discerning in what they are willing to learn, more questioning, and more resentful of being told what to learn. They need to see more clearly how what they are being asked to learn will benefit them; for adults, learning is much more utilitarian than it is for children.

Whether for children or adults, learning theories abound. We could consider the theories of Thorndike, Pavlov, Guthrie, Tolman, Hull, Skinner, the Gestalt theorists, Piaget, Freud, Knox, Knowles, Kolb, Bruner, and others. An exhaustive treatment of them, however, would consume this book and more. A variety of good books summarizes these theories; references for some of them are given at the end of this chapter. What we want to do here is to outline the chief characteristics of some practical models of adult learning that can provide a basis for discussion and inform your preparations for teaching.

Malcolm S. Knowles

Malcolm Knowles has been a pioneer in the field of adult learning and is a strong proponent of the position that adults do not learn like children. In several works (including *The Adult Learner*), he presents a series of assumptions, patterned after the work of Eduard Lindeman, that guide his view of adult learning:

1. Adults are motivated to learn from being in situations in which they see a need to learn. Consequently, adult learning settings should begin with topics that address the adult audience's current learning needs.
2. Adults are oriented to the broad range of affairs in life, not to narrow subjects. Thus, adult teaching should be multidisciplinary rather than subject-oriented.
3. Adults learn from their experience. Therefore, the most productive adult learning comes from the analysis of adult experience.
4. Adults have a deep need to be self-directing. Therefore, teaching adults should be involved in setting the agenda for their learning.
5. Individual differences broaden and harden with age. Therefore, adult teaching should make allowance for differences in style, time, place, pace, focus, and method.

Knowles has been very active in propounding this set of principles for teaching adults and even refers to them by a distinctive name, andragogy, by which he intends to separate the principles from those used in pedagogy, the teaching of children. Knowles argues that the andragogical principles are quite different from what happens in most of our school systems where the model is that the instructor knows best what is to be taught and learned and where students are expected to learn the same things in the same ways. Clearly, children in elementary schools don't have the experience to draw from to set their own learning agendas. Somewhere before college graduation, however, they do develop interests and preferences that beg for an andragogical approach. Yet most university courses continue to run on the pedagogical model: instructors as disseminators of knowledge and students as empty pots to be filled. Knowles's andragogical message is that effective adult teaching begins with where the students are. Adults will learn faster if what they are studying has an immediate effect on their current situation in life. That is not to say that the instructor cannot alter the students' intellectual whereabouts by adding new information to them,

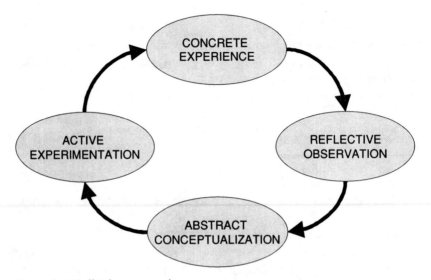

Figure 3.1 Kolb's learning styles

only that the adding will be more effective if it builds on the foundation of interests and understanding already in place.

David Kolb

David Kolb comes at the question of adult learning in a different way. Kolb's theory is that all people learn in the characteristic four-step pattern as shown in Figure 3.1. First, a person has an experience. Then, he or she reflects on that experience, analyzing it and trying to make sense of it before attempting to fit the experience into a broader conceptual framework of the world. This latter involves fitting the sense of the experience into an individual's collection of theories about how the world operates. Once he or she has done that – in effect, formed a hypothesis about how things work – the person tries it out, and this experimentation, in turn, leads to another experience from which he or she can retreat and reflect. Kolb's notion is that this four-step cycle goes on in our lives many times a day and that reinforcing cycles add to larger structures of beliefs or hypotheses that we carry with us throughout our lives.

Kolb also notes that, over time, people begin to favor some of the steps more than others. Some people, for instance, might become more comfortable with experimenting with things (Active Experimentation),

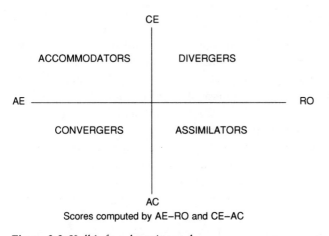

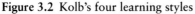

Figure 3.2 Kolb's four learning styles

while others become more comfortable conceptualizing how an experience might fit into a bigger view of how things in life work (Reflective Observation). Thus, people develop characteristic learning styles or patterns, which Kolb reasoned can be measured.

Indeed, Kolb developed a learning style instrument (marketed through the Hay Group) that attempts this measurement. The articles in the scholarly literature indicate mixed results on the validity and accuracy of this instrument, but the theory has a certain face validity, and the instrument is easy to use, which makes the package attractive to those interested in exploring learning styles.

This instrument, the Learning Style Inventory, produces scores for each of the four steps in Kolb's theory. Those scores can then be combined to produce a single point on the grid shown in Figure 3.2. Kolb sets the Concrete Experience and Abstract Conceptualization steps and the Reflective Observation and Active Experimentation steps at opposite ends of independent continua. After calculating the differences in the scores on each continuum, an instructor then plots a single point to get an overall categorization of the student's learning style. Kolb then offers descriptions of the characteristic ways that each of the four basic types (Accommodator, Diverger, Converger, and Assimilator) approaches learning. He also gives examples of people in various occupations who seem to rely on one of the styles more than the others. To avoid biasing your view if you plan to use the instrument, we won't explain more about the instrument but rather encourage you to try it.

Akin/Pearl/Clawson model

Gib Akin conducted a study of managers and the way they learn. Akin's qualitative interviews of 60 managers indicated that managers used six learning themes: mentoring, role-taking, practical accomplishment, validating, anticipatory, and personal growth. Individual managers, Akin reported, used distinctive thematic approaches to learning situations and tended to rely on those distinctive approaches.

In Akin's view, learning themes are action-oriented rather than cognitive or analytic. Themes refer to what people actually do when they are confronted with a learning situation rather than what they say they might do or how they might reflect on learning. In this sense, you can think of a learning theme as analogous to landing an airplane at a large, multirunway airport. The pilot, the learner in our analogy, approaches the airport, the learning situation, and circles. Considering wind, other planes, and other factors, our learning pilot has the freedom to choose how he or she will approach this airport. Left alone to choose, each pilot will select an orientation and approach to the airport that suits him or her best, one that he or she is comfortable with, have used before, and is confident will lead to efficient and effective results. Being allowed to approach the subject matter (airport) from his or her preferred approach, the pilot is able to make a smooth, comfortable landing (grasping the material). If forced, however, because of teaching style, materials, setting, or program culture to approach the airport from another perspective, the pilot may indeed make it down, but may experience a bumpy, perhaps jarring, landing. In that analogy, there is no "right" way to land – or to learn. Rather, people have preferred styles and, if permitted, will utilize those styles when entering into a learning situation.

Gail Pearl and I undertook the task of reviewing Akin's work and attempting to replicate it. In an attempt to corroborate the existence of the six learning styles and to measure them, she interviewed MBA students, developed an instrument, checked her preliminary results with expert raters, and administered three waves of questionnaires to MBA candidates at the Darden Graduate School of Business Administration. In the course of that work, we concluded that managers (as approximated by MBA students with years of experience in industry) do indeed have distinctive learning styles, but that Akin's six-category model was broader and less consistent than the data we observed. Consequently, we winnowed the categories down to five: social, role-taking, practical, anticipatory, and scientific.

Social. Some people like to learn from other people; they would rather ask someone how to do something than look it up in a book or simply start trying to do it. Such a social-oriented learning theme may grow into a full-fledged mentor-protégé relationship, but more often it is simply peers working together to learn the ropes of new jobs or assignments. Hence, Pearl and I have retreated from the mentoring terminology that Akin used and dubbed this learning theme or pattern "social." People with a social learning theme typically describe how they tried to find a person who knew something about the learning target, how they would ask several people what they knew about a subject, how they would confer with others about a new area, and how they found that approach both rewarding and efficient. For social learners, acquiring new knowledge and skills means talking with and working with other people. For them, the key question is *Who knows about this stuff, and how can I work with them or pick their brains?*

Role-taking. Role takers have a mental image of what a person who has a certain title does. Whether accurate or inaccurate, they view the world as a series of caps and gowns people don as they assume new assignments, jobs, and careers. The more a role-taker can learn about what that cap and gown signify, the better prepared that person will be to put the garb on, wear it, and become that role. Consequently, when confronted with a promotion, role takers will attempt to clarify the expectations that they have, that society has, and that the organization has for people who fill that role; they then try to live up to and fit into that definition, that set of expectations. In that way, learning for role-takers is much less personalized – fitting the learning to the self – and much less social than it is for the social learner. Role takers want to fit themselves into the role rather than the other way around. Role takers want to learn from broad, abstract expectations rather than from another person's perspectives.

For role-takers, the key questions are *What do people in this position (managers, section heads, executives, etc.) do? What do people expect of them? How can I look like one? How can I behave like one? How can I perform like one?* If their view of the demands placed on a certain role is sufficiently flexible and adaptive, their learning can be effective and efficient. If their view is distorted or inaccurate, however, role takers, trying to do what it is they think they *should* do in order to fill the role, may appear to others to be playing a game, acting out the job, putting on airs, or otherwise behaving insincerely.

Practical. Practical learners emphasize Kolb's Concrete Experience step. They are risk takers who have high confidence in their ability to figure things out for themselves. They seldom wait for guidance and they seldom trust or place much value in socially defined ways of doing things. They want to find their own way, to discover for themselves the connections that exist, and they believe they can best do this by diving in, trying things out, discarding whatever doesn't work, and trying a new way until the problem, learning issue, or situation is resolved.

Practical learners tend to be impatient, in a hurry, and intolerant of those who wish to slow down and sort through things more carefully. Receiving a box from UPS, the practical learner will open it eagerly, discard the instructions, lay out the pieces, and begin assembling them. Consequently, practical learners often find themselves in the middle of situations with something of a mess and may not be sure how to get out of it. They tend to have positive attitudes, though, and will optimistically, if with a bit of frustration, disassemble their work and try again until it comes together. Then with great pride and, indeed, a deep insight into how the "target" actually functions, they add this experience to their base of knowledge.

It's easiest to picture practical learners in situations with tangible things such as machinery and hardware, but they often take the same approach in social settings as managers, companions, and team members. Practical learners are more inductive in their learning style: they want to generate their own results and rely on them rather than build on what others have thought or written. For the practical learner, the key question is *What are we waiting for? Let's get to it!* and, later, *Hmmm. That didn't work. What else can we try?*

Anticipatory. Anticipatory learners don't like surprises. They like to know what is going to happen before it happens and they tend to postpone action in favor of careful understanding of a situation. Anticipatory learners are, therefore, often at odds with practical learners, but if the two can work together, they can complement each other's styles. Anticipatory learners take a measured pace and are careful and thorough. They like to lay out the instructions, consult manuals, read additional books and materials on a subject, and reach a conclusion about how to go about things before actually beginning them. They like to have a map, an overview, a plan of what's going to happen and how it's going to happen. They tend to be deductive thinkers, in that they search for the framework or formula that (they assume) has already been established and then, when they are confident that they understand what will happen, apply it to the learning situation. For the anticipatory learner, the key questions are *What books are there on this subject? Where are the manuals? Do we understand the instructions thoroughly? Do we know what will happen if we do this or that?*

Scientific. Scientific learners closely follow the model taught in elementary science courses: They become enamored of a question (of practical need or not), formulate a hypothesis about how things might work, try it out in a controlled, experimental way, and then reflect carefully on the results to see how the experience can be incorporated into a broader conceptual view of the world. In Kolb's terms, these people would be balanced learners, those whose Learning Style Inventory profiles are relatively even, without heavy emphasis on any particular style. Scientific learners are neither fast nor slow, social nor asocial. Rather, they are searching for verifiable principles that can be applied again and again. They collect data, draw inferences, experiment, and review results. For the scientific learner, the key questions are *What do the data show? What conclusions can we reach from the data?*

Those five categories leave out Akin's *Validating* and *Personal Growth* groupings. In the former, Akin said that people would learn something in one way or another and, encountering it again in a learning setting, muse, *Oh yes, I knew that. So,* that's *what I've been doing.* Here, learning has already occurred, in the sense of being functionally available to the individual, but the individual just doesn't know what to call it. In this light, validating learning can be viewed as awareness of learning rather than the learning itself. In amending Akin's model, we were more interested in how the "validating" or any other kind of learner learned what he or she knew in the first place.

The Personal Growth category for Akin comprised individuals who spend their time and energy on personal habits and characteristics. These people subscribe to personal health journals, buy self-help books, and focus their growth on improving their physical or intellectual selves. For Pearl and me, this delineation was more about *what* was learned rather than *how* it was learned. We thought that the learning themes should outline just how a person learns and not become confused with the object of that learning. A person can choose to learn about self, business, management, assembling furniture, or whatever, but it was the learning process itself that we wanted to examine.

Neither Akin nor Pearl and I believed that an individual uses one learning theme to the exclusion of others. We reasoned that people probably use each of the themes to one degree or another, but that individuals have a preferred mode, a style that fits and feels right. When circumstances allow, we choose that style and apply it to the learning situation at hand. The learning style measure that Pearl and I developed demonstrated that, indeed, individuals had scores on all dimensions but tended to have dominant styles.

Learning contingencies. In the course of our investigation, though, Pearl and I encountered a confounding factor relating to the question, "Do people use the same learning theme when they approach fundamentally different kinds of learning situations?" We tested this question, and the answer seems to be no. When confronted with learning about organizational networks and managerial role demands, people tended to use social means. When those same people encountered the task of learning about a new computer program or about how to install a new computer system out of the box, they tended to use anticipatory techniques. We concluded that the style or theme applied to a situation was a function of, at least, the preferences of the individual *and* the characteristics of the learning target. We might go on to surmise that, in formal learning settings like classrooms, the learning style applied is also affected by the mode of instruction and the demands of the instructor.

Myers-Briggs Type Indicator

The Myers-Briggs Type Indicator (MBTI) is an instrument a mother-and-daughter team developed over a period of 40 years. Their interest originated in a desire to understand the daughter's husband and his (what was to them) unusual behavior. Carl Jung's publication of *Psychological Types* in 1921 fueled that interest, and over the years, they developed and refined an instrument that is widely used in industry and psychological counseling today. The MBTI yields scores on four dimensions that combine to form 16 basic psychological types. Some of those dimensions relate to learning style and are relevant to our discussion here.

The first Jungian dimension is Extraversion/Introversion. In the MBTI, these terms are not used exactly as they are in lay English. Rather, they pertain to the tendency of individuals to be oriented to the outside world or to the inside world, especially as the individuals process information. Extraverts (Es) in the MBTI view are those who draw energy from a crowd and are invigorated by discussion. They would probably be social learners in Akin's scheme. Extraverts also process information socially. They like to talk about things with others.

Introverts (Is), on the other hand, process information internally. They do not like to deal with data in a social setting, but will retreat inwardly to consider quietly and personally the meaning of what they have encountered. To them, silence is nothing to be avoided; it may, in fact, indicate considerable effort and work being done by the introvert as he or she processes what is going on.

Sometimes in teaching, you will be faced with a very quiet group. Students may tend not to discuss among themselves; they may indulge in lengthy pauses before answering questions; and they may seem distant. That silence may be very disconcerting to you. You might wonder whether or not the class is following the instruction, whether you have said something either too stupid or too erudite to stimulate the group, or if, as has happened on occasion, you have brought the wrong material into the wrong room at the wrong time. The real reason may be none of these; you may simply have a class with a lot of Introverts in it.

How you deal with classroom silence can make a big difference in your effectiveness as a teacher. I've seen situations where an instructor was so distraught over the silence of the class that he stopped and asked them what was wrong and whether he had offended them. The class was utterly surprised and sidetracked by the intervention. They wondered what was going on, began worrying about their relationship with the instructor, and lost touch with the subject matter of the class. All because there was more silence in the room than the instructor (probably an Extravert) was used to. In most teaching settings, you will have both Extraverts and Introverts in class. If a group happens to be more commonly introverted, that kind of silence may simply mean that people are thinking and working hard on the topics you have introduced.

Assessing the degree of Extraversion/Introversion in your students and in yourself provides clear benefits. For Es, the pull is toward the conferences, the classroom settings, the committee meetings, and the social aspects of the learning industry. For the Is, the attraction lies in the quiet meditative office hours, the stimulating research to be pursued in solitude, and the opportunity to think alone. Ask yourself which one you are and how that might affect your teaching style and your ability to relate to and communicate with your students.

A second MBTI dimension that relates to learning is the Perceptive/Judging scale. Perceivers (Ps) are open to outside information; they will delay making decisions in hopes that late-breaking news may help them make a better decision. The humorous conception of Ps relates to a family of Ps who went on vacation. They loaded up water skis, snow skis, beach equipment, and climbing gear, and headed out. Only when they reached the outskirts of town and pulled onto the freeway, did they begin to ask each other which way they wanted to go! They were prepared for any result but just weren't concerned about destination until they were on their way.

In contrast, Judgers (Js) have clear ideas about what they like and don't like and tend to impose their preferences on all situations. Js find it more difficult to accept new information and incorporate it into their view of the world. Thus, in the classroom, while Ps tend to be more receptive to new information but perhaps less able to act on it, Js may be more resistant to restructuring the way they already think about things. But once Js "get it," they apply it consistently and well.

The third learning-related MBTI dimension is Sensing/Intuitive. Sensing (S) types tend to be skeptical of ideas or information that do not come to them through their five senses. They like to be able to see things, to touch things, to feel the reality of things. In Kolb's language, Sensing types would rely more on concrete experience than Intuitives (INs), who respond to ideas and abstractions. INs like to see the whole and then to expand it. They daydream, imagine, create, and innovate. They are willing to act on hunches or impulses and trust their feelings much more than Sensing types. Ss like to have things laid out in logical order, in sequence, one after the other. Intuitives like to see the big picture, to ingest it all at once, to see the connections among the parts of the whole. Obviously, the way you explain things in class determines the extent to which you reach one type or bypass another.

The MBTI is an easily administered instrument that can be scored quickly. The interpretation of the scores can take hours or days, however, depending on the skill of the interpreter and willingness of the group to pursue the nuances of the data. Although I don't advocate that you give this instrument to every person in your classes, I have found that understanding it and your own profile can help you communicate more clearly with others and help them be comfortable with their learning style. It will also help you be more tolerant of other people's learning styles and of institutional biases for one style or another. I do encourage you to take this instrument, receive some guidance in its interpretation, and reflect on how your type can influence your effectiveness in the classroom.

Neurolinguistic programming

John Grinder and Richard Bandler are generally credited with establishing a line of study called neurolinguistic programming (NLP). Although this chapter won't pursue all the characteristics of NLP, it will outline some aspects of NLP that are useful when thinking about adult learning. NLP posits that over their lifetimes people develop physiological highways in their nervous systems. When we receive sensory data and respond, we use a neuromuscular-linguistic link or pathway. The more we use that particular pathway, the more that pathway becomes familiar, comfortable, and a preferred way of sending signals from one part of the body to another.

The analogy often used is that our nervous system, especially the brain, is like a tub of firm gelatin. When a hot rock, a neurological electrical impulse, is added to the system through our five senses and moves from one place to another, it burns a pathway into our system. It is easier for subsequent impulses or signals to follow the same pathway rather than forge a new one. After repeated use, the pathway becomes the neurological equivalent of a freeway with thousands and thousands of impulses passing over the same pathways rather than less used, less familiar alternatives. Recent research on the brain seems to confirm that general model.

Since the process begins with sensory input, it produces, according to NLP, three basic information-processing styles in people: visual, audio, and kinesthetic, based on sight, hearing, and touch, respectively. The idea is that some people prefer to receive and process information through their eyes and are thus typed as "visuals." Others prefer to hear things ("auditories"), while some prefer to get data by touch and feeling ("kinesthetics"). NLP goes further and argues that people will reflect their preferred information gathering and processing styles in their speech (hence the link to "linguistic"). Visuals, for instance, will often use phrases like, "Don't you see?" or "I see what you mean" or "Let me show you what I mean." Auditories will use language like "I hear you" or "Do you hear what I'm saying?" or "Let me explain it to you." Kinesthetics will say things like "That feels right to me" or "I need to get in touch with so-and-so" or "I can't quite grasp what you're talking about."

One obvious connection between this theory and teaching is the importance of providing information through communication channels that will be familiar to and accepted by receivers. In teaching, major course ideas that are not presented visually, audially, and kinesthetically will be missed by some and ill-understood by others. NLP strongly suggests that instructors provide for visual, audio, and kinesthetic examples for all major concepts being taught.

Conclusion

People learn in different ways. They may have some adaptability in their learning styles, but we seem to prefer certain ways of approaching and working through learning situations. We receive and process information in different ways. We think and decide in different ways. The more sensitive you are to the variations in your students' cognitive styles and to your own cognitive, learning, and teaching styles, the more effective your teaching will be.

Beware, also, of the danger of "overteaching." Michael Polanyi in his book, *Personal Knowledge*, introduced the concept of logical "unspecifiability," the idea that there are processes in the world that become more impossible to do the more one tries to analyze and understand them. Hammering a nail and riding a bicycle are good examples. If you tried to teach hammering or riding a bike with the laws of physics – describing the force vectors (with their power and direction) and their relationships to centrifugal forces and gravity, and introduced the mathematical equations to describe these processes along with techniques of measuring them to the novice, then the behavioral tasks of actually hammering or bike riding would become more difficult, even impossible, to do. The same is true of the golf swing. At some point, you must just do it, and from the doing, learn.

The same danger also exists in your learning about teaching. This book is intended to help you see aspects of the teaching/learning relationship that you may not have examined before. But if it causes you to freeze up in the classroom because you are trying to remember all of the principles and guidelines, then it serves no good purpose. On the other hand, we can no longer assume that teaching will teach us to teach effectively. The middle ground, which comprises ongoing learning about teaching and continued development of practical and artful skills of teaching, is the balance we want to strike. As usual, the solution lies not in either/or answers, but in the both/and answers. When you enter the classroom, as when you begin a golf swing, you must let your previous training, preparation, and skill development take over and let it happen. If you try to control excessively either your teaching or the golf swing, your results will be jerky and less effective.

Further reading

Bloom, Allan, *The Closing of the American Mind*, New York: Simon & Schuster, 1987.

Buzan, Tony, *Use Your Head*, London: BBC, 1974.

Cattell, Raymond B., *Personality and Learning Theory*, New York: Springer Publishing Company, 1979.

Christensen, C. Roland, *Teaching and the Case Method*, Boston: Harvard Business School, 1987.

Gragg, Charles I., "Teachers Also Must Learn," *Harvard Educational Review*, 10 (1940) 30–47.

Hayakawa, S. I., *Language in Thought and Action*, 4th edn, New York: Harcourt Brace Jovanovich, 1941.

Hilgard, Ernest R., and Gordon H. Bower, *Theories of Learning*, 4th edn, Englewood Cliffs, NJ: Prentice-Hall, 1975.

Knowles, Malcolm, *The Adult Learner*, 4th edn, Houston: Gulf Publishing, 1990.

Knox, Alan B., *Adult Development and Learning*, San Francisco: Jossey-Bass, 1978.

Kuhn, Thomas S., *The Structure of Scientific Revolutions*, 2nd edn, Chicago: University of Chicago Press, 1970.

Mager, Robert F., *Preparing Instructional Objectives*, Belmont, California: Fearon Publishers, 1962.

Mager, Robert F., and Peter Pipe, *Analyzing Performance Problems or "You Really Oughta Wanna,"* Belmont, CA: Fearon Pitman Publishers, 1970.

North, Alfred, *The Aims of Education: and Other Essays*, New York: The
  Free Press, 1967.
Polanyi, Michael, *Personal Knowledge*, Chicago: University of Chicago
  Press, 1958.
Porter, Lyman W., and Lawrence E. McKibbin, *Management Education and
  Development*, New York: McGraw-Hill, 1988.
Rogers, Carl R., "Personal Thoughts on Teaching and Learning," in *On
  Becoming a Person*, Boston: Houghton-Mifflin, 1961: 273–78.
Skinner, B. F., *Science and Human Behavior,* New York: The Free Press,
  1953.

4 | *Planning a course: trips and tips*

JAMES G. S. CLAWSON AND
MARK E. HASKINS

Let our children grow tall, and some taller
than others if they have it in them to do so.
– Margaret Thatcher,
former British Prime Minister

At a very fundamental level, dreaming about, then designing a framework for, then developing the content of, and then delivering the classes in, a course is one of the more entrepreneurial activities an instructor does. For a brand-new course, it may occur only a handful of times over the span of a career. It occurs repeatedly, albeit in a slightly different way, when you conscientiously revisit and revise a course that may be going into its twenty-seventh offering. In either instance, course planning is akin to mapping a road trip – identifying the destination, knowing the students' "you-are-here" position, choosing the best vehicle(s) for the journey, identifying the best routes, selecting the most conducive speed to travel, and highlighting the memorable scenes along the way that all contribute to a strong, lasting, effective learning experience for students. Indeed, it is about creating a journey that invites and entices students to experience and internalize as much of the trip as they possibly can so that they learn and, to use Thatcher's analogy, grow as tall as they can.

Course planning is about...

Anticipation

Planning a course, at its most basic level, brings to bear an instructor's best thinking about how to craft an effective learning experience for students. This applies to a university-based semester-long course as well as to a one-day nondegree executive development seminar. The challenge in course planning is to plan without knowing the specific

49

strengths and weaknesses of those who will be in the course and without knowing the specifics of what happened in each preceding class.

Although we as instructors may not know such specifics, there is always information available that allows us to anticipate, in general ways, useful baselines. For example, there are colleagues (at our own institutions or at another) who have taught similar courses before; there are advance class rosters identifying those who have tentatively signed up; there are the insights we have gleaned from our own prior classes; there is our own subject matter expertise and sense of a logical topic flow and pacing; and then there is the bold and creative side of our psyches that prompts us to try something different. All such factors can help an instructor to anticipate what is likely to work best in a course. The very act of anticipation engages your mind to consider possibilities, wrestle with a host of interesting "what ifs," and to be on the lookout for new materials and examples. Avoid procrastination: It is the antithesis of anticipatory course planning, producing none of these positive benefits. In fact, it can sour an instructor's outlook for an impending course and drain vast amounts of mental energy in needless excuse-making, feelings of infringement on your work, and ultimately in last-minute worry about getting a course ready to go.

Destination, motivation, and fascination

The process of anticipation is largely focused on (1) envisioning the learning destination desired for students; (2) wanting to cultivate a sense of fascination for the subject matter; and (3) seeking to fuel students' motivation to learn. To identify a destination, instructors must decide whether the course is a broad overview course or a more narrowly constructed, dig-deeply course. Is the objective primarily to develop an appreciation for the subject matter or to develop mastery? Is this a stand-alone course or does another, subsequent course rely on this course's ending point as its starting point? To cultivate a sense of fascination, instructors should contemplate interesting and creative ways to explore the subject matter's principles, shortcomings, and applications (e.g., in an accounting course comparing the parallels between IBM's balance sheet and a balance sheet constructed for one of the course's students). To fuel students' motivation, instructors should think about how best to convey the relevancy of the course (e.g., using outside speakers, contemporary news articles, videos, DVDs, testimonials from graduates) and their own enthusiasm for the course content.

Preparation

Once an instructor has anticipated the course aspects of destination, motivation, and fascination, it is time for preparation to begin. Preparation is putting in place the plans for, and the mechanisms to, execute the ideas chosen to move students toward the envisioned destination, while motivating them to take the journey, and fascinating them along the way. The value in advance preparation is that it allows time for operational issues to surface and get dealt with; it provides a litmus test for the feasibility of an idea at a point in time when the idea can still be modified or abandoned and replaced with another; it is respectful of support staff's time and efforts. And, quite simply, some things require lead time to get done (e.g., invitations to outside speakers, obtaining copyright permissions from publishers for news articles or other reprints). We have found that the crafting of a course syllabus, at least one with the general contents described here, is an extremely useful aid to course preparation. We have found this to be true not only for our degree-program courses, but also for the one- and two-week executive education programs we deliver. In effect, putting a syllabus together serves as a comprehensive, dynamic "To Do" list, and the finished syllabus serves as a road map for the course.

Syllabi

A robust, detailed course syllabus is the culmination of an instructor's planning and the starting point for students' course trek. The syllabus is the course road map – with just a glance, it provides a sense of location amidst busy calendars, gives direction on where to proceed next, facilitates course execution, and, if followed, can lead both instructors and students to the positive destinations of learning and satisfaction. A good syllabus presents your course as a journey worth taking, making the strong statement that you have identified a clear destination and know how to get there.

It is tempting for an instructor to simply compile a reading list and hand it out to students as the course syllabus. Sometimes, instructors do not even have a complete course reading list to hand out at the beginning of a course, preferring instead to hand out assignments week by week or class by class. In all but perhaps a current events-type course, that approach creates the view that the instructor is only one step ahead of the class; indeed that may be the case. The overall effect is to give students an early impression that the instructor lacks preparation or interest in the course. It may also leave students confused about the way the course will be administered, and about where they are going and how they will be evaluated – minimal issues that, we believe, should be dealt with in a syllabus. These feelings can combine to undermine any positive sense of anticipation and enthusiasm for the topical journey about to begin.

Creating a detailed syllabus, well in advance of a course's start, can help produce great results in the classroom. Developing a well-conceived syllabus is not a trivial task, but a worthwhile endeavor. Despite some instructors' fears, a good syllabus need not be constraining; it can be modified and adapted while a course is under way and saved for use in subsequent academic terms, with amendments as necessary in years to come. The following sections highlight some of the more important aspects of course planning and creating a strong syllabus.

Syllabus contents. A robust, informative syllabus should contain most, if not all, of the following items:
- A title section that simply notes the title of the course, the name of the instructor (including contact information and office hours if formally set) and the school, and the date of the course.
- A statement of learning objectives for the course.
- A clear listing of the required materials for the course and where those materials can be obtained.
- A comprehensive statement describing the grading policies to be used in the course along with the classroom norms the instructor seeks to establish and any other rules of conduct or practice that are expected (e.g., an attendance policy).
- A complete course calendar depicting the days and dates the course meets, daily topics, each class' chronological number in the course, and major readings. To help students plan their academic time, the course calendar should also include exam and paper dates, and special holidays or other events.
- A detailed communication of daily assignments. For each class listed on the course calendar, instructors should indicate the class topic, the

reading assignment(s), any pertinent study questions, and any special notes to students.

- In anticipation of some students wishing to pursue additional reading pertinent to the course, it is useful to provide a supplemental reading list in a syllabus. If included, it is important to clearly mark such readings as not required and not the focus of any exam contained in the course.

Clearly, this syllabus outline suggests that creating a syllabus is not a last-minute activity. When students receive our syllabus, we want their first impression to be positive and to create heightened interest. We want them to sense our commitment to the course and to feel that this is going to be worth their while – to be both challenging and fruitful. We want them to set aside the time they need to devote to it, to plan their vacations, trips, job recruiting, and other activities around the course's meeting times using the syllabus calendar. We want them to understand our ground rules so there is no misunderstanding.

Let's take a chronological look at crafting a syllabus along these dimensions. What happens first?

Calendar checks. The practical reality is that a course is taught within an institution's calendar structure. At a minimum, there are starting dates, ending dates, exam periods, paper-writing periods, holidays, sporting events, and other calendar events that affect a course's flow. Inadvertently scheduling an important conceptual class on the day before Thanksgiving probably means that some students will miss it and others will only be partially prepared and attentive. There are also other courses and other commitments that students have running concurrently with yours. Practically speaking, it may not be possible to learn much about the major assignments and events that other courses have scheduled, but instructors are wise to consider the implications of students' concurrent commitments as best as possible to ascertain the share of students' minds and energies available for their course.

Clearly, the rationale undergirding this calendar check is to add the students' view of the term to the sequencing of course materials and deliverables. One way to get this view is to create a table of the academic period with columns for the date, the course classes, school events, national and other events (see Figure 4.1). Using such a table, it is easy to see how coincident events might impinge on, or be leveraged by, one's course. Begin by asking questions such as, "Where are the clusters of classes that are available? Where do the weekend breaks come? Where

DATE	COURSE EVENTS	SCHOOL EVENTS	NATIONAL EVENTS	OTHER EVENTS	TO DO

Figure 4.1 Background factors in course planning

are there large gaps in the schedule? Where are the major holidays and sporting events that will conflict with student preparation and the scheduled classes?" With answers to these questions in hand, the most important parts of a course can be scheduled when the most favorable class sequences are available, and the less critical course content can be scheduled during the more disjointed or busy parts of the calendar.

In calendar planning, do not forget the demands on your own time that a course will make. Collecting papers or exams the day before a major holiday or professional conference, for instance, has a way of ruining what may have been a much needed three-day break or personal development sojourn. Remember to schedule enough slack in your own calendar to grade papers and exams and to get the renewal needed to remain sharp and energized.

Within the executive education, single-company, short-course program context, it is critical to add the sponsoring company's calendar issues to this phase of the course planning process. For example, we can recall conducting an executive program for a large client when the attending managers' performance reviews for their direct reports were due. Needless to say, we did not have much of their attention for the 24-hour period prior to the deadline. We had no choice but to lower the participative content of the program for a day and have the teaching team step into a more directive, lecture-oriented mode.

We also conducted a program near the end of the client's fiscal year for company executives who needed to be in close contact with their teams to properly close out the year and a number of pending deals. Because we knew beforehand, we were able to schedule 60-minute morning and afternoon windows expressly for "cell-phone time," and we even provided spare cell phones for attendees whose own cell phones malfunctioned.

Sequencing modules. The next chronological syllabus-building step is to decide on the logical clustering and flow of course topics. These clusters become modules (groups of classes sharing a complementary focus) in the finished course, and their flow presupposes a carefully considered pace for the course as well as a series of leverageable connections. Sorting this sequencing out is simultaneously a teaching issue, a learning issue, a calendar issue, and a conceptual issue. From the teaching perspective, it is important to consider whether or not the materials for each module are available during the tentative time planned for that module. Constraints on ordering materials, scheduling classrooms (or other facilities), and getting speakers and your own pedagogical preferences all influence whether a certain sequence of course modules works better than another.

On the learning issue, it is important to carefully consider the sequence of classes that would be most conducive to students' learning. Are the topics arranged so that they make sense for students? Would one module work better for them in front of another module or vice versa? For instance, in our school, we became concerned at one time about the effectiveness of the student study groups that meet throughout the first year of the MBA program. Originally, the required Organizational Behavior course began with a module on individual behavior and then led into the topic of small-group behavior, but we reversed this sequencing to better address the school-wide concern for more effective study groups.

The calendar can also affect module sequencing. If a particular module requires six classes to cover it effectively, but the natural sequencing of that module puts it on the calendar where only three classes fall together uninterrupted, the module might be better served by resequencing. Take care not to ignore the impact of large gaps between classes in a module or between related modules: They can add to the difficulty students may have in understanding and retaining material.

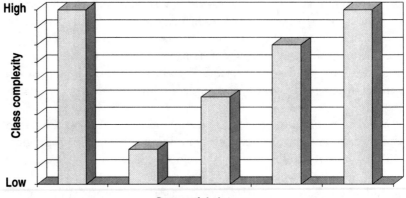

Figure 4.2 Conceptual flow for course module designs

In summary, module sequencing is something of a mental, linear programming endeavor – that is, there are constraints and objectives within which a course sequence must be programmed to achieve maximum student learning. The optimal sequencing may not be the one that you experienced as a student or saw a colleague do or that you tried the first time you taught the course nor the one you would have chosen without such constraints present, but it may be the best one for facilitating student learning for this semester's course offering.

Module Building

The structure of classes within a module greatly influences student learning. Sherwood Frey, a colleague of ours, introduced us to a module structure framework that makes great sense and works well in its rollout. Although the following description of that structure is tailored to case method instruction, the same principles can be applied to other teaching methods. The starting point underlying this module structure framework is one of "creating a need to know" in the minds of the students and then satisfying that need.

As Figure 4.2 shows, an effective module structure begins with a practical but complex set of materials wherein students discover how important and intractable the problem/issue is, given their existing capabilities. The second class addresses the frustration they experience coming out of the first class by dropping to a lower level of complexity and including some theoretical training on the topic. In our school, the second case in a module is often the least complex, and it is usually accompanied by a reading that introduces conceptual frameworks that can be applied to the situations that will arise thereafter in the module. This second class might focus on a single subset of the questions raised in the first class or it might treat all of them at a more basic level. The case or exercise associated with class No. 2 should be simple relative to the case the day before so that it allows everyone in the class to grasp and complete the assignment well. That approach gives students a sense of accomplishment that can replace the frustration of the first day. It also helps students to see that no matter how complex a new and real problem may seem, it can be dealt with in an effective manner.

Subsequent classes in the module gradually build in complexity – each class is a bit more challenging and comprehensive than the last because it adds additional considerations, introduces nuances of the practical applications, or poses similar issues in more complex situations. Finally, the last class in a module is as complex as the first one and has no accompanying supporting materials. The students are left on their own, after the careful coaching and development of the middle classes, to wrestle with a difficult situation. We expect that their experience will be very different from the first day of the module because of their increased understanding and analytical capacity. If an instructor takes care to point it out, students can see how much they have grown. Students often leave the last class of such a module fired up about their abilities and the ways that the course has developed them and eager to test their new skills. Then, they encounter the first class in a new module, and the cycle begins again.

For executive education short courses, this concept for module design is applicable with one alteration. For the first class in a stream of topical classes, when the entire stream is likely to only be four to seven classes long, it is not critical to have the first class "create the need to know." Generally speaking, if an instructor has performed due diligence in assessing the needs and interests of the course's executive attendees, the design of *each class* will generally follow the module design pattern we describe. Thus, within a single 90- to 120-minute executive education, nondegree program class, the first 15 to 20 minutes are used to posit the "need to know" via the presentation of a business situation that the participants can relate to. The next 20 minutes are generally spent introducing the fundamental analytical tools, skills, and/or mental models for addressing that issue. Next, we would spend about 45 minutes conducting the analytical approach suggested, followed by discussions germane to implementing the decision the analysis points to. The subsequent class may then simply present another identical opportunity in the same general subject matter arena for additional practice or reinforcement. If class sessions are scarce for a subject matter stream, the next class may pose the same learning sequence, but for another topic within the stream.

Faculty version of the syllabus

We recommend developing two versions of a syllabus – a faculty version (Figure 4.3) for instructor eyes only as well as the disseminated student version. A faculty syllabus includes all the elements of the student version with the following changes: First, reserve an entire page for each class. Second, separate the student assignment from the rest of the page with a solid line. It is the material below the line on each class page that defines the faculty version; here, add three sections: Objectives, Tentative Teaching Plan, and Notes.

Objectives. Every class ought to have some specific objectives. They may be as simple as, "To have everyone introduce themselves and get to know at least five classmates a bit better," or as complex as, "To have students demonstrate their level of understanding of PERT techniques given the data in the Sun Oil case." Disciplining yourself to think about and write specific objectives for each class is a powerful focusing device. It sharpens preparation and clarifies the value of each of the teaching techniques or tools tentatively selected for use in a class. Some may think that writing objectives for each class is confining or even counterproductive and that an instructor should not write objectives. We disagree. Explicitly articulating class objectives clarifies and sharpens what is to be accomplished at the end of a collective investment of time and effort for both instructor and students.

Our thinking here has been influenced by Robert Mager. In two classic books, *Preparing Instructional Objectives* and *Analyzing Performance Problems*, he provides useful guidance on the topic of educational objectives. In brief, he recommends setting objectives for each teaching session and framing them in behavioral ways so that students demonstrate their learning. Thus, the subjects in the subject-verb construction of most "Magerian" objectives are the learners. The verbs are

Figure 4.3
Faculty version of a syllabus for an MBA career management course

Course Objectives

This course is intended to:

1. Help you develop skills in generating and using personal data in making career decisions.
2. Provide you with a conceptual picture of the second semester job search process and a plan for managing it.
3. Help you develop skills in knowing what kind of job data is relevant to you and in generating that data in your dealings with organizations.
4. Provide you with a bilateral (individual/organizational) conceptual framework of career development and some opportunity to practice applying it.
5. Develop your skills at an essential managerial skill, inductive logic or reaching conclusions under uncertainty from large pools of data.

Grading

Your grade will be composed of 35% Self-Assessment Paper (SAP), 35% Career Development Paper (CDP), and 30% class participation.

Required materials

Self-Assessment and Career Development (SACD). 2nd edn, by James G. Clawson, John P. Kotter, Victor A. Faux, and Charles C. McArthur, Prentice-Hall, Englewood Cliffs, NJ. Available from Publications Department.

Supplementary Case Packet (CP)

Faculty

Professor James G. Clawson	Tel: 924–7488 (Room 315)
Course Secretary Mary Darnell	Tel: 924–7486 (Room 323)

Figure 4.3
(contd.)

COURSE CALENDAR, Fall Semester

I. Introduction
1.   M   9/6   Introduction

II. Self-assessment
2.   T   9/7   The Figure Test
3.   W   9/8   Cognitive Style
4.   M   9/13   Values
5.   T   9/14   Interpersonal Style
6.   M   9/20   Life Styles
7.   T   9/21   Written Interview (Written Interviews due)
8.   W   9/22   Developing Life Themes
9.   M   10/4   Strong Interest Inventory
10. T   10/5   Completing a Self-Assessment
11. M   10/11   Canceled for Dyad Exercise

III. Self-assessment paper
12. T   10/12   Personal Theme Development. SAP Assignment
13. W   10/13   Canceled to Write Self-Assessment Paper
14. M   10/18   Canceled to Write Self-Assessment Paper
15. T   10/19   Implications of Self-Assessment (SAPs due)

IV. Generating opportunities
16. M   11/1   The Job Search
17. T   11/2   Written Sources (Résumés and Annual Reports)
18. M   11/8   Correspondence and Interviewing
19. T   11/9   Corporate Culture
20. M   11/15   Managing Job Search
21. T   11/16   Negotiating and Deciding I
22. M   11/22   Negotiating and Deciding II
22b. M   11/22   Two Person Choosing (Optional)
23. T   11/23   Managing Joining Up

V. Individuals and organizations
24. W   11/24   The First Year Out
25. M   12/6   Developmental Relationships
26. T   12/7   Managing Plateaus
27. M   12/13   Renegotiating the Contract
28. T   12/14   Issues Day
29. W   12/15   Managing Careers Over Time (CDPs due)
         No final exam.

Figure 4.3
(contd.)

Class #1. Introduction to the Course

Assignment: Read this SYLLABUS (CP), INTRODUCTION (SACD), THE SELF-ASSESSMENT PROCESS (SACD). Read also DAN AND MANDY (SACD).

Study Questions: What decisions do Dan and Mandy need to make? What kinds of information do Dan and Mandy need to make their decisions? How should they make their decisions?

In Class: We will discuss the course and the major assignments in some detail. After a discussion of the case, the WRITTEN INTERVIEW (SACD) and the STRONG INTEREST INVENTORY will be assigned.

Objectives:
1. To generate students' enthusiasm and get their thinking about the kind of data they need to make the choices they may be facing this year.
2. To establish realistic expectations about the course by discussing workload, calendar assignments, grading.
3. To set up and assign the Written Interview and Strong Interest Inventory.

Tentative Class Design:
1. Discuss case (40 min.)
2. Outline course objectives, calendar, workload, grading, and overall approach. Use overhead of the calendar page to point out heavy work periods. (30 min.)
3. Assign Written Interview, Strong and Background Data Sheet; explain next class, remind to bring texts. (10 min.)

Notes:
1. Don't come across too rationally. They have to feel safe in such a personalized course.

Figure 4.3
(contd.)

Class #2. The Figure Test
Assignment: Complete the Strong Interest Inventory.

Begin writing your Written Interview. DO NOT POSTPONE IT. It helps
to write it in 2 or 3 sittings rather than in a marathon exercise. You
will get better data. The Interview encourages you to take a break
after Question #4, but feel free to leave your writing at any point.
The sequencing is important (don't skip ahead), but the time spent
in each sitting or on each question is up to you.

In Class: The Figure Test will be administered, scored, and analyzed.
DO NOT DO THE FIGURE TEST BEFORE CLASS! BRING YOUR TEST TO
CLASS.

Due: Hand in your completed Strong Campbell and your Background
Data Sheet.

Objectives:
1. To allocate all preparation time to the Written Interview.
2. To model data generating and analyzing process we will use
   throughout the first half of the course. (Take instrument, Feelings
   Record, Read note, Read case – if there is one, Analyze the case,
   Score own data, Analyze own data.)
3. To generate and analyze Figure Test data.

Tentative Class Design:
1. Any questions about the Written Interview? (5 min.)
2. Figure Test (administer, analyze, and score) (60 min.). Don't spend
   too long on the matrix. Save time to score.
3. Make entries in Feelings Record.
4. Analyze the Tom Wilson case. Then, leave time for them to work
   on their own data.

Notes/Development Ideas:
1. Check overheads. Redo so they are neater.
2. Need to develop a simple, reliable Cognitive Style instrument.

. . . and so on for all class sessions

---

action verbs that are observable, and the criteria for adequate performance of the verbs are specifically laid out in terms of quality and time. For instance: "Three or more students will describe the application of 'Rogerian' listening techniques to a performance review situation provided in today's case study to the instructor's satisfaction before the end of class." That objective is "Magerian" in that it identifies who will do what and to what standard of observable performance. That kind of objective has strong implications for what should happen during the class. More vague notions of a class goal, such as, "Cover Rogerian listening," make it harder to focus on learning rather than teaching and to know if students are learning.

Tentative Teaching Plan. A tentative class plan simply lists the major sections of a class. These may each be associated with a question that will guide the class for a period of time. This plan is tentative and may be revised as the actual class day approaches. Writing this skeletal teaching plan along with the syllabus, though, facilitates remembering the logic employed in constructing the course. Sometimes these tentative plans follow the same order as the objectives for the class; often they do not. One way to organize this section in case-oriented classes is to list the major questions that ought to be addressed in that class. These may be questions you will actually ask or just questions that will guide your thinking about how the class unfolds. Asking the right questions is an essential teaching skill, and planning for the tentative unfolding of the class provides another opportunity to practice forming good questions. As discussed in a later chapter, comprehensive case teaching notes often provide a starting point for a tentative class plan, galvanizing in-class questions and discussion timing.

Notes. In this context, there are two kinds of notes – pre-notes and post-notes. Pre-notes serve as reminders of any unusual audiovisual arrangements or special orders that need to be made in advance of a class. These might include reserving a room, ordering a self-assessment instrument, or checking out audiovisual equipment. Make a habit of checking your pre-notes a week or two ahead of time.

Post-notes refer to important thoughts captured after having just taught the class. During the class, you may have observed a better way to teach the subject, a new question to ask, or a different, more effective way you could have conducted the class. Record those notes and keep them readily available for reference when revising the syllabus for the next iteration of the course.

Other Examples of Syllabi

As we noted earlier, mapping the journey with a syllabus is also important in the short-course, executive education arena, even when the
course lasts only a week or two Executives tend to prefer short, synoptic communications, so bear that in mind as you work. We often
provide them with (1) a narrative overview of the entire program; (2)
a narrative overview of each of the program's subject matter streams;
(3) a flow diagram of the combined subject matter streams; (4) a day-
by-day pictorial schedule of the program materials and topics, and
(5) specific class session assignment sheets. In essence, these materials
stand alone and in combination: They communicate all that is needed
for a program from the most general to the most specific. Figure 4.4
provides some examples of these items as they apply to a two-week
executive education program for one of our large corporate clients.

Recently, we have discovered an interesting, promising approach to
course syllabi: A graphical depiction of a syllabus that can be a substitute for, or a complement to, the more traditional narrative approach
discussed throughout this chapter. Biktimirov and Nilson (2003, p.
311) present and discuss such a syllabus for an introductory finance
course. The beauty of such an approach is that it visually conveys the
flow of topics and materials, across the semester and in relation to
one another. We encourage such experimentation with syllabi and find
the graphical approach to have great appeal.

Conclusion

It's your choice: Preparation of a course syllabus can either be a chore
or a pathway to a classroom adventure. It is intriguing to think about
the route (i.e., the points to be connected in sequence over a semester),
the distance to be covered in a day (i.e., the pace at which topics are
introduced and dealt with), the sights to stop at and dwell on (i.e.,
the examples and stories to share related to the topic of the day), the
detours to take (i.e., the connections to make to other courses, the purposeful doubling back over prior material to reinforce the lessons, etc.),
and the vehicles to ride (i.e., the role of cases, DVDs, CDs, lectures,
outside speakers, and current events).

At many institutions, course syllabi are centrally collected by the
registrar or in the library. They are available to instructors and students.

Figure 4.4
Syllabus for a two-week executive development program

Panel A: Narrative program overview

The purposes of this program are to
(a) facilitate the development of an enterprise view,
(b) enhance the analytical business skills, and
(c) strengthen the leadership capabilities of those company leaders attending.

This program is premised on the belief that the future of the company will be determined by you and your cohorts' abilities to implement strategies, quickly assess realities, seize opportunities, avoid setbacks, and effectively work together.

One aspect of the journey during these two weeks will be to focus on developing "strategic thinking" in regard to changing environments, value chains, and the opportunities you face and create. Professor Jeanne Liedtka (JL) will lead these discussions and they will serve as the bookends for the program as well as its connecting thread.

A critical aspect of fully utilizing strategic thinking capabilities, is to exercise them in the context of one's daily operations and imperatives – to do so requires systems thinking and state of the art thinking in regards to service excellence. Professor Bob Landel (BL) will facilitate the classroom conversations and exploration of operational excellence.

Leaders must challenge assumptions about customers and competitors. Who are they? How can we serve them? How should I be partnering with them? Why can't I simply try to be better at what I already do? Professor Robert Spekman (RS) will encourage you to think "out of the box" in regards to markets, customers, partners, and innovation.

Financial data is at the heart of knowing where a person is and where he or she aims to go. Shareholders expect value creation. What does that mean? What gets measured is what gets done so the "right" things better get measured. Professor Mark Haskins (MH) will facilitate conversations that address becoming more financially savvy in operational decisions and in understanding organization-level performance.

The company's future is yours to define, shape, and create. Personal leadership skills can be learned and enhanced. Leveraging the capabilities of those who work for you and who you work with is one of

Figure 4.4
(contd.)

the most important leadership skills you can acquire. Professor Lynn Isabella (LI) will encourage you to ask yourself tough questions, consider alternative ways of leading, and share with you "best practices."

Throughout the program, we will strive to develop a clear picture of the positioning of the different company businesses in today's market, while looking to the future and envisioning the possibilities to both defend and grow each business. We'll come together as a class to share what each business group sees as the top opportunities for the company. Finally, we'll pull it all together, on our final morning, by returning to where we began: With the strategic challenges facing the company. Working in learning teams, we'll ask each individual to review the learning and insights generated over the past two weeks, and to identify one key opportunity that he or she is personally willing to commit to that will begin the process of addressing the challenges faced.

Panel B: Overview of the "performance" stream
Session # 1
Material: Company annual report
Theme: Financial statement savvy
Learning objectives:
- To explore the content of this primary means of communicating to shareholders and reporting performance for the enterprise
- To understand the basic premises on which the three key financial statements are built
- To introduce "financial picture thinking"

Session #2
Material: Company annual report and additional handouts
Theme: Company and industry financial analysis
Learning objectives:
- To perform a basic DuPont-model financial analysis on the company's financial statements
- To compare and contrast the company's financial results with other industry players
- To ascertain the direction and magnitude of performance results necessary to lead the industry group and to begin to raise ideas for how to bring about that performance enhancement

Figure 4.4
(contd.)

Session #3
Material: Sparta Glass Works case
Theme: Contribution and risk analysis
Learning objectives:
• To understand cost behaviors and the need for that understanding in responding to a market request/need
• To introduce and execute a basic risk analysis, sensitivity analysis, and contribution analysis

Session #4
Material: Mobil Oil case
Theme: Implementing strategy: the balanced scorecard
Learning objectives:
• To review one company's use of the balanced scorecard in bringing about successful strategic and operations-related change
• To explore a general framework for a performance management/ measurement system
• To consider aspects of your company's performance measurement systems that are perhaps missing or undervalued and ideas for addressing that

Session #5
Material: Horizon Insurance Co.
Theme: Outsourcing and creating value
Learning objectives:

Figure 4.4
(contd.)

- To identify the proper framework for contemplating an outsourcing opportunity
- To understand and execute a relevant cost analysis in the context of an outsourcing option
- To introduce the basic financial considerations involved in creating shareholder value

Panel C: Entire program content flow overview

Performance	Financial Statement Savvy and Analysis	→	Value Creating Analysis	→	Performance Measurement
Strategic Thinking	Industry Analysis	→	Developing capabilities within the firm and across the value chain	→	Company value chain and opportunities workshop
People	Leading Change	→	Leaders, differences, and teams	→	Thinking like a partner and teacher
Processes	Service Excellence	→	Supplier/customer collaboration and dynamics	→	Implementing business strategies
Markets	Segmentation →		Sustainable competitive advantage	→ Alliances and Partnerships →	Innovation

Panel D: Week 1 of 2, calendar overview

Monday	Tuesday	Wednesday	Thursday	Friday
Breakfast	Breakfast	Breakfast	Breakfast	Breakfast
Program overview (MH) Strategic challenges debrief (JL)	Developing a marketing focus – Sealed Air case (RS)	Segmentation is KEY and not all customers are created equally – Signode case (RS)	Transforming the business: Is there sustainable competitive advantage? – FedEx/UPS case (RS)	Contribution and risk analysis – Sparta Glass case (MH)
Break	Break	Break	Break	Break
LT	LT	LT	LT	LT
Understanding industries – article and Disney case (JL)	Assessing service reliability and improvement opportunities – Arrow Electronics case (BL)	Leadership and strategic change – Peter Browning and Continental Whitecap case (LI)	The process of changing – Johnsonville Sausage case (LI)	Exploring the value chain – Compaq/Intel article (JL)

Figure 4.4
(contd.)

Lunch	Lunch	Lunch	Lunch	Lunch
LT	LT	LT	no LT	LT
Annual Report discussion (MH)	*Company and industry financial analysis (MH)*	*Service excellence: Operating processes – Southwest Airlines at Baltimore case (BL)*	*Building capabilities across functions and business units – Park Nicollet video case (JL)*	*Supplier-customer collaboration – GE/Carrier case (BL, RS)*
		Break		*Group photo*
		Tour of Academical Village		
Individual prep Dinner LTs	*Individual prep Dinner LTs*	*Individual prep Dinner LTs*	*Individual prep Dinner LTs*	*Individual prep Dinner LTs*

Panel E: Example of a "performance" stream assignment sheet

Topic: Outsourcing and creating value

Material: **Horizon Insurance Agency** (UVA-C-2140, Rev. 1/04)
Chapter 3, **EGMACS text**, pp. 3–14 (optional background reading)
Chapter 5, **EGMACS text**, pp. 8–9 (optional background reading)

Assignment:
1. Please complete the worksheet presented at the end of the case. It is designed to create a comparative financial analysis of a "status quo" option versus the "outsourcing" option, with the final column capturing the financial differences between the two. (You should feel free to complete your worksheet in Learning Team or to check out your completed worksheet with your Learning Team.)
2. In general, how should we determine whether this outsourcing option adds value to Horizon Insurance? With that in mind, should the contract be signed? Why or why not?

Note: The reading provides lots of details. It is not important that those details be studied. Rather, please focus on the major issues presented in those pages.

We encourage instructors to peruse those syllabi from time to time to simply get a feel for some of the more appealing formats our colleagues use. If something is appealing to you in that regard, try it – chances are, it will also appeal to your students. In addition, seeing what your colleagues do is an easy way to identify some of the more creative course components and pedagogies they are using. Consider seeking out that colleague to learn more about how well something worked and what challenges it presented.

In the end, investing a conscientious level of effort and time in planning a course and crafting its related syllabus is time and effort well spent. That effort will minimize the need for continual overhauls of a course in an attempt to get it right. Moreover, the investment will be obvious to students, and a well-planned course is more likely to deliver on its promise of providing students with a worthwhile, positive learning experience.

Further Reading

Biktimirov, E. N., and L. B. Nilson, "Mapping Your Course: Designing a Graphic Syllabus for Introductory Finance," *Journal of Education for Business* (July/August 2003), 308–12.

Mager, R.F., *Analyzing Performance Problems,* Belmont, CA: David S. Lake Publishers, 1984.

Preparing Instructional Objectives, Belmont, CA: Lake and Management Training, 1984.

Marcis, J.G., and D.R. Carr, "The Course Syllabus in the Principles of Economics: A National Survey," *Atlantic Economic Journal* (September 2004), 25.

5 | *Planning a class: no detail is too small*

JAMES G. S. CLAWSON AND
MARK E. HASKINS

> The teacher's task is not to implant facts
> but to place the subject to be learned in
> front of the learner and, through sympathy,
> emotion, imagination, and patience, to
> awaken in the learner the restless drive for
> answers and insights which enlarge the
> personal life and give it meaning.
> – Nathan M. Pusey, President,
> Harvard University, *New York Times*,
> March 22, 1959

Once you've designed a course, probably with topics for each day as outlined in the previous chapter, you'll need to begin designing the individual classes. You may decide to break your course into modules and then into individual classes. We'll address briefly the issue of modules and then address some tools and techniques for designing classes themselves.

Modules

Modules are groups of classes that address a single topic or a set of closely related topics. You may decide, given the constraints of calendar, range of topics in the course, and level of your students, that you will put anywhere from two to ten classes in a module. Modules of two classes can be very useful in the beginning of a one- or two-year degree program to establish an overview of the topics and frameworks that a course will explore over the program. Likewise, ten-session modules can be useful in developing behavioral skills in courses designed to leave students prepared to do specific things on the job. In our experience, however, modules of two are often too short to do much more than introduce a framework, while modules of ten take up too much space

71

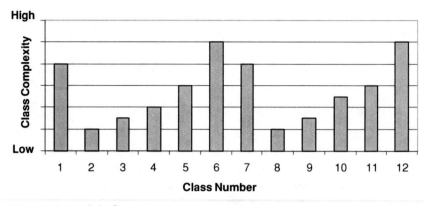

Figure 5.1 Module flow over time

in a course and can leave students feeling like they're beating a dead horse.

In an executive education program, we'd argue that five- to ten-session modules are about right: they allow you to open the module with a set of complex ideas that create a "need to know" on the part of the student and then work up to being able to deal with a similarly complex set of issues by the end of the module, but with much more success. So, on a chart of class complexity over time, a well-balanced module would begin with a complex case, move to a simple case with one or two issues, then gradually increase in complexity until at the end of the module, students are facing a complex set of issues again, but with the tools to deal with them. If you design a module beginning with the simple issues, the students may not get the energy to deal with the issues until the end of the module and by then, many learning opportunities have been lost. A "complexity" chart over two modules, then, would look something like that in Figure 5.1.

The effective module designer carefully considers the sequence of topics in each module so that the simplest and most foundational concept is introduced in class #2 and each of the additional concepts added in subsequent classes builds on and adds to that first concept. Then, by the time students get to the cumulative conceptual complexity in the last class of the module (Classes No. 6 and 12 in Figure 5.1) they will have seen the conceptual progression of the module and feel capable and competent. The next class, the first class of the next module, then introduces a new set of problems and issues that the students find compelling but a bit overwhelming and the process begins anew.

Planning classes

Once you've laid out your modules, you can begin thinking about the details of each class – and there are many to attend to. You have to think about the sequencing of the concepts (presumably done during the course or module design), the materials, the study questions, the objectives for each class, and a variety of administrative and pedagogical issues surrounding each one.

We often use the class planner shown in Figure 5.2 to guide our thought process for designing a class. We've found that this planner is useful in MBA programs where secretaries, administrators, the student affairs office, the program chair (interested in overall work load and integration issues), and others need to see what's happening in each class. It's also useful in executive education settings where a program assistant may be charged with making the arrangements and needs to know just what is required to make the class ready to go. Using this planner, instructors, program assistants, secretaries, materials procurers, the audiovisual staff, room reservers, and anyone associated with the class can see in one glance what's required to set the stage for the class.

Let's consider each of the elements of this planner and how they fit together. In general, note that everything above the dark line between Study Questions and Objectives is intended to go to the students, while everything below that dark line is only for the instructor and administrators. You may decide to draw the dark line in a different place: For example, you may decide to include session objectives in the material you send to the students; that's your choice, obviously.

Program and Instructor. Beyond identifying module title and course number, the instructor cell lets a program administrator know who designed this class, and if he or she has questions, whom to call. These two lines keep the class plan linked to the appropriate program, whether it's an executive education one-week program called Managing the Corporate Aviation Function or a year-long MBA First-Year Accounting.

Topic. The topic of the class may or may not be revealed to students as you wish, but recording it here exactly as it occurs on the course outline allows you to link your topic flow and keep track of what the class is intended to address. If you choose to show this to students, it helps them to link to the course outline as well.

Figure 5.2
CLASS PLANNER

Program:	
Instructor:	
Week #/Day/Date	
Class #/Topic	
Read:	
Study Questions:	
Objectives:	
Time for Class:	
Learning Team?	
Handouts:	
Audiovisual: *Films, overheads, etc.*	
Tentative Teaching Plan:	
Notes and Developmental Needs:	
Transitions and Bridges:	Leading in: Leading out:

Read. Here, list the assigned readings to the students. These may be technical notes, chapters, reprinted articles, cases, or other material. All the readings that the students should prepare in advance should be listed here, but not the handouts that you'll reveal to them in class. If you include references here, program assistants will be able to find the materials without having to call you and inquire where to locate them.

Study Questions. You may or may not want to have study questions in your assignments to the students. Some classic case method instructors only use an assignment question like "Prepare the American Toy Company case." The thought there is that the more guidance you give students about how to approach a case, the more you build in an unintentional dependency on the instructor for guidance as to how to deal with it. On the other hand, depending on your students and the location of this class in the module and in the course, you may choose to guide their reading and analysis of the case in question with a series of questions.

We encourage careful thought to framing the study questions. The right study question is golden; the wrong study question can anger and frustrate students and leave them at the beginning of your class ready to spew forth their resentment. Naturally, you'd rather have them bursting with eagerness and anticipation.

For many case situations, the generic sequence of study questions is a simple three-part structure:
1. What are the problems here? (What do you see?)
2. Where do these problems come from? (analysis) and
3. What would you do if you were in Mr. X's position? (action)

You may choose to devise variations on this basic structure and there are many. Let's consider some of the pros and cons associated with some of these variations.

If you use this three-part structure too often, students will catch on to the rhythm and can, over time, become bored with it. So, it's good just for variety, to mix up your study questions *or* the way you begin class to keep them engaged.

Some instructors only ask the third question – or a weaker variant of it: "What should Mr. X do?" If you begin always with the action question, you may be unintentionally encouraging students to adopt a "Fire, Fire, Ready, Aim" approach to solving problems, something that North Americans are often accused of in international business settings. On the other hand, that approach does ensure that you do not get bogged down in overanalysis, something that can happen if you take the three basic questions in sequence.

A clear danger of the 1–2–3 approach is that the class becomes so engaged in figuring out what we should be working on and what those problems are (the analysis), that it never gets to the action section. That is in part a time management problem and in part a philosophical one. If you want your students to be "action-oriented," you'll need to take care that you don't allow them, unintentionally, to get mired in analysis class after class.

To encourage thorough discussion, we encourage the use of open-ended questions in place of closed ones. Closed questions are those that imply a "yes" or "no" answer. For example, "Should American Toy Company sell its southeast subsidiary?" Unless you add "*why?*" you may encourage students to make a simple superficial choice and come to class not expecting to be drilled on their reasoning. A better question might be, "What are the rigorous reasons why American Toy Company should or should not sell its southeast subsidiary?" With that approach, you are clearly signaling to students the need to prepare their analysis – on both sides of the action question. "Should American Toy Company sell?" allows you to take a vote at the beginning of class, and votes are *very* useful both in helping students commit to a plan of action and in setting up an instructive debate in class. But unless the underlying analysis question is also stated, your class may or may not get your *implication* that they need to do their analysis.

Similarly, phrase the action question in a way that advances your discussion. "What should Ms. Y do?" is really irrelevant. No one cares as an instructor what Ms. Y should do, only what students *would* do. We are careful always to frame these questions as follows: "If you were in Ms. Y's position, what would *you* do?" That helps to make the discussion less of an academic, arm's-length conversation, and more of a personalized, engaged, "I'm-in-the-situation" exchange. Be sure to ask the question you really want the answer to. Often it's not the first question that comes to mind.

We also encourage you not to use too many study questions. Again, the issue is overly guiding the students and taking away from them the need to think about the situation and "see" what needs to be done, rather than passively being told what needs to be done. For example, "Use the Black Scholes method to analyze this case" is so specific that it doesn't give students the chance to think through what approach they should apply, which is a big part of managerial wisdom. Depending on your objective for that particular class, you may have an objective that focuses on a specific technique (a "drill class") or you may wish to have somewhat more vague assignment questions so students can choose which techniques to use. This will allow you to create an opportunity for some "Aha" moments.

The nature of your study questions may vary depending on the position of the class in your module framework. The first case in a module, if you follow the framework outlined earlier, would probably emphasize Question 1 in the basic study question sequence, "What are the problems here?" The purpose of this first, highly complex case is to let students see a variety of related issues in a topic and in a situation that is credible but very difficult to solve. This enhances their "need to know" how to address this class of problems.

In your second class, the simplest of the module, you may have a more direct set of study questions – something like, "Use the framework on page 6 of the technical note to analyze this case." Though you wouldn't want to use this kind of specific question throughout, here it focuses students on the foundational concepts you want them to get before moving on to successively complex situations. So the first case might have the generic sequence and the subsequent class might devote more time on Question 1 whereas the second class might only use variants of the second and third questions and focus on the analytic framework at the center of the topic. By the time you get to the last case in the module, your study questions might return to the generic sequence, but the class focuses most heavily on the third one, action planning and implementation – since by then the students should be prepared to identify problems quickly and as well as skilled in doing the analysis using the core framework.

Objectives. We believe it's important to have clear objectives for each class. These may or may not be behavioral objectives,[1] but you should identify what you are trying to do with each class. If you have more than two or three objectives, you may be expecting too much out of the class. On the other hand, one or two simple objectives may capture your intent – particularly in early parts of a module. For example, you may state: "to introduce the problems associated with plant floor design planning" as the objective for the first class on a module that will introduce concepts like bottlenecks and materials flows. Similarly, in Class 2, the objective might be "to develop skill in applying the 7-S model," if you're using that framework in your organizational design module. By the time you get to the last class of a module, you may have more sweeping objectives like "to allow students to demonstrate how much they've learned about company valuation." Here your goal is clearly to help them feel good about what they've learned since the opening case of the module when they likely floundered.

---

[1] Robert Mager, *Analyzing Performance Problems: Or, You Really Oughta Wanna*, Center for Effective Performance, 3rd edn, 1997. Robert Mager has been considered by many over the years as *the* reference for how to set educational objectives. We refer you here if you'd like to learn more: Robert F. Mager, *Preparing Instructional Objectives*, Palo Alto, CA: Fearon Publishers, 1975.

Time. This line allows you to designate how much time you need for this class. If you're teaching in a regularly scheduled framework, you may not have the option to adjust how much time each class gets. On the other hand, if you're using this planner in an executive education program, you may have 60, 75, 90, or even 120 minute classes, depending on the material and the difficulty of the subject.

Learning Team. This cell allows you to declare whether or not students should meet in their learning teams to discuss the case/class beforehand. Sometimes learning team meetings are very beneficial; other times you intentionally do *not* want them to meet beforehand – as when a class is entirely "self-contained." You may need to advise students of this in the assignment section of the planner, but for the program administrators, it's very helpful to know whether or not to reserve the study group rooms and when.

Handouts. This section of the planner allows you to note the materials that you wish to hand out in class. It may be the B Case or the rest of a case series or simply an ancillary article or copies of your over-heads or PowerPoint slides. Listing them here helps ensure that you won't forget them later on and be rushing around at the last minute worrying about whether you've got your handouts ready to go or not.

Audiovisual. This is the section where you outline any AV needs you have: film clips, overheads, tapes, DVDs, and so forth. If your AV department is involved in helping you set these up, you can send these class planners to them and they can set up their schedule to fit yours well in advance. This section also reminds us of our discussion about adult learning theory and how important it is to make provisions for a variety of kinds of learners in the classroom, including the visuals as well as the audios and kinesthetics.

Tentative Teaching Plan. We find that when we're planning a course or module or class, we have lots of ideas about how the class might unfold. Since this planning takes place well before the delivery of the class, we sometimes forget those cool ideas when the time for the class itself comes around. This section is a place where you can collect and retain those initial ideas about how the class would unfold, so that when you get to the two or three days before preparation time, you'll be reminded of what you were thinking early on. We try to include rough ideas about what our time allocation to various activities during the class might be so we can stay true to our intentions for the class, particularly in the complexity sequencing.

Notes and developmental needs. Here we intend to capture thoughts about what we'd like to develop for next year's offering of the class. Sometimes we make these notes before class ("pre-notes"), during preparation, and sometimes after class ("post-notes"), when we've seen something we didn't anticipate. Having this section is a way to remind us next year of the kinds of things we thought would make the class go smoother next time.

Transitions and bridges. This cell is a place to think about how this class connects with the class that went before it and the one that comes after it. These little statements help remind us what we were thinking about the logic of this class in juxtaposition with its neighbors in the course and with others the students may be taking or have previously taken. These conceptual links to the rest of the course or module are important for instructors to keep in mind, and perhaps even articulate in class to help students put the class in the context of the course.

Final preparations for class

This class-planning framework is a way of capturing the major ideas and concepts that one needs to keep in mind when preparing for a particular class session. That said, it's only the starting point. The day before the class, you are faced with the existential realities of what to do during each part of the class. This is when the nitty-gritty details of what will happen in class come rushing to mind.

One such issue is pacing. A good way of addressing it is to use a class outline in which you lay out the time allocation for various topics and structures, and, word by word, the key questions one will ask to open up each section of the class. What you are doing here is taking the "tentative teaching plan" from the class planner and refining it in careful detail. The challenge is to lay out a map of a class that addresses the objectives but in a flexible and yet targeted way. A sample class outline is shown in Figure 5.3.

The sequence of events that you choose to follow is a complex and difficult set of choices. Further, depending on the discussion, you may or may not be able to follow your plan and still follow the energy of the students in the room. It's a balancing act to get both student energy and your teaching objectives lined up and in the same direction.

If you use our planner system, you'll see a section for updating your experience so you can use your notes as input to next year's class

Figure 5.3
Class outline for Ed Norris and the Baltimore Police
Department (A) case

(Typically a first class in the complexity sequence with lots
of attention to the range of problems in managing
large-scale organizational change.)

5 mins.	Introduction: Why would we study a police department to learn about managing change in businesses?
10 mins.	Would you have taken this job? Why or why not?
45 mins.	If you had taken the job, what would you have done and why?
10 mins.	How is Commissioner Norris behaving like a businessperson?
5 mins.	Assignment for tomorrow. Bridge: Today we explored the complex interactions of a host of problems related to managing large-scale organizational change. These included issues of race and diversity, history and tradition, funding, political sensitivities, technology, organizational structure, career management, competition, and the surrounding business climate/environment. Tomorrow, we'll look at a simpler case that will allow us to refine our views of change, the change process, and models for implementing change in organizations, and to develop more skill in planning and managing a change process or initiative.

planning. After each class, we encourage you to make notes about
what went well, what didn't go so well, what the students said, what
questions came up, and so on, so you can remember to fold these things
into your teaching for the next iteration.

Further, if you're careful, you'll make some notes about how your
class fits into the other classes the students are taking and find ways to
connect or integrate your material with what they are learning in other
courses. The instructor who does this is viewed as clued in and on top

of his or her experience and program. Most instructors don't do it. But the ones who do have a much stronger impact on students' learning.

Finally, if you have information about students' backgrounds, where they came from, previous work experience, their hobbies, and career aspirations, for example, you can utilize that information in your planning so you can call on people at appropriate times to bring up issues you wish to raise. This also cements in the students' minds how much you know about them and how hard you're working to make the class a seamless, integrated, joint learning adventure.

Conclusion

We find every aspect of planning to teach to be exciting and engaging. Sorting out what a course should focus on and how it would unfold as outlined in the last chapter is fun. Filling in the details can be just as enjoyable. In this chapter we've laid out an approach to planning for the individual classes that populate a course and its modules. Issues about what materials to assign, what study questions to assign, what if any handouts or audiovisual materials to use, how to start, what questions to ask, how to manage the discussion, how much time to allocate to each topic, and how to end the class are all pertinent and important. The alternatives are endless – and because they are endless, some instructors feel inundated by them. We offer here a time-tested method for planning a class and an appendix that outlines a way of thinking through highly interactive case-oriented classes. We hope you'll find them as useful as we have.

Further Reading

Girgin, K. Z., and D. Stevens, "Innovations in the Classroom," *European Business Forum*, 21 (Spring 2005), 63–64.

Heron, J., and P. Reason, "A Participatory Inquiry Paradigm," *Qualitative Inquiry*, 3 (1997), 274–94.

Kavanaugh, K., "Teaching the Language of Work," *Training & Development*, 53, 4, 14–16.

Mager, Robert F., and Peter Pipe, *Analyzing Performance Problems: Or, You Really Oughta Wanna – How to Figure Out Why People Aren't Doing What They Should Be, and What to do About It*, 3rd edn. Center for Performance Effectiveness, 1997.

Napell, S., "Six Common Non-Facilitating Teaching Behaviors," in *Teaching and the Case Method,* L. Barnes, C. Christensen, and A. Hansen, eds., Boston: Harvard Business School Press, 1994.

Nash, L., "Seven Questions for Testing My Teaching," in *Teaching and the Case Method,* L. Barnes, C. Christensen, and A. Hansen, eds., Boston: Harvard Business School Press, 1994.

Palmer, P. J., *The Courage to Teach: Exploring the Inner Landscape of a Teacher's Life,* San Francisco: Jossey-Bass, 1998.

Pusey, Nathan M., *New York Times,* March 22, 1959.

6 | *Lecturing: the possibilities and the perils*

JAMES G. S. CLAWSON AND
MARK E. HASKINS

> I would hesitantly ask if I should do the
> Darwin lecture with or without songs.
> – Richard Milner, anthropologist

Lecturing is probably the most common form of organized instruction in the world. For many of us, the notions of college teaching and lecturing are so closely aligned that we automatically think of the latter when we think of the former. Indeed, many universities officially designate certain faculty appointments as Lecturer. That lecturing is so common does not, however, make it necessarily the best method of instruction nor does it mean that it is not amenable to the best features of other instructional styles – even singing!

Six preliminary points

Before focusing on a variety of lecture-related specifics, six overarching points are important to note. First, lecturing requires special attention and practice to become skilled at it. Effective lecturing is neither the mere reading of notes nor the casual regurgitation of facts. At its most fundamental level, lecturing is the verbal conveyance of one's robust topical understanding to another. Doing that in less time, more poignantly, and with greater student retention is a skill to be crafted through thoughtful planning, trial and error, frequent reflection, careful craftsmanship, and the observation of others.

The second point is that good lecturers work with the differences in learning styles resident in their audiences. The earlier chapter on adult learning described the stream of research called neurolinguistic programming that posits three fundamentally different learning patterns: audio, visual, and kinesthetic. Any moderately large lecture audience is likely to have each kind of learner in it. Effective lecturers embrace all three dimensions in their lectures so that each kind of learner may learn most comfortably. This means that the lecturer chooses words carefully for the audio learner, adds slides, films, and drawings for the visual learner, and stories and examples that evoke affinity feelings for the kinesthetic learner.

The third point is that attention to process enhances the content rather than diminishes it. Some educators opine that attention to the lecture presentation process is vain and demeaning to the subject matter. "Scholars are not entertainers!" they declare. It is, however, in our opinion just the opposite – inattention to presentation demeans the subject matter. A lecturer that really cares whether or not the topic is comprehended by the listeners thinks carefully about how the audience is likely to hear, relate to, and internalize the information being presented. With such a concern, any and all legitimate lecture aids should be considered.

The next point is that pride can erode an instructor's ability to lecture effectively. Pride can get in the way of a willingness to learn how to improve the conveyance of knowledge. Students sometimes speak of a instructor's putting on airs and behaving in a condescending way. Yes, a lecturer is extremely knowledgeable about the subject and perhaps even world-famous for that knowledge. He or she may even be a kindred spirit with Oscar Wilde, who when asked by a US customs agent if he had anything to declare upon returning to the United States, is reputed to have said, "I have nothing to declare but my genius." A love of the subject and a concern for student learning means, however, that instructors should begin at the students' level, with a frame of reference they can relate to and a pace they can manage.

Another point to consider is that it is a lecturer's task to excite an audience about a subject, not merely to cover it. Many lecturers think their task is to "cover the material." They look at a course calendar, divide the "material" into roughly equal sections, and begin speaking. A good day, they say, is when they have "covered" what they intended to, and a bad day is when they didn't "cover" all the material. Our view is that "covering the material" does not guarantee that the students have learned it. Rather, a lecturer should be thinking about how much their students can assimilate from one lecture.

This leads us to the last overarching point: Personal styles are more effective than mimicked ones. Although it may be tempting to emulate other effective lecturers, it is rarely a successful approach. It is important, over the long term, to develop your own style. Certain complementary techniques that others have used can be useful. The key point is to be natural, to be yourself in order to avoid losing touch with your own love of the field and becoming stilted and awkward. With good preparation and a comfortable approach, enthusiasm for the subject matter shines through. Students will tolerate all sorts of idiosyncrasies from their lecturers, even coming to view various idiosyncrasies as quaint or endearing trademarks of a favorite lecturer, as long as the lecturer is genuine, engaged, organized, and interested in the students. Be yourself, but a self that is concerned about how well students are learning, not just how much has been conveyed to them.

Advantages of lecturing

In spite of the denigration it sometimes receives as being boring, monotonous, or an excuse for poor teaching, lecturing is a powerful instructional tool that has many advantages: Efficiency of transmission of new material; the ability to communicate with large audiences; the option of taping for later use, perhaps at other institutions; the chance to add emphasis to written materials; to dramatize key points; and the opportunity to add material that is not contained in sources available to students elsewhere. Moreover, for people for whom listening is easier than reading, lectures provide a comfortable avenue for getting new information.

Because a lecturer can go directly from key point to key point, lecturing is more efficient in disseminating information than discussions or case method. Likewise, lecturers set their own pace, determine when (or if) to field questions, and decide how and when to cover topics, and which topics to include. All told, such control can be used to maximize the efficient conveyance of data, facts, theories, and opinions. It is important to note, however, that even though lecturing is often quite efficient in the dissemination of information, that is not necessarily the same as effectiveness of learning.

Lectures can reach large audiences. The only constraint on the number of people who may benefit from a good lecture is the available technology for voice transmission and the number of seats available. Clearly when a lecturer's face and expressions are so far away as to be unclear, some effectiveness is lost. Even then, a powerful speaker can still motivate and galvanize an audience. We've seen speakers standing in front of 15,000 people with nearly all of them standing and cheering as the lecture came to an end. Optimal use of technology and the right room selection allows large numbers of students to receive the same information in the same way efficiently.

Lectures also allow an instructor to add emphasis to certain points that students may or may not have picked up from a reading assignment. A lecture gives the instructor an opportunity to point out which portions of assigned written material are more significant than others. A lecturer savvy to the role that overstatement can play in communicating to large audiences can dramatize major points in ways that help students to remember better.

Finally, lectures have the advantage of allowing an instructor to introduce late-breaking theories or additional conceptual ideas and data that are not included in textbooks or other written materials the students have. Sometimes an instructor can abuse this opportunity by repeatedly rushing in with late breaking insights as an excuse for not being as organized or as clear as he or she should be. Such situations should be the exception, not the norm, however, during a lecturer's course.

Disadvantages of lecturing

The lecture method has a number of disadvantages including the relative passivity of the learner, the minimal amount of real-time feedback between learner and instructor, and paradoxically, the pace of instruction.

Perhaps the greatest drawback of the lecture method is the relative passivity of the learner. Sometimes in crowded, and not particularly comfortable settings, students are asked to sit quietly while a single person in the front, one whose face and gestures are not readily visible, drones on for lengthy periods of time on subjects that may or may not be of interest to the student. Since the human mind and auditory system work at several times the rate at which most people speak, as much as 70 percent or 80 percent of the mental time spent listening to a lecture is down time. What do listeners do with this down time? Their minds wander, they fidget, they check their email or read the news online, or they stay stuck on a lecturer's comment they didn't fully understand. These mental and physical barriers exacerbate further understanding and retention of information that is presented in the lecture. In addressing this problem, lecturers should consider the likely and potential passivity of their audience and thus vary their pace, their tone, their props, and their examples in order to keep the audience physically, emotionally, and intellectually involved.

Because lecturing is primarily a one-way means of communication, it affords little opportunity for the instructor to gain feedback on what the learners are thinking and feeling or how they are reacting to the lecture. While the lecture is better than broadcasting methods and written methods in this regard, it is difficult to know in real-time how the lecture is going. In giving a lecture to audiences that include three remote locations in the same building and seven satellite-linked remote locations scattered around North America, you can still and should ask questions, listen to answers, and field questions from participants. There are other indicators, though, of how you are connecting with the audience. Rustling papers, shifting in seats, and the number of people apparently not paying attention, are all cues to the receptivity of the audience.

Another disadvantage of lecturing is that students cannot "re-do" the experience for later review. After reading a chapter, a student can flip back and confirm certain facts, but in a lecture there is a tension between listening and writing. People write much more slowly than they listen. When a student uses time to write, he or she may be caught up in writing and miss the next important point. Thus, a set of notes will never be as complete as the lecture or as robust in its connections and informational nuances. There are solutions to offer students: The mind mapping technique developed by Tony Buzan is one means of accelerating note-taking and minimizing that attention gap. (See the appendix to this chapter for a brief overview of this technique.)

Pace of instruction can be a detriment. With written materials, students can go at their own pace, but in a lecture the instructor dictates the pace, which should be an engaging one. If an instructor tends to speak slowly, students may have even more mental down time than in a typical lecture. Some students will always be behind and some will be bored waiting to go on. It is a judgment call to know how fast or slow to go. We suggest varying the pace at different times during a class and across a course. This altered rhythm is appealing to most listeners and permits an instructor to "discover" the best pace for certain topics and places in a course.

Preparation

Mark Twain once noted that, "It usually takes me more than three weeks to prepare a good impromptu speech." We echo his point in observing that smooth, brisk, fresh, effortless-looking lectures require a lot of preparation. There are a number of things to do in preparing a lecture to make it most effective. Writing good objectives, carefully considering the student level of understanding, knowing the subject matter content extremely well, practicing public speaking skills, and assessing the physical lecture setting in advance are all things that can be done ahead of time to make a lecture go smoothly and effectively.

Every lecture ought to have a good, clear set of objectives. Without them, a lecture can wander, bouncing from one point to another, leaving the listener with a less than clear idea of how the points are related or if they even are. Likewise, explicit objectives foster the architecture of a lecture so that an instructor can capture the leverage (e.g., enhanced student learning, less time to cover the same topic) arising from clearly connected content. Sharing a lecture's explicit objectives with students at the start can aid their listening and note-taking.

Far too often, we have all been forced to sit in lectures where the content is either so far beyond our understanding or so far below it that we tune out. A careful lecturer does some advance scouting, either informally or formally, to understand the mix of students in the class and their understanding of the subject matter. That step helps in preparing appropriate examples, conceptual frameworks, and details of the subject matter that fit the level of understanding of the audience. To ignore this step is to invite potential disaster. At a minimum, in teaching the second or third class in a sequence, a lecturer should find several students to talk with and ascertain how much they really got out of the class.

A public speaking or acting course is excellent preparation for lecturing. If there are such courses available, we suggest taking one as a means of sharpening one's command of the space and the attention of those in a large lecture hall. One professor at the University of Virginia had to give his large lectures in Old Cabell Hall, the school's richly appointed and extensively decorated theatrical auditorium. For several weeks, he had to deliver his lectures on economics in front of the elaborate set for Shakespeare's *Midsummer Night's Dream*, which was being presented in the evenings by the school's drama department.

What a challenge! Without the equivalent presence and skilled techniques of a leading actor, how could he have ever commanded such a setting as that?

The room itself is a critical component in course planning. In some rooms, the acoustics are such that unaided speech can be heard clearly. In others, amplification is absolutely essential. We recall one lecture recently in which the person introducing the speaker addressed the audience from a podium with a microphone. In that setting, with that equipment, the introducer's voice was thin, difficult to understand and seemed very, very far away. When the speaker took the stand, though, it was clear that he was experienced and had checked out the room in advance. He had brought with him his own amplification system. No doubt he had been disadvantaged in other settings. He wore a small, almost invisible, clip-on lavaliere microphone with no visible wires. A transceiver device was plugged into the wall at the side of the stage and into the room's speakers. With this equipment, he was able to freely move about the room and be easily heard. He could speak softly and be heard and raise his voice for emphasis. He could approach the people in the front row and roam the aisles as he felt necessary. The impact was powerful. Although the room was large, the effect for the students was of engaging him face to face.

This kind of advance assessment of a setting is essential. Go to the room well in advance when no students are there. Practice walking up and down the stairs or aisles, getting to the places where you can walk, noting places where you might trip over cords or loose carpet, fall off a stage, or down the steps. Learn where the light switches are. Bring a friend who can stand on the stage and speak while you go to different parts of the room to learn how well voices carry and how difficult it might be to hear in such a setting. Then remember that when the room is full, it will be even harder to hear; bodies absorb sound, and the students are rustling and making their own competing background noise.

Check out the heating and cooling systems, too, if possible, to make sure that the room won't be too hot or cold. Uncomfortable temperatures are a major distraction for students. There are situations, however, where this is not controllable. We remember one setting in which the students noted that the only control of the temperature was the door. Unfortunately, that meant that the student sitting next to it received a constant series of requests to open or close the door throughout the course; it was very disrupting, but short of finding a new building to meet in, there was nothing to be done.

Delivery style

We have identified several concepts with which to perfect your lecture skills:

Clarity. Foremost among the points to consider with regard to the actual delivery of lectures is clarity. Most of the prior suggestions in this chapter are intended to help provide greater clarity. In addition, select the main content points that are key for students to understand and build the lecture around those ideas. Emulate the example of the great short story writers for whom each word, each phrase is carefully calculated to build a particular impression. Anything more is superfluous and anything less is ineffective. Focus preparation to deliver those ideas clearly and well. Remember, "Don't try to do too much." Remember also the power of frequent "sound bytes." Of course, a short, pithy phrase or sentence does not capture the full elegance of a theory or the breadth of a debate. A sound byte does, however, lodge in peoples' memories like a favorite song or smell that brings back a flood of related thoughts and memories.

Authenticity. Don't put on some kind of professorial face that is not natural. Rather, allow your personality, interest, and familiarity with the subject matter to come through. This approach will resonate with students, inviting them to be more attentive. For the lecturer, this approach can be much more sustainable and less draining.

Outlining. A good opening set of remarks is to present an overview of the day's lecture. One difference between pedagogy and andragogy (although it has not been demonstrated that the same approach doesn't work well with children, too) is that adults want to know where the learning agenda is headed. Showing adults what's coming up appeases their desire to know what's going on and helps them to remember what's coming. It also provides an opportunity for students to anticipate parts that are of particular interest to them.

There are several ways to organize a lecture. The University of Minnesota's Center for Teaching and Learning Services' website notes the following general possibilities. Lectures can be organized according to cause/effect, time sequence, topic, problem/solution, pro/con arguments, and ascending/descending order of importance, familiarity, or complexity. An intuitively appealing, logical clarity to the path a lecture will take can help students stay focused, attain a sense of progression/accomplishment, and can underscore the building-block nature (or other connections) of the material presented.

Transitions. Students come to class from a variety of places. It takes a little time for them to adjust their attention. It is constructive to begin a lecture with a quick bridge comment or two that helps them remember what happened in the last class and how this class fits into the overall course perspective. Bridge comments are useful at the end of a class session, too, to help students summarize the day's material and to anticipate what's coming in the next lecture. These bridges can be done verbally and visually through the use of a handout or an overhead transparency (or Power Point slide) that shows the connections to other classes.

Although transitions from one part of a lecture to another may be obvious to the lecturer, it may not be as obvious, or obvious in the same way, to many listeners. A change in voice or body language, along with explicitly articulated connections, all signal that we're moving on to a new area.

Relevancy. An important challenge in any lecture is relating it to real-life situations. With that in mind, one good way of starting a lecture is to present a difficult problem that the audience can relate to. Couching the introduction to a subject in the context of a pressing problem invites students to anticipate the answer. Simply saying something like "If you want to calculate net present value, here's the answer," won't do the trick. Exercise some imagination to identify a class of problems that fit a topic and then select one that is close to home for the students (e.g., in selling your car today, would you rather receive $5,000 right now or $5,100 in six weeks?).

Liveliness. Use hooks that grab students' attention and keep them tuned in for the underlying principles. As one award-winning professor recently noted, "I believe the single greatest contributor to interest throughout a lecture are examples" (Glaser, 2002). Pick problems and examples that students have had experience with or can easily understand. Indeed, consider two lectures on leadership: one that purely lists and defines the five most often cited characteristics of a leader and one that does the same but begins with a scene from the movie *Braveheart* in which William Wallace is rallying the Scottish peasants. With the image and words of William Wallace as context, the lecture is bound to have an increased probability for student learning.

Stories that are humorous or emotionally powerful help individuals remember the conceptual framework, the point, or the principles presented to them. For example, in a lecture on some of the recent changes in the federal laws pertaining to corporate governance, photographs of high-profile former CEOs and CFOs being arrested simply but powerfully underscored the seriousness of the new laws and the intolerance for old ways of corporate governing.

Voice modulation. Do not underestimate the importance of voice variations. Monotonic, unvaried cadences can numb students no matter how scintillating the subject. Most instructors find that what they think are significant variations in voice are barely discernible to the listener. They are even less discernible in front of large audiences. Thus, it is important to exaggerate voice changes for them to be recognized by students in the back of the room. Again, the lessons of the actor's stage are poignant. Stylized ways of communicating emotions and points of emphasis help an audience hear and internalize what they hear.

Humor. Humor can do a great deal to break up the monotony of a lecture. It is also another way of providing hooks for people to remember certain points and ideas. Humor that is either somewhat self-deprecating or that points out oddities in the subject matter is usually well received. Beware of sarcasm, though, and humor that comes at the expense of any subgroup of people – it often backfires.

Variety. Injecting variety into lectures helps students see and retain what they hear, in helping signal changes between sections of lectures, and in maintaining one's own interest. Indeed, in one study of undergraduate students that explored the question, "What constitutes a good lecture?" variety was an oft-cited attribute. The report noted that an instructor's style "was not as important as the ability to 'break the trance' with demonstrations, examples, and changes in tone" (Lacoss and Chylack, 1998).

There are a number of ways to add variety to a lecture – movies or film clips, demonstrations, and slides, and even breaking the audience into two- or three-person buzz groups to talk about a particular concept for a few minutes. Such techniques vary the delivery and provide students with some intellectual change of pace to keep them more attentive. One good rule of thumb suggests that an audience should be involved in some way at least every ten to fifteen minutes.

Energy. Energy is infectious. If an instructor is clearly enthusiastic about the subject matter and energetic in the delivery of it, people in the room begin to feel that and to catch it. They are likely to generate a similar kind of energy and enthusiasm for the subject. How about the legend of the professor who jogged into an operations class focused on product performance with a chainsaw in hand, started it up, sawed a chair in half, and screamed, "Did this product do what it was suppose to do? DID IT? I CAN'T HEEEEAR YOU!" Think what that would do in garnering student interest in, and anticipation of, the lecture that the instructor was about to deliver.

Eye contact. Eye contact is an important way of catching attention. Many of us have sat in audiences and felt for a few seconds that the speaker was looking directly at us and speaking directly to us. Remember how powerful those few seconds were? Maintaining eye contact with the audience is important, as is shifting it from side to side and front to back, making sure to focus on individuals in all parts of the audience. We've all watched teachers who gazed at the ceiling or the far corner of the room as if to portray "wisdom" or some other academic posture; it can be very distracting.

Spontaneity. Spontaneity is another important dimension of lecture delivery. If a lecture comes across as an old, well-worn, methodically scripted presentation in which even the humorous lines are delivered with a certain overfamiliar flatness, listeners tune out. Work from a detailed outline rather than sentence-by-sentence notes, in order to stay on track but with ample room for spontaneity. Do not read a lecture. Think of yourself as teaching the students, not the "stuff."

An open forum. Invite questions along the way to get variety into a lecture and to generate some needed feedback. Handling questions is an art, since some of them may be completely unanticipated and fairly obtuse. Even that fact, though, is good feedback. Use questions and answers to gauge how well the audience is tracking the lecture. Anticipate the most likely questions and have a ready, coherent response. Keep a list, with your lecture notes, of the questions students asked – such information is helpful in (1) anticipating the questions likely to be raised the next time the lecture is given, and (2) revising the lecture itself. If a question is asked that you don't wish to pursue or don't find useful, find a way to respond without embarrassing the questioner. Instead of saying or implying "That's a stupid question! Weren't you listening?" try responding with, "Perhaps many of you didn't catch the way I presented this topic. Let me try it a different way," and proceed to do that. If the question raises a subject related to the topic but not one to be pursued now, suggest that answering the question deserves a more careful and more reasoned response than can be done today or in class and invite that student to meet with you outside of class. Perhaps a group of students interested in that topic might be asked to wait until after class to pursue it.

Repetition. The military method of "tell 'em what you are going to tell them, tell 'em, and then tell 'em what you told 'em" works well in any lecture. Having presented your outline and covered the content, summarize at the end, with intermediate summaries along the way. Summaries help students to confirm the key points and the outline of the lecture. Finally, draw the bridge to the next lecture and to the course as a whole.

A proper close. Near the end of lectures, students get restless and eager to move on to their other classes or appointments. Therefore, don't try to put anything of importance in a lecture in the last five minutes. Realize that students are beginning to disengage – to close their laptops, collect their papers, put on their coats – and are not likely to be breathlessly dwelling on the content of those final few minutes. Review, point out the bridge to the next lecture, but make sure that the key points were hit earlier, not crammed into the end.

Listening to a lecture

Now, consider the other side of the coin for a moment, listening to a lecture. George Odiorne, a distinguished professor of organizational behavior, once gave a lecture titled, "How to Listen to a Lecture." In that talk, he made some interesting points that reinforce how learning, even in lecturing, is a two-way street involving transmission and reception. Odiorne noted that the retention of lecture material by listeners immediately following a lecture tends to be about 50 percent of the material. Two months later, retention drops to 25 percent of the material, and a year later to 5 percent of the material. He also noted that most universities are devoid of classes on how to listen, even though 75 percent of the work done in communication in general, and in university learning situations in particular, involves listening. He then highlighted several bad listening habits and provided insights germane to speakers, anticipating these listening proclivities. You may find it worthwhile to share these insights with your students:

1. *Listening for facts.* Instead of listening for facts, try to get a view of where the lecturer is going. Look for the ideas and the direction and then for the corroborating evidence to the main points.

2. *Avoiding the difficult.* Focus and concentrate on the difficult instead of avoiding it and see how it compares with your current level of knowledge. Concentrate on the new and obscure ideas that you have not encountered before, for that is where your learning will be.

3. *Prematurely dismissing the materials as irrelevant or boring.* Many listeners want only to be entertained. Pay attention, and ask, regardless of how boring the material the important things to receive. G. K. Chesterson, an English philosopher, once noted, "In all the world, there is no such thing as an uninteresting subject, only uninterested learners."

4. *Concentrating on the lecturer's appearance.* Don't let the dress or appearance of the speaker keep you from paying attention. The speaker's credentials can have a similar influence on listeners. Listen attentively for the golden nuggets. It may be that the very fact of the speaker's not fitting a preconceived notion of look, style, or credentials is all the more reason to listen.

5. *Taking notes.* Paper-and-pencil listening without thinking well leads to writing only the last phrase, thought, or idea presented and not relating it to the central theme of the lecture. When taking notes, think about major themes rather than trying to be a stenographer/recorder.

6. *Avoid voting "for" or "against."* Don't let negative or positive emotions evoked by a speaker override a rational assessment of the points made. You don't have to agree with a lecture to understand it or find something of value in it.

7. *Not using the gap.* Remember that we can listen faster than we can speak, up to 1,000 words per minute with 90 percent retention. The typical speaker goes at 100 to 300 words a minute. Thus, your mind spends a lot of time waiting; time that you can use to connect the speaker's ideas to your own.

8. *Summarizing during the gap.* Be patient. Let the lecturer make his or her point and then reflect on the conclusions and summaries. Don't jump ahead and try to interject your own thoughts and conclusions before the lecturer has done so and before the data that he or she is

presenting have a chance to tell their story. Learn to exercise patience
in that difficult time when your mind is waiting for something to
listen to.

Ready for prime time?

As for the performing arts, rehearsing lectures on videotape can be
very helpful. Personal mannerisms, habits, repeated phrases, and any
number of other quirks, some positive and some negative, become
obvious. View a tape and notice the things that help or hinder your
presentation. Look for clarity of speech, choice of words, the visual
and kinesthetic parts, movement, and gestures that indicate interest and
enthusiasm, transitions, summaries, and other features of the lecture
that are valuable. Make notes and select a few (not a lot of) items to
work on. Keep annual tapes and review them from time to time to see
how you have developed and improved over the years.

Conclusion

Lectures are a prevalent form of instruction. Carefully prepared and
presented, they can be highly effective. All instructors should have this
capability in their repertoire. Constantly reassess your own lecturing
abilities by using student feedback, videotapes, and peer reviews so that
month by month, year by year, and course by course, your lectures will
become increasingly compelling and interesting to attend.

Further reading

Aigner, P., "Lecturing Doesn't Have to be Boring or Long-winded," *Presentations* (August 2001), p 74.
Buzan, T., "Mind Mapping," *Success*, April 1997, p. 30.
Buzan, T. and B. Buzan, *The Mind Map Book*, New York, NY: Plume Publishing, 1996.
Edwards, H., B. Smith, and G. Webb, eds., *Lecturing: Case Studies, Experience and Practice*, London: Kogan Page Ltd., 2001.
Glaser, S., "Effective Lecturing," http://tep.uoregon.edu/resources/librarylinks/ articles/lecturing.html, 2002.
Goodwin, L., "Enliven Your Teaching," *Management Accounting*, December 1991, pp. 54–55.

Kaufman, J., "A New Species of Instruction: The Musical – Lecturing with Lyrics," *Wall Street Journal*, 8 May 2002, p. D.9.

Lacoss, J., and J. Chylack, "What Constitutes a Good Lecture?" *Teaching Concerns* (Newsletter of the Teaching Resource Center at the University of Virginia), fall 1998, pp. 1–3.

"Lecturing Tips for Professors," http://www.thehumorsource.com/joke-647.html, September 15, 2002.

MacFarlane, B., and R. Ottewill, eds., *Effective Learning & Teaching in Business & Management*, London: Kogan Page Ltd., 2001.

Odiorne, George, "How to Listen to a Lecture," presentation at the OB Teaching Conference, Harvard University, May 21, 1976.

"Suggestions for Effective Lectures," Center for Teaching and Learning Services, University of Minnesota, http://www1.umn.edu/ohr/teachlearn/MinnCon/lecture1.html, 2003.

APPENDIX

Mind mapping[*]

Strange as it may seem given the attention education receives in our society and the extensive amount of time so many people spend in formal learning situations, there is almost no attention devoted in educational programs to helping people learn how to learn. More specifically, we are not aware of any business instructors (ourselves included) having received any instruction in ways to enhance human memory and learning. Generally, students are simply thrown into the "educational process," usually a setting in which students listen and take notes while an instructor speaks.

One easily learned, high-payoff endeavor that can enhance students' learning is what we consider a superior approach to note-taking and review. The approach has been termed "Mind Mapping" and is the classic life's work of Tony Buzan, a well-known English author and lecturer.

Recall

The remembrance of facts, linkages, and insights is a critical capability if learning is to be cemented, useful, and cumulative. Our recall

---

[*] We are indebted to our colleague Brandt Allen for an earlier version of this material.

ability, especially the recall of details, declines rapidly over time. Perhaps 80 percent or more of detailed information is lost within twenty-four hours of a one-hour learning period (Pollitt, 1999). (Another detail you may promptly lose.) Buzan argues, and perhaps it is a tautology, that recall can be increased by short, frequent reviews (e.g., within half an hour of the end of the session, again the next day, and again one week later) of the material studied.

One key to the effectiveness of the reviews is the structure of the notes initially recorded and subsequently revised. Memory, the source of recall, is based on neurological linking and associations. Consequently, Buzan asserts that note taking should reflect this natural mental structure. In short, the objective is to create a mental picture or map of the material covered that approximates our memory structure. The central principles in mind mapping, therefore, are to:

1. Select with great care the key words that form the elements of the mind map, and
2. Connect the key words in logical ways that reflect their relationships.

Key words

At the most fundamental level, note-taking is a process of condensation – of putting down on paper only a few words and pictures that represent the key elements of a lecture (or any other learning session for that matter). For each of us, words are associated with other words – the mention of one word triggers the thought of another. Each person should use key words that trigger the recall patterns that undergird their memory of details and of understandings. Thus, the first skill in the art of better note taking is learning to record only key words that spark recall. The second skill is patterning those key words for richly informative recall.

Patterned note-taking or mind mapping

Chances are that if our students received any formal instruction at all in note-taking it was likely the sequentially linear, outline form. Such a linear pattern may indeed reflect the structure from which an instructor speaks, but it probably does not reflect the form in which listeners receive and store the words they hear. Listeners "hear" in the

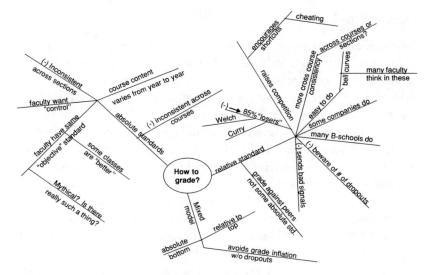

Figure 6.1 A mind map of an MBA faculty meeting on grading

context of their own realities, their own "Ahas," their own curiosities, and their own contexts. What adds texture, tone, and meaning for one is likely to be different for another. For example, one person's notion of a "loss" may be centered on athletics while another's is centered on a death in the family. Likewise, "trust" may be a construct for one that is rooted in "trusting someone only as far as you can see them" while another's may be rooted in a deeply religious context. Buzan argues that memory and recall are enhanced if notes are constructed in ways that resemble how our brains work – they link and integrate concepts. Hence, note-taking should be structured in a similar fashion. In essence, notes should portray a map of the concepts heard and seen that approximates the storage map the brain uses.

Mind mapping begins at the center of a page where the main idea of the learning session is placed. Related ideas are then connected to the central idea with branches as shown in Figure 6.1. With just a quick scan of this map, it is clear that: the central issue is prominently displayed; relatively more important ideas are closer to the center; conceptual links are evident by the lines; subsequent thoughts/insights can be easily inserted where appropriate; and rudimentary pictures can denote emphasis.

Detailed to-dos

Buzan offers some suggestions for using the mind-mapping technique. First, he suggests that recall words should be printed in capitals. Printed words give a more photographic, more immediate, and more comprehensive picture for storage and therefore are more suited to creating mind maps designed for later recall. The little extra time that it takes to print is amply made up for in the time saved when rereading the notes later. Second, the printed words should be on lines, and each line should be connected to other lines. This is to guarantee that the pattern has basic structure. Third, in creating a recall pattern, the mind should be left as "free" as possible. Any thinking about where things should go or whether they should be included will simply slow down the process. The idea is to recall everything the mind thinks of around the central idea. Do not worry about order or organization at this stage as this will in many cases take care of itself. If it does not, a reordering of the material can be done during the first subsequent review.

Remember, when taking notes, key words and phrases are essentially all that are needed. The structure of the mind map may not be evident until near the end of the lecture. The first round of mind mapping notations will therefore probably be semi-final rather than final copy. Patterned notes in their final form are usually neat and it seldom takes more than ten minutes to finalize an hour's notes on a fresh sheet of paper.

Beyond mere note-taking

Mind maps are an excellent device for facilitating brainstorming sessions and for preparing to give a presentation. For the former, begin by putting the topic in the center of a chalk board or a piece of paper and then writing all of the thoughts/connections that come to peoples' minds. It is amazing to see how one word or one concept sparks a new one, enhances another, or completes an earlier one. In such a setting, don't worry about drawing the connections right away unless they seem immediately obvious. Let the process proceed till it runs out of energy. Then, with the help of those in attendance, go back and draw the connections, the enclosures (boxes, circles, triangles, etc.), and the symbols that complete the map.

Mind maps are useful in preparing presentations. In a fashion similar to the brainstorming scenario just described, they can be used to help in the initial organization of a presentation; checking the comprehensiveness of a presentation; and in helping prioritize the parts of a presentation. A lecturer's final rostrum notes can still be crafted in the more traditional outline form, but if such an outline is based on a mind mapping endeavor, it is more likely to: make the most provocative connections; emphasize what can most benefit from emphasis; underscore a multi-dimensional array of forces bearing on an issue; highlight the weak and strong arguments in a debate; reveal the areas wherein an issue sparks emotion vs. reason; and posits the indirect versus direct nature of other pertinent views/facts/beliefs.

Conclusion

We have three colleagues we know of whom we would characterize as quintessential mind mappers. They have learned the art, and felt the freedom to use mind maps to stimulate meetings, capture student comments on a chalkboard, and summarize discussions. At the risk of sounding trite, one mind map is worth a thousand words. As we have observed our colleagues in action with their mind maps, and as we have been in the audience of a mind mapping facilitator, and as we have begun to use the technique ourselves, we must agree with Buzan (1994, p. 9) when he states, "Using mind maps, you will greatly increase the effectiveness of your note taking, improve your memory, enhance your creativity, and have more fun."

Further reading

Buzan, Tony, *Use Your Head*, London: British Broadcasting Company, 1974.
Buzan, Tony, *Use Both Sides of Your Brain*, New York: Plenum Publishing, 1989.
Buzan, Tony, "Mind Mapping," *Executive Excellence* (August 1991), 3–4.
Buzan, Tony, "Presents of Mind," *Executive Excellence* (January 1994), 9.
Buzan, Tony, "Mind Mapping," *Success* (April 1997), 30.
Buzan, Tony and Barry Buzan, *The Mind Map Book*, New York: Plume Publishing, 1996.
Hogath, Christine, "Mind Mapping: Some Practical Applications," *Training & Management Development Methods*, 8, 1 (1994), 3.01–3.18.

Mento, Anthony, Patrick Martinelli, and Raymond Jones, "Mind Mapping in Executive Education: Applications and Outcomes," *Journal of Management Development,* 18, 4 (1999), 390–407.

Pollitt, D., "Mind Maps Chart the Way to Business Efficiency," *Training & Management Development,* 13, 1 (1999), 3.01–3.04.

7 | *Managing discussions*

JAMES G. S. CLAWSON

> A good question is worth a thousand
> answers.

Socrates, probably the most famous discussion teacher ever, developed
the dialectical approach of asking questions that stimulated student
thinking and subsequent discussion. Although the discussion technique
has this long and well-established history, it is for many instructors a
focus of concern and fear. The idea of relinquishing some control over
the focus of a class and the uncertainty of what questions students will
ask can be daunting to those of us with lesser intellect and confidence
than Socrates. It need not be so. The key is to let go of the often-held
idea that the professor has to know it all and to accept that it may be
legitimate and professional to say, "I don't know. Let's find out."

The issue of control is a critical one. The first related premise here
is that the people in the room have some background, experience,
intelligence, and insight to share. Without making that assumption, an
instructor is not likely to look for ways to bring all those things out
and into the class. Without that assumption, the instructor is likely
to continue trying to control the "air time," concepts introduced, and
direction of the class. Without that assumption, the instructor is likely
to lecture.

So, in some ways, managing a discussion is like conducting an orchestra. There are a variety of melodies to play, experiences to benefit from,
intellects to open up and discover, and theories to examine. With the
appropriate waving of questions as batons, the instructor can bring all
those elements together in a way that produces a harmonized whole
for everyone in the room. If the instructor does not hold the assumption that all in the room have some value to add, however, then the
instructor becomes a soloist rather than a conductor – an a capella
soloist with no supporting band or orchestra.

If you, the instructor, assume that everyone in the room has some valuable experience and insight, then the discussion technique becomes a means of discovery. Through thoughtful questions and searching answers, students can be led to understand things that they did not before – by relying in large part on the contributions of their peers along with those of the instructor. Discussion technique is much more, though, than simply asking, "Are there any questions?" That careless beginning does not do justice to the range and depth of things that can be done to make this approach a vibrant, instructive teaching method.

Perhaps the discussion technique is best viewed as a pedagogical bridge between lecturing and the case method. It is not really either, for it is more participative and bilateral than lecturing and yet less problem-focused and less participative than case method. Discussions may be used both within lectures and case classes for particular purposes.

Since discussions potentially can arise in almost any kind of educational setting, there are many aspects to learning how to manage a discussion well. We'll consider several of them here. Let us consider the benefits, advantages, types, concerns in planning for, questions in, getting participation in, the importance of periodic summaries, and the use of audiovisual techniques in orchestrating effective classroom discussions.

Benefits

The discussion method has many benefits for both students and instructors. First, discussions allow the instructor to see the attitudes and level of understanding of the students. The unilateral approach taken in lecturing does not naturally bring to the fore what the students are thinking or how they are reacting to the material.

The discussion technique also helps to build a more cohesive learning team among the students. This sense of membership in a group whose purpose is to study and discover together can add significantly to the learning motivation of the students. Discussions help the students to understand not only the material but also each other better. This often leads to continuing discussions outside the classroom, which of course levers the instructor's influence beyond the class hours.

Discussion also allows students to clarify gaps in their knowledge. If material has been covered too quickly, discussions invite students to fill in what they missed with questions and to explore areas that they want to probe more deeply.

Such insight into the students' depth of understanding also serves the instructor. Though only one student may voice them, any questions raised usually represent more than one student's concerns. Instructors should respond to questions as if speaking to all. Students who are shy or confused welcome discussion breaks so that some of their questions may be voiced by others.

Discussion also brings the experience of the students in the room to bear on the topic. Some instructors view the classroom as a group of empty heads waiting to be filled. If you view the students instead as a group of people with widely varying experiences and backgrounds and beliefs, then the ensuing discussion becomes an opportunity to tap that richness and variety. With such a perspective, students become partners in the classroom teaching, and by virtue of what he or she may see and explain, an instructor becomes a partner in the learning.

Finally, to the extent that learning is more effective when it is participative, discussion technique involves people more directly than lecturing. While minds may doze during the attention gaps common in lecturing, it is difficult to stray far from the subject when asking a question or being asked how your thoughts compare with those of the last person who spoke. This managed involvement builds a more natural engagement of the topic, as your peers begin to express their thoughts and relate the subject to their own experiences and understandings.

Disadvantages

Discussions have disadvantages, too. A major one, as we have already mentioned, is the need for the instructor to relinquish some control over what "happens" in the classroom. We use the word "happens" to refer only to outward behavior. Inward behavior, what people are thinking and feeling, is, paradoxically, under less of an instructor's control in lecturing than in any other technique. Lecturing creates the illusion of learning by virtue of the passive outward behavior of the students. Human behavior occurs, we can easily assert, at three levels. Level One is behavior that can be captured on film, the things that people say and do. Level Two is conscious thought which may or may not align with Level One. (People can be sitting quietly in class and daydreaming about something quite different.) Level Three is people's semi-conscious values, assumptions, beliefs and expectations (or VABEs), which have a major impact on shaping both Levels One and Two.[1] Most observers would agree (from previous discussions) that learning often begins with Level Two, migrates to Level Three, and eventually to Level One. Skinnerians, of course, disagree, arguing that deep learning (Level Three) begins with conditioning at Level One.

Many instructors believe that if students are seated quietly and respectfully, learning is taking place. Quite the opposite may be true. In fact, it may be that students have learned over the years that if you sit quietly (at Level One), you do whatever you want at Level Two (thinking about last night, tonight, or whatever). So, although some instructors fear that discussions mean less control, in fact, discussions are an avenue to gaining at least some influence on Level Two thinking and Level Three believing. Yet yielding the floor still seems to many instructors a loss of control. Some are afraid of being asked a question they cannot answer, or of being confronted with mistakes in what they have said, or of being asked about "irrelevant" matters, or perhaps most commonly, of not being able to "cover" everything planned for the day. To some, this loss of control is a major disadvantage of discussions.

Discussions also create a more equal classroom. To conduct discussions, instructors must at least recognize students and engage them on a personal and direct level. At the same time, students must, at whatever level of understanding they have, engage the instructor. For some, that is a disadvantage. It means that the students are getting too "close." I've heard one instructor comment, "the prisoners should not control the prison." Wow. Yet for others, that "loss of control" and the resulting increased intimacy of the relationship between student and instructor are a good thing.

To be fair, there is risk in classroom discussions. Discussions can hurt people. A student may present a train of thought or analysis that the rest of the class concludes is poor, indicating their disapproval with giggles, snickers, sighs, bored expressions, or outright catcalls. The instructor him- or herself may react with a caustic comment. Weathering such storms can be an advantage if it helps the student to gain confidence speaking in front of people and defending his or her position. If the

---

[1] See James G. Clawson, *Level Three Leadership*, 3rd edn (Upper Saddle River, NJ: Prentice Hall, 2006).

possibilities for personal pain are not managed by the instructor or the other students, however, it can be a devastating experience that causes people to retreat from further participation.

The pain is not restricted to the students either. Cutting comments, hostile behavior, and derision can also be directed at an instructor. We are aware of at least one situation in which the open hostility of a class toward an instructor led, in large part, to the instructor's suicide.

These possibilities for discomfort can lead some instructors to avoid discussion-oriented classes. Some don't feel "qualified" to handle the variety of situations that might occur. This is, to us, unfortunate. Teaching is a social profession. It requires us to be comfortable and facile with social exchange and to develop skills that enhance learning for our students. We must learn to anticipate, to allow some tension for learning's sake, and to be willing to stretch ourselves and our students intellectually and emotionally. People are more resilient and more adaptable than we sometimes assume. We can, if we are aware of what's happening in the room and truly value for learning and personal growth, make some mistakes and still have an overall positive effect on our students.

In the end, the underlying issue is an instructor's self-confidence. The degree to which we allow our self-esteem to be determined by others (external locus of control) will shape our willingness to participate in discussions with students. If we as instructors are able to say that our self-esteem does not rest entirely on the opinions of the students in the room, then we can allow ourselves to be vulnerable by engaging discussions. If we assume that instructors should know the answers to all questions, we may never engage in discussions. If, however, we assume that no one could ever know all the answers, we can enjoin a discussion and not be upset if someone asks a question we cannot answer. Rather at that time, we can model the very thing we hope of all our students – that they will become life-long learners – and offer to either find the answer ourselves and report back to the class or assign the student who asked the question the task of researching and reporting back with the answer.

The discussion mode is also less participative, less problem-oriented and more instructor-dependent than the case method. Those features may cause discussions to become overly abstract or theoretical and therefore less applicable to the students' immediate needs and concerns.

As with other modes of teaching, settings have a big influence on the success of a discussion. If someone is assigned to teach in a room arranged in the usual elementary school fashion with students lined up in rows facing the front, it is difficult to get students to talk to each other. They cannot see each other easily, cannot face each other, and end up talking to the instructor or the chalkboard instead of each other. Discussions require a different kind of setting (e.g., horseshoe seating) to be conducted well, and such a setting may not be available – at least without some effort and planning in advance.

Types of Discussions

There are several types of discussions, including developmental discussions, gripe sessions, buzz sessions, and the problem-solving discussion.

Developmental discussions are those that begin at a particular point of knowledge in an area and are intended to move step by step toward a higher or broader level of understanding. In this type of discussion the instructor has a clear map of where he or she wants the class to go and has formulated questions that will move logically, developmentally, from one learning platform to the next. Carefully planned developmental discussions allow the instructor to retain a large proportion of control over what happens in the classroom. It is important not to give a lecture "in a discussion's clothing" since students are likely to see the charade and disengage.

Gripe sessions are where students vent their feelings and resentments and hence where little learning is likely to take place. Some instructors and, indeed, some managers discount discussions in general as little more than opportunities for gripe sessions; they avoid participative discussions all together. That is a mistake. Gripe sessions can be turned into productive sessions if the instructor is skilled and knows how to do so. It's an important skill: Refusing to allow students (or employees) the opportunity to vent their feelings can lead to disengagement and frustration.

People in educational settings, including degree programs and executive education programs, often build up resentments, frustrations, concerns, and strong feelings about either the subject matter or the process being used to introduce it. Gone unarticulated and unrecognized, those emotions can seriously impair the learning process. Sometimes the cause of the emotions reflects characteristics of the students themselves; maybe somebody was sent to the program who really doesn't want to be there or maybe he or she have just had a fight with a family member or is overwhelmed by other aspects of the program. Other times, things the instructor is doing cause those feelings: designing a course in a way that doesn't fit the students, not taking time for student questions in order to continue "moving ahead."

Allowing students to express their feelings, concerns, resentments, and frustrations may be essential to revitalize the learning motivation and to really move ahead. Taking the time for such a discussion signals to the students concern for their learning. The need for such a session is often foreshadowed by certain signs: angry faces, short comments before class, a disproportionate number of people reading other material or not paying attention.

If it seems that students are at odds with a course or an instructor, you can stop and ask them, "What's going on?" In our experience, it is best not to draw conclusions about where the signals are coming from but rather, to describe what you see and ask them, "You seem uninterested in this class. I see people nodding, others reading, and others whispering. What's going on here?"

That invitation and a little silence usually produces some comments and discussion about what is bothering the group. It may only take five minutes or it may take the rest of the hour. Regardless, an instructor's sincerity in hearing what the students have to say and openness to deviating from a plan is critical. In a recent executive program class in which we stopped to do this, we never got to the day's case. Later though, participants' evaluations almost uniformly mentioned that class as the best of the seminar because it showed faculty flexibility and sensitivity to the condition of the people – who were struggling to link concepts they had heard in several different classes and just couldn't input any more new information before resolving the issues they had at the moment. We didn't cover the material planned, but we greatly accelerated the group's learning.

When one or two in the group actually begin to respond to an instructor's invitation to express what is wrong, invariably other hands will go up. After a while, the comments will often begin to be repetitive. That is a sign that the venting has come full circle. You can then point out that the group is beginning to go around in circles and that it is time to move ahead. You can also point out that it is easy to raise complaints but it is much more difficult to suggest what should be done. This is the segue for inviting the group into a problem-solving discussion. Remember, as the instructor, you are an active part of that discussion too, and you have a voice in the ideas offered and the resolution agreed on. It is this persistence in developing action suggestions that elevates a "gripe session" to a productive participative discussion.

Again, unless an instructor is willing to adjust plans to fit the objectives of both the course and the people in it, this exercise will become counterproductive. It is better not to ask than to ask and ignore. We have not yet seen a group who could not be turned from complaining to productive problem-solving when the people in power (in school, the instructor or the administration; in business, the leadership) were willing to recognize the complaints and invite the complainers to become involved in the solutions.

A problem-solving discussion involves identifying a particular problem and asking students how they would solve it. The idea is to use problems that students can relate to in order to engage their concentration. In this it is similar to the suggestion we made above about starting lectures, but the problem discussion is really much closer in content and style to the case method, which we discuss in a later chapter. Use problems of your own choosing or invite the students to present problems related to the subject matter from their experience.

Buzz groups are a common and effective technique for creating more discussion among students during a class, regardless of how large the class is. Break the class down into groups of two, three, four, five, or six and assign a topic of discussion for a brief period of time, perhaps as little as two minutes or as much as fifteen or twenty minutes. With several questions, or a particular focus to work on, and the go-ahead to begin, the room will erupt almost immediately into a high level "buzz" of conversation. This is an excellent way of getting everybody in the room in a situation where they can express their thoughts and feelings. The noise level is a good monitor of student energy for the assignment given them. When the noise begins to drop a little, announce, "Okay, two minutes!" and the energy level will increase as people hurry to finish their assignment before the time runs out.

When time is up, you can debrief these sessions either by inviting reports from various groups or alternatively, asking for brief samples of conclusions from many groups until suggestions and solutions begin to be repetitive. Some instructors feel it important to hear from each group to continue the principle of allowing all to be heard (which is a main reason for having the buzz group in the first place), but this can become repetitious and boring. If you're bored, the students probably are, too. The debrief process can be accelerated by asking, "Do any of the remaining groups have anything *different* to add; that is, things that are not minor variations of what we've already heard, but that represent something really new?"

The **solidifying discussion** is another type of discussion in which the instructor is providing an opportunity for students to identify their misunderstandings or lack of understandings and to clarify or solidify the basic principles that the instructor was trying to teach. This give-and-take discussion, at the end of the presentation of a conceptual framework, can be extremely important. In this type of discussion, the instructor asks, "What are the key points you think we should take away from this discussion?" Usually several people will raise their hands to highlight and clarify the key points. If they don't include all the points you as the instructor thought important, you can add to them at the end. This approach is much more effective than listing your ideas of the key points at the end of each class – in which case the students will be conditioned to waiting to hear your list and sitting passively throughout the rest of the discussion until you get to the specified takeaways.

Planning for discussion classes

As noted earlier, beginning a discussion requires much more than simply asking, "Are there any questions?" There are several things you can do to plan effectively for a discussion class. Perhaps the most important thing is making sure that the participants have something to discuss. The discussion method presumes that the students in the room have enough information, data, or experience with the topic in order to comment on it. Given that premise, it's important to make sure that a lecture or the materials assigned provide this foundation for the students. The content doesn't necessarily have to present more than one viewpoint, but it should have a clear position to which the students can react. Take sufficient care in delivery or in the choice of assigned readings that the students will be able to enter the discussion period with a sufficient understanding of the theoretical constructs or the concepts that they can comment upon them.

In his book, *Learning through Discussions*, William Hill also stresses, among other things, the importance of clear definitions of terms and concepts.[2] Discussions that use different definitions of the same terms quickly become chaotic and confusing and undermine the learning process – although they do provide an opportunity for a "lecturette" to clear things up if the instructor has thought through the conflicts and developed his or her own answer.

Questions

The single most important tool available in conducting an effective discussion is a high-quality question. There are two basic principles that are important to remember in framing questions. First, frame questions that have no single right answer, that cannot be answered merely yes or no, but that ask the student to describe something, to compare something or express their opinion on a particular topic of principle. Asking a question in the heat of the class, live in real time, that comes out in a yes/no format is like slamming on the brakes of a car traveling at 65 miles an hour. The class comes to a skidding standstill, an awkward silence develops after the student says yes or no, and everyone is left wondering what to do.

One way to avoid yes/no questions is to ask comparative questions for which students are asked to contrast one theory with another, one management style with another, and so on. As they do so they will begin to identify the pros and cons of each side and to distinguish both approaches with some overarching larger principles.

Don't let questions become too abstract or theoretical. When that happens students may lose interest and will be unable to see the relevance to what they are trying to accomplish. Although that may not be true in the higher levels of the mathematics and natural sciences, for management classes, it tends to be all too common.

Another discussion-generating approach is to ask for the arguments for and against a particular framework, theory, or set of concepts presented in an article or in a lecture. As students articulate the pros and cons, they not only deepen their understanding of the subject but they learn what other views are and how they might embrace or counter them. That is a central technique in debate and legal training and applies well to many learning situations.

---

[2] William Hill, *Learning Through Discussions* (Beverly Hills: Sage Publications, 1977), 51–54.

One useful discussion opener is, "Who could use this [concept, framework, or principle] and why?" That will stimulate the students to think of not only immediate applications but also to find creative applications of the topic.

Of course, the old standby is "Why?" If you happen to pose a yes/no question, the follow-up question "Why?" can save the day. Usually after one student has given his reasons, another will be eager to jump in to show that there are better reasons for doing this or not doing this or for this concept and not that one. A common and powerful technique in developing good discussions is to ask for a vote on a topic, for instance, on their assessment of a leader in a situation. Or ask for a distribution of votes – for instance, "How do you assess the leader here on a scale from 1 to 5?" After the votes are taken, ask those who voted in the tails of the distribution (say the 1s and the 5s) to give their reasons; as a result, a nice discussion is likely to develop.

When probing a student's thinking, try to find how deep and how broad it goes, with the "Why?" question. Remember, there is a fine line between probing and attacking. If students are put on the defensive, their openness to learning goes down. That is not to say they shouldn't be challenged and pushed. To attack and humiliate them does them no good. We've known faculty who, for instance, would "nail" somebody for weak thinking. Sometimes that galvanizes a student to work harder next time. Sometimes it leaves a wound that never heals.

The difference between those two outcomes has to do with the motivations of both the instructor and the student. For example, consider the oft-told story of Socrates, who was asked by a young person if he could join his school. Socrates sized him up and took him to the beach where he put him under the water until he was nearly drowned. When he came up gasping for air, struggling and panting, Socrates declared that when he desired knowledge as much as he desired air, then he might reapply. When we take this kind of pressing, intense approach with students, we ought to ask ourselves how we view our craft. Are we there only to deal with the brilliant who would shine with or without us? Or are we there to deal with people where they are and travel with them as far as they can go? Or are we there to help people all along that distribution relate to and learn from each other?

Students don't have the depth and experience in our fields that we do. Our job, in part, is to motivate them toward the field. If they feel attacked and overwhelmed and associate bad experiences with us, what is their likely motivation to continue learning on their own in our area when the class is over? If we ask them questions that lie around the borders of their understanding and encourage them to expand their boundaries, then they are more likely to carry on without our pressure later. We can stretch them without embarrassing or attacking.

One more comment on questioning: avoid the Easter egg hunt, the technique that revolves around the instructor's "best answer." The instructor has a word or an answer in mind that he wants students to find and he keeps asking different questions trying to get them to say the exact word or answer. That practice is extremely transparent and frustrating to students. Learn to accept students' responses and not to have a preferred "instructor answer" as you ask questions.

Getting participation in discussions

Discussion questions and topics that have little emotional content make it difficult for students to engage. Try to frame questions or select approaches to topics that have the potential of engaging students at more than an intellectual level. If the discussion topic is medieval history, for instance, and the students are falling asleep, begin by asking them what they would do if soldiers had come down the dormitory halls that morning and stolen all of their food for the president of the university. After getting them engaged at this level, shift to the perspective of the serfs in feudal manors and proceed from there.

On the other extreme, be careful not to choose topics that are so emotional that students won't touch them. That is rare among adult students, but there *are* taboo areas. A student's relationship with his or her parents is not often something that they want to or can discuss very well. There are some topics that are too emotional for them. Religion and sexual practices are two topics that they may want to avoid.

In between those poles, select emotionally charged issues that relate to the focal topic areas and find ways to bring students to the subject through them. The intent is to engage students at a level that allows them to remember and learn. Legislative outcomes, recent business discussions or events, political activities in which there is a good deal of controversy all can provide an emotional as well as an intellectual gateway to the subject at hand.

Another approach is the "two column" method, in which both sides of an argument are placed on a chalkboard and groups of students work on both columns, identifying and clarifying pros and cons. Or ask the entire class, for instance, to work on argument A even though they don't all believe in it, and subsequently to work together on column B, or you may divide the class in half and encourage them to take sides and argue the points for and against each of the two columns, regardless of their personal beliefs. That helps proponents and adversaries to see the strengths of the other side, a useful managerial skill. And, of course, it is another form of the dialectic approach mentioned in the opening paragraph of this chapter.

For difficult subject matter, you can call on people with no special knowledge and ask something gentle along the lines of "This is a highly complex and difficult subject. There are many people in the country – and in the room – who may not have special understanding of it. Would you tell us what your assessment of this situation is?" That approach works with topics about which anyone could have an opinion, even if special training or experience would give one greater insight. But be careful not to send signals that "We want to hear from you dummies who don't get it." If you add, "We'd like to hear from you as a repre-sentative of the group that doesn't understand this subject," you can cut deep and actually create the opposite reaction to what you hoped for.

On the other hand, it might be useful to call on people who do have a special knowledge in the topical area. That technique can have the effect of creating a lot of participation in the short run but of shutting down participation thereafter, since the other, less knowledgeable peo-ple in the room may feel intimidated and not want to offer anything after the "expert" has spoken. As a rule of thumb, save experts for later in the class and let them try to fill in gaps or straighten out con-fusions created by the others. It is the creation of the confusion and its unraveling that can be more educational for the rest of the class than the alternative of simply listening to the expert share what he or she knows.

Another discussion generator is to ask why this particular article, case, or subject is being introduced in the course at this time. That question can help students to think about the flow of the course and how each piece fits in.

Another good question is, "What is the key message or theme that the author is trying to present?" This question encourages students to put themselves in the author's mind and consider the main points and concepts that they are trying to communicate. The class can then decide how effective the author was in making those points and learn from that about their own means and skills of communication. In addition, ask what arguments, either for or against the author's case, have been omitted or were under- or overplayed.

Asking students to frame the questions that they should consider for a class or set of materials is another excellent way of engaging them. At the beginning of a class this can be done by asking something like, "We have 90 minutes to use here, and I want to make sure that we use it to your best advantage. What questions do you think we should consider today?" List these on the board and when the main ones are out, add a couple of your own and then ask for the logical sequence of addressing them.

This approach points out to the students several things. It shows them how difficult it can be to ask the right questions. In their own professional settings, they will be left on their own to decide the major questions to consider, and this is good practice. It also points up to them and to the instructor how dependent a class can become on an instructor through such seemingly little things as who asks the first question. You as the instructor can also learn a great deal about the students' real level of understanding and insight into your topical area. This can be a humbling approach; you learn how much they really know, that is, what they can do and how they think when left to their own devices. As instructors we can lull ourselves into a false sense of accomplishment if we allow the quality of classes we have shaped and directed alone to inform our sense of what the students are learning. One warning: don't use this approach if their questions will not influence the class. It's not fair to ask their questions, and then reject them in favor of your own.

Peter Frederick in his article, "The Dreaded Discussion: Ten Ways to Start," also suggests reading key quotes from the articles assigned. Sometimes there are inspirational or especially dense sentences or paragraphs that seem to capture the essence of a piece. Reading these carefully chosen parts at the beginning of the discussion may help to focus and drive the group further.

Another discussion generator is to ask the whole class or buzz groups what the main takeaways from the day's class are. This often works well as a summary, one that the students then own. Takeaways are the "true statements," as Frederick puts it, that students should glean, retain, and use. This is particularly effective among executive students, who are more concerned about the effectiveness of each class than younger people tend to be.

Periodic summaries

Periodic summaries are an important feature in the effectiveness of the discussion approach. When students are winding up a discussion of a subtopic or beginning to get a little confused, it is wise to pull things together by either inviting a student to give a summary or offering one yourself. Reviewing where the class has been, what the key points are, and how these fit in with where the class is going will help cement the key points for those who have been down in the trenches of the discussion and need to pause, rise up, and get a larger perspective. The use of a separate flip chart or chalkboard to periodically note key points as they arrive during the class can be an effective mechanism. Then, when it is time for a summary, there is already a list of key points to refer to. This saves the time of trying to rewrite those points, too.

Conclusion

The discussion technique is a powerful teaching technique. It requires provocative and well-framed questions. In comparison with a lecture class, it demands relinquishing some control. In return, it facilitates gaining a better view of where the students are. It engages bright, young minds at their boundaries, and offers the real possibility of seeing a topic in a new learning light for you. When introduced with a set of materials that provides the students with knowledge, skill, and understanding of the topical area and when guided by well-phrased and well-timed questions, the discussion technique can be an enormously effective approach to learning. Good discussions are fun and can encourage students to learn more in a topical area. Approached as an afterthought with only spontaneous questions and ideas, however, the discussion technique can be boring and even dangerous.

Further Reading

Blouin, A., "Creating an Environment for Collaborative Learning," *Association Management*, 57, 14 (2005), 14.

Frederick, Peter, "The Dreaded Discussion: Ten Ways to Start," *Improving College and University Teachings,* 29, 3, 109–14.

Hill, William Faust, *Learning through Discussions*, Beverly Hills: Sage Publications, 1977.

Lundman, Joseph, *Mastering the Techniques of Teaching*, San Francisco: Jossey-Bass, 1984. (See especially Chapter 6, p. 119, "Enhancing Learning through Classroom Discussion.")

Mier, Nif, *Problem Solving and Discussions and Conferences: Leadership Methods and Skills*, New York: McGraw-Hill, 1963.

Spitzer, Q., and R. Evans, "The New Business Leader: Socrates with a Baton," *Strategy and Leadership*, 25, 5 (1997), 14.

Tootooncki, A., P. Lyons, and A. Hagan, "MBA Students' Perceptions of Effective Teaching Methodologies and Instructor Characteristics," *International Journal of Commerce and Management*, 12, 1 (2002), 79–93.

8 | *Case method: fostering multidimensional learning*

JAMES G. S. CLAWSON AND MARK E. HASKINS

> Thinking is the mind talking to itself.
> – Plato

> It can be said flatly that the mere act of
> listening to wise statements and sound
> advice does little for anyone. In the process
> of learning, the learner's dynamic
> cooperation is required. Such cooperation
> from students does not arise automatically,
> however. It has to be provided for and
> continually encouraged.
> – Charles I. Gragg

Case method refers to instruction that utilizes descriptions of actual situations to provide a basis for discussion among students and instructor. These descriptions are usually written, but they may be oral, videotape, CD-ROM, or Web-based. The underlying intent of the case method is to narrow the gap between theory and practice by placing students in the midst of a real situation they are likely to encounter, then to press them to analyze the situation, make a decision regarding a course of action to take, and then defend that decision in the midst of their peers. Cases were first used in medical instruction, then in law. The approach was adapted for use in business instruction early in the twentieth century (see Garvin, 2003).

In a typical case-method course, students are given a written case in advance of each class. The case may or may not be accompanied by an additional reading requirement that introduces a theory or an analytical framework that the students can apply to the case. Sometimes, the instructor will present the theory in lectures either before, during, or after the case discussion. Students are expected to read the case in advance, analyze it, reach a conclusion, and then come to class prepared to join with their classmates in an active debate of the issues in and related to the case. Case method, in its primary form, is highly participative. The goal of case method is to *involve* students in their learning and to bring to bear on a set of problems all of the participant experience in the room, to find the participants' limits of understanding, and then by discussion, to extend those limits.

Variations in case method

There is no one case method. Rather, a range of approaches often fall under the conversational use of the term. Perhaps the most clarifying taxonomy is the elegantly simple, classic one of Dooley and Skinner (1977) in which the proportion of instructor versus student talking is used to create a classification scheme of case use. In "classic case method," the instructor may speak from 0 percent to 15 percent of the time. In other classes, designated by their instructors as "case method" because they use written cases as a basis for some classes, the instructor may speak up to or more than 90 percent of the time, which really, then, is a lecture in which the case is merely an illustration. And some instructors will vary the proportion of teacher talk versus student talk over the breadth of a course or course module, depending on student preparation and objectives. In our view, classes in which the instructor speaks more than 50 percent of the time, even though they may be using a case as an illustration or as the center of analysis, are more accurately termed discussion classes or lectures (Figure 8.1). An instructor can give a lecture in which a case analysis is presented, but that does not make the class a "case class." Thus, the essence of case method includes two key elements: (1) decision-oriented descriptions of actual professional situations and (2) significant student involvement, that is, students talking for most of the time.

Types of cases

We may distinguish between descriptive cases, methodology cases, and decision-oriented cases. Descriptive cases pose no unresolved situation requiring a decision about a course of action to be taken. Such cases just describe a process or a decision already taken in order to exemplify a good or bad implementation of an idea or tool. Methodology cases are extended story problems that put the elements of a certain

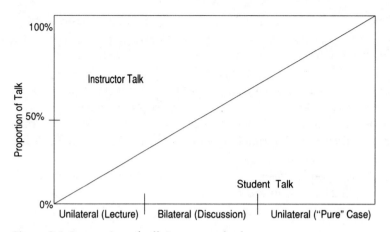

Figure 8.1 Proportion of talk in case method

methodology into a case format to give students practice at pulling out the elements and applying them. Decision-oriented cases, on the other hand, end with a problem that needs to be solved or a decision that needs to be made. It is the pressing decision that provides energy and enthusiasm when the students get involved. In our view, it is the students' participation in the analysis, discussion, and making of decisions about actual, practical, and current situations that defines the classic case method.

Student involvement in a practical problem is what makes case method an extremely powerful learning venue, one that can engage students at a deeply intellectual and emotional level, and which can greatly strengthen their abilities to deal with the realities of their professions. If the cases used are not "real" or are perceived to be outdated, student enthusiasm for engaging them declines, consistent with Knowles's theory of adult learning discussed in an earlier chapter.

Case method is applicable to most forms of professional development. We have seen instructors teach finance, marketing, quantitative analysis, medicine, law, real estate, accounting and public administration as well as organizational behavior and strategy taught very effectively. Although you might not use case method to introduce theoretical constructs in the natural sciences or mathematics, we can easily see how you could: Descriptions of research dilemmas and previous studies could deepen students' understanding of and ability to apply those constructs.

Cases need not be long. What's required in a case is enough information for students to see a situation and develop a perspective on it (so they can debate it). Cases are *not* news articles, because the student should *not* be lead to a single conclusion, but rather have the legitimate basis for pursuing several alternatives. That is one reason, in our experience, why seasoned journalists often do not make good case writers – they are too imbued with the need to lead the reader rather than present a situation with much of its ambiguity and noisy data. It has been said that a good case reads like a mystery – all the clues are there for making a good decision; it is just not clear, prior to a vigorous class debate, which clues point to which decision.

Benefits of case method

The case method *works* – that is, it intensifies students' learning precisely because it engages them in real issues that they are likely to face. Malcolm Knowles (1990) points out that adult learners learn best when they are actively involved with a problem that they are, or envision, facing. Case method engages students. It puts before them, if the cases are well chosen, problems they are likely to face or have faced. It stretches their thinking, develops their speaking and persuasion skills. It forces them to adopt a decision-oriented mind set. In the executive education classroom, executives love to solve problems and when a case presents a problem they identify with, they are quite willing to dive in and strive to solve it, especially in debate with their peers.

Applied well, case method builds a variety of skills, notably context assessment, priority setting, data analysis, critical thinking, decision-making, inductive logic, planning, social persuasion, courage, public speaking, extemporaneous speaking, debate, and "presence." Every case method class is a "leadership laboratory" in which each participant must convince not the instructor but his or her peers. If a person's analysis, decision and presentation are not persuasive, classmates will argue for different approaches. All of that strengthens the mental, emotional, and engagement skills of the participants.

Participation in a case discussion tends to foster the Level Three learning we described earlier. Passive listening and note-taking while sitting in a lecture class may or may not leave a lasting impact at Level Two, thought, let alone at Level Three (values, assumptions, beliefs, and expectations). However, when 20 to 90 people get involved in a debate about how to handle a business situation, emotions sometimes, even often, run high and the participants are engaged at all levels of learning – behavioral, mental, and emotional. Elsewhere, others (e.g., Rees and Porter, 2002) have discussed some of the benefits of case method. We agree with many of theirs and in our experience, we assert the following four benefits.

Involvement. As suggested above, perhaps the case method's strongest benefit is the way in which it can grab students' attention and torque it into full-fledged enthusiasm. There is no escape from the question, "What would you do?" Everyone can answer that question. Merely asking it of a person conveys a message of the worth and value of the person asked and this alone can pull the individual into the arena of ideas and debate. Case method does not allow a student to sit back and day dream, not so much by reason of force as by enticing invitation to engage his or her peers in a lively debate.

The case method also presses one to be more involved in the material even before class begins. Knowing that one may be called on to speak extemporaneously does marvelous things for a person's energy for preparing for class. Whereas a student might skip some reading assigned for a lecture class, they cannot do that in a case class without risking public embarrassment in front of one's peers. This is not necessarily an opportunity for public ridicule, although the tone and demeanor of the instructor does a lot to model to the class how to handle those who are ill-prepared or thinking shallowly, but rather a natural human desire to look good, especially among one's own reference group.

The case method involves people. We have known colleagues visiting another colleague's class to get so caught up in the case discussion that they began to speak out or raise their hands, wanting to join in. We have known parents visiting class who simply could not restrain themselves, but vigorously requested a chance to be heard. We have seen forests of hands rise instantaneously when one person begins to conclude. When that happens, there is electricity in the air that makes the hair on the back of the neck rise, that causes the heart to beat faster, that brings a tickling to the stomach, and flushes the face. When you have experienced this in a dynamic case discussion, it is difficult to return to a more unilateral, less exciting, yes, mundane kind of instruction.

Focusing on students' level of understanding. A major benefit of the case method is that it keeps the focus of the discussion close to students' own boundaries of what is known. Because people, in a group feel the constraint to not repeat what is known to all and also not to hold forth on that which is distantly unknown to the group, there is a certain self-governing system at work in the case method. People will tend to explore the boundaries of their own knowledge and beliefs as quickly as they, in a group, can. This collective "pushing of the envelope" provides an inviting, somewhat forgiving/safe context to wrestle with new ideas, thoughts, and emotions.

The case method's focus on sharing wisdom and insight points to the importance of the composition of the group. Classes composed of people from the same background sometimes flounder because the students are unable to see new perspectives on the problems presented in the cases. Classes with people from diverse backgrounds often develop the most interesting discussions because people are approaching identical problems from different viewpoints. In this situation, people find themselves learning from their own, and others', thinking.

This self-governing system works well too, to stretch the marginally less able and to give pause to the marginally more able. For the former, there is the social pressure to keep up with the group, to think harder, to prepare more carefully, to concentrate more fully. For the latter, there is the realization that life, especially in the social sciences, must be lived with other people and therefore one must learn how to communicate with and manage others, others who may not be as quick or as insightful. Both of these key insights are taught not as intellectual concepts, but as a result of simply being a part of the case method class and having to deal with its immediate constituent realities.

Ongoing feedback from students about what they "get." Another benefit of the case method is that it allows the instructor to continuously monitor the level of understanding and skill development in the class. While discussion methods also do so to some extent, they tend to give more data on the students' level of understanding than on their skill development. In case discussions where not only analysis but also decision-making is required, the instructor can see how emotionally and intellectually prepared the students are to present their conclusions and to persuade others. We have often noticed students who wrestle with making a commitment to a point of view, others who struggle with finding the rationale to support their conclusions, and others who struggle with the details of plans needed to implement their decisions.

Some criticize the case method for being unreal and artificially decision focused (see Jennings, 2002; Mintzberg, 2004). Yes, cases are not a real-time business situation, and you are in a classroom. And yet, the discussion *does* center around real business situations and it *does* involve the convincing of real people, peers who are focused on the same issues. If students engage peers in discussions of ideas and opinions about the problems in the cases, they are practicing and developing leadership skills for the workplace.

Skill development. Skill development also occurs in case classes. When a student prepares a case, discusses it with his or her study group in advance of class, presents ideas in the larger class setting attempting to present briefly and cogently an analysis, a decision, and the steps for implementing a decision, and then has to respond to comments, criticisms, suggestions, or sheer apathy from their classmates, that student is learning to analyze, decide, persuade, muster courage, develop constancy of image among peers, become more efficient at reading, analyzing, presenting, and responding, and interacting with colleagues.

Disadvantages

The case method is not the answer to all teaching challenges; it has some disadvantages. One is that it can become heavily instructor-dependent. Some instructors can facilitate a case discussion in a provocative and penetrating way, while others, with the same material, may be boring and superficial. Some of that has to do with the personality of the instructor and some of it has to do with the relationship between the material and the instructor. The instructor who comes across as dull with one case because of its content and focus might be dynamite with another case with a different focus. The challenge is for each instructor to find ways and cases to repeatedly create vibrant discussions and lasting learning.

The case method's allowance for questions and challenges from students means that the case method instructor is much more vulnerable to the class. For instructors who don't mind that, case method is fine; for those who do, it can be very threatening. Students see how you handle questions and challenges to your authority, to your knowledge of the theory or the industry in question as well as to your level of preparation and ability to think and act in real time. Case method instruction demands a *relationship* with the students, whereas lecturing may not. Differences in the relationship between instructor and students can be so pronounced that in case courses this "pedagogical slack" makes it more difficult for course designers to ensure that students receive a uniform experience across the program.

Case method is also time-demanding. It often takes us five to 10 hours to prepare a new case for a 90-minute class. As an instructor repeatedly teaches cases, he or she develops a repertoire, much like a performing artist. Critics will say that encourages an instructor to become obsolete and not keep up with the field. Although that is possible, we would counter that the dynamism and excitement latent in a great case discussion motivates one to stay current, stay fresh, and settle for nothing less than the best class possible.

Over the years, case instructors compile teaching files with teaching notes, charts, anecdotes, case maps, and other related materials that often accelerate later preparation time. Once an instructor has taught a case five or six times, it is possible to anticipate the usual routes the discussion will take and preparation time is often dramatically shortened. The challenge then is first, to be willing to find and utilize new and more current cases and invest the preparation time in these new materials with their requirement for new repertoires; and second, to be open to new ways of structuring or unfolding case discussions so that one truly engages the students rather than simply attempts to lead them through a time-worn pathway that may or may not fit the current class's interest and focus.

On this latter point, many instructors see the less canned, less structured aspects of the case method as a disadvantage. They argue that they have certain material to "cover" and open-ended case method sessions leave them with too little control to ensure their teaching objectives. Our response is that "covering material" doesn't ensure that learning has occurred, and if we aren't in touch with students' learning, or lack thereof, we aren't doing our jobs. It's what the students know well enough to use when they leave our courses that determines our success. If a class doesn't get all the learning objectives for a particular class, an instructor may have to come back later to some of those points, or develop more skillful ways of managing the discussion to touch on all of the "necessary" stops on the learning tour for the day.

Case method can leave the instructor at the opening of each class uneasy and perhaps actively concerned about what direction the discussion will head and how well equipped he or she might be to handle the diversions. Frankly, we find that emotion healthy and good for stimulating more careful preparation and attention to the plan for the class. That said, it is true that case method demands some courage of us as instructors, courage to reveal ourselves in the way we handle myriad situations in class and courage born of confidence to recognize and manage the unknown.

Case method and efficiency

Is case method less efficient than simply telling students what to do, why to do it, and how to do it? We don't think so. It may seem so when only the delivery of subject matter content is considered. But if you look at student learning as extending beyond subject matter content, case method excels. In that sense, learning includes not just hearing about an idea or tool, but understanding and knowing how to apply it as well. A concept heard, vaguely understood, and not used is not learned. When students deal with case after case related to a broad topical area and each experience presses them to apply, reexamine, and wrestle with peers' applications of concepts in that area, they begin to see similarities, dissimilarities, and obstacles not only to understanding but to implementation. They form conclusions about what works in what situation and what the more portable concepts and principles may be. This sort of learning goes beyond what is most likely possible from lectures.

There is a danger in attempting to manage a case method class so that students arrive at a particular conclusion or theoretical construct. If an instructor controls the discussion so closely that he or she can plan each step and makes certain that the class takes each step, the experience becomes a thinly veiled lecture with the case as an illustration. In this format, the power to the students of the discovery process is largely lost.

At the other end of the case discussion spectrum, there is also a danger in allowing the class to go wherever they want without more experienced guidance. As with most things, the challenge is to find the useful middle ground not the extremes. There the students experience some genuine control over what they talk about, the thrill of discovering truths in their area of inquiry, and how to deal with the intimidation of making a decision, and all this amidst the patient and probing support of the instructor.

Case Method and Theory

Some observers argue that case method is ineffective in transmitting theory. In our view and experience, case method and rigorous theory work rather well together. Case method provides the means for allowing students to make their own theories-in-action in a forum where they can be re-examined in ways that are not likely to happen elsewhere. Moreover, case method instructors can, and do, introduce rigorous theoretical constructs throughout their courses. Learning how to do this in a way that connects the theory to practical application is the challenge and privilege of the case teacher. The real question is whether or not students will ever USE the theory in practice – the case method allows instructors and participants to jointly explore and assess that potentiality.

Instructors have a responsibility both for crafting learning opportunities and for the accuracy of that learning in the classroom. Lecturing offers one opportunity to ensure accuracy of teaching, but does little to test accuracy of learning or of skills in the application of that learning. Case method provides a good channel for the latter. We often assign theoretical notes and readings along with cases and often give lecturettes in class to either introduce or further explain relevant theoretical constructs. What separates these unilateral communications from the typical lecture is that students have pushed themselves to the point of needing that additional information and are therefore open to it and the information is unfolded in a context where the utility of the lecturette is immediately apparent. This approach is consistent with all of the principles of adult learning or *andragogy* introduced earlier.

Case method can also be used to develop theory. If a case, rich in data on relevant dimensions, is used without a theory-based reading, the case material can be the mechanism for the students to develop the theory themselves. Is this reinventing the wheel? Perhaps, but with the additional benefit that the inventors seldom forget their discoveries and are always able to find ways to use them. Recipients of free theoretical gifts, as recipients of free tangible gifts, seldom value them as much as those who wrestle with a problem and find their own solution.

Case method can also be used to help students make their own operating theories explicit. When a student explores one line of analysis as opposed to another line, an instructor can ask, "Why that route?" This "meta-analysis," an analysis of the student's analysis, urges the student to make clear the thought process that guided his or her behavior. Revealed in this way, the assumptions and beliefs that comprise a student's thought process, and hence theories-in-use, can be reexamined and perhaps modified, especially if peers in the room begin to express reservations.

The more direct method of simply telling someone that their approach is wrong and they should try it another way seems on the surface to be more efficient, but again, consider the student's openness to the feedback and what they will do with it. Sending the message and having it not only heard, but incorporated into a person's set of operating values and beliefs (at Level Three) are two different things.

Finally, we do not hesitate to give students theory when it seems necessary. If their own explorations, for whatever reasons – their dullness, our dullness in leading the discussion, or the overpowering scent of red herrings – do not lead them to what we may consider necessary conclusions, we may either interrupt the discussion to lay out some theory-induced concepts or we may ask them to consider more carefully a theoretical reading we've assigned in connection with the current discussion.

So, we say emphatically, case method does not preclude the introduction of, the writing of, the understanding of, and the application of good theory. Rather, it invites it. But it does so in a way that makes students and instructors more open to theory and more able to use it. Rather than theory and cases being anathema, we find them to be complementary avenues that work well together.

What case method demands of the instructor

Case method makes many demands on the instructor. It takes time to prepare, it requires a more personalized demeanor in the classroom, and it typically requires case writing to add to the pool of first-class materials. An instructor must have an ability and willingness to relax a desire for total control in the classroom, and an interest in and awareness of the learning of the individuals in the room.

Careful course design includes excellent materials (there are a lot of bad cases out there). Among the best case publishers are Harvard Business School Publishing, Ivey School at Western Ontario, Simmons College in Boston, Darden Business Publishing at the University of

Virginia, the European Case Clearinghouse, and the North American Case Research Association. Browse their on-line bibliographies, read the abstracts, perhaps order inspection copies and read the cases (always a good idea before actually assigning one). It takes time, but choosing well is important: Sometimes the cases are old, poorly written, or just not appropriate for the kind of discussion that you want for a particular part in a course.

Having the wisdom and insight to ask good questions is essential to the success of a case method class. Indeed, perhaps no skill is so important to case teaching as this one. If you misphrase a question, or ask the wrong question, a class can degenerate rapidly and be very difficult to resurrect. Good questions do not have yes or no answers, but rather invite the respondent to describe their thinking and make a case for why others should accept it. A good question and response should stimulate a solid 10 to 20 minutes or more of subsequent discussion. Sometimes, depending on the skill of the group and the clarity of the discussion, an instructor need do no more than nod in the direction of the next speaker. Other times, a bit of introduction and background may be necessary to present a question and have it understood and connected to the rest of the discussion. A common flaw for new case method instructors is that they pay too little attention to the wording and content of their questions. The best instructors ask precise, probing, provocative questions – a skill nurtured via careful planning, thought, and experimentation.

Instructor questions must be timed just right so as to not preempt students' mental processing of various inputs and so as to not preempt posing just the right question themselves back to a classmate or to the class at large. At times, an instructor may find a leading question appropriate and useful (e.g., "John, what do you conclude from the VP's comments in the case?") and other times, not. Questions posed by an instructor should generally seek to do one of three things: open up a new arena for the class discussion (figuratively opening the gate into a new pasture for the class to graze); turbocharge the debate (e.g., "Sara, how would you argue against Scott's recommendation?"); or probe for additional explanation/understanding. There is no prescribed moment for any one of these sorts of questions – truly, the exact moment is when you, as the instructor, sense that it is the right moment, in that class, with that discussion to date, and with that cadre of students.

No matter the course, no matter the case, no matter the class, there are some tried and true questions to have in one's repertoire and at the ready. Here is a baker's dozen of such questions:

1. Why would you do that?
2. What other approaches did you consider and why did you choose the one you did?
3. How would you do that?
4. John, what is your response/reaction to Jane's analysis and suggestion?
5. How would you explain that to grandma who never went to business school?
6. What has been overlooked in the discussion so far?
7. What could happen, and how would you address it, that might negate/derail your plan?
8. What other resources/perspectives might be helpful in this situation?
9. What's the real problem/opportunity/issue here?
10. What are a couple of enduring principles that we can posit from our case discussion today?
11. What assumptions are you making?
12. In what ways does this case connect to a prior case we have discussed or another course you are taking or have taken?
13. How would you know if your plan of action failed/succeeded in six months' time?

An instructor's ability to manage a case discussion depends on a key set of skills. Managing beginnings, whom to call on and when, when to talk and when to be silent, how to deal with silence, managing conflicts, interjecting input and theory, and managing endings and conclusions all pose challenges.

Managing beginnings is important to successful case courses, not only for the first class, but for every class. The impression you make upon entering a room can either add to or detract from the learning environment. The first words you speak can do the same. If you are critical, overbearing, or apologetic and disorganized, you set a tone for the class and perhaps for the course. Careful instructors are aware of these influences and while they may not manage them compulsively (some do), they will attend to them and strive to improve class after class, course after course.

Beginnings establish direction and ground rules as well as acceptable and unacceptable behaviors. Beginning a case course with a lecture, for instance, will confuse the students who came ready for a case discussion. Beginning with a case introduction before a group ill-prepared for it, however, can also disrupt their readiness to learn. We carefully think about when we are going to arrive, what we're going to do, how we're going to dress, and what we're going to say in the first five minutes. Tony Athos, a friend/mentor at Harvard Business School, takes management of beginnings very seriously: he mingles with students in advance to find out what they're thinking and talking about to get his mind and experience more closely aligned with theirs so that he can from the outset, reduce or eliminate as many barriers between them and him as possible. Throwaway phrases from an instructor (such as, "I didn't have much time to sort this out this morning, but we'll work through it") can seriously demotivate a class. Beginnings are important, think carefully about everything you'll say and do and consider the consequences your choices will have on the students. We recommend videotaping several beginnings to observe how your beginnings affect the atmosphere in the classroom.

Whom to call on is an important beginning consideration. Do you call on the person obviously prepared (who may have even come up before class to volunteer to begin the discussion), or randomly pick a student, or is it best to select someone who may be struggling with the material, or someone who seems unprepared? Students' backgrounds may also influence this decision. Do you call on those with extensive experience in the industry highlighted in the case or someone who doesn't know it and might bring a fresh perspective? What about balance in calling on men and women, majorities and minorities, and one that you might not even think about, the left side of the room versus the right side of the room? Right-handed instructors may naturally turn clockwise from the chalkboard to face the class, meaning they will face the left side of the room first. With a tendency to call on the first hand seen, instructors may select an inordinate number of hands on the left and very few, backed up by frustrated faces on the right. Again there is no best answer to these questions – we pose them merely for instructors to consciously consider so that the choices made in these regards are not haphazard or by default.

Sometimes it is best for the learning of the group to call on a person who is struggling with the material because that person becomes a surrogate for the rest of the class – the embodiment of their questions and concerns about the material. Working with them provides a means for the majority of the class to follow along and is a superior approach to calling on the bright or experienced one who can sail through that particular analysis and perhaps intimidate and "lose" the rest of the class in the process.

To foster and facilitate debate, it is sometimes useful to ask, "Who disagrees with the last point of view?" Indeed, if everyone seems to be agreeing, you may begin to worry about groupthink and the subsequent shutting down of the learning process.

When to talk and when to be silent is another issue of case class instructor management. If an instructor speaks too much, or attempts to solve disagreements too soon, the class will soon learn to wait and listen for the instructor's "right" answer. Allowing students to explore an issue, to flounder a bit, and to debate until they've exhausted their resources, and then having the wisdom and insight to recognize that point and to step in with some new ideas to spur their discussion is a skill developed by case instructors over time.

Case instructors also need to develop means for keeping track of students' contributions to the daily discussions. In degree programs (MBA) we record students' contributions to each class's discussion with a relatively simple spreadsheet, "Evaluating Students" (see Chapter 18). Such information is necessary for assigning grades and for keeping track of who has been silent (and thus in need of an invitation/opportunity to join in) and who has been too dominant. Some experienced case teachers believe that no more than 10 to 15 students out of 60 should talk in a class since any more is an indication of shallowness and a mere collection of so-called "chip shots." In our experience, classmates will tend to censure long-winded, off-the-mark, or trivial comments so as to not waste the group's time. In that kind of environment, we can have as many as 20 to 30 contributing at a substantive level during a 90-minute class.

Case method also demands that instructors become skilled at managing silence. Sometimes, what seems like lengthy silence is exactly what the class needs in order to think about the issue, to formulate arguments, and/or to reflect on the previous comment. Yet most of us are uneasy with silence, particularly in an educational setting. It somehow seems that to allow silence is to renege on one's responsibility either as a conversationalist or as an instructor. Yet the opposite can be true.

Silence can punctuate emotions, underscore important points, and produce poignant questions. Pressing for premature answers may yield immature thinking. A good case teacher is comfortable with silence and knows how to use it to the advantage of the group's learning.

In any setting that encourages discussion there will be disagreement. How that disagreement is dealt with can make a big difference in the openness of the class and in its learning. With cases, one often tries to foment moderate conflict by seeking students with differing opinions and calling on them to lay out their rationales. If an instructor is skilled and a little lucky, it is possible to get emotions connected with the various viewpoints. This is desirable, because it heightens the learning possibilities for the class. When a student is emotionally, as well as intellectually engaged, memory is more highly activated and the intensity of concentration is raised. When these conditions lead student to personally examine their closely held values, methods of analysis, or goals for business, it is enormously helpful in the educational process.

When emotions tip over into the irrationally held, but not-open-for-discussion zone, the debate is likely to become divisive and unproductive. Out of fear of the latter, many instructors actively avoid emotional encounters in the classroom. Our belief is that instructors can learn to handle such situations. A key goal is to make sure that there is a balance between points of view.

Another worthwhile case method goal is to encourage people to reason out their positions publicly so that they can learn: (1) whether they are really committed to their viewpoint or not, and (2) what it takes to make a rational, convincing argument for their position among peers. It is important to make certain that discussants focus on the issues and the situation in the case rather than attacking each other personally. One cannot always avoid that. In that situation, an instructor has to remember that students must take responsibility for their own actions. It is not the instructor's responsibility to protect everyone in the class, either from the attacks of others or from the backlash to their own behavior. It is the instructor's responsibility, should such a situation arise, to help the people in the room gain some experience with those kinds of situations so that it becomes a learning experience.

Most case classes have a certain structure. There are several common structures: the problem first, the answer first, and the free form are perhaps the three most common. In the "problem first structure," the classes are usually divided into three sections, problem identification, analysis, and action plan. Most of our classes follow this three-part structure because we believe it is hard to work on the solutions until one has a clear idea of what the problems are. We usually spend about 20 percent, 40 percent, and 40 percent, respectively on these three class sections, although that may vary depending on the needs of the class. Earlier classes in a course may focus more on problem identification, while later classes may emphasize more action planning, but each class has some of these three elements in it. The analysis period is when we bring theory and conceptual frameworks to bear: How did we get into this mess? What are the dynamics of this situation? How do you make sense of this situation? What are the causal links here? All of these questions are appropriate queries to pose to the class.

In the "answer-first structure," instructors begin the class not with "What are the problems here?" but with "What would you do?" The rationale for this start is that the students' case preparation has led them to that point and they have immediate energy for letting that out. In this structure, instructors allow the class to flesh out several alternative action plans and then back into the analysis and problem identification by asking students for the underlying rationales that led to their proposed action plans. This is an effective technique if done well, but it can be demoralizing for others if one student is so compelling with his or her recommendation that the rest feel they have nothing to add. Further, if a student develops a rigorous action plan that does not address what some feel are the main issues, it can be used to highlight the point that we need to know what we're working on before we charge off with solutions. Near the end of a course, this approach can be powerful and efficient in that students steeped in problem identification and analysis will be able and willing to incorporate into their answers the rationales for why this solution and not another one, thereby covering the problem and analysis sections seamlessly in concert.

The "free-form structure" allows students to set the class agenda. This may be explicitly done by asking them at the outset of class "What questions or issues do you think we should answer (or work on) today?" or by simply asking someone, "to begin." This approach assures the instructor that the class is where the students are and can be a good means two-thirds or three-quarters of the way through a course of doing an exam preview. Without structuring the students' beginning discussion, an instructor can find out what they know and how they think. This has been a humbling experience in the past and it has highlighted again how often the gap between what we think they know and what they really know is too large. If the class ignores the conceptual frameworks already introduced and the practice they've had already in using them, we should probably conclude they have not yet learned how to use the frameworks or accepted their utility thus exposing a disconnect in the learning we were striving for and what was achieved.

Interjecting theory is an important part of case discussions. Consider for a moment comparing the case class to a hole of golf. If lecturing were the only technique we could use, it would be like playing a round of golf with only one club. But if a player has several clubs at his or her disposal, then he or she can pick and choose when to play which club and under what circumstances. Knowing when to play a 7 iron or a sand wedge requires skill with both clubs and experience and judgment. Knowing when to interrupt a case discussion with a short lecturette requires some skill at making the lecturette, at the interruption, and at building the bridge back to the case. Poor interruptions leave a class flat and with no enthusiasm or sense of direction. In practicing the various teaching techniques introduced here as well as your own, you'll find some you feel more at home with than others. If you allow yourself to use only a few techniques, your breadth of skills will diminish and you'll be playing the golf course of andragogy with but one or two clubs in the bag.

Managing endings and conclusions are also critical to case teaching. In "classic case method" there might be no ending, just the recognition that the time is up and that students should leave. In a more controlled approach, instructors may attempt to give the "right" answer at the end of the period. This can be equally deflating to the students since it undermines their desire to study the next day. ("Why study if he/she is just going to give us the right answer at the end anyway?") In between, there is (1) the choice to occasionally let the discussion hang, (2) to report what actually happened in the real case situation and discuss whether or not that was a *good* decision, and/or (3) to build a bridge from this class to the next one which might include articulating the next assignment to give students a sense of the overarching framework that the sequence of cases fits.

Class-to-class bridges are much more important in short courses (three days to three weeks) where you have less time to build a conceptual arsenal of tools and skills. Indeed we find that practicing managers in our executive programs have less tolerance for rediscovery although we are convinced that similar principles of learning apply equally to them as to MBAs. Consequently, we tend to build more explicit bridges between classes in our shorter courses, building the near-shore span at the end of class and the far-shore span at the beginning of the next class (e.g., "Remember that in our last class, Sturdivant Electric, we talked about how to manage interpersonal conflict and how to deal with limited resources under conditions of pressure? We build on that theme in today's class by examining a broader context, how conflict develops and can be managed in work teams and under less stressful conditions.")

What case method demands of the student

Case method makes some significant demands on students as well as on instructors. Students have to be willing to prepare in advance, to attend class, to speak their opinions, to show some courage in conversing with their classmates and to respond to instruction from all sides. If they won't prepare and won't talk, it is difficult to hold a case discussion. Sometimes getting these two elements is a matter of expectation and acculturation. In some institutions, students are not generally expected to behave in this way and they may not until otherwise encouraged or coached. Having a large proportion of one's grade dependent on class participation helps in this regard.

The case method asks students to have the courage to make decisions and have them examined by their peers. Some people don't like to do that. It is an excellent refining fire, though. Students who, for whatever reason, refuse to take a position and to defend it are likely to find the case method threatening and overwhelming. But consider what kinds of settings they will encounter in their careers. Don't most careers demand that a person make decisions and defend them and act on them? Yes, and the case method is excellent training for such a need.

In an interesting study, Rosier (2002) found that students' learning from case method instruction was greatly enhanced by the writing of post-class "reflective reports." Indeed, excellent pre-class preparation and lively in-class discussion can often benefit from some sort of reflective process. Most of the time, instructors simply assume students will review their notes, reflect on the discussion, and thus embed their learnings. This approach, although common, leaves the reflective process to the discretion and initiative of students. With a modest nudge from instructors via an assignment to write a one-to-two page reflective report within two days of the class, learning and retention can be enhanced. Rosier (p. 593) suggests several guiding questions for the reflective reports.

- *What would you now do differently if you could have a second try at this case?*
- *Can you apply what you have learned to your work, to your studies, to another case, or to any other aspect of your life (past, present, or future)?*
- *What else have you learned from the case, from the study group discussion, and/or from the class discussion?*
- *What have you learned from writing this reflective report?*

It may seem a bit odd to require structured reflection from your students, but we believe the use of reflective reports has merit. We have had students use learning journals to capture insights – reflective reports both expand and organize reflection to yet a greater extent. As with many aspects of our craft, we encourage experimentation, and this practice has appeal for us all to try and refine.

Corporate case instruction

There are many, especially corporate clients that we encounter, who believe cases and case method are too time-consuming and expensive. For many corporate education buyers or providers, the preferred model is a self-contained seminar (no advance preparation) with presentations by an instructor. These are clearly Level Two experiences – the participants are to "get" the concepts and skills from listening to an instructor. In these roles, instructor dynamism is critical and often carefully scrutinized. The underlying message seems to be, if the material and the delivery method are deenergizing, we'd better make sure we have a powerful instructor to "keep their attention" during the seminar. Participants often come to corporate educational settings with that back-of-mind assumption – here I am, teach me!

We have a number of corporate clients, however, who are willing to let us use cases more and more frequently in their corporate educational environments. The benefits are apparent: higher levels of classroom energy on the part of all concerned, more responsibility on the participants rather than instructor to seize the topic, and the beneficial shared experiences and insights from everyone in the room, not just the "sage on the stage."

There are challenges with using the case method in corporate settings, however. The first is the issue of whether to use "inside" cases. Many companies say they want cases based in their industry and in their company in order to maximize the learning potential. There is a strong rationale for this. The downside however is twofold: first, for inside company cases, many participants will have some limited experience with the case and often will either tune out or debate the accuracy of the case with the instructor. This result undermines learning for everyone in the room. The second downside is that it takes lots of time and money to develop good cases and most corporations are not willing to do what's necessary to develop those materials – or release them for wide use once they are written.

Usually, a better alternative is to select cases from related industries or companies with similar issues that the participants can approach in an arm's length fashion, and then discuss in class. Then, at the end of a class session, participants are invited to think about how to apply the learnings to their own situations. Such an approach requires an instructor to have learned a fair amount about the client company so that appropriately poignant and critical questions get asked. While most companies think their issues are unique, in our experience, most business situations have been experienced and learned from before.

That said, we have clients, including three large government agencies, who are developing their own case libraries. In the world of law enforcement, for example, many government agencies carry the responsibility of training not only their own employees, but also the officers of domestic and foreign local and national enforcement agencies. In these situations, short and well-written descriptions of crimes or investigations including the data signs at the time, reports, and a complete description of the evidence and situation are helping new and experienced law enforcement officers enhance their analytic skills. These cases need not be long – they can be one to three pages depending on the volume of relevant data necessary to render a decision.

Conclusion

Case method is a very powerful teaching tool. Some shy away from it because it demands time and talent from both student and instructor alike, but these concerns ought to be considered in the broader view of adult learning. The ability to use, leverage, enhance, and enliven course concepts should be the measure of educational effect not the volume of material covered or the speed with which it is covered. Your institution, university, corporation, or consulting firm may have a culture that doesn't encourage active participation and shared problems on which to focus. Perhaps they should. In our experience, there's nothing quite so energizing and informative as getting 30 to 50 experienced people in a room and focusing their talents on a relevant, important, and shared business issue. We've seen cases work in a wide variety of settings with a wide variety of participant/student types and have become convinced that they can be very effective in a large number of settings.

Further reading

Barnes, Louis B., C. Roland Christensen, and Abby J. Hansen, *Teaching and the Case Method,* 3rd edn, Boston: Harvard Business School Press, 1994.

Clawson, James G., and Sherwood C. Frey, Jr., "Mapping Case Pedagogy," *Organizational Behavior Teaching Review*, 11, 1 (1986–87), 1–8.

Dooley, Arch R., and Wickham Skinner, "Casing Casemethod Methods" *The Academy of Management Review*, 2, 2 (1977), 277.

Garvin, David A., "Making the Case," *Harvard Magazine* (September/ October 2003), 56–65, 107.

Jennings, D., "Strategic Management: An Evaluation of the Use of Three Learning Methods," *Journal of Management Development*, 21, 9 (2002), 655–65.

Knowles, Malcolm, *The Adult Learner, A Neglected Species*, Houston: Gulf Publishing, 1990.

Mintzberg, H., *Managers not MBAs*, San Francisco: Berrett-Koehler Publishers, 2004.

Rees, W. D., and C. Porter, "The Use of Case Studies in Management Training and Development – Part I," *Industrial and Commercial Training*, 34, 1 (2002), 5–8.

Rosier, G., "Using Reflective Reports to Improve the Case Method," *Journal of Management Development*, 4, 8, (2002), 589–97.

Turner, Arthur, "The Case Method Revisited (A)," *Journal of Management Education*, 6, 3 (1981).

Vance, Charles M., *Mastering Management Education*, Newbury Park, CA: Sage Publications, 1993.

9 Role-playing

JAMES G. S. CLAWSON

> I have always thought the actions of men
> [are] the best interpreters of their thoughts.
> – John Locke

Role-playing can stimulate learning by bringing abstract conceptions alive for students, push them to focus on significant details that they otherwise might ignore, help them to see others' points of view, help them see the differences between concept and reality, provide on-the-spot variety in the classroom, and give enormously useful data to an instructor. Whether role-plays are set up extemporaneously as the opportunity arises or planned for and managed well in advance, they are a valuable teaching tool for any instructor's repertoire. This chapter outlines some of the benefits of role-playing and addresses some important role-playing issues such as when to use the technique, how long to use it, how to set up role-plays and assign roles, and how to effectively debrief participants.

Benefits of role-playing

Role-plays can dramatically galvanize a sleepy class into one charged with attention and the electricity of concentrated learning. The pressure of having to present your ideas in a simulated, but live, conversation often causes students to think more deeply, more quickly, and more emotionally than they do when they present their ideas as part of a detached, impersonal analysis.

Role-plays are an excellent avenue for bringing abstract discussions and action plans alive for students. Without role-plays, students can easily gloss over the implementation issues in their proposed action plans. When students remain concerned only with the concepts, they often talk in poorly examined abstractions and assumptions. Students may assume, for example, that: they can move easily from one step

141

to the next in their action plans; they will get approval for their suggestions; abrasive personalities will melt before their persuasiveness; strong conflict will evaporate under their guidance; a key supporter will materialize at the right moment; and even that they can hire a replacement in a day's time. That is lazy thinking, and it bores listeners, leaving them, as well as the speaker, insensitive to the realities of a manager's task to get something done through other people.

Unless students make the crucial distinction between concept and reality, they are likely to exhibit many of the criticisms leveled against students of management: overanalysis, underattention to implementation detail, obliviousness to the practical realities of organizational influence and power networks, and the inability to think in real time on one's feet. The role-play is a superb vehicle for bringing the distinction between concept and reality to the fore.

Role-plays help students confront mental laziness and think through the barriers that lie between them and the simulated implementation of their ideas. Herein lies much of the value of role-playing. There is a big difference between saying, "I would have a meeting with John Doe and get his agreement to my plan and then go see the boss" and confronting a live person representing John Doe and having to persuade that person that your plan is the right thing to do. Role-plays provide the opportunity to push students to see if they have thought through implementation details and are prepared with contingency plans to deal with unexpected outcomes. Used repeatedly, role-plays require students to add to their class preparation a careful mental review of their plans – managerial mind experiments, if you will – in which they think through each step of a proposed plan to see if it will work.

Another benefit of role-playing is that it can help students see the merits of another's position, either because the other role-player has expressed him- or herself well and has been convincing or because the student has been asked to role-play a point of view opposite from his or her own. Used in this latter way, the role-play strengthens a student's ability to empathize with, to experience, and to understand another's perceived reality. This experience sheds additional light on the individual's own view and clarifies the weaknesses and strengths of that position.

For the instructor, a role-play is a way of playing devil's advocate in an instructional setting and doing so in a way that leaves students more likely to learn insights than if you simply pointed them out. This technique is used in debate and the law for highlighting both the armor and its chinks in an opponent's position.

Its ready availability provides an immediate means of breaking the sameness of your usual teaching approach. Unannounced and spontaneous role-plays can immediately inject variety and freshness into a class. Constructing role-plays on the spot may be difficult, however, so we recommend that instructors sketch out one or two in advance of each class just in case they are warranted during class.

Role-plays also yield data about the level of understanding and skill of the students. After a role-play, it may be a bit deflating to realize that many of the skills, concepts, and principles taught earlier are not being used by students. Making this discovery while there is still time to teach them is a good outcome, however. Remember, students do only what they know and can do. Their behavior reveals how much they've learned, and this information can do much to help you assess students' understanding and to revise your teaching plans if necessary. Maybe the concepts are in the students' minds but they just don't see the relevance of them in this particular role-play, or maybe the concepts are not practiced enough for the students to feel comfortable using them. Role-plays can foster greater comfort with and help cement the application of concepts.

Finally, role-plays can show the students themselves how much they know or don't know. Some students, when listening to another's comments about a point in class, blithely think to themselves, "I could have said that! And said it better! This is no big deal; I know this stuff!" Their conclusion is often naïve, of course. The listening students may indeed have held some thoughts similar to those their classmate articulated, but the translation from thought to action is not as easy as students believe. When students have to role-play their own action plans, they quickly discover that finding the right words and style to persuade someone else is not easy. They begin to see that their mental plans and their behavior are not one and the same.

Carl Rogers suggested that there are two congruencies critical to effective interpersonal relationships. The first, internal congruency, is the degree to which one's experience (i.e., feelings and emotions) overlaps with a person's thoughts.[1] Businesspeople tend to value rationality

---

[1] See Harold S. Spear's article, "Notes on Carl Rogers' Concept of Congruence and His General Law of Interpersonal Relationships," in Tony Athos and Bob Coffey

and logic, and they often suppress their feelings, their immediate experiencing, to appear "professional." In those moments, their thinking does not match their feelings, and they become, for the moment, internally incongruent. Daniel Goleman similarly noted that the inability to recognize our own emotions and to manage them in dealing with other people is a major barrier to success in the business world.[2]

External congruency is the degree to which a person's thoughts are consistent with their behavior. If a person thinks one thing and says another, Rogers terms such a scenario as "externally incongruent." Sometimes a person's external behavior – what we can observe or hear – is more congruent with the person's experiencing (feelings and emotions) than with their thinking. People who are flushed, agitated, and shaking but trying to speak in a logical and controlled manner manifest the tension that often exists between feeling, thinking, and behaving.

We all process our experiences internally and translate them into thoughts or mental plans. We translate those mental plans into the things we say and do (Figure 9.1). Why then, all too often, do we find ourselves saying, "That didn't come out quite right" or "That wasn't what I meant to say"? To paraphrase the popular Hollywood film, something was lost in translation.

So, when students sit back and tell themselves that they're learning as much by observing as they would by participating, they deceive themselves. When individuals are called upon to speak, to persuade, to present – in short, to make those internal translations on the spot – many suddenly find themselves ill prepared. To be able to recognize feelings and to translate them accurately and effectively into thoughts and actions is a skill. Fortunately, also, it is a skill that can be practiced. Role-plays provide an excellent opportunity for students to develop such skills and to practice their abilities to frame and communicate their thoughts and feelings in effective, productive ways among peers.

A common theme in the benefits of using role-play is that the technique can bring abstract discussions alive, and, in so doing, expand students' willingness to learn. In a role-play, the student is confronted with real people – either the instructor or a member of the peer group. Role-plays thus produce close to real data for the students to work

(eds.), *Behavior in Organizations: A Multidimensional View* (Englewood Cliffs, NJ: Prentice-Hall, 1968).
[2] See Daniel Goleman, *Emotional Intelligence* (New York: Bantam, 1995).

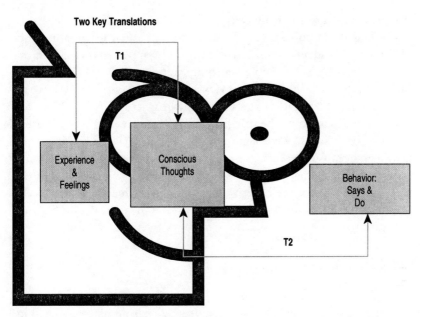

Two Key Translations

T1

Experience & Feelings

Conscious Thoughts

Behavior: Says & Do

T2

Figure 9.1 Rogers's two translations

with and respond to. Role-plays demand that the players and those who identify with them (usually most of the class) engage the situation viscerally as well as intellectually. It is this compelling feature of role-plays that can cause a class to come alive.

When to use role-plays

As with other teaching techniques, knowing *how* to use a role-play and knowing *when* to use it are two different things. Role-plays can be used to start a class. As an example, ask students to play out a key conversation suggested by the case reading or assignment. In this use, a role-play simultaneously highlights the key issues in the case and grabs the students' attention.

More often, however, we find role-play more useful in the last third of a class. For us, most case classes have three major segments: problem identification and clarification; analysis (addressing such questions as "What are the causes of the problems we have just outlined?" and "What are the underlying dynamics of these causes?"); and action planning. In this last portion of the class, students build on their view of the problems and their analysis of the causes to suggest things that one might do to solve them. These action-planning discussions only begin with a student's plan, because the real test of a manager is in the "how." "How do you implement your action plan?" "How do you bring Mr. Smith to your point of view?" "What barriers do you expect to encounter?" "What do you expect the boss to say?"

In these discussions, the role-play can effectively sensitize a student to new possibilities. We are careful not to *end* a class on a role-play, however, because there needs to be time for alternative role-plays and the debriefing. A major benefit of ensuring debriefing time is that the role-players' classmates can give the role-players feedback. Peer feedback is often more direct and more powerful than anything the instructor can say.

How long should a role-play last?

Role-plays can take a lot of time; if they last too long, they can bore the rest of the class. Long role-plays may teach the role-players the limits of their peers' tolerance for listening to them, but this insight comes at a heavy cost in class time. Thus while keeping an eye on the content of the role-play, it is also necessary to gauge the interest of the observers.

Sometimes role-playing students become stubborn and refuse to stop even when it is apparent that their counterpart is not responding and that the rest of the class is unengaged. Like a chess game nearing checkmate, a role-play can have a clear outcome long before it actually occurs. In this case, stop the role-play and ask, "Where is this headed?" If they say, "Nowhere!" then ask "Why?" and the ensuing discussion becomes a personal feedback session to the participants, one which they usually find hard to ignore.

Generally, we find that two to five minutes is adequate for a role-play growing out of a student's action plan. (Of course, more time may be needed for more involved role-plays such as simulated performance reviews.) In five minutes, one can get a very clear view of the objective the student had in initiating this discussion and can have a decent debrief of the interchange. Sometimes we've stopped a role-play after the first comment, i.e., after 15 seconds; we often do this when the person initiating the conversation has said something that will color the whole rest of the conversation ("Bob, you have a problem!" is an example of the kind of comment that can point a conversation in one particular direction); but sometimes it is also worthwhile to wait until the end of the role-play and ask students what they saw in the opening comments.

Choosing the role-players

Choosing the right students to participate is an important part of a successful role-play. The obvious choice criterion is experience with the topic of discussion. An instructor can pick a student experienced in the topic area either because of their ability to show the rest of the class how a person experienced with that field would approach the topic or because the instructor wants the experienced student to flounder a bit and become more open to learning in the area.

On the other hand, it may make sense to choose a student *not* experienced in the topic area to help them learn what the topic is like. Then, choose someone experienced in the subject as the counterpart so that the inexperienced person will be pressed more effectively. For instance, having an experienced bond trader interview a Wall Street hopeful for employment can teach the hopeful person a lot about whether or not he or she has what it takes to thrive in that environment. Important criteria other than experience that warrant consideration, however, are ability to suspend fear of looking stupid to classmates and ability to get into the role. The personalities of some people may make them ill-suited for role-plays, and self-conscious students can destroy a role-play opportunity.

Some people feel very uncomfortable "play acting," as they put it. Instructors can explain that the student is not to act but, rather, simply to be him or herself in that situation. Even then, some people begin with something like, "Well, first I would explain to the people the importance of the situation and then I'd motivate them to follow my lead." In this case, the student is not role-playing but talking *about* the situation. We would interrupt here and say, "Wait. I don't want you to talk about the situation, I want you to say what you'd say to these people as if they were the real people in that situation. Don't talk about it, DO IT!" This is usually enough to get people out of their reluctance, but not always. If a person just cannot speak directly to the role-play situation, then thank them for trying and move on to someone else.

Picking someone who is quiet and/or shy is a high-risk tactic. People who, for whatever reason, don't participate much in class are unlikely to bring much energy to a role-play. This is not always true, however. In role-plays, they might display a different kind of commitment to their positions than they usually do in class and be very effective.

One method for finding good candidates for role-plays is to ask who in the room agrees with one of the points of view in the discussion. Pick someone from this group and then ask who subscribes to the opposite view and pick one of them for the role-play counterpart. In this way, people who are likely to have real points of difference are selected and are thus likely to produce a good discussion. Random choices may produce two people who think the same and cannot do much more than say, "You're right, let's go ahead." This outcome is terribly deflating when their goal was to highlight differences in approaches or the difficulties in implementing a particular plan.

Role-plays can certainly highlight differences in style among the students. When an instructor wants a role-play to motivate a student to think about his or her style (as when a student may be seen as overly assertive or abrasive, or when the role-play calls for a person to wrestle with a known personality type and, therefore, requires some acting), it is often best for the instructor to play one of the roles. In this way, the instructor can then insure that certain viewpoints or certain interpersonal styles are brought to bear. One caution however: instructors should not overdo role-plays in which they take part. An instructor's background, strength of feelings, determination to press the other role-player, confidence, position of authority as the instructor, and expertise can all combine to overwhelm the student. If an instructor is always a part of role-plays and/or manages them so that the instructor's view always prevails, the class will grow discouraged and retreat emotionally and mentally from role-playing. Therefore, strive to have the preponderance of role-plays between students, especially early in the course.

Another approach is to structure role-plays so that the whole class can participate. There are at least two ways to do this. First, have the class pair up and role-play a situation simultaneously. A variation of this approach is to have a third person assigned as an observer who takes notes for later feedback. Alternatively, assign various segments of the class to certain group roles, such as the board of directors, shareholders, or unionized employees. These groups may interact with a student who has suggested a meeting or react to a student making an announcement as an officer of the company. These whole-class role-plays can be extremely powerful and can reveal key issues very rapidly.

Setup planning begins with a focus on how the room should be arranged for the role-play. Are the chairs needed? Lights dimmed? Name tents? A table? Props? Handouts can really help a role-play setup.

The in-class setup of a role-play takes careful explanation. Make sure the students understand the roles and the setting before starting the role-play. Choose the players at the beginning of the setup so that, while explaining the role-play to the rest of the class, the role-players can be "getting into" the role. A two-minute introduction to review the data for each role can enhance the actual role-play enormously. Don't be afraid to use some silence, also, to give the students time to adjust mentally and emotionally to their roles and put themselves into the setting. Be clear about who and/or what the roles are. For role-plays involving several people, have name tents, signs, or some other means of identifying everyone.

The instructor's verbal setup can profitably include a review of basic facts that were outlined in the case or discussed earlier in the class. For example, in setting up a role-play involving the entire class, in which one person is the chief executive officer (CEO) and the rest are members of the board of directors, we assign the CEO role first (so that the student can collect her or his thoughts and notes), and while that person is thinking, we talk through the nature of the board of directors with the rest. "How old are you? What are your educational backgrounds? How liberal are you? What concerns do you have about the firm? Why did you get into this business in the first place? How do you feel about risk?" This kind of session is particularly important when you are asking students to portray positions in a case that may not align with their own. In this case, for instance, the young, assertive MBA students would be prone to respond differently from more elderly board members. If the students respond as themselves, the difficulties facing the young manager in the case, i.e., trying to convince an older board of directors to change corporate strategy, might not emerge.

Our experience is that after several role-plays with careful setups, the students become accustomed to the technique and are able to get into role-playing much more quickly than at first. We have found it useful to use some signals the students are familiar with to get them into the role-playing mode more quickly. Here are some we use. We almost always conduct role-plays from a chair in the front of the room. After two or three times, the students know that when we get the chair out, they are about to role-play. Pulling up the chair often creates a stir in the class, in fact, because they know that they're about to have some fun, see some difficult situations, and have to pay attention because they may be in the middle of it. After two or three classes, the students respond in almost Pavlovian fashion, sitting up and leaning forward to concentrate. When we sit in that chair, we never speak as the instructor. Students know we are in role-play. Only when we stand are we back in real time.

Sometimes it's useful to take a "time out" during the role-play. As a convenient signal then, Jim makes a T with our hands to signal time out, or bumps the edges of his hands together like the take signs on movie sets to signal "scene one, take two!" We use a similar gesture to signal "time in" ("Roll 'em!" on the movie set), that we're back in the role-play.

In time outs, we often talk to the side of the class opposite from our student role-player counterpart as though that side is our alter ego or a group of confidants. We ask for their advice and counsel, "What should I say? How should I respond?" Their answers help reduce the impression that we aren't reasonable and or behaving like a "real" businessperson, which forces the student role-player to deal with what we say rather than discount it, thinking, "A real businessperson wouldn't do that!" Time outs also give the student role-player additional time to think about and consult others nearby on how to carry on from that point forward in the role-play.

Who are you playing?

Students often wrestle with the question "Who am I?" in role-playing. Usually, the one best answer for this is "You are YOURSELF in this person's situation. You have all the data we've discussed so far, you have the benefit of this analysis on the board, and you are you, not the person in the case. We want to know what YOU would do in this situation, not what you think the protagonist would do." Students who try to be cute and play someone else or play the opponent's advocate actually undermine the role-play because they interject a dimension of dramatic falsehood into the situation. These students maintain and build the gap between concept and reality in the classroom; acting out another person in a role-play is a means of avoiding engaging the situation and the class, at an emotional as well as a conceptual level.

Press students to be themselves in the case situation. No one has to act, and hence, can opt out by saying, "I'm not a good actor." We don't want actors, we want people to deal with a situation as they would if they were there. As they do so, they build experience and insight that will serve them well later.

Debriefing

As with experiential exercises, debriefing of role-playing is very important. Here it is important for instructors to try to see what the students saw in the situation. Try to help them make the "obvious" explicit because it may not have been "obvious" to others. Ask them what they saw happening, what suggestions they would give to the role-players, and see how they deal with both giving and receiving feedback. Sometimes it is useful to interrupt their discussions to interject observations or to lighten or reinforce a message that may be either too direct or too obtuse.

A common, useful debriefing question is "What other approaches could Susan have taken?" Sometimes this question leads to another role-play. A student will say, "Well, I would have asked for her permission in the first place!" whereupon we pull up the chair and sit in it – and immediately everyone knows that now this student has a chance to try his or her hand at the conversation. In any case, it always gets some response, because almost everyone in the room secretly wishes to have been in the limelight showing how they would have handled the situation.

Finally, it is important to modify the conclusions they've drawn from the experience. "What does this experience teach you? What principle or principles do you glean from this experience? How will this change the way you think about your action planning for tomorrow's case? How will this affect the way you analyze a situation?" Students often say they want to pay more attention to the other key people described in the cases and how those individuals might influence their action plans.

Conclusion

Role-plays are powerful teaching tools. They always engage the students – MBAs and executives alike. Role-plays narrow the gap between theory and practice, infuse spirit into the class, and add a healthy dose of realism to the discussions. On MBA and Executive Education evaluation feedback forms, role-playing is often noted as the most engaging and exciting part of the course. Role-plays require careful setup, careful time management, and an instructor who is willing to take some risks to learn from an experience. Practiced and used appropriately, role-plays can greatly facilitate students' learning.

Further reading

Alexander, Jean, *Let's Get Down to Cases,* New York: Department of Interreligious Cooperation Anti-Defamation League of B'nai B'rith, 1957.

Anonymous, "Teaching Engineers How to Manage: Role-Playing for Better Team-Playing in R&D Management," *Management Review,* 76, 3 (1987), 10–12.

Armstrong, Scott J., and Philip D. Hutcherson, "Predicting the Outcome of Marketing Negotiations: Role-Playing Versus Unaided Opinions," *International Journal of Research in Marketing* (Netherlands), 6, 4 (1989), 227–39.

Benfari, Robert C., and Harry E. Benfari, "Intelligence and Management," *Business Horizons.* 31, 3 (1988), 22–28.

Bensman, Joseph, and Robert Lilienfeld, *Between Public & Private: The Lost Boundaries of the Self,* New York: Free Press, 1979.

Biddle, Bruce J., *Role Theory: Expectations, Identities, and Behaviors,* New York: Academic Press, 1979.

Burridge, Kenneth D. et al., *Element Masters: Fantasy Role-Playing Game,* 2nd edn, revised, Scottsdale, AZ: Escape Ventures, 1984.

Corsini, Raymond J., and Samuel Cardone, *Roleplaying in Psychotherapy: A Manual,* New York: Aldine de Gruyter, 1966.

Fein, Melvyn L., *Role Change: A Resocialization Perspective,* Westport, CT: Praeger Publishers, 1990.

Fine, Gary A., *Shared Fantasy: Role-Playing Games as Social Worlds,* Chicago: University of Chicago Press, 1983.

Gordon, Gerald, *Role Theory & Illness,* New Haven, CT: College and University Press, 1966.

Gygax, Gary, *Role-Playing Mastery,* New York: Perigee Books, 1987.

Hardy, Margaret E. and Mary E. Conway (eds.), *Role Theory: Perspectives for Health Professionals,* 2nd edn, New York: McGraw Hill, 1988.

Hawley, Robert C., *Value Exploration Through Role-Playing,* Oxford: Hart Publishing Ltd., 1974.

Jaquays, Paul, *Central Casting One: Heroes of Legend*, Task Force Games (www.task-force-games.com), 1988.

Kamen, Vicki S., and Cynthia Bentson, "Roleplay Simulations for Employee Selection: Design and Implementation," *Public Personnel Management*, 17, 1 (1988), 1–8.

Kipper, David A., *Psychotherapy Through Clinical Role-playing*, New York: Brunner/Mazel, 1986.

Kirkman, Frank, "The Theatre of Life," *Management Decision* (UK), 25, 1 (1987), 9–17.

Klapp, Orrin E., *Symbolic Leaders: Public Dramas & Public Men*, New York: Irvington, 1964.

Livingstone, Carol, *Role-play in Language Learning*, Singapore: Longman, 1983.

Milroy, E. (ed.), *Role-Play: A Practical Guide*, New York: Pergamon, 1982.

Parisi, Lynn, *Creative Role-playing Exercises in Science and Technology*, Boulder, CO: Social Science Education Consortium, Inc., 1986.

Rossi, Alice S. (ed.). *Gender & the Life Course*, New York: Aldine de Gruyter, 1985.

Shaw, Malcolm E., et al., *Role-playing, a Practical Manual for Group Facilitators*, San Diego: University Associates, 1980.

Thompson, John F., *Using Role-playing in the Classroom* (Fastback Services No. 114), Bloomington, IN: Phi Delta Kappa Fastback Publications, 1978.

Van Ments, Morry, *The Effective Use of Role-play*, revised edn, New York: Nichols Publishing, 1989.

Whetten, David A. and Kim S. Cameron, *Developing Management Skills*, Glenview, IL: Scott Foresman, 1984.

Williams, Norma, "Role Taking and the Study of Majority/Minority Relationships," *Journal of Applied Behavioral Science*, 25, 2 (1989), 175–186.

Wilshire, Bruce, *Role-playing & Identity: The Limits of Theatre As Metaphor* (Studies in Phenomenology & Existential Philosophy), Bloomington, IN: Indiana University Press, 1982.

Wohlking, Wallace, and Patricia J. Gill, *Role-playing*, Danny G. Langdon, (ed.), (Instructional Design Library), Englewood Cliffs, NJ: Educational Technology Publications, 1980.

Wood, Bob and Andrew Scott, "The Gentle Art of Feedback," *Personnel Management (UK)*, 21, 4 (1989), 48–51.

10 | *Case writing: crafting a vehicle of interest and impact*

MARK E. HASKINS

> We ought to be able to learn some things
> secondhand. There is not enough time for
> us to make all the mistakes ourselves.
>
> – Harriet Hall

Late at night, Lt. Col. Hal Moore pores over the military history of the French in Vietnam. Soon, he will lead the US Army's 7th Cavalry into battle there. In the movie *We Were Soldiers*, Moore (played by Mel Gibson) sits at a desk littered with open books. The camera zooms in on one particular book, opened to the battlefield pictures of a massacred French army unit. Moore is making terse, blunt notes as to the mistakes he believes the French made. The unspoken line of the moment is, "I will not make the same mistakes!" Later, we see Lt. Col. Moore training his men in battlefield simulations with as much noise, chaos, and the need for on-the-spot decisions as he can create – all to prepare them for what is to come.

Such is the intent of case method instruction, and in particular, case writing. Indeed, one of the most important aspects of case writing is the development and use of provocative scenarios that enable students to learn, using Harriet Hall's term, "secondhand." Done well, some good cases are useful for several years, and some great cases for many years. Consequently, the questions that arise are: "Should I consider writing a case?" "Where can I find good cases?" "Where can I find promising case leads?" and "How do I craft effective, enduring cases?"

Why write a case[1]

New cases are developed for a number of reasons:

[1] We are indebted to our former colleague William Rotch, who was the consummate case teacher and case writer. This section is from his Technical Note titled "Case Writing," UVA-G-0364, © 1992 by the University of Virginia Darden Graduate Business School Foundation. Used with permission.

154

- to allow students to explore a topic in a real-world setting
- to demonstrate the nuances, challenges, and judgments inherent in managerial decision-making
- to create a venue for student debate, discussion, and decision-making
- to foster the integrative aspects of management.

Different kinds of cases fit different purposes, and a case's learning objective(s) shape the selection of what is put into it, as well as the way it is presented. Some cases are intended to come early in a course or module and, in that position, should avoid unnecessary complexity. Later cases might be less focused and richer in their description of the setting. Early cases are likely to be more methodological and highly structured; later cases may have more emphasis on implementation issues. In short, cases can be as in-depth as the instructor wants to make them, and make it possible to embed a single class, a module of classes, or an entire course in a situational context.

The current case pool

Perhaps the largest single producer of business cases is Harvard Business School (Boston, Massachusetts), from which, through its HBS Publishing arm, more than 7,500 cases, teaching notes, pieces of software, videos, and other related teaching materials are available. Other well-known sources of business cases include Darden Business Publishing at the Darden Graduate School of Business Administration at the University of Virginia (Charlottesville, Virginia); the Richard Ivey School of Business at the University of Western Ontario (London, Canada); and IMD (Lausanne, Switzerland). One centralized distribution source of cases from around the world is the European Case Clearing House (ECCH), co-headquartered at Cranfield University (Bedfordshire, United Kingdom) and Babson College (Wellesley, Massachusetts). As the world's largest single distributor of business cases, ECCH distributes cases from all the aforementioned schools as well as cases produced by other schools such as IESE in Barcelona, Spain, INSEAD in Fontainebleau, France, and the Center of Asian Business Cases located at the School of Business, University of Hong Kong.

Over the last several years, journals dedicated to the development and dissemination of business cases have been created. These include such double-blind reviewed journals as the *Business Case Journal* (http://www.sfcr.org/bcj/edpol.htm), the *Asian Case Research*

Journal (http://www.worldscinet.com/acrj/acrj.shtml), and the *Journal of Finance Case Research* (http://www.jfcr.org/journal.html). Likewise, many academic business disciplines have chosen to publish their own education journals, many of which frequently contain business cases (e.g., *Issues in Accounting Education, Journal of Marketing Education*). For those academic groups not publishing separate educational journals, many include an educational section (often presenting cases) within their existing journals (e.g., *Journal of Applied Finance, Interfaces*). Not to be outdone, various interest groups also publish their own general business education journals that are not exclusively case oriented and yet, many times contain cases and/or articles on case pedagogy. Examples in this regard include journals such as: *Journal of Management Education, Journal of Learning and Education, Journal of Business Education, Training & Development*, and *Journal of European Industrial Training*, to name just a few.

Think in terms of a 2 × 2 × 2 cube

What would a business-oriented discussion be without the always-in-vogue, destined-for-the-business-professors'-hall-of-fame, 2 × 2 matrix? Incomplete, probably. Therefore, in that spirit, we invite you to think in terms of a case-writing focus fitting not into a 2 × 2 matrix, but rather, a 2 × 2 × 2 cube. Visualize one axis of the cube positing decision versus descriptive cases. A second axis of the cube portrays field-based versus non-field-based cases. The final axis of the cube simply denotes paper-based cases versus multimedia-based cases. Each of those dimensions and dichotomies is discussed below.

Decision cases versus descriptive cases

In thinking about the types of teaching cases in the marketplace, or that an instructor might consider writing, instructors have historically thought in terms of two archetypes: the decision-oriented case and the purely descriptive case. The classic notion of a decision case is that it poses a dilemma, an opportunity, a conflict, an emergency, a quandary, a problem, and/or any other situation where the case protagonist must make a decision and propose action steps. A decision case is written from a decision-maker's viewpoint and includes data and information that the decision-maker likely had at the time of the case. The decision-maker is usually confronted with a variety of options, not one of which is an immediate and obvious best choice. The power of that kind of case lies in its ability to invite readers into the case situation and ask them to identify the issue to be addressed, the alternatives they consider germane, a process for reaching a decision, the decision they would make, and the likely outcomes springing from that decision. At each stage of a typical decision case discussion (including problem identification, analysis, and action planning), the case provides a strong base for discussion and learning.

Descriptive cases have been traditionally viewed as akin to a newspaper article in that they report on a situation. In doing so, such a case generally describes a situation, the related facts and deliberations, the decision, and the outcome(s). Descriptive cases are often used to exemplify the good or bad application of a technique, process, or framework. As such, they must faithfully represent the full array of pertinent facts and forces at play so that students can, in some sense, replicate in their minds the focal techniques, processes, or frameworks. Many times, a descriptive case is "turned into" a decision case when an instructor asks students if they would have pursued the same path, applied the same technique(s), or evaluated the possibilities in the same way(s) as described in the case, and why or why not?

In setting out to write a case, it is important that an instructor think about whether: (1) the information contained in the case will be extensive or minimal, totally germane or not; (2) the case problem or situation will be obvious or not; and (3) whether the students' intended task will be clearly delineated or not. If, at the outset of writing a case, it is not clear where the case should fall along these lines, it is always best to err on the side of more information not less, more structure not less, and decision-maker centered. The reason for this assertion is that, as the case writer becomes more familiar with the facts, gains greater clarity as to how and where the case might be used, and struggles with actually crafting the case story, it is always easier to modify the first draft by taking information out of it, making it less structured (i.e., more ambiguous), and casting the case as a purely descriptive case.

A typical structure for decision-oriented cases

Many classic and long-lived decision-oriented cases depict a common structure. They often begin with a statement of the problem(s) facing the decision-maker as described from his or her point of view. That introduction highlights the central focus of the case, introduces the protagonist, and is generally less than a page in length. Framing the problem(s) and the key protagonist at the beginning helps students read the case with a general sense of the issue to be addressed, which helps them interpret and evaluate what they then read. The choice to include this kind of introduction depends in part on how well students are prepared for the case method. Students steeped in case methodology and targeted for improvement of their skills in sifting out problems from masses of data and contextual information may be given cases without an introduction of this kind. But for the most part, like a symphony or musical, an "overture" that previews the key players and the key issues starts the reader down a purposeful path without guaranteeing they will see the problems clearly. The clarity with which a case introduction lays out the problems will depend on the teaching objectives for the case material.

The second section of the case then takes a big jump from the present set of problems to begin, as it were, back at the beginning. Having set the context for the decisions to be made, a good case then jumps back and begins to build a carefully constructed story that leads again, ultimately, to that same time and place by its end. This structure allows the case writer to build tension, to introduce relevant historical data, and to create urgency about the situation. Typically, the historical roots of the problem are described in a company and/or industry background section and then more immediate data/information pertaining to the problem is folded in.

The background section represents the body of the case and includes sufficient data for the reader to analyze each of the options that are described or implied. In addition to financial data, historical facts, and a description of trends and processes, the background portion of the case often includes quotations from firm employees with various perspectives to depict pertinent opinions, values, beliefs, and perceptions. That component adds a significant dose of reality to a case. It is important that the perspectives presented in the case not lead the reader to a single conclusion; that is more likely if the case writer interviews only one or two people. Multiple perspectives should be included to allow the student to wrestle with the pros and cons present in almost every situation when viewed from different perspectives.

Finally, a well-crafted case comes full circle to present a reprise of the original problem statement. By that point, the student is prepared to understand and deal with the case problem(s). Now, the student has the benefit of the company's history, the relevant facts pertaining to the situation, data that suggest one or more possible avenues. Furthermore, if the story is well written, the student has, in the process, become a part of the situation. With that preparation, the student can formulate an approach, conduct an analysis, reach a decision, and consider the problems of implementation.

Excellent decision cases are true to reality; provide some guidance as to the topic or focus of the situation; hint at or include statements of a problem (or set of problems) that requires a decision; have a clear and compelling structure and style that gives relevant, multifaceted, and important information for making decisions; and imply several viable options that pose a dilemma or choice for the case protagonist.

A typical structure for descriptive cases

The general structure for a descriptive case is not all that different from that of a decision-oriented case. There are two key differences, however. The first is the descriptive case is likely to follow a chronological path in its description of a company event. So, even though the case may start by posing a problem confronted by a decision-maker, the descriptive case usually goes on to describe the actions and decisions made by the case protagonist(s) – it is as if time has progressed past the point of having to make a decision to some point in time after the decision has been made. (That is in contrast to the decision-oriented case, in which the reader is virtually placed at the point in time when and where the protagonist must render a decision.)

The second difference is that a descriptive case is likely to be much more complete in the data it presents than a decision-oriented case. The reason is that a robust descriptive case generally provides the data students need to recreate the manager's analysis; execute a focal technique (e.g., a linear programming solution); and/or juxtapose the pro and con arguments germane to the considerations feeding into the manager's deliberations.

Field-based versus non-field-based cases

Field-based cases. For the new case writer, one of the most daunting aspects of case writing can be finding companies that permit their story to be told in the form of a teaching case. It is often easier to gain company access for research cases, since those are more easily disguised and less likely to be discussed in the public classroom. In either instance, here are some suggestions for developing field-based case leads.

One of the most productive sources of case leads is an instructor's former students (either degree-seeking students or participants in short continuing education courses). Both groups are frequently captivated by the case method since they have played the role of a learner using cases and are then often eager to identify and describe a problem they have encountered that they think represents a good case-writing opportunity. Another source of case leads is current or past work colleagues. We have, from time to time, called a former colleague whom we know has contacts within a certain company or industry and asked that colleague to introduce us to a contact there who might be receptive to a case on a certain topic. Finally, although cold calls on companies or individuals whose stories have been chronicled in the business press are not always successful, the few opportunities that do open up through this entree are also viable avenues for developing a case lead.

There are several key elements in the relationship between case writer and case protagonist/sponsor that must be understood and managed for the experience to be positive for both parties. The most important issue is credibility. If the case subjects do not trust the writer's skills and knowledge, they are unlikely to participate. Early conversations for company access and scheduling should also include a discussion of the case writer's experience, training, writing skills, and any other information that can give the case protagonist a sense of confidence in the author.

When approaching a new case-writing opportunity, it is important to make clear and explicit at the outset to the case protagonist that his or her company will be asked to sign a release on the final case, authorizing the writer unrestricted use of the case. Introducing a form like that in Figure 10.1 can provide the focus for such a conversation, and it makes clear that the company will be asked to sign a release on the final case. This conversation will generally bring to the fore any concerns the protagonist has regarding the nature and extent of information they are willing to give, their desire for the case to be disguised, and the overall likelihood of it being released at the end. It is at this point that the case writer must determine: (1) What are the odds of a disguised case (if insisted on by the case protagonist) being a viable instructional vehicle?

Figure 10.1
Typical case release form

The Darden Case Collection
The Darden Graduate School of Business Administration
University of Virginia
P.O. Box 6550
Charlottesville, VA 22906

As copyright Licensor/Owner, I hereby grant permission to the Darden Graduate School of Business Administration to use the materials indicated below for educational purposes, and the reasonable promotion thereof, in business case studies and other learning materials in print and/or electronic format. The case studies and learning materials will be used by the Darden Business School and its professors for MBA, Executive Education, and other educational programs, and may be distributed to other business schools, companies, or academic institutions for the purposes of a pedagogical tool. The materials desired for use in the —— case and materials are the logo(s), video, audio, print materials, or other image(s) used in the case and materials (including future revisions of the case or materials). This Agreement may be executed with a facsimile signature.

_____

Signature (Licensor/Owner, or authorized agent)

_____

Printed Name

_____

Title

_____

Organization

_____

Date

_____

(2) Is the chance of nonrelease too high to warrant the investment of time and effort needed to write the case? (3) Will the protagonist be forthcoming with the information needed to make a rich and useful case? If the answer to any of these sorts of questions is suggestive of a less-than favorable outcome, the writer should seriously consider not doing the case. Even with all of this upfront caution and conversation, once the case is completed the protagonist (and/or his/her company) may judge it to be too sensitive or too negative in tone to be released. Writers are then cast in the role of negotiating the changes that are required to acquire the signed release, and to insure those changes do not destroy the learning potential resident in the case.

Field Routine.[2] The research activities undertaken in the field are likely to vary with the type of case to be written. Here are some field tips that experienced case writers have found helpful:

• Your contact person will not necessarily have explained the project to everyone with whom you talk, so expect to take a few minutes to do that with each person. Often the people you meet have simply said okay to the boss's request, which was, "Will you talk with John Jones from the Darden School?" They do not know Darden, what a case is, or what you want to know.

• Review the schedule. Try to get some unoccupied time so you can review notes, make lists of questions and needed information, and start an outline. That time is more valuable than conversation with the sixth person in a row.

• Do not be afraid to attend a regular company meeting if the subject is related to your case. You can often learn a lot about what is going on, though don't expect anyone to stop and explain things.

• If interviewees ask you whether you would like a copy of something, always say yes. It may be useless, but nuggets can be hidden in masses of apparently irrelevant data. The importance of a company memo or presentation sometimes becomes clear only later. If you think you might want a copy, ask for it, and make a list. Try to get copies made before you leave; if that is not possible, give your list to a specific person so you can follow up.

• If you see public information, pick it up. Sometimes waiting rooms have company information such as brochures or newsletters lying about. Sticky fingers help.

---

[2] Ibid.

- Keep two note pads. Except perhaps for the names of people seen, leave the top pages blank; you may not want your 11 a.m. interviewee to see what you discussed with your 9 a.m. interviewee. Use one note pad for raw interview notes; use the second pad for secondary notes, such as your ideas, thoughts, and questions. The second pad will be used during quiet times, in the evening or while waiting on hold for someone to answer the telephone.
- To help keep track of which information is confidential, try the technique of one of our colleagues. As soon as a source says, "This is strictly confidential," pull out a different colored pen – a signal to your source, and a reminder to yourself, that the information is privileged.
- Throughout this phase of the research, be particularly alert for related points of controversy. When those issues are identified, try to document all sides and to obtain supporting information. For instance, the visit may have been planned as part of research and writing about a debt/equity decision. In the course of the interviews, however, you might discover that a change in dividend policy had also been debated but not adopted, or that the capital-structure decision originally included certain alternatives that were discarded after considerable debate. Inclusion of these unexpected factors may enrich the case.
- Some case writers use tape recorders; others find them more trouble than they are worth. Some use them only for recording thoughts and impressions after an interview. Recording an interview or a meeting certainly helps to capture quotations and the nuances of a discussion, and such features can help the case writer add flavor and excitement to a case. On the other hand, a meeting with the assistant plant accountant to determine how overhead is allocated might not be expected to produce quotable material.
- An approach that often produces unexpectedly revealing responses is to ask near the end of an interview, "Is there anything else you think I ought to know?" You may hear something that you never knew enough to ask about.
- As you leave, you can pave the way for the future by outlining what you expect to happen next. With your main contact, describe what you see as the next steps, with a rough time sequence. This discussion shows your commitment to progress and may reveal that your contact will be away just when you would like a draft reviewed. With

other interviewees, note that you may be back to them on the telephone if further reflection reveals some things you don't understand.

- Be sure to follow up your visit with letters to all interviewees thanking them for their time and help. You may want to take this occasion to reinforce the possibility that you will want more information. Generally, clearing sections of a case that came from specific people is not necessary, but it is sometimes a useful check on accuracy.

- Try not to let your notes get cold, because the nuances fade quickly. Notes have a half-life of about eight hours. This requirement often means writing up notes on the trip home – a difficult task because the writer is usually worn out by then. But reconstructing conversations is even harder a day or two later.

Non-field-based cases. There are at least two non-field-based sources that represent additional viable inputs for the creation of teaching cases. First, if an instructor has a wealth of business experience in a particular arena, that experience can be used to craft provocative teaching cases. Sometimes referred to as "armchair cases," such cases may be structured in the same way as the field-based cases, albeit with vaguely fictionalized dialog, characters, circumstances, issues, and companies. Although they are sometimes viewed as less realistic, less authentic, and thus less worthy of an instructor's attention, we have written such cases, used them, and found them to be valuable classroom learning vehicles.

A second non-field-based source for cases is articles in business magazines and newspapers. The advantages of using the business press for crafting a case study are that a company story is often chronicled over time so the case writer is able to craft a longitudinal case without having to be involved with the company over many months or even years. Another advantage is that there is no need for a company signed release so that negatively oriented case studies are possible – companies typically will not sign a release for a field-based case that casts them or their managers in any sort of negative light. One obvious additional advantage is the fact that the case writer need not have to invest the time and money in traveling to a company's site. The disadvantage of these sorts of cases though is that the story only gets told through the filter of the business press author. One way to moderate that disadvantage is for the case writer to call the company and ask for a phone interview with the appropriate manager(s) to verify the business press reporting or to get an additional, maybe even an alternate, viewpoint. Another disadvantage is that the case generally ends up full of citations, which can make the writing and the reading of the case cumbersome and cause it to sound more like an academic tome than like a report drawn from first-hand sources.

Once a case is written, finalized, and ready for classroom use, it is a good idea to create a catalog of case information for easy and ready access. The case registration form that the Darden School uses for all its cases includes title, author, a short abstract, whether the case's use is as a restricted, prerequisite case, or a related case, the subject area, keywords, the country setting, the size of the organization, and any pertinent dates. That sort of synoptic information makes it easy for a potential adopter of the case to get a quick sense of the case's relevance to his or her needs. Such information aids in the case adoption decision and in the case files management process.

Paper versus other-media cases

Paper cases. By far, and not surprisingly, the most dominant form of cases available in the market place are 100 per cent paper versions (as a handy example of one, see the Appendix to this chapter). For those of us who are accustomed to this medium for communicating our scholarly insights, thinking, and depictions of observed phenomena, it is a very comfortable medium. Several points, however, are worth noting if this is the medium of choice. First, *longer cases are not necessarily better cases.* We have found that students, especially Executive Education, short-program students and those students whose first language is not the language in which the case is written, do not appreciate having to spend more than half their allotted preparation time for the case to merely reading it. In accounting, we find cases that require extensive numerical analysis work best if they are five to 10 pages long (including exhibits). In organizational behavior, a comfortable page length is in the 6–18 page range. To present students with a 30-page case that will be used for just one class is, in our opinion, too much.

A second point especially true for paper cases *is that more editing is better than less editing.* It is perhaps obvious, but things such as typos, data columns that do not add up, incorrect grammar, and narrative inconsistencies tend to easily and quickly annoy students. The more

that they encounter such correctable aspects of a case, the less seriously they tend to take the case and its preparation. The case writer
should proof, edit, double-check, and repeat those tasks until his or
her attention begins to wane due to having read it, thought about it,
and scrutinized it so much that it becomes difficult to concentrate when
re-reading it. At that point, it is a good idea to have a second person,
preferably a professional editor, work their magic on it. Only after a
second pair of eyes has reviewed it can a case writer be most confident
that the case, at least as a written document, is ready for prime time.

A third point to note is to consider the time-period specificity of the
case setting. *The shelf life of a written case can be extended through the
avoidance of dates and time-specific environmental factors.* For example, if the manager in the case actually faced the problem discussed
in the case in June 2006 and that date has no substantive bearing on
the learning objectives of the case or the nature of the intended discussion, omit the date. On the other hand, if the focal decision was
shortly after the September 11, 2001, demise of the Twin Towers in
New York City, chances are that that event is an important contextual
factor that has to be included in the case. Likewise, if one of a focal
company's main competitors is a company that changed its name after
the case time frame (e.g., Philip Morris switching to Altria), it is better
to simply refer to the competitor in generic terms (e.g., a large, multinational competitor). Sometimes it is tempting to include in the case
a reference to exogenous economic or world events that do not have
any real bearing on the learning agenda for the case (e.g., John Smith,
the newly appointed head of the sales group had just returned from
the opening ceremonies dedicating the new World War II Memorial
in Washington, DC). Such facts add to the human interest of the case
narrative but date the case quickly. If, in the example just given, it is
important for the reader to have a hint of John Smith's sense of history or patriotism, it is fine to cast that fact in a more timeless fashion
(e.g., John Smith, the newly appointed head of the sales group, had just
returned from a weekend trip to view the World War II Memorial in
Washington, DC).

And finally, more company history is not always better. We can
think of several cases where it seems that the case writer devoted
way too many pages to conveying 30 years of company history when
the salient points of that history could have been codified in one or
two pages. Resist the temptation to include in the case all you have

learned about the company – be selective and purposeful in what is included.

Other-media cases. Teaching cases need not be in the form of paper pages to be read by the students. For a number of years, video, CD-ROM and DVD, and Power Point™ media have been around as supplements to the traditional paper case. Often, you will find a video interview of a key company manager accompanying an organizational behavior paper case or a CD with various data files on it or analytical models already set up on it (e.g. an EXCEL™ spreadsheet) that facilitates students' numerical analyses of a finance case. Of late, however, video- and CD-based cases have become more than just traditional case supplements, they have become primary case vehicles in their own right. Of course, the same set of precursors also applies here. What special issues arise then in regards to the creation of video- and CD-ROM based cases?

Video cases can capture the "ambience [of a place and the people] – the language people use, whether they're laid back or intense, how competitive the environment is, and how people talk to [and about] one another" (Stringer, 1999, p. 54). That is very true, and crafting a video- or CD-based case that is successful in this regard is not easily done. Indeed, our colleague Jeanne Liedtka (2001) wrote an article on the "promise and the peril" of going down the video case path. We recommend that article to anyone contemplating creating a video case. In short, she discusses several things that we all wish we had known before embarking on developing a series of video cases together. The video cases we crafted with her were the most basic type of video case – that is, interviews of key executives at our focal firms. In total, we had more than 40 hours of tape to distill down to three 30-minute videos. What did we learn from this experience?

1. It is imperative to formulate an interview guide in advance and to give the questions to the interviewees ahead of time so that they have some time to formulate substantive responses. Rambling and roaming conversations are enjoyable and tempting to pursue but once the camera starts rolling and the subsequent task of editing the tape looms on the horizon, succinct, on-point discussions are all you want on the tape.

2. An efficient and constructive way to edit an extensive amount of videotape is to have it time-coded and transcribed. The transcript should be linked to the videotape via the time code. The editing

process can then work from the transcripts, to the tape, in an iterative fashion.

3. It is easy to underestimate the time and expense of creating a video case. We have found that it took us about 10 hours of tape to formulate 30 minutes of pithy, provocative, seamlessly appearing finished tape. In addition, professional-grade videotape cases will cost in the thousands of dollars (perhaps between $5,000 to $20,000), not hundreds.

4. Finished videotape cases must have eye and ear appeal or students will lose focus and interest very quickly. One "talking head" on tape for longer than a minute or two runs the risk of dulling the listener's attention. Speakers on the tape who have one or more of the following speaking styles make it very difficult for listeners to stay engaged – monotonic sounding, speak very slowly, ramble, use lots of "uhs" or colloquial expressions, and/or articulate their logic in a very circuitous route. One visual scene during the course of a video also tends to numb the listener's attention. Even if all the taping is conducted in one office, change the camera angles, change the pictures on the wall, change the stuff on the top of the desk, and change the lighting from speaker to speaker.

5. If at all possible, use professionals for the videotaping.

6. As a listening guide for the video case, consider creating a workbook that has the speakers' pictures in the order of their appearance on the tape with space beside each picture for students to make notations concerning what they heard that person say at that juncture in the tape. Listening to a 20-to-30-minute tape does not lend itself to note-taking at the end; it is best to facilitate student note-taking with such a workbook while they listen to the tape. The workbook can also pose issues, questions, and concerns to be listening for as the tape plays.

In a related vein to video cases, audio-only cases can be a powerful teaching medium. On one occasion, we sought to create a classroom discussion that galvanized executives, all from one company, to deal with some tough personnel issues that many in the decentralized parts of the organization felt were being ignored and/or mishandled. A paper narrative of the field managers' concerns seemed like it would trivialize and sterilize the intensity of their feeling. Video cases seemed like an option, but the people we approached to be on tape to voice their issues were rightfully concerned with maintaining anonymity. We decided to do audio-only tape recordings. These worked really well, and many of the production foci noted above in regard to video cases also applied in the audio-only setting. Production costs were substantially lower than for a video case because we were able to line up interviewees for taped phone conversations – thus there was no travel required and no professional videographers needed. We did find it again useful to have the audiotapes transcribed for our editing purposes, and we did create a listening workbook (without pictures of the speakers) that identified the general position, functional area, and years with the firm of all speakers, in sequence with when they were heard on the final tape. In the end, the taped voices, played in a quiet classroom with no video stimuli, made for a very powerful medium.

CD-ROM-based cases are fast becoming an option for use and for creation. Such cases have the cachet of the times and also provide pedagogical flexibility due to the nonsequential access to various video clips, interviews, animation, etc. that they allow. Moreover, they are portable and easily viewed by students anywhere they can carry a laptop. It is important to once again state the obvious, though: For a CD-ROM-based case to be effective, it needs to appear professionally produced. Contemporary audiences are accustomed to the slick visual images of, and the nuances in, any number of CD-ROM-based games and tutorials, not to mention the professional-caliber Web sites most students navigate daily. For a CD-ROM-based case study to not measure up to that same level will immediately cast it as a second-class, unprofessional, or outmoded item. Assuming such quality in the CD-ROM-based case production can be attained, what are some additional issues to consider prior to and during the creation of a CD-ROM-based case?

1. Be sure that the medium (a CD-ROM) fits the message. As one of our colleagues frequently reminds us, CD-ROMs are great vehicles for short video clips, television ads, movie clips, color pictures, and animation (e.g., depicting the flow of financial data through an accounting system to create a set of financial statements) – they are not very well suited for text or tables, unless they are adapted for a full multimedia treatment.
2. Even with CD-ROM-based cases, some printed materials can be very helpful including:

    a. a directory to the content of the CD

    b. an executive summary of some of that content

    c. a stipulation of some up-front questions that give students some idea of what they are looking for as they go through the CD

    d. instructions regarding the systems requirements to play the CD.

3. Because CD-based case material comes in "chunks" that can be randomly accessed, if there are parts that an instructor expects all students to view, it is important to note those as such.

The final medium sometimes effectively used for case material is simply a basic Power Point™ series of slides. Such a medium is especially useful for the (B), (C), etc. series of cases epitomizing the "prediction-type" cases described earlier. In just three or four well-crafted slides, an instructor can convey the facts pertinent to an ongoing situation first spelled out in an earlier installment of the case series. Such an approach economizes on the time taken in the classroom for students to read the longitudinally rolled-forward series of events and outcomes. This efficient means of presenting updated information also affords the instructor the opportunity to explore several alternative endings to a base case, each provoking their own set of classroom conversations.

Characteristics of effective cases[3]

The best way to judge any case is from the vantage points of: (a) teaching a number of cases like the particular type of case being judged; and (b) having a clear sense regarding the intended role a particular case will play in a course. Against these two backdrops, both of which are enhanced and sharpened by continued case experience, one can read a case and usually assess the likelihood of it successfully meeting its desired learning objectives. From this dual backdrop, effective cases generally share several common attributes. Those attributes are:

1. *Intrinsic interest.* Does the case engage the student? Does it involve a significant problem? Is there a managerial role in the case, or can a management perspective be developed?

2. *Buried rewards.* Does the student's learning reach new levels as he or she works with the case, discusses it in class, or thinks about it afterward? Success in this respect has been variously labeled:

[3] Ibid.

the "Easter egg effect," "the rabbit discovery," or the "aha phenomenon."

3. *A wider context.* Does the case allow the analysis to capitalize on related issues in other functional areas or relevant chapters in a textbook?

4. *A deep analytical challenge.* Does the case require clear thinking, especially in defining the problem (perhaps differently or more deeply than the case's characters do)? This aspect is sometimes called "peeling the onion."

5. *Creative alternatives.* Does the case challenge students to develop alternatives, perhaps some not explicitly stated in the case?

6. *Clear presentation and organizational style.* Is the case tightly and efficiently presented, including information that is appropriate to the teaching objective? Is it free of unintended "red herrings" or unnecessary material? Is important information included rather than merely shown in the teaching note where students won't see it?

7. *Exhibits.* Are the exhibits carefully selected and constructed? Are they appropriate for the teaching objective?

8. *Multiple teaching objectives.* Although not always possible or appropriate, some of the best cases support multiple purposes and uses with different levels of students.

Revising cases

In our experience, it is very difficult to get a case just right without having taught it. After teaching it once or twice, you will likely recognize gaps in the data as well as unclear accounts of certain contextual circumstances. Cases, no matter the medium or the style, should be subject to refinement after a few test drives. We encourage case writers to keep careful notes following the first and second teachings of their new cases. Those notes should point to ways to improve them. Revisions may involve shortening/lengthening the case, changing its style, adding/deleting data, and/or focusing/obfuscating the main issue. One caution is in order: If it is a field-based case with a signed company release, substantive revisions may warrant going back to the company for a new release. Generally, if the revision does not alter the essence of the company story contained in the case or introduce previously unreleased company data, no new release is needed.

Teaching Notes

We believe that no case is complete unless accompanied by a teaching note that presents the author's view and experience regarding how the case can best be used. A well-written teaching note can save a new or experienced instructor a great deal of time in preparation and also suggest ways to fully mine the riches buried in the case. The next chapter provides information for crafting a teaching note.

Conclusion

There is nothing quite so pleasing to an instructor as identifying an instructional materials need in your course, an applicable case lead, writing the case, using it in class, having it be effective, and then jotting down a few notes for its use next time. We would even assert that there is a mutually beneficial synergy between case method teaching and case writing – each enhances the other. We encourage you to try writing a case, circulating it to a few colleagues you know who use cases, and committing yourself to be not just a user of others' cases, but a contributor to the instructional inventory of cases that others can use.

Further reading

David, F. R., "Strategic Management Case Writing: Suggestions after 20 Years of Experience," *SAM Advanced Management Journal* (Summer 2003), 36–42.

Jennings, D., "Researching and Writing Strategic Management Cases: A Systems View," *Management Decision*, 37, 2 (1997), 100–05.

Liedtka, J., "The Promise and Peril of Video Cases: Reflections on their Creation and Use," *Journal of Management Education* (August 2001), 409–24.

Naumes, W., and M. J. Naumes, *The Art & Craft of Case Writing* (Thousand Oaks, CA: Sage Publications, 1999).

Nelson, E., "Producing and Using Case Material for Research and Teaching: A Workshop for Partners in Know-how Transfer Projects," *Journal of European Industrial Training*, 20, 8 (1996), 22–30.

Stringer, D., "Case Writing 101," *Training & Development* (September 1999), 53–57.

APPENDIX

An Effective Decision-Oriented, Non-Field-Based Case

CONSUMER SERVICE COMPANY (A)

Consumer Service Company was established to take advantage of the young, professional, and affluent baby-boomer population. It was apparent to John Hurdle, the founder of the company, that a major part of the economy comprised upscale households, where both adults were employed as professionals or where both had other significant interests that occupied their time. These two consumer segments seemed to offer great opportunity for a company that provided a variety of quality services, saving consumers time and enhancing the quality of their lives.

The company began by offering a housecleaning service. Initially, its regional offices were headquartered in the larger East Coast suburbs, and each had well-trained janitorial employees, who were available to perform housecleaning on a weekly, biweekly, or monthly contract basis. Recent additions to the service portfolio included exterior home maintenance, automobile maintenance, and landscape maintenance. The concept was powerful, and the business grew exponentially.

The basic concept was demonstrably sound, and was the root of the company's success. Part of the company's success could also be traced to its organizational structure (Figure 1). All four services were performed from regional offices located in a number of cities across the United States. Each regional office had a manager for each of the four service lines, and it was each manager's responsibility to hire and train the staff, supervise the day-to-day work, and conduct the local marketing. The office administrators managed the offices, but were not involved in the functional operations. Each of the four service lines was managed as a division, by a national director. The national directors were responsible for the supervision of their respective field-service

Figure 1
CONSUMER SERVICE COMPANY (A)

Organizational Chart

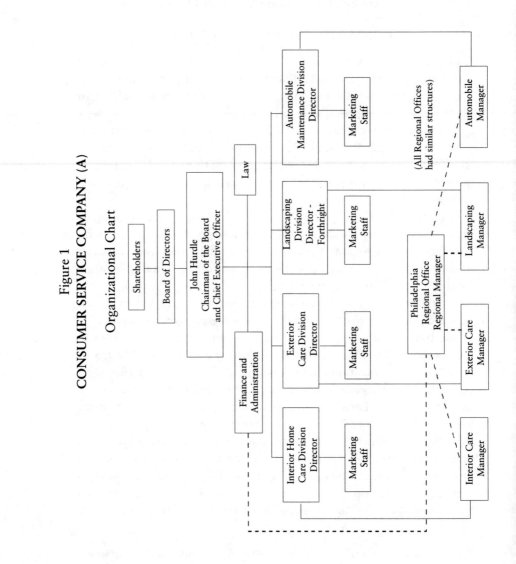

managers and for the national marketing of their service line. Hurdle had rightly understood that the four services the company offered involved different consumer decisions, and his decision to orient the company's marketing and service directly toward the interests of the buyer had fueled a large part of the company's growth.

Working out of the company's headquarters, in Morristown, New Jersey, the four product-service directors had small marketing and administrative staffs. The corporate office provided accounting, computing, legal, and administrative assistance to the divisions and the regions. Each of the four service-line directors (and an administrative vice president) reported to Hurdle, the chief executive officer. He was the very model of an entrepreneur. In addition to being the founder of the company and the developer of the consumer-services idea, Hurdle had put all his personal capital at risk in the venture. Consumer Service's stock was owned by several institutions and by about 300 individuals. Hurdle's 30 percent share of the company's stock made him a wealthy man. Of late, he had begun thinking about opening a European operation modeled on the successful US operations. After all, he could finance the start-up himself, the challenge was intriguing, and his two sons could head it up.

Every fall, the division directors were responsible for developing a profit plan for their division, committing their group to a deliverable level of sales and profits before taxes. Sales were billed to customers based on time spent on the job by the Consumer Service employee, multiplied by a standard hourly rate. Because employees were paid only for time they actually worked on jobs and because fixed costs were relatively small, profit levels for the company were fundamentally a factor of sales levels. Indeed, division directors primarily focused their efforts on hours sold and average rates charged.

To help develop the sales plan, division directors asked their field-service managers to provide an estimate of the sales level they expected during the next year. In addition, each division's marketing staff was asked for projections as to what the division's sales would be. In previous years, the division directors had met with Hurdle during the first week in October in a seaside resort to establish the profit plan for each division and for the company as a whole. Together, they reviewed prior years' results for each division, and, in a collegial discussion, established the coming year's sales and profit plans. Hurdle always made an inspirational speech at the start of the proceedings, and he challenged any division director who seemed to be proposing a lazy plan. But he also believed the directors were to be treated as managers of their own businesses, and so he did not pry too deeply into the details of the division plans.

The profit plans were used to keep things on track during the year – if a division fell behind plan, the director would investigate, and, if necessary, change marketing programs, increase field training, or take some other action deemed necessary. The division plans were also used to forecast demand for accounting and computer services from headquarters. In fact, once the division plans were established, the headquarters budget was crafted, and each division's profit plan was allocated a share of the corporate costs. This allocation was not changed during the year, regardless of the division's actual sales results.

The division plans were important, not only to the company, but also to the division directors. The division directors' annual compensation was based on the following formula:

Base pay ($25,000)	+ 2.5% of planned sales for the year	+ 0.5% of sales over plan	– 7.5% of sales under plan

The time for establishing the profit plan for the coming year was fast approaching, and Hurdle proposed a modification of the previous years' procedure. He suggested that the company would save time and money if the division directors met with him individually in his office to finalize plans for their division. He asked Ms. Forthright to meet with him at 2 o'clock the next Thursday, October 17. She was relieved because that appointment would give her a week to study carefully the data from her field managers and her division's marketing staff. As the week passed, however, she became anxious. She learned from the grapevine that she would be the last of the four directors to meet with Hurdle. The other three had found the meetings to be quite unpleasant, and were now committed to a plan they thought would be difficult to execute.

(Additional facts available only to Forthright and to Hurdle will be provided by your instructor. See chapter 11, appendix.)

11 Case teaching notes: getting from here to there

MARK E. HASKINS

> Even with the best of maps and instruments,
> we can never fully chart our journeys.
>
> – Gail Pool, Professor of Anthropology,
> University of New Brunswick

As discussed in an earlier chapter, well-crafted teaching cases are rich in what is and is not stated; bringing to life the case characters; detailing the situational context and how it arose; and in giving students a sense of where the issue/situation is headed. Thus, cases are like a richly textured aerial photograph of a landscape with an arrow on it pointing to a spot that says, "You – the student assuming the role of the businessperson facing a decision and having a particular learning agenda – are here." Well-crafted teaching notes, on the other hand, are a map of that landscape. That map poses for the case discussion leader, ideas, suggestions, and routes for getting students from here to there on two levels. One level pertains to the business situation in the case that warrants a plan of action to address a business problem or seize a business opportunity. A second level pertains to the means for crafting a high-potential learning experience for the students who are discussing the case.

In regard to a case's business situation, the teaching note map metaphor highlights the reality that there are often: multiple routes that can be taken to any one destination (i.e., frequently there is more than one good answer to a business problem, opportunity, and action plan); mountains, rivers, borders, and deserts that often get in the way of a simple, direct route (i.e., businesses often face a number of varied obstacles in implementing an action plan); a number of communities identifiable along the map's many roads and highways (i.e., business decisions always involve one or more constituencies such as customers, partners, colleagues, and competitors); and there are intermediate stops to be made when the distances to be traveled are great (i.e., long-term business objectives and goals often require the identification of milestones and metrics for assessing progress). In regards to the issue of facilitating a classroom discussion of a case intended to create student learning, the map metaphor highlights the need for a teaching note to: pose ideas for how to achieve a set of learning objectives; identify potential student pitfalls and stumbling blocks; provide suggestions for involving other people and/or materials in the case discussion; and to detail suitable analyses for evaluating intended outcomes from students' likely suggestions for action.

Purposes of a teaching note[1]

Case teachers are the intended audience for a teaching note. Though the format, style, and content may vary from one teaching note to another, the main test of any teaching note's quality is how helpful it is to the instructors who use, or are thinking of using, the case. A teaching note can help case teachers in at least five ways:
- the *selection of cases* to use in a course (teaching notes should convey an idea of the case's scope and intended teaching objective[s]);
- the *use of a case* (teaching notes should contain an analysis of the case, some proposed teaching questions, and an overview of at least one possible classroom discussion plan);
- the *anticipation of student questions and difficulties*;
- the *connection(s) of the case with other cases* in a course or with a series of cases within a course; and
- the *coordination of a group of instructors' joint use of a case.*

Let's be clear: Case teaching notes are not the same as what is commonly found in a textbook's solutions manual. A solutions manual generally provides only the answer to a problem and implies that there is a single, correct answer. Cases are usually too complex to have single right answers, although there may be good analysis and bad analysis. Often the teaching objective of a case has more to do with an analytical and decision-making process than with any specific answer. Thus, preparation of teaching notes is a far more complex process than that of providing single solutions to problems. Moreover, teaching notes

---

[1] This section draws on a document prepared by our colleague William Rotch titled "Teaching Notes for Cases" (UVA-PHA-0028, © 1985 by the Darden Graduate Business School Foundation). Used with permission.

are concerned with how a case might be used in a classroom or other educational setting. A solutions manual usually is not. With cases, an instructor's teaching *strategy* is an important element and a teaching note should posit one or more effective strategies that take into consideration the student audience (i.e., their level of experience and competence; the size of the group), the time available for the case discussion, and the positioning of the case in a course. Thus, a case teaching note has a wide range of important matters it must discuss in order to be helpful, of which the specific "solution," or results of analysis, is only one. Indeed, "effective preparation for [case] discussion classes takes more time, because instructors must consider not only *what* they will teach, but also *who* and *how* [thus necessitating a] simultaneous attention to process (the flow of activities that make up a discussion) and content (the material discussed)..." (Barnes et al., 1994, p. 23). If that is the classroom challenge faced by case instructors, quality case teaching notes must rise to that very same challenge.

Content of a teaching note

The appendix to this chapter contains one teaching note that portrays the features discussed here. Please note that it is our belief that any teaching note can always be improved and thus, we put forth this one teaching note as an example and invite you, the conscientious instructor, to consider how it might be improved.

The content of a robust, useful case teaching note generally includes the following sections:[2]

1. A brief statement as to the case's objective(s), where it might fit in a course or training sequence, and how it connects to other potentially useful and related cases

For instructors considering the adoption of a case for their course, this section of a teaching note provides a quick and easy means for ascertaining the role a particular case can play. For instructors who have used the case before, this section of its teaching note provides a succinct reminder of the learning objectives for that case's classroom

---

[2] The numbered headers in this section, with the exception of number nine, are based on Rotch, UVA-PHA-0028.

discussion and it quickly helps to get an instructor's thinking into sync with the overall agenda for the case. If a case has multiple objectives and multiple themes of varied importance to the case situation, they should be clearly set forth in this section in such a way as to distinguish between main and secondary objectives/themes. The listing of thematic key words, as found in an online library search engine, makes it easy for an instructor to garner a quick overview of a case, and such words impose a discipline on the teaching note writer to be precise in identifying objectives and themes.

2. A short synopsis of the case facts and situation

If the learning objectives and themes of a case under consideration are appealing, an instructor is then generally interested in knowing the case setting and a few highlighted case facts. For example, is the business featured in the case a manufacturer or a merchandising company? Is it a $2 billion company or a $1 million company? What position does the case protagonist hold? What is the immediate issue to be addressed by the protagonist? Geographically, where is the company located? Such information can be helpful to potentially adopting instructors as they strive to diversify the case settings represented in their courses. For instructors who have used the case before, such information is one more means by which they can get reimmersed in the case and its use.

3. A set of suggested study questions/instructions to assign with the case

Some case method teachers prefer to not assign specific study questions to accompany a case. One oft-cited reason for this approach is the belief that part of the learning to be gleaned from a case is for students to identify the issue(s) to be addressed. Indeed, such a viewpoint has a great deal of merit. Other instructors, however, may choose to be a bit more directive and assign several study questions to go along with the case. Including suggested study questions in a case's teaching note addresses the more directive desire of this latter group while not closing off the use of the case to the former group who can simply choose to not use any of the study questions.

Each of the suggested study questions presented in a teaching note should be subsequently discussed and addressed in the teaching note.

In addition, any study questions assigned to students should constitute part of the classroom case discussion – we have found that students get frustrated from working on specific, assigned questions only to find that they are never discussed during class.

There are two general types of suggested study questions to include in a teaching note. One type is the nonspecific. Examples include, "What should the CEO do?" or "How would you address the problem faced by the division manager in the case?" or "Should the company out-source their printing department?" These sorts of questions simply signal to students that you do not want to provide any more guidance on the case than that, and it clues students into what might be the open-ing discussion in the class devoted to the case. The more specific type of assignment instructions serves to direct students to perform some specific, focused preparation. Examples in that regard include, "What is your assessment of the situation faced by the division manager?" or "Calculate the net present value of the proposed investment," or "Identify two or three additional options the CEO should consider in addition to those noted in the case," or "Be prepared to detail for your assistant, in a role play during class, the steps you want taken to correct the customer's complaint presented in the case."

If it is best that students prepare the case by working in pairs or in a team, the case assignment should instruct them to do so. If students' case preparation can benefit from an additional reading (e.g., a recent newspaper article to which you can direct them online or in the library), the assignment should make that clear. If student learning is enhanced by turning in a case write-up or their case analysis at the end of class, the student assignment should note that requirement. Thus, any task that fits within the confines of the time frame students can reasonably be expected to devote to a particular case's preparation and that enhances their learning from the case should be offered in the case assignment section of a teaching note.

4. An analysis of, or commentary on, the study questions

If a case is accompanied by a specific set of assignment questions, tasks, or deliverables, a comprehensive teaching note should have a section that poses ideas and insights to prime an instructor's thinking along the same lines as was asked of the students. For example, if specific questions were assigned to students, suggested answers or potential debating points should be presented to instructors in the teaching note. If specific tasks were assigned to students, an appropriate amount of, and placement of, class time should be devoted touching on those tasks. Thus, if students were asked to read a recent newspaper article, they should be asked about it and the teaching note should suggest ways for an instructor to connect the article to the case (e.g., as an introduction to the case or as a capstone to the discussion or as a mid-class contemporary example of an issue just surfacing in the discussion). If students were asked to calculate an NPV, the teaching note should construct that calculation. If students were asked to prepare a deliverable on the case to be handed in, instructors should be sure to collect it, and the teaching note should provide suggestions on how to leverage those deliverables into the discussion (e.g., one student can be asked to present the content of his or her deliverable or deliverables can be traded among the students for comment or evaluation). It is good to remember that if a question or task was worth asking students to spend time on, the teaching note should devote some attention to the content and pedagogical aspects of that request.

The analysis of a case often extends beyond what was assigned to students to also include analyses pertinent to the issues likely (or needing) to arise during the class discussion as a result of an instructor's teaching plan. For each of the facilitative questions or comments identified in the teaching plan (see the next section), the teaching note should also present insights into, or suggestions regarding, the accompanying analyses (numerical or otherwise) that students should have either done prior to class based on their own wrestling with the case or are expected to do in real time in class as the discussion progresses.

A special comment on numerical analysis is warranted at this juncture (see also Maister, 1985). We have all been guilty of, and been witnesses to, the phenomenon frequently referred to as "getting lost in the numbers." Besides triple-checking the accuracy of any numerical analysis contained in a teaching note, authors should provide only essential numerical analyses, with clear linkages to where the data came from in the case and how the numbers were calculated. Elegant, but marginally beneficial numerical analyses are not usually very helpful and thus should not be a part of a teaching note. Moreover, a clearly stated purpose for a particular numerical analysis is quite helpful as it positions the analysis in the context of a process for decision-making or for gaining greater clarity on an issue. If computer-based printouts are deemed appropriate for revealing a particular analysis, it is important to have an accompanying legend that keys readers into the construction of some of the critical numbers appearing on the spreadsheet printout. In fact, it is our preference that if you find it expedient to include a spreadsheet printout in a teaching note as part of the numerical analysis, then it is better to simply include a computer CD or disc with the spreadsheet model and results on it as part of the teaching note package. Another alternative is to post the spreadsheet model and results on a Web page and simply reference that Web page in this teaching note section, making sure to discuss some of the numerical results as they apply to the case issues under discussion.

5. A detailed, robust teaching plan for facilitating the class discussion of the case that takes into account the learning objectives for the case, the time allotted for the case, anticipates where students are likely to have difficulty, and includes questions an instructor can use during the class to facilitate the discussion

It is in this section, along with the analysis section, that high-quality teaching notes are distinguished from lesser quality ones. Two thoughts to keep in mind as you craft this section of a teaching note: First, in many ways the ease with which this section comes together for the case writer can be used to gauge how well the case has been crafted. In other words, if the articulation of a teaching strategy seems disjointed or forced, chances are the case is missing some important information that would provide the foundation for a smoother classroom flow for the discussion. Second, many instructors believe that this section of a teaching note cannot be written until after they have taught the case once or twice. They would argue that an untried teaching strategy is not as valuable as one that has been tried and found to work. It is our belief that all teaching notes should, at a minimum, contain a preliminary teaching strategy that is then refined and revised after the case has been taught. Our discussion here will not differentiate between preliminary and final drafts of this section of a teaching note as the content and considerations are the same in both.

With an eye to the overall approach to writing this section of a teaching note, it is best to begin by envisioning the classroom discussion. In order to do this, instructors should be very familiar with the case, the assigned questions (if any), the nature of the classroom discussions leading up to this class, and the students' familiarity with the topic, contexts, and skills presented in and demanded by the case. With those perspectives in mind, envisioning the class discussion should occur at two levels – the classroom conversation likely to occur and the classroom conversation desired. Seldom will these two be exactly the same, left to their own accord, without some careful instructor preparation and discussion facilitation. Indeed, the conversation likely to occur prior to any instructor considerations of guidance and goals is rooted in where students are (in terms of knowledge, skills, and attitudes) and their natural tendencies, while the latter conversation is rooted in the instructor's pre-class learning agenda morphs into a real-time learning agenda as the classroom conversation is underway. From an instructor's point of view, the goal is to facilitate a conversation that is student driven, begins where students are, and seamlessly progresses toward maximum learning and appropriate positioning for the next class.

One of the most important decisions in crafting a teaching strategy is deciding how to open each class (see McKeachie, 2002, esp. Chapter 4). Some effective possibilities to pose in a teaching note:

(a) Ask a student to recap the case facts and the issue to be addressed (this is an approach that can be used to make sure everyone is in agreement on these dimensions and/or provides an opportunity for a student who has been silent in class to date to have an easy entry into the conversation).

(b) Ask a student for an overview (i.e., a road map) of how he or she went about making the decision called for by the case situation (this approach provides everyone an opportunity to see where the discussion is heading before the class embarks down a path, thus affording others the opportunity to revise or embellish the designated path the class will follow; this is often a useful opening question when a case is complex or prone to tangential analysis and unproductive avenues of inquiry).

(c) Ask a student for his or her recommendation and defense of that recommendation (this approach starts with an outcome and then the rest of the conversation backfills the rationale, the analyses, and the debates; this is often a useful opening when part of the learning agenda is for students to develop decisiveness, an ability to communicate and enlist others in their decision, and to listen for possibilities from others while exercising courage in their convictions).

(d) If the case ends with a decision contemplated by the case protagonist, a modified version of (c) is to ask a student if he or she agrees with what the case protagonist is about to do and why or why not.

(e) Ask a student to address one or more of the assigned study questions (this approach is perhaps most appropriate when the case is a descriptive rather than a decision-oriented case and the learning agenda is comprised of making sure students understand the processes, analyses, or principles embedded or displayed in the case).

Once the class has begun with an appropriate opening, the teaching note should identify and discuss some of the avenues springing from that start. The teaching note should suggest follow-on questions that instructors should have at their ready to fuel the conversation. Sometimes those follow-on questions may be nothing more than encouraging other students to react to, or comment on, the opening student's comments/analysis. To some extent, such a follow-on question is one that should always be asked, probably more than once or twice, during a class discussion.

In thinking about follow-on questions, it is useful to think about the case discussion in the context of a shepherd and a flock of grazing sheep. This metaphor was offered to us a number of years ago by a former colleague, John Rosenblum. Now, it is important that you suspend all preconceived ideas you may have regarding the IQ of sheep and the relative challenges and appeal of sheep-herding as a vocation. In the context of a case discussion and a case teaching strategy, think of the discussion as comprising several "pastures" where you would like the students to graze. As a facilitator of that discussion, the task is to know what questions to ask that prompt students to explore the richest corners of that pasture and that, at the appropriate time, open the gate from one pasture to another. As noted by Brookfield and Preskill (1999, pp. 87–91), there are several types of queries:

(a) "Questions that ask for more evidence" (e.g., on what do you base your conclusion? what evidence in the case would suggest that your plan might not work?).

(b) "Questions that ask for clarification" (e.g., can you explain that accounting concept to someone who is not familiar with accounting terminology? how could that point be illustrated using a local example?).

(c) "Open questions...to provoke the students' thinking and problem-solving abilities" (e.g., what is the central problem you

see in the case? Why do you think the manager in the case dis-
trusted his employees? In general, does such a view have merit and
why?).

(d) "Linking or extension questions . . . [to] actively engage students in
building on one another's responses to questions. . . [and to] prompt
student-to-student conversation" (e.g., How does your position differ from John's? How does your idea connect to our conversation
yesterday? If this were a strategy class discussing this case instead
of a finance class, in what ways would the discussion be different?).

(e) "Hypothetical questions [that] ask students to consider how changing the circumstances of a case might alter the outcome" (e.g., if
the manager had been a male instead of a female, how might the
discussion portrayed in the case have been different? If you were
the manager, what is your recommendation?).

(f) "Cause-and-effect questions . . . [which] are fundamental to developing critical thought" (e.g., how might changing the company's
bonus plan affect the behaviors of the sales force? if your recommendation is implemented, what sorts of problems might you
expect).

(g) "Summary and synthesis questions . . . [which] call on students to
identify important ideas and think about them in ways that will aid
their recall" (e.g., Recap the four reasons Scott gave for opening
the new store. . . which one or two were the most persuasive and
why? As we think about finishing the case analysis tomorrow, what
more information do we need and for what purpose?).

We would add another category of question to this list, questions
that instructors may find provocative to use in class, and that is simply
to ask students what questions they have and, if they (the students)
were the manager in the case under study, what questions should that
manager ask. All of these and other properly placed instructor questions and comments during a class discussion can help students plumb
the depths of a case situation and the thinking of their classmates. The
importance of asking the right question, at the right time, of the right
student cannot be overestimated nor can such a skill be formulaically
prescribed for one instructor by another. It is a skill, an art that instructors develop a sense for and get better at when it is viewed as a skill
worthy of conscientious consideration and careful reflection. Indeed, as
the famous French playwright Eugene Ionesco is credited with saying,
"It is not the answer that enlightens, but the question." Teaching notes,

especially those based on having taught the case several times, should offer instructors an array of questions that can be purposefully and positively used to achieve the case objectives. For each question suggested, the teaching note should also highlight possible student responses and how those comments are likely to open the door to further follow-on questions and comments.

As part of this section of a teaching note, it is also important to give instructors some sense of the timing of the conversation that needs to take place in order to allow for a student-centered discussion, facilitated with well-timed instructor queries, comments, and other conversation nudges, while attempting to address most, if not all, the learning objectives for the case. Such guidance may be nothing more than suggesting: instructors allow no more than five minutes for students to recap the case facts at the start of class; at the halfway point in the class the first student action plan should be summarized on the front board and the conversation should be opened up for others to ask him/her questions about the plan; and with 10 minutes left in class a final, refined action plan should appear on the front board and students should be in the mode of getting their final questions addressed by one another or the instructor.

From time to time, a case discussion can be enhanced by the use of an outside guest speaker or the use of some different pedagogy (e.g., role-plays, buzz groups, videos, etc.). If that is true for the class for which the teaching note applies, their use should be noted in this section of the teaching note.

6. A discussion of the case's relationship to any underlying theory base, conceptual framework, analytical methodologies, or well-known business examples/stories

Not only is a case discussion intended to cast students in the role of a real decision-maker facing an actual business issue, the discussion should also provide an opportunity to take a specific situation (or several specific situations) and extract generalizations. These generalizations often take the form of tools and techniques added to a student's repertoire (e.g., role and methodology of calculating free cash flows); frameworks for organizing important considerations (e.g., Michael Porter's five forces); methodologies for addressing a situation (e.g., SWOT [strengths, weaknesses, opportunities, and threats] analysis); bringing to light contemporary theories (e.g., the efficient markets theory) and research (e.g., Kouzes and Posner's diagnostic work on the leadership practices inventory instrument); and of creating memorable corporate icons representing certain business To Do's or To Don'ts (e.g., Enron). Such generalizations should connect to the learning objectives for a case. Moreover, a series of cases may be needed to fully craft and cement the generalizations. To the extent that a single case begins, contributes to, or provides a capstone for a case series, its connection to the case series' objectives should be clearly stated.

7. A summary of the case's sequel, or what happened next, if known

For some cases, though not by any means most cases, the teaching note author knows how the issues in the case were actually addressed by the case protagonist(s). If known, a short paragraph or two in the teaching note presenting that information is useful. It is useful not in the sense that it represents the "answer," because the actions and decisions that business managers take are not always the best, the most creative, or even the most defensible. The actions taken do, however, provide one more opportunity for instructors, usually near the end of the case discussion, to pose another question of the sort, *"Here is what the company actually did. In some ways our discussion today has touched on some of the same ideas. In what ways though do you see what the company did as different from what you proposed, or as particularly creative, or more (less) likely to succeed?"*

8. A suggested list of supplementary readings (or other resources) that could be assigned for student study and/or used in class

Another valuable component of a high-quality teaching note is a short list of references that instructors might find informative as part of their preparation for facilitating the case discussion. Useful references generally fall into three categories. First, references that pertain to the company and the situation in the case can be helpful as background information, context enrichments, and/or case sequels and updates. If such sources are available, instructors need to be mindful that students only have the information contained in the case. A second category of references pertains to the theme(s) of the case. For example, in the teaching note presented in the appendix to this chapter, the case it pertains to involves a budgeting role-play. Thus, there are references pertaining to the role of, the shortcomings of, and the debates surrounding the use of budgets in business settings. A third category of references that are sometimes provided in a teaching note pertains to other cases that instructors might find useful as substitutes for, prerequisites to, or follow-ups to the focal case being discussed.

9. Suggestions to encourage and facilitate student reflection

An often overlooked aspect of our classroom teaching, course designs, and teaching notes has to do with creating mechanisms for student reflection. Because "reflection is intimately linked with the process of learning" (Moon, 1999, p. 100), suggestions for how to encourage, or how to orchestrate, some reflective student activity are valuable additions to a teaching note. Clearly, at the end of class the summarizing and synthesizing category of questions mentioned above is helpful in this regard. Likewise, at the start of a class, calling on a student to summarize and synthesize yesterday's discussion is another reflective technique. Within a case series, including an assignment question with each successive case that asks students to link that case to the prior one in terms of identifying the lessons brought forward that were helpful in this case is another means for explicitly inviting reflection. One other mechanism is, at the start of the course or at the start of case series, to provide five minutes at the end of each class for students to journal three or four insights, ideas, and/or questions for further study springing from that day's case discussion. If certain reflective ideas or processes seem particularly appropriate for a specific case, the conveyance of those ideas in a teaching note will be a welcome addition to those instructors adopting the case.

Some teaching note miscellanea

Writing teaching notes during the case-writing process.[3] Developing preliminary teaching notes while the case is being written almost always improves the case itself. When developing a case, especially a

---

[3] This section is from Rotch, UVA-PHA-0028.

field-based case, the case writer is engaged in a number of activities, often at the same time. The case writer is gathering information, shaping the case's purpose, smoothing the pathway to case release, recording statements to be used as quotes, and organizing the sequence and hierarchy of case presentation. Experienced case writers know that one does not get a good case by collecting reams of data and then seeing what it means; one must do an analysis at the same time that the case is being written in order to ascertain where the case needs additional clarity, additional data, or can benefit from opposing views. Therefore, along with all the other activities just cited, case writers ought to be thinking through an analysis of the material and how the case might be used in class. The discipline of setting these ideas down as "preliminary teaching notes" helps a case writer be sure that all the necessary information is in the case. One experienced case writer has said that the time to write a case's outline is in the company parking lot as you leave, to which one can add that it is also the time to outline an analysis and a preliminary set of teaching notes. Preparation of teaching notes should not be put off beyond the time of case writing. While it is important to recognize that notes can seldom be considered final, it is equally important to start work on teaching notes even before the case is finished.

Teaching notes are not scripts. Even though the format with which a teaching note is written and organized may have the appearance of a script, teaching notes should not be viewed as strict scripts to be mechanically followed. Instructors should always be on the watch for classroom discussion paths to pursue that are raised by the students in that discussion and instructors should constantly exercise the freedom to diverge from the teaching note's plan as situations warrant and appear beneficial. It perhaps goes without saying, but we will say it anyway: Individual instructors are responsible for their own facilitation of a case discussion. Thus, teaching notes are best viewed as merely the starting point for an instructor's own case preparation.

Silences. Much of a teaching note comprises a teaching plan that poses possible questions for instructors to use and the attendant discussion points springing from those questions. Indeed, we have asserted that this part of a teaching note is what distinguishes good ones from not-so-good ones. The inference here, and even when a variety of good teaching notes are reviewed, is that all instructor questions garner immediate, precise, clear student responses. This is simply not the reality. In fact, one could argue that good questions prompt silence – silence that is full of real-time student thinking. One of the hardest skills to master as an instructor with an exciting teaching plan, in the midst of a high-energy discussion, with the clock ticking and several learning objectives not yet met, is to fill the silence and answer your own question. But as instructors we must master "silence as a second language. It is priceless" (Groneberg, 2003, p. 34). Silence can indeed be priceless in the learning process, and we encourage instructors to not be seduced by the steady flow of a teaching note's class strategy and plan. Be prepared to use 20 or 30 seconds of silence after asking a question – even if it feels like 10 minutes – for students to formulate their responses to your question. Do not be guilty of "insufficient wait time [and] rapid rewards" (Napell, 1994, p. 199) for early responders.

Conclusion

Teaching notes are an invaluable source of information, insights, and ideas. In some important ways, a teaching note serves as a map for a case discussion. But making the journey from here to there (i.e., from the start of class to the end of class), remains the primary and professional responsibility of the classroom instructor and his or her students. Teaching notes foreshadow a case discussion, provide suggestions for facilitating that discussion, and can expedite an instructor's own case analysis. They are dynamic documents in that they should be continually revised with the case in the classroom.

Further reading

Barnes, L. B., C.R. Christensen, and A.J. Hansen, *Teaching and the Case Method*, Boston: Harvard Business School Press, 1994.

Brookfield, S. D. and S. Preskill, 1999, *Tools and Techniques for Democratic Classrooms,* San Francisco: Jossey-Bass Publishers, 1999.

Groneberg, T., *The Secret Life of Cowboys*, New York: Scribner, 2003.

Maister, D.A., "How to Avoid Getting Lost in the Numbers," HBS Case #9-682-010, Boston: Harvard Business School Publishing, 1985.

McKeachie, W. J., *Teaching Tips: Strategies, Research, and Theory for College and University Teachers*, Boston: Houghton Mifflin Company, 2002.

Moon, J.A., *Reflection in Learning & Professional Development*, London: Kogan Page Ltd., 1999.

Napell, S. M., "Six Common Non-Facilitating Teaching Behaviors," in *Teaching and the Case Method,* Barnes, L.B., C.R. Christensen, and A.J. Hansen, eds., Boston: Harvard Business School Press, 1994.

APPENDIX

Sample Case Teaching Note*

CONSUMER SERVICE COMPANY (A)

Teaching Note

Case summary

Consumer Service Company offers interior home cleaning, exterior home maintenance, vehicle maintenance, and landscape maintenance services. The company is organized regionally and centrally into four divisions representing the respective services. Each fall, the division directors are responsible for developing a profit plan for their division, committing the division to a level of sales and profits before taxes. In years past, the four division directors met with the CEO in a retreat setting to establish division profit plans as well as a plan for the company as a whole. The discussions were typically collegial in nature and the projections for each division were shared. The overall company sales and profit plans were built on the consensus divisional plans. The division directors' annual compensation was based on a formula of base pay plus bonus (minus a penalty) for exceeding (failing to meet) sales projections.

For the current year, the CEO has changed the profit planning process. In lieu of the retreat, he is holding individual meetings with each of the division directors without sharing information among them. The director of the landscape division is the last of the division directors to meet with the CEO. The new process is somewhat unsettling because

*This note was prepared by Professor William May, University of Southern California, and by Professors Robert J. Sack and Mark Haskins, University of Virginia. Copyright © 2004 by the University of Virginia Darden School Foundation, Charlottesville, VA. All rights reserved. *To order copies, send an e-mail to dardencases@virginia.edu. No part of this publication may be reproduced, stored in a retrieval system, used in a spreadsheet, or transmitted in any form or by any means – electronic, mechanical, photocopying, recording, or otherwise – without the permission of the Darden School Foundation.*

the division director does not know what goals have been set for the other divisions. The director hears that the other directors had rather unpleasant encounters with the CEO.

Information sheets for the CEO and the division director covering the previous three years of the landscape division are appended to this teaching note (Exhibits TN1 and TN2). The CEO has three years of projected and actual sales figures; the division director has additional information on which annual projections were based. It is clear from the information sheets that the division director has been "sandbagging" in preceding years. It is also clear that the CEO is projecting a percentage increase for this division that far exceeds previous annual increases.

At the heart of this case is a budget negotiation role-playing exercise in which each of the players has information not available to the other player. The discussion of the ethical issues involved in the profit planning process springs from students' observation of the role-playing.

Teaching objectives and possible uses of the case:

This case provides an effective means for uncovering, highlighting, and discussing principles for the development of a sales budget *and* the ethical issues embedded in the relationship between individuals charged with developing and implementing the budget. The case is best used as a follow-on to a prior class (e.g., Oriole Furniture) that has introduced students to the purposes and processes of budgeting. It can be used in one, 60–90 minute class.

Suggested student assignment:

1. Read the Consumer Service Company (A) case prior to class.
2. Be prepared to be called on for a role-play, for which you will receive some additional information in class.

Teaching strategy

• Distribute the case, without the additional information sheets (Exhibits TN1 and TN2), to the class for reading prior to the session in which it will be used.

Exhibit TN1

Establishing the sales plan –

The Role of Mr. Hurdle

Mr. Hurdle, President of Consumer Service Company, has the following information available to him as he prepares for his October sales planning meeting for the coming year with Ms. Forthright, the director of the Landscaping Division.

A. History

Year	Sales committed to in landscape's sales plan	Actual sales reported
current	$5,200,000	$5,400,000 est.
last	$5,000,000	$5,100,000
prior	$4,500,000	$4,600,000

B. All of the other divisions have signed up for their sales plans for the coming year. To make Mr. Hurdle's sales goals for the company as a whole, Ms. Forthright is going to have to come in with a 10% increase to $5,940,000. The other divisions (one of which is having a particularly difficult time because the director is having personal problems) are similarly stretched.

C. Consumer Service's stock price has been virtually flat for the last two years except for a brief spike several months ago when rumors of a tender offer pushed the price up temporarily. Mr. Hurdle was torn by the tender offer rumor – as the largest single stockholder, he would have benefited from a high-priced buyout. But it is also true that any such buyout would have ended his plans to bring his two college-age sons into the business and to explore a European expansion. The company's investment bankers have assured Mr. Hurdle that the rumors are quiet for now, but they have also told him about criticisms about the company they have picked up on the street, such as "lost their hustle" and "management has relaxed."

Exhibit TN2

Establishing the Sales Plan –

The Role of Ms. Forthright

Ms. Forthright, the director of Consumer Service's landscape divisions has the following information available to her as she prepares for her October sales planning meeting for the coming year with Mr. Hurdle:

A. History

Year	Sales projected by Field managers	Sales projected by Division marketing	Sales committed to in the plan	Actual sales reported
current	$5,400,000	$5,250,000	$5,200,000	$5,400,000 est.
last	$5,200,000	$5,100,000	$5,000,000	$5,100,000
prior	$4,800,000	$4,400,000	$4,500,000	$4,600,000

B. The aggregate sales projections from Ms. Forthright's field managers, for the coming year, are $5,500,000. The division marketing staff projects sales of $5,400,000.

C. Some marketing studies have shown increased competition from both local and national landscaping companies. It may be that the division's unique position is about to be seriously challenged for the first time.

- In class, select two pairs of students to independently play the roles of Mr. Hurdle, the CEO, and Ms. Forthright, the division director. Give each role-player only his/her respective additional information sheet and ask them to leave the room for 20 minutes to prepare, on their own, to play their assigned roles in a budget planning meeting to be conducted in front of the class.
- During the time that the role-players are out of the room, give the rest of the class the two additional information sheets so that they have the complete story and, in a class discussion, develop on a flip chart, overhead transparency, or a computer projected image the budget planning principles which the class would hope to see in the role-play discussion (i.e., the normative discussion) versus those they actually expect to see. Just before the role-players return, instruct the

class to be observant regarding how the participants treat each other, what they say/don't say, and their general approach to the meeting.

- Each role-play should take about 10 minutes. It can be terminated when the two parties agree to a plan for the landscape division or when it becomes apparent that no consensus will be reached.

- During the remainder of the class, facilitate a debriefing discussion by first asking the role-players to step out of character and comment on what they were thinking and sensing while engaged in the role-play. Then, ask the class what they observed and what each role-player seemed to be striving to accomplish. Continue the class discussion by asking such questions as those presented in the analysis section below.

Analysis:

A number of budgeting principles and ethical issues should emerge from the role-playing and the class discussion will be somewhat different each time the case is used. Nonetheless, the discussion should embrace most, if not all, of the issues mentioned below.

Budgeting principles

The case provides the occasion to make the following points: (1) a budget is best developed from the bottom up and should not be imposed from the top down; (2) to be effective, a budget has to be "owned" by the operating units; (3) effective budgets are built from detailed projections; and (4) there should be trigger points embedded in the budget plan for mid-course changes if certain pre-established circumstances/events arise.

Ethical issues

(a) Honesty, integrity, and truth-telling

Virtually every company code of ethics begins with a statement about honesty and integrity. Truth-telling is a basic norm in our society. Yet, withholding information, deception, and game playing are not always seen as ethical violations and certainly fall far short of lying, which is always wrong.

- *Does the division director's past sandbagging (***Exhibit TN1*** shows actual results in excess of budget) constitute a violation of honesty and integrity? Why, why not?*
- *Does her sandbagging fall within acceptable limits of withholding information or deception? Why, why not?*
- *To what extent does the past climate of sandbagging, undoubtedly known by the CEO, justify such behavior?*

(b) Respect for persons

A basic norm in our society is to treat individuals as persons and not as means. This norm is often tested in the kinds of relationships that people have in the workplace.

- *To what extent, if at all, did the role-players violate the norm of respect for each other in the information that they presented and the information that they withheld?*
- *Does the compensation plan that Mr. Hurdle has developed create excessive pressure on Ms. Forthright or cause her to be deceptive? Why, why not?*
- *To what extent is Mr. Hurdle's 10 per cent increase for Ms. Forthright's division justified in light of his personal needs and in light of the division's past performance history?*

(c) Loyalty to oneself vs. loyalty to the group

The facts in the case often create a tension in the two role-players, and that tension reflects a real ethical dilemma. The class may want to explore the role players' response to that tension.

Over the past three years, Ms. Forthright's compensation has been

Year					% Increase
Current	$25,000	+ $130,000	+ $1,000	= $156,000	
Last	25,000	+ 125,000	+ 500	= 150,500	> 3.6%
Prior	25,000	+ 112,500	+ 500	= 138,000	> 9.1%

If, for the coming year, Ms. Forthright accepts the $5,940,000 sales plan desired by Mr. Hurdle, and only delivers actual sales of

$5,500,000 her compensation would decrease to:

$$\$25,000 + \$148,500 - \$33,000 = \$140,500$$

- *Did Ms. Forthright accept the challenge offered by Mr. Hurdle – for the good of the company – or did she balk at the salary risk involved in accepting a stretch budget?*
- *How did she trade off the personal risk against the potential good for the group? Was her response proper? Why or why not?*
- *Did Mr. Hurdle impose his personal interest on Ms. Forthright? Is he entitled to ask for that level of performance from her because of their respective positions? Why or why not? Is it better if he tells Ms. Forthright why he needs a stretch goal? Why or why not?*

(d) Creating an ethical climate

A code of conduct does not create an ethical company. On the other hand, it remains clear that an ethical climate can develop without a code of conduct in a situation where people respond ethically to day-to-day business challenges.

- *If Ms. Forthright is now committed to a budget which exceeds reasonable expectations, how is she likely to react to the resulting pressure? What kind of pressure will she impose on her field managers?*
- *How might this budgeting process affect the integrity of the company's reporting process?*
- *If you were the controller of this company and knew that the budgets had been developed in this way, what countervailing controls might you think necessary?*
- *To what extent would this budget process work in a non-US setting and create similar or dissimilar behaviors from mangers? Why? Or why not?* (Note: this question is best posed to non-US students)
- *What would you expect the budgeting process in this company to be like next year? How will Ms. Forthright approach the negotiation next year, with the experience of this year in her mind? Do you think this process would work in non-US settings? Why or why not?*
- *Imagine an important business issue confronting the landscape division sometime during this year – e.g., an accidental poisoning of a child as a result of improperly applied chemicals. How would you expect Ms. Forthright to react? How will she and Mr. Hurdle handle*

*it? How might their handling of that issue be different if the budget
had been developed in a different way?*

With 15 minutes remaining in a 90-minute class (adjustments to the
timing of the discussion posed in this note are left to instructors if class
periods are different from 90 minutes), instructors should pose two
final, codifying-type questions.

1. *Given the discussion we have just had, what are some of the major
   concerns embedded in the budgeting process?* (This question simply
   opens the door for students to reiterate and underscore the key issues
   raised in (a) to (d) above as areas for concern.)
2. *What two or three things were raised in our discussion that would
   help moderate these concerns?* (This question allows students to
   synthesize normative takeaways.)

Special note to instructors

As we publish this case, budgets are under close scrutiny – their very
usefulness is being questioned and companies are beginning to eliminate them or completely overhaul long-standing budgeting processes.
Instructors may find it useful to peruse the following articles (with brief
quoted excerpts from each) in order to both deepen and broaden the
budgeting discussions that they facilitate in the classroom. Moreover,
these references might also form the basis for students fulfilling a term
paper or speech requirement pertaining to the contemporary budgeting
debate.

Ericson, Richard, "Incentives Ought to make the CEO's Job Easier,"
  Financial Executive (June 2003).
Fisher, Liz, "Budgeting – One Step Beyond," *Accountancy* (March
  2002).
Jensen, Michael, "Corporate Budgeting is Broken – Let's Fix it,"
  Harvard Business Review (November 2001).
Neely, A., Sutcliff, M.R., and H.R. Heyns, *Driving Value Through
  Strategic Planning and Budgeting* (a research report from the
  Cranfield School of Management and Accenture, 2001).
Parmenter, David, "Abandon Budgets and Set Your Enterprise Free,"
  New Zealand Management (October 2003).

Finally, instructors are encouraged to explore the rising promi-
nence and ever-expanding work of the Beyond Budgeting Round Table
(BBRT). This group is quite active in publishing, conducting seminars,

and working closely with major international companies to radically alter traditional budgets and processes. The organization's Web site (www.bbrt.org) provides lots of useful information.

Some publications springing from, or related to, the BBRT's work include:

Hope, J., and R. Fraser, "Figures of Hate," *Financial Management* (February, 2001).

Beyond Budgeting, Boston: Harvard Business School Press, 2003.

"Who Needs Budgets?" *Harvard Business Review* (February 2003).

12 | *Action learning*

LYNN ISABELLA

One must learn by doing, for though you
think you know it, you have no certainty
until you try.

– Aristotle

There can be no action without learning
and no learning without action.

– Reginald Revans,
"Father" of Action Learning

Action learning at its most basic is learning by doing. It was created by Professor Reg Revans in the 1940s as a means to improve coal production in the United Kingdom. Revans observed that learning had two components. Learning garnered from authorities, such as academic theory and concepts, and learning from student questioning of their own experience. Without both learning components, Revans asserted, learning was incomplete. Thus, practice, reflection and doing began to garner as much attention as abstract models.

Action learning, as a management education concept, has come to incorporate the creation of situations through which students can solve real problems and thus learn by doing. Much of its interest has come about to redress what is seen by many as a flaw in management education, specifically the opportunity to practice.

Currently a great deal of attention is surrounding action learning in the context of executive development. Company based action learning projects, through which teams of managers work on issues of strategic importance within their corporation, are threaded through executive education curricula. Clearly, action learning has become a dominant learning vehicle in non-degree programs. However, it is also becoming increasingly important in degree programs.

This chapter focuses on the many expressions of action learning within business education. First, we will discuss the benefits of action learning, including the factors necessary for action learning activities to succeed. Then we offer a range of action learning activities available to instructors of business. Finally we also discuss the negative side of action learning and strategies for avoiding action learning pitfalls.

Why include action learning as a learning option?

More and more in business education, it is not enough to simply offer theory or conceptual frameworks. Application of knowledge in real time to real situations brings learning out of the classroom and onto the business playing field. There are a number of advantages to action learning.

At its best, action learning has the *potential for being a high-impact learning experience, requiring engagement and investment.* Given that most managers have a learning profile that includes experimentation and experience (Kolb, 1984), students will learn best by experiencing actual situations as opposed to reading about what others did or might do. Action learning is not theory, but theory in action. Thus through action learning students can "experience" real situations, people, and issues. At its most impactful, the student is a co-creator of the experience, immersed in a learning experience that has not been pre-organized or pre-scripted.

Action learning also creates a *practice field for students to try, get feedback, and make mistakes without severely detrimental consequences.* Management is one of the few professions into which individuals are parachuted without proper training. Imagine if airline pilots flew planes or if doctors treated patients without benefit of hours of practice to build skill and knowledge. I often ask my students, for example, how they learned to conduct a performance appraisal. The universal answer: I just did it, or more precisely worried about it obsessively and then did it completely wrong. No soccer player ever makes goals consistently without practice. Why should we expect managers to be good managers without practice and the benefit of missing shots without the pressure of performing at game time?

On the other hand, action learning allows individuals to *see and feel the consequences of poor actions taken.* While discussions can be heated in a case discussion about potential action alternatives, students never have to implement the decisions that they take in class. Action learning is different. Students must live with the consequences of their actions. During computer simulations, a wrong product decision in a competitive market has consequences on that product's positioning and share of market. A company with a dominant share suddenly loses ground to a competitor. The student or student team finds themselves lying in the bed they just made.

Finally, action learning can *open the door for individual self awareness through feedback*. There is nothing like the opportunity for personal reflection to increase learning through experience. Although personal learning can arise from an understanding of basic concepts, it is another matter to observe your engagements in a role-play. Too often I've had students articulate a very coherent and reasonable strategy for talking to a difficult employee. When challenged to do it live against a student role-playing the difficult employee, there are few links between proposed actions and executed behaviors. What they do looks nothing like what they said they would do. Thus, the platform for self-awareness is generated. Perhaps the students believed they were being understanding and caring, when in fact their behavior was experienced as condescending and without compassion.

Expressions of action learning

The benefits of action learning are substantial. And there are many different expressions of action learning available to instructors of business education, some of which have already been the focus of chapters in this volume.

As Figure 12.1 outlines, action learning can be viewed along two critical dimensions. One dimension is the *level of engagement*, specifically individual or group. Some types of action learning are engaged in solely by the individual, while other types of action learning involve activities done by a team or group. Action learning at the individual level can be focused and specialized to meet the learning goals of the student. It usually involves a student as the principal action taker, and thus learner. Action learning based on team activities offers learning from the task as well as the relationships established and team dynamics created. Thus, the layers of potential learning increase. Unfortunately, also increasing are layers of noise and distraction for the learning. We all know how complicated team projects can be. Even a great project task can

		Activity base	
		Individual	Group or Team
Potential degree of impact on learner	Low	Case studies, guest speakers, company visits	Team paper, case project, outdoor challenge
	High	Role-plays, in-class exercises, retrospectives or self-narratives, reflective exercises or activities, individual practicums or internships	Behavioral simulations, computer-based simulations, company project, consulting project

Figure 12.1 Expressions of action learning

be overshadowed by the interpersonal and team dynamics created by the interactions of team members. While those dynamics are certainly at their best grist for the learning mill, they also can detract from the team's ability to deliver on the project and thus on a big component of the learning.

The other dimension to consider is the *degree of action impact.* Relatively speaking there are action learning experiences where the action impact is minimal. This to me means there are few, if any, repercussions or negative long-term consequences for the actions taken. This is not to say that an individual's learning is low; it is to say that the impact the action learning will have on oneself or others is minimal. Case studies are one example. Cases are intended to provide an immersion for the student into a real-life situation. While the student immerses in determining the correct option price or number of batches to be processed, the student never implements his or her recommendation. That is not to say that the student has not learned about calculating economic order quantity; it is to say that the decision is devoid of making it so.

On the other hand, there are also action learning experiences where the action impact is high. These are situations in which the actions or decisions taken have real-life consequences and/or students see the results of their actions. Such high impact action learning activities are ones that put the student in a problem-solving situation as an active participant whose actions have a direct bearing on the outcome. Certainly the MBA's summer internship is a type of action learning as is a work issue that an executive education program participant is in the midst of or has recently addressed. No longer is the challenge articulated through a problem in a text book or to be discovered within the pages of a case.

What all action learning activities share

Despite where in the learning matrix an action learning activity falls, there are several commonalities.

First, *action learning requires the involvement of and participation by the learner*. It is active in the sense that the student is an active participant in the experience. What the student does or says impacts the decisions taken or the recommendations preferred. In a case study, for example, that may mean putting oneself into the shoes of the protagonist and attempting to see the situation through their eyes. For an in-class exercise, engagement might mean taking the exercise seriously enough to try to participate meaningfully.

Second, it is a *collaborative and co-created learning experience* between students and instructor. No one has absolute knowledge. All involved in the experience create the learning experience through their engagement with each other. For a company project, the executive sponsor might have expert knowledge of his marketing area, but the students in the action learning initiative have to figure out how to tap into that knowledge or reconstruct it in a way that opens new doors.

Third, *action learning builds in opportunities for reflection and processing what just happened*. While the notion of reflection will be more fully discussed later in this chapter, all action learning activities contain some method of stepping away from the experience to learn. It may be simply stepping back from a role-play to ask the question, "So what did we just learn about managing our boss?" Or it might be a more extensive review of how the team ended up as the lowest performing team in the simulation. Or the stepping back might happen at various points during the action learning activity, such as time outs during a simulation to take stock of actions or keeping a journal of ideas or emotions triggered by the experience.

Finally, *focus is relevant to the participant's work environment.* This means for projects that the issues are real to the students and company. Issues are not made up or make work. Especially for more mature students with extensive work experience (or who might be working concurrent with their study), outside team projects or inside classroom activities must be grounded in something meaningful.

The downsides of action learning

Action learning activities are not without their difficulties and downsides. First *action learning initiatives take time and require external contact and connections.* When the action learning involves a company project or consulting-type engagement, company contacts need to be made and maintained. Projects can be especially insightful for students, but the crafting of the project becomes essential. If projects are too big or burdensome, students will be overwhelmed. If they are too contained or insignificant, students will wonder why they are being asked to spend so much of their precious time on what they perceive to be busy work.

While action learning is about practicing, it does not connote leaving a student without some basic skills to succeed. Thus, *action learning requires support and coaching* to help students over the inevitable pitfalls. When teams are the delivery mechanism, support and coaching becomes even more critical, not to mention time consuming. Teams need coaching in the project content *and* they may also need support or coaching relative to their team process. To not deliver both of these is to shortchange the student's learning.

Another downside is that frankly *not every student likes action learning* as a learning mode. My personal experience in orchestrating many action learning experiences is this: About 20 percent of the students don't get it, don't want to get it, or don't see the value. If you expect that 100 percent of individuals will see the value or invest totally, you will be disappointed. Remember the classic saying, "You can lead a horse to water, but you can't make it drink." The same is true with action learning initiatives. Not everyone embraces the learning potential. Fortunately many more students do than do not.

Why might some portion of students dislike action learning? These kinds of experiences *can be threatening to an individual's self-understanding.* Any given student might not be ready to learn or be confronted by the issues in question. Role-plays can confront students with the difference in what they say versus what they do. Behavior leadership situations can be even more disconcerting. A number of years back, as course head for our First-Year Organizational Behavior course, I used the Looking Glass simulation from the Center for Creative Leadership. This behavior simulation created an organization and individuals were assigned to various positions (with various embedded business problems) within that company. The focus of the simulation is about how the participant orchestrates his or her role. One particular student who saw himself as a commanding leader was confronted with subordinates who would not follow and one who actively rebelled at the leader. The simulation created an experience that put that student's leadership ability under the microscope. And the results did not fit the student's self-perception. It can also squarely let the students know what they don't know and this can be threatening.

Finally, some *action learning initiatives can tap painful and personal events that make learning difficult.* Over several years our Darden students have participated in an outdoor challenge experience as part of the orientation activities for the learning teams. Over the day students were confronted with a variety of team challenges, such as getting all students over a 10 foot high wall or through a spider's web. For a student who has been raped, the experience is not about the team conquering the wall, but about being touched. While perhaps a dramatic example, it is an actual example of the trauma one student felt about issues raised by this action learning initiative.

Project-based action learning experience

Although the downsides of action learning are real, I believe that overall the value of action learning more than outweighs any difficulties. In essence, action learning offers a practice field so needed by future managers and by current managers needing or wanting new or better skills. One of the very best practice fields is an action learning project. It offers students the opportunity to work on actual company problems and take responsibility for making real and tangible recommendations. Such projects require special attention. The rest of this chapter will focus on project-based action learning.

Here are some tips to insure project-based action learning is at its best:

Insure that the project is manageable and challenging. Crafting projects that are challenging without being overwhelming, that require real solutions, not just academic ones, and that stand a chance of implementation so students don't feel as if they are doing make-work is a big challenge. Time and effort need to go into collaborating with the sponsoring company and its executives to learn about project possibilities. Better projects are ones the company really wants to learn about (not ones that the company already has explored), that are tied to the strategic direction of the company, and that have the highest level of sponsorship possible. In addition, if students know that their work stands a high probability of being implemented because the company is highly invested in their research, the project takes on additional meaning.

Be attentive to team composition. There is also this issue of team selection or construction. One advantage to such projects in an MBA environment is the proximity of the students to each other. The complexity mounts if the action learning project is done in an EMBA environment where the students are not physically proximate and may, in fact, be located in different countries. This requires a level of technology and infrastructure to allow participants to converse in chat rooms, through conference calls, or via other technology.

Sometimes there is the question of giving students a choice in project or team. It is clearly the purview of the instructor to balance choice against learning goals. For example, if the goal is to encourage students to learn about areas they might not know really well, then allowing them to choose a project in their area of expertise would not be consistent. On the other hand, putting a student on a project in which he or she cannot invest may mean that then student learning, not to mention project results, may suffer.

Provide ongoing coaching and support, but not explicit direction. Although the instructor may clearly understand the project issues and the agenda of the student, the student, as the learner, may not be clear and require direction. The question of just how directive to be is a critical one. Since the intent of action learning is to learn by doing, directions that interrupt the natural struggles and challenges for the students are unwelcome. Despite the temptation to tell students what to do, I advise letting the students struggle. That does not mean, however, that you should deny students the benefits of coaching.

They very much need assistance through listening, questioning, offering conceptual clarification, or team facilitation. Although there can be a high degree of ambiguity in the project, learning how to deal with the ambiguity may not be what students like, but it is often an important aspect of the action learning agenda.

Encourage frequent contact and feedback. Direction is not optimal, but students do need direct feedback about how they are doing. Is the project at a level of development consistent with the time spent on it? One of my own most substantial learnings as a coach is telling project teams exactly how far they are (or in many cases are not) from completion. Sometimes certain teams just don't pull together and need a "kick in the pants" to really appreciate how much work they have left. It can be difficult to do, but sometimes the harsher the better, especially if the client results are at stake.

Coach the sponsors. Although students are the most obvious recipient of coaching, it is easy to forget that the organization's managers who are sponsoring the projects need coaching themselves. Those executives may not know how to work with a student team or how available to be. I have found that a brief session with the sponsor initially as well as ongoing phone calls to see how the project is progressing from their viewpoint go an awfully long way.

Time for reflection

There can be no action learning without opportunities to reflect upon the experience. Creating ways to encourage, no demand, that reflection are essential to completing the action learning loop.

With the amount of time and effort that goes into planning and executing a major action learning initiative, delivery of the final project results is greeted with relief. Echoes of "we're done" or "phew – that's over" resound loudly. The problem is, the experience is only half the learning. The learning needs to be identified, solidified, and assimilated. That only happens through reflection and review following. There are many ways to do this:

- *Use journaling* to focus emerging learnings. Actually passing out journals gives students a physical reminder to chronicle their experiences and impressions. It is important to stress that getting thoughts on paper is more important than the quality of the writing.

- *Conduct a formal "after action" review.* If the journal chronicles emerging learnings and impressions, a more formal review of the entire process creates another critical learning context. Such a review is more than "What did I learn?" or "How did we do?" It is a considered exploration of what worked, what didn't, and what might have been done differently. For such a review to create maximum learning, it has to be done without blame or evaluation, without recrimination or judgment. The review merely explores best practices (what worked well and why), missteps (what didn't work so well and why) and opportunities not taken (what we could do differently next time). The point is for a team to review what actions or processes accounted for the results they achieved.
- *Require a reflective paper* that forces students to consider their own role and behavior in the activity. Those reflective papers are more than "I did this" or "I did that" or "We visited this plant or this location." Truly strong reflective papers are the result of a serious introspective journey and willingness to see oneself and one's actions honestly. While students may resist such papers, those who embrace the opportunity create documents that are truly inspirational. If there was ever any question about the value of action learning, a good reflective paper would take away any concern.

Powerful learning

The more real the situation to what the student's action learning experience is, the greater the impact and potential learning that can be achieved. This is why action learning is potentially so powerful. Because the student is involved and engaged in his or her learning, and doing something that ties directly to an organizational activity, the relevancy and connections are immediate. Learning can be faster and deeper.

Action learning affords one other advantage: By engaging in action learning, students are implicitly learning skills for a lifetime. Yes, they are learning from their experiences, but they are also learning *how* to learn from their experiences. In addition to the business knowledge that action learning provides, students are learning a method for linking experience and learning. All those role-plays, all those projects, simulations, visits, exercises are more than instructional vehicles for content. They are springboards to encourage students every day to consider their own lessons of experience.

Further reading

Brown, David, "Action Learning Popular in Europe, Not Yet Caught on in Canada," *Canadian HR Reporter*, 18, 8 (April 25, 2005).

Dilworth, R. L., and V.J. Willis, *Action Learning: Images and Pathways*, Malabar, FL: Krieger Publishing Co., 2003.

Hale, Richard, and Charles Margerison, "Adding Real Value with Work-Based Learning Questions," *Training Journal* (July 2004), 34–39.

Honey, Peter, "One More Time: What Is Learning to Learn?" *Training Journal*, (April 2005), 9.

Kolb, David A., *Experiential Learning: Experience as the Source of Learning and Development*, Englewood Cliffs, NJ: Prentice-Hall Inc., 1984, 14–15.

LaRue, Bruce, and Robert R. Ivany, 'Transform Your Culture', *Executive Excellence*, 21, 12 (December 2004).

Marquardt, Michael, "Harnessing the Power of Action Learning," *T + D*, 58, 6 (June 2004), 26–32.

   Optimizing the Power of Action Learning, Palo Alto, CA: Davies-Black Publishing, 2004.

Taylor, David W., Oswald Jones, and Kevin Boles, "Building Social Capital Through Action Learning: An Insight into the Entrepreneur," *Education & Training*, 46, 4/5 (2004), 226–35.

13 | *Experiential methods*

JAMES G. S. CLAWSON

Experience is the best teacher.

Experiential teaching methods are those that rely on data generated during the exercise/learning experience rather than on data prepared in advance as with lectures and cases. Experiential methods engage students in experiences that simulate social phenomena. They include games such as Starpower, Gazogle, Global Markets, Sub-Arctic Survival, and the Organization Game as well as computer simulations like Markstrat, Sentra, Cogitate, and CapSim. These exercises, and a host of others, are available worldwide for instructors to purchase and use.

By engaging students in simulations of business situations, experiential methods generate their own data for students to consider and digest. Unlike the case method, in which the case provides the information to deal with, and unlike the lecture where the instructor and the text provide the information, experiential methods establish a platform for students to generate their own information and then to analyze and use it. What a student analyzes and learns from is not the written introduction to the exercise, but what happens in the exercise itself. In this sense, the increasingly common outdoor exercises (often called "ropes courses" because many include rappelling or rope-bridge construction and use, etc.) also fit into the category of experiential exercises. And in a sense, role-playing, as described above, is a mini-experiential exercise embedded in a class the same way a lecturette can be embedded in a case discussion.

Michael Polanyi (1962) said that some kinds of knowledge are logically unspecifiable. The more someone analyzes, for example, riding bicycles and hammering nails, the more *unable* he or she is to perform them. Can you imagine a parent trying to teach a child to hammer a nail by carefully measuring and explaining the force vectors that result in dynamic equilibrium that keeps the hammer head moving on

212

a smooth arc to land exactly perpendicularly on the head of the nail? The more a parent (or teacher) tried this, the less able the child would be to strike the nail. Polanyi argues that this knowledge, how to hammer a nail, is thus logically unspecifiable. An instructor, accepting this line of reasoning, would go about the teaching of hammering in a very different way. The instructor might create a controlled environment (e.g., with specially constructed hammers with a large head, padded gloves, large nails, etc.) and administer experiential exercises designed to help students develop personal familiarity with hammering nails.

The same is true of other kinds of activities. Of course, not all learning is logically unspecifiable; we would not ask surgeons to perform surgery without some specific instruction. And some specifiable skills are better taught with some practice as well. So the usefulness of experiential methods extends across both the logically unspecifiable and specifiable realms.

Experiential learning theories such as David Kolb's suggest that personal experience tends to cement the learning of specifiable conceptual principles and render it more available in the future than it otherwise would be. In experiential learning, material is completely learned, recalled, and made a part of an instructor's usable subsequent repertoire. Experiential learning thus can be more powerful in the learning environment than many other techniques.

The primary appeal of experiential methods is their ability to touch the student emotionally and physically, not just intellectually, at Levels One and Three as well as at Level Two. This multidimensional student involvement is exhilarating for both instructor and student, and as long as the learning is explicitly recognized and clearly established, such an experience makes this approach a wonderful tool. While this kind of power sometimes frightens instructors away from using experiential methods, the well-prepared instructor need not be unduly hesitant to use the method. Most experiential materials come with an instructor's manual to guide the user through the materials step by step. Moreover, as you use the materials, your own experience and wisdom in their application is enhanced.

Because experiential methods usually involve groups ranging from 3 to 20 people (and we have done exercises with up to 240!), they are often associated with course work on interpersonal relationships and small-group dynamics. These methods can be used for a variety of teaching objectives, however, and with much larger groups. There are both computer and non-computer exercises that can be used with several hundred people that address multiple aspects of business. In some of these, group issues are secondary if considered at all.

Tim Hall (1975) has suggested ways to determine if experiential methods are a viable classroom alternative. He says that if you believe that:

1. Learning is more effective when it is an active rather than a passive process;
2. Problem-centered learning is more enduring than theory-based learning (Hall writes, "When a person has a problem to solve and then scans for and applies knowledge which will help solve that problem, she has been internally motivated to master that knowledge");
3. Two-way communication produces better learning than one-way communication;
4. Participants will learn more when they share control over and responsibility for the learning process than when this responsibility lies solely with the group leader (which follows the philosophy of andragogy introduced earlier); and
5. Learning is most effective when thought and action are integrated. Experiential methods in the classroom present a rich teaching and learning possibility.

then you might consider using experiential methods. The rest of this chapter outlines some pros and cons of experiential methods and makes some suggestions for finding and using these tools.

Advantages of experiential methods

The biggest and most obvious advantage of these techniques is that they immerse the student in the learning situation. A person cannot be in an experiential exercise and not have some kind of experience. It may not be great, it may not be what the instructor intended in every case, but there will be an experience. Each individual's experience, in turn, contributes to the experience of the whole class, and if a good debriefing is performed, all the students can learn a lot about the central concepts of the exercise and their ability to relate to other people as well as themselves.

A sort of positive cheerfulness usually goes along with these experiences, because experiential methods are usually fun, which helps to engage students. These methods are fun in part because they represent a break in the traditional routine of lecture or case method courses; they are something different, something mysterious, something new. We often hear lots of buzzing about what the objective of a new exercise is, as students try to figure out in advance what it all means. This attendant, positive cheerfulness engages students and holds their interest.

Experiential methods also engage the instructor. They are an excellent way for a teacher to get out of a rut, to try something new, and to experiment. Experiential exercises can help an instructor learn new ways of teaching and can help to recharge your own energies and attitudes. The challenge is in finding experiential ways that grab the students' attention, that hold it in a concentrated way, and that have a positive and edifying outcome.

Most experiential techniques are also flexible. They usually allow for many variations and modifications to fit the needs of the individual instructor or the intended participants. You can often modify the instructions, the materials, or the ways the materials are used to emphasize a particular interest or course objective.

Experiential methods also help forge strong links between theory and action. Coleman (1977) claimed that unlike classical learning, experiential learning erects no hurdle between symbols and action.[1] "When consequence is perceptively connected to action, then such experiential learning provides a direct guide to future action," he wrote. In other words, unlike other forms of instruction, experiential methods allow students to experience a phenomenon directly – you don't have to work through the ambiguity of words and language. And since action occurs near the beginning of the learning process in experiential exercises, the motivation to learn, to understand what's happening in a relevant situation, is built in. If the exercise is well constructed and chosen for its relevance, the students' needs to learn exist concurrently with the learning exercise. With lecture and case materials, students can only anticipate the situations in which they will be motivated to apply the concepts introduced.

Experiential exercises also teach leadership and management well. Kolb (1984) found that students using experiential methods reported very high learning in the areas of new attitudes, communication skills,

---

[1] James S. Coleman, "Differences Between Experiential and Classroom Learning," in *Experiential Learning: Rationale, Characteristics, and Assessment* (San Francisco: Jossey-Bass, 1976).

and self-awareness, all of which are productive managerial and leadership attributes.[2] In courses where leadership, group dynamics, and getting things done are major topics of concern, experiential methods can add a dimension of realism and insight not possible with other approaches.

Finally, and in that connection, experiential methods are an excellent complement to other teaching techniques – lectures, cases, and other instructional approaches. Lectures, for example, are most useful for transmitting information but of little use in changing attitudes. Experiential exercises are effective tools for prompting students to examine their attitudes and values. Cases can help students understand real business problems, while experiential methods can help them see how they arise and what to do about them.

Disadvantages of experiential methods

Experiential methods often require careful, perhaps time-consuming, preparation. Sometimes special rooms or breakout areas for the small groups or special electrical equipment or visual props need to be found. If the materials for the participants are not in the right place at the right time or if the logistics of moving groups and giving clear assignments are not well in hand, the experience can turn into a chaotic disaster. It is important to think through every step, every detail, and as many contingencies as is possible in preparing an experiential exercise. What happens if a computer crashes – either the one(s) the participants are using or the main one that is calculating results? What if the weather is inclement? What if there aren't enough small-group meeting areas? What if the expected interactions don't occur? What if students don't find the exercise relevant or engaging?

It is also important to think about how to introduce the game to the participants. How can the rules and principles of the game be introduced most effectively and efficiently? Should there be a trial run to make sure the participants understand the procedures? Should there be a detailed schedule posted so participants know what will be happening when? Depending on the exercise, the introduction can require very careful and detailed planning.

---

[2] David A. Kolb, *Experiential Learning: Experience as the Source of Learning and Development* (Englewood Cliffs, NJ: Prentice-Hall, Inc., 1984).

Experiential methods can be time-consuming to implement. They seldom fit into the usual 50- or 90-minute class period. Special permission may be needed in scheduling an experiential class period over two, three, even eight hours. Other instructors may see this as intruding on the remainder of the academic program and voice their objections.

As previously mentioned, experiential methods also have the risk of getting out of hand. It is possible that some aspects of a game can trigger emotional reactions lying latent in the class. Some individuals under pressure in an experiential situation may revert to disruptive but previously successful coping behaviors such as retaliation, yelling and shouting, leaving, or sabotage. Others may reveal their personalities more than they do in class and classmates may conclude that the person was either nicer (or smarter or whatever other adjective you choose) or not as nice, and so forth, as previously thought. These things are not bad in and of themselves, however, as some instructors might believe; they can simply lead to increased learning. Indeed, it may be *only* under conditions of stress and emotionality that students can really gain an insight or see what they have not yet seen.

Knowing when to intervene in a developing situation is a judgment call. We step forward to dampen the situation when we see signs of two things occurring simultaneously: loss of rationality and the personal focus of an attack. As long as the people involved are thinking and aware of their "experiencing," meaning that they know both what they are thinking and what they are feeling, and are not being critical of another's quality as a human being, we let the exercise proceed. But when someone becomes irrational or personally abusive or inconsiderate, we intervene and, based on the situation, either invite the people to pause, think, and focus on the ideas and behavior rather than the people involved, or stop the conversation altogether. In our experience, such a necessity has rarely arisen.

A final disadvantage of experiential methods is one that can be avoided by a strong debriefing. When a group uses an experiential exercise but does not take the time, nor have the proper guidance to debrief it, the exercise becomes little more than a pleasant break in the curriculum. Coleman speculated that the weakest link in the experiential process of learning lies in generalizing from the particular experiences to general principles that are applicable to other circumstances. An Arabic proverb asserts that the wise learn from the mistakes of others, the smart learn from their own mistakes, and fools never learn. These caveats point to a danger in almost all experiential exercises: people will have fun, they may even become so engaged that they lose track of the time, but they may dismiss the experience and carry on as before unless they pause adequately to question the value and forward-looking meaning of the exercise.

Some proponents of experiential learning exercises insist that anything that can be taught at all is better taught through this method of instruction. They point to the very young student's experience of learning simple math and spelling in grade school as evidence of the method's efficacy. Only because students later gain a much greater facility with a symbolic medium, language, they argue, do educators change the method of teaching. We posit that experiential learning exercises, like all other teaching methods, should be used at the proper times and in the proper way to ensure their continued effectiveness. They are an excellent way of augmenting or introducing conceptual material.

Sources of experiential exercises

Many consulting firms publish business related experiential exercises. The names of these change over time with mergers and acquisitions, so be aware that the copyright owners may migrate. Temple, Barker and Sloane of Boston produce Cogitate and Wise, two computer simulations that ask participants to make decisions on a variety of products manufactured and sold in international markets. Capsim is another popular computer simulation, based on the Web. In these simulations, students must deal with exchange rates, transportation costs, human-resource-training lag times, and a variety of other problems in making their decisions. These games facilitate training of a large number of students and can be run over as many periods as an instructor has time for so students can get to see the "long-term" results of their calculations and decisions. Computer simulations generate two kinds of data, computer-generated results from decisions made during the game and the experience of working as a team in making those decisions. Both can be profitably debriefed.

Non-computer simulations are marketed by various firms. Some common ones are "Bafa Bafa," "The Looking Glass," "The Organizational Game," and "Starpower." These games set up organizational interactions around certain themes (distribution of power in "Starpower," for example). As participants operate in the game, exchanging resources, constructing products for sale, or managing an in-box, they generate their own data and situations that require response. These situations provide the basis for learning, real time and later during the debriefing.

Academic institutions also have experiential exercises for distribution. "Global Markets" and "Gazogle" are two that the University of Virginia's Darden School faculty have prepared and made generally available. "Global Markets" introduces students to international resource allocation and is a great way to help new students in a program get better acquainted early in the program. "Gazogle" is an operations game based on Lego blocks that teaches the interaction between production organizations, team work, managing quality, and customer service. A description of our first use of "Global Markets" can be found in the *Organizational Behavior Teaching Review.*[3]

Which leads to the last and perhaps most exciting source of experiential methods, your own creativity. Trying to figure out ways to engage students in meaningful exercises is not only a challenge but engaging; contemplating what students need to learn and figuring out ways to help that learning occur is rewarding and fun. Simply telling students to learn something so often just doesn't do the trick. We encourage instructors to devise their own experiential exercise to meet their specific need. The exercise may not work just right the first time, but it can fine tuned until the desired nuances and results flow from its use.

It was very rewarding to create "Global Markets" and watch as students responded to the design and threw themselves into the exercises. Similarly, Howard Raiffa of the Harvard Business School reportedly one day offered to sell a dollar bill to the highest bidder at the luncheon table in the Harvard faculty lounge under the following rules: The highest and the second highest bidder both had to pay, but only the highest bidder would get the dollar bill. He warned the group at the table not to do it, then opened the bidding at $0.10. Some 15 minutes later, he accepted a check for $20 and a second check for $19.90 from 2 colleagues. This simple experiential exercise became even to experienced instructors a powerful lesson on human behavior. The point is that you could explain that kind of behavior to people but they wouldn't likely believe it. Experiencing it among themselves, even Harvard professors were persuaded.

[3] James G. Clawson and Phillip Pfeiffer, "Global Markets," *Organizational Behavior Teaching Review*, 14, 2 (1989–90) 70.

Examples of experiential exercises

There are, as we have said, a multitude of experiential exercises out there. We introduce a few here for your awareness.

Performance review. There are a number of performance review cases and exercises available. One comes from Len Greenhalgh at Dartmouth. The purpose of this exercise is to practice skills in performance appraisal and supervision of subordinates and to develop skills in communication and problem solving. Three pairs of students, in turn, role-play a performance appraisal in front of their peers. The remainder of the class is divided into halves and has read the background on either the appraiser or the appraised. After the role-plays, the instructor initiates a discussion with questions that might include: "What did the two individuals do to facilitate the discussion of performance? To hinder the discussion?" and "What could the two of them have done differently to help the discussion?" This exercise takes from 40 to 60 minutes and can be done with a group of any size.

Desert (and NASA Moon and Sub-Arctic) Survival. In another exercise, intended to teach the value of group versus individual decision-making and the dynamics of small-group behavior, the class reads an account of a crash landing in the region specified by the exercise (desert, moon, or sub-Arctic). Individuals consider a list of 15 items and rank them in order of their importance to their survival. Then the group is split into small groups of five to nine people to develop consensus lists of the rank-ordered items. The entire group then compares their individual and group rankings with the rankings of a professional group expert in survival in that area. In the vast majority of cases, regardless of the degree of "expertise" of any individual, the group decisions turn out to be better than the individual scores. This exercise is usually a significant learning experience, especially for those who tend to make decisions on their own. We've seen variations on this approach depending on instructor needs and interests. For example, one instructor grouped the students *after* they did their initial individual ranking in order to put certain kinds of people together and to demonstrate over confidence in team decision-making.

House of Cards. In this exercise, a number of groups of from five to ten people are assigned the task of building a structure out of cards. Playing cards or old-style computer cards or any stiff card stock will work. Instructors can select how long they have to complete their structure. One member from each team serves on a review board that evaluates the structures at the end of the exercise. The winning group will be the one with the largest value where revenue equals the board-appraised value of the building times the number of square inches of floor space it covers. The main purposes of this exercise are to explore the effects of objectives, planning, and organization on group production and output, and to examine different factors that may affect profitability in a production company. Possible discussion questions here include: "What was your primary objective in this task?" "Did your group members attempt to influence the real estate board either before or during the appraisal?" "What factors in your group's efforts do you think account for its success or failure in this task?" "How did your group's division of labor and coordination of efforts affect your group's performance?" Any number of groups may participate in this exercise, which can be done in less than an hour.

Star power. This game explores the affects of the uneven distribution of power in an organization or system. Participants are randomly divided into three equal groups and then given chips they can trade with other participants. As the trading progresses, it becomes apparent that the rich are getting richer and the poor are getting poorer. Finally, the rich are allowed to make the rules for the game and in so doing generally create a major social upheaval. The game then becomes the foundation for discussion about power and its distribution in society, in organizations, and in communities and families.

Capsim. Capsim is a computer-supported international management simulation that asks teams of players to make business decisions about manufacturing, finance, personnel management, marketing, and distribution. The game is managed on the Web so that local instructors don't have to worry about running the computers or the back office operations. The scope of the game is international and takes into account exchange rates and differences in doing business in various countries. Students' teams are organized into industries and compete against each other as they make several rounds of decisions and receive results in the form of income statements, balance sheets, and market surveys. Capsim offers a number of add-on modules that emphasize other aspects of managing a business according to an instructor's particular needs.

Helium Pole. This is a fun exercise that points out the difficulty of reaching simple goals with engaged, interested team members. A team of 10 or more players is asked to divide into two groups and face each other with index fingers extended toward the opposite line of players. The instructor then gives two instructions: every player must be touching the pole at all times with their index finger, and your task is to lay the pole on the ground as a team. When the instructor lays the lightweight tent pole on the interlacing (zippered) index fingers, it magically begins to rise! Players are shocked, laughing, shouting, and struggling to understand what's happening. It seems so simple, yet the tiniest upward pressure from 10 different people in their attempts to maintain contact with the pole collectively propels the pole upward, faster and faster.

As can be seen from these examples, experiential exercises cannot recreate exactly the experience of the workaday world. They do provide stimulating and powerful situations, however, which can simulate experience in the classroom to the advantage of the students' learning.

Preparing for experiential methods

The first thing in preparing to conduct an experiential exercise is to get the materials well in advance. You should not only order them early, but also allow enough time to work through them and to become thoroughly familiar with them yourself. This process will take longer than it will for the students, at least the first time, because of the need to be familiar with as many questions and alternative problems and scenarios as possible. Being or appearing to be unfamiliar with the exercise or its outcome is deadly to its success, because the students will lose confidence in the facilitator, withdraw their own involvement, and distance themselves from the learning potential in the situation. If at all possible, stage a run-through with friends, colleagues, and/or assistants. This rehearsal can be an enjoyable event, particularly if the exercise has some self-assessment aspects so the colleagues or teaching assistants can learn from it even if it doesn't go perfectly. A rule of thumb: It's better to overestimate the time needed for ordering, study, and practicing than to be hurried and lack confidence when the real session begins.

Check out the facilities. Each exercise has its own set of needs for space and equipment. Although most can be adapted to a variety of settings, walk through the facilities, check places for charts and overheads for the large group sessions, examine the space for breakout sessions and administrative setup. This preview is best done after receiving the materials and studying them enough to get a good feel for the sequencing of the exercise and how it works in real time. In the popular "Starpower" exercise, for instance, you will needs places for three groups to meet. Although the game specifies groups no larger than 30, we have purchased two sets and run a group of more than 50 with good success. The game was flexible, but finding the right room(s) in our building to handle three, 18-person groups with space for negotiating and places to hang the instruction charts, etc., took some planning, wandering, and conferring with building managers.

Don't underestimate the importance of practicing the introduction to the game, how it will be run, and how it will be debriefed. This mental preview will help in anticipating any awkward positioning of the basic elements of the exercise. This same advice applies to computer simulations. Where will the machines be? Where will the results come out? How will the groups pick up, analyze, and resubmit decision data? What happens if the machine goes down?

Solicit help. Well-staffed exercises can be a pleasure; understaffed exercises can be a madhouse full of frustration for instructors and participants alike. In planning the exercise, imagine what would make the experience administratively seamless for the participants. That is, how can instructions, guidance, calculations, data, results, or whatever the game calls be disseminated in a smooth and uninterrupted fashion? In administering "Global Markets," for instance, to 240 first-year MBA students, we planned that we would need 4 instructors for the introductions in 4 different section rooms, 2 people to distribute the new capital infusions to each team's mailbox between each round, 4 people to collect and check the team scores as they were handed in at the end of the exercise, and another person to do the calculations on the scores while the first 4 instructors were conducting the debriefing. We learned in the first offering that we could consolidate some activities and run some others in parallel. We got more efficient the next time around with better advance preparation and reduced the number of assistants needed. The first time, though, the extra people really paid off by helping the participants feel that everything was under control and proceeding as planned. (We also learned that involving other instructor helped them to see our objectives and learn more about the benefits of the exercise than was likely if they had only observed the exercise from afar.

Experience the exercise. Experiencing a game from the participant's point of view can really uncover the kinds of questions and problems that will occur in any experiential exercise. The experience will help an instructor be more empathic about the participants' situations and reactions and help in answering their questions with confidence and conviction.

Conducting experiential methods

Conducting an exercise has at least three parts, the introduction, the exercise itself, and the debrief. It may be tempting to get started by simply giving students advance reading on the exercise, but we advise caution here. Simply handing out a manual may or may not be the best way to introduce the students to the exercise. Some manuals are more confusing than helpful. We have colleagues who, in some instances, have rewritten manuals or handed out supplements to the manuals to help students work through the specifics of a simulation or game. Advance reading has the advantage of saving time in the introduction session, but it robs the instructor of control over students' first impressions of the exercise. If possible, introduce the exercise within the first class, to create student enthusiasm and avoid confusion.

Remember also the Audial-Visual-Kinesthetic triangle of communication from neurolinguistic programming (NLP) theory that we introduced earlier. People have preferred modes or channels of giving and receiving information, some emphasize the sound channel, others the visual, and others the kinesthetic or emotional. A good introduction, then, will include words, visual aids, and examples or stories to communicate each major point.

Once the exercise is under way, instructors should circulate through the groups to help answer questions that arise or resolve conflicts and dilemmas. Be available. Practice "MBWA" (management by walking around) during the exercise. Visit the small-group meetings. Observe the trading sessions or whatever the main activity is. A demonstrated commitment to the exercise will influence the students' reactions to it and enhance an instructor's chances of being in tune with and able to understand the events of the exercise.

Most exercises involve individual work, small-group work, large-group work, faculty interventions, and off-line breaks. Manage the transitions from one aspect of a game to another carefully. Make certain participants know what's happening next and how they should move from the present section of the exercise to the next section. Again, maps, charts, and other visual aids along with anecdotes and stories and the usual verbal instructions, help clarify the boundaries and transitions. Post charts that show the overall flow of the exercise, with times, places, and participants, conspicuously to help those who either forgot, didn't get it during the introduction, or simply want to make their way from point to point more quickly and efficiently.

Debriefings

The debriefing is absolutely critical to the learning success of experiential methods. In some ways, the game is nothing more than a data generating device, a feeder, to the debriefing. Spend as much time anticipating the debrief as planning the administration of the exercise. Questions should be carefully thought out and phrased in advance. Think about those questions and collect likely answers from listening to various groups during the exercise. Use such real-time insights to guide the discussion toward clarifying the activities and learning. Some possible questions include, "What did you learn from this exercise?" "What were the main themes of this exercise?" "Describe how your team worked together," "What would you do differently if you could do this over again and why?" "What connections does this exercise have to business situations?" "How were you able to use concepts we've used in the course previously?" "What was frustrating to you in this exercise and what can you learn from that?" "What lessons or principles should we takeaway from this exercise?"

Ethics of experiential methods

There are some ethical issues connected with the use of experiential methods. Because they tend to involve people in an intense and often personal way, some instructors feel obliged to announce a disclaimer at the beginning saying that participation is voluntary. Personally, we believe that these exercises are no more optional than any other class, case, or assignment *unless* they explicitly involve revealing personal data that a person does not want to divulge. Attending case discussions or discussion classes in which someone might be embarrassed by what he or she does is not optional. People sometimes embarrass themselves in experiential exercises just as they do in other educational settings. Embarrassing or not, people do what they do. In this regard, experiential exercises are no different from other teaching techniques. The ethical question is whether or not objective learning (learning about things other than the self) is mandatory whereas subjective learning (learning about the self) is optional. Of course, participants always retain the right to vote with their feet on any experience and simply leave.

Sometimes, to avoid revealing themselves, participants try to assume a role in an exercise. That is, they try to act the part of the devil's advocate (always taking the contrary view), their boss, the obstreperous colleague, their mother-in-law, or some other imagined personality suggested by the exercise. Sometimes this is a signal that they are uncomfortable being themselves in the situation. We encourage people to avoid playing roles and to be themselves. Part of becoming an effective manager (and an effective teacher), is to develop the courage and confidence to be yourself and then to accept responsibility for self and finally to learn to deal with others as they are.

Experiential methods provide an excellent avenue for developing this courage and practice in dealing with people, but only if people work at being authentic, during the exercise.

Conclusion

Experiential methods are powerful teaching tools. They engage the participants emotionally as well as intellectually. Although they take considerable time on the front end, such exercises can create learning that is more deeply seated and retained longer than with other methods. Experiential methods may not be the best way of explaining theory or concept, but they are often the best way of demonstrating them. Exercises exist or can be created for virtually any aspect of management or education. Experimenting with and experiencing a variety of experiential methods will add another andragogical tool to your teaching skills portfolio.

Further reading

Brooks-Harris, Jeff E., and Susan R. Stock-Ward, *Workshops: Designing and Facilitating Experiential Learning*, Thousand Oaks, CA: Sage Publications, 1999.

Coleman, James S., "Differences Between Experiential and Classroom Learning," in *Experiential Learning: Rationale, Characteristics, and Assessment*, San Francisco: Jossey-Bass, 1976.

Hall, Douglas T., et al., *Experiences in Management and Organizational Behavior.* Chicago: St. Clair Press, 1975.

Keeton, M. T., *Defining and Assuring Quality in Experiential Learning*, San Francisco: Jossey-Bass, 1980.

Kolb, David A., *Experiential Learning: Experience as the Source of Learning and Development*, Englewood Cliffs, NJ: Prentice-Hall, Inc., 1984.

Polanyi, Michael, *Personal Knowledge*, Chicago: University of Chicago Press, 1962.

14 | *Enhancing the conversation: audiovisual tools and techniques*

JAMES G. S. CLAWSON

A picture is worth a thousand words.

Regardless of the method of instruction a person chooses, audiovisual (AV) tools can significantly enhance the impact of that method. Learning to use AV tools effectively can take time, but the long-term gains in learning for students are worth the early investments. Visual aids are especially important for the visual learners who like to see what they're learning, but even for others, the extra reinforcement of a visual image can make the difference between a student's vague awareness and clear memory of a concept. For visual learners, a picture is worth a thousand words. Similarly, audial aids can enhance learning for word-oriented students. Indeed, some evidence suggests that certain kinds of music can prepare the mind to learn at phenomenal rates regardless of its orientation.[1] Whatever an instructor's preferred and dominant instructional style, proficiency with a variety of AV tools can increase his or her teaching effectiveness.

Audiovisual tools can include everything seen and heard in the classroom, from how an instructor dresses and gestures, to the arrangement of the room, to the chalkboard, flip charts, props, slide-and-tape programs, tape recordings, overhead projectors, films and videos, and computer projections.

Instructor dress and gestures

An instructor is an AV tool. Students see and hear an instructor and what they see and hear will either add to or detract from the learning they take away. A class focusing on production-floor dynamics conducted by an instructor wearing, for example, suspenders and a

---

[1] See, Sheila Ostrander and Lynn Schroeder with Nancy Ostrander, *Superlearning* (New York: Dell, 1979).

228

pin-striped suit sends a mixed message to the audience, and, subtly, undermines the credibility of the session. An instructor in corduroys and topsiders somehow doesn't fit a class on Wall Street investment techniques in the students' minds. Okay! We clearly agree that you can't tell a book by its cover, and that substance is more important than style. But we also argue that effective learning is a function of everything that happens in the classroom, and if several features of that learning environment are out of alignment, the learning is diminished.

Take, for instance, bringing a coffee cup into the room. Many faculty do so; some students have picked up the habit by watching their instructors and concluding that somehow it is a part of the professorial role, something that instructors do, and that therefore they can, too. Focus on that chain of influence for a moment. What signal does it send to students? The message, at the least, is that the instructor is less than fully focused on the class or the material, because his or her own thirst, comfort, or need for wakefulness is taking up some mental and physical energy. Furthermore, what is the effect on the class's attention when the cup gets knocked over or coffee sloshes out during class as it often does? As students emulate such behavior, many people in the room soon will be sipping, spilling, cleaning up, apologizing, and in the process be distracted from the learning events in the room.

Instructors have other habits that can distract the students. We know of an energetic and respected instructor who had two unusual and somewhat distracting gestures: As he talked vigorously, little flecks of foam would collect around the corners of his mouth, so he would form his index and middle fingers into a V and wipe both corners at the same time. Then, when he paused for a moment, he would place the palm of his right hand on the back of his head, mostly bald, and wipe slowly up over the top and down across his face, removing, we guessed, the perspiration from his head and face in one fell swoop. Now, he was a great instructor, but many students became so aware of these two gestures that they used to make pools on how many minutes into the class he would do each. All of which detracted from his excellent messages. So, one might ask, "What are my personal tics? Have I filmed myself in class lately to identify them? Do I have a sense of when and why I do them? Can I manage them so their influence on the concentration of the students is minimized?"

By the same token, instructors who use AV techniques effectively can enormously enhance learning. Behavioral cues about when to start class, for example. One of my mentors at Harvard had a set routine, almost like a golf pre-swing routine, where he'd walk into class, stand behind the pit table, remove his jacket, hang it up, unbutton his sleeves, roll them up, open his case folder, lay out several yellow sheets of paper, and by then, the class "knew" that it was time to go to work and had settled down. And he never had to say a word!

The seamless introduction of video clips, PowerPoint slides, or over-head transparencies can also have a big impact. Too often though instructors are not polished in these transitions and either project the overhead on the ceiling or out of focus or have the video clip mis-cued so the transition from discussion to audiovisual is clumsy and distracting. Well done, these enhancements can really accelerate learning.

In short, when instructors walk in the room, they are immediately a mass of visual cues and suggestions. If those cues are carefully managed, they can do much to increase the learning that ensues.

Arrangement of the room

In earlier chapters, we have touched on the way in which the physical setting can add or detract from the learning environment. Indeed, the arrangement of the room in which one teaches is perhaps the most pervasive visual cue in the learning setting. Chairs set in rows like an elementary school classroom make it difficult to focus on or talk with anyone other than the instructor up front. For that reason, most discussion and case method classes are arranged in a horseshoe pattern, often on sloped, amphitheater-style floors. That setup allows the instructor to be in the midst of the students, allows them to talk to each other while still being able to see things on chalkboards or flip charts at the front of the room.

Using the chalkboard

Most instructors have a chalkboard in the room, and many use it with-out giving much thought as to how. We've gone into some colleagues' classrooms after classes were finished and looked at the boards and been shocked: we couldn't read *any* of the words written on some, couldn't see *any* connection between various portions of the boards in others, and found virtually nothing on the boards at all in still others. We might not have been surprised or confused if we had sat through each of the classes in question, but in those rooms, the utility of the chalkboard as a major visual opportunity was lost. The chalkboard provides a chance to reinforce ideas, to summarize, to anticipate, to structure, and to cement new learning. Too often that chance is squandered. Ideally, the chalkboards should provide a solid visual summary of the concepts and discussion held during the class. Students at the end of the class should be able to look at the chalkboards and "see" the progression of the class laid out before them.

There is no one best way of using the chalkboard, but there are some basic principles to consider. First, learn to write legibly. If it's important enough to be put it on the board, it's important enough to have people be able to read it.

A second way to improve your use of chalkboards is to make tentative plans for them before class. At our school, we have three main vertically movable boards at the front of the room and one or two smaller boards on the sides of the room near the front. We often make paper diagram mockups of that layout before class and, imagining how the discussion will progress, try to allocate space for each segment of the discussion to various portions of the board layout; we often delineate ideas for board use in the teaching notes we write for cases. That kind of planning eliminates the all-too-often-observed embarrassed fumbling over the boards as an instructor tries to make one concept visible to the class without covering up another or having to erase because there wasn't enough space left to record the next key point. This may seem like a trivial issue, but the middle of class is not the time to be grappling with the switches or arrangement of the boards or having to take time to erase. Treating board use as an afterthought can cause disruptions in the class and its learning.

On the other hand, if boards are so tightly laid out and structured that they dictate the structure of the class, the students can also be put off. Writing "bin titles" on the top of several columns on the boards before class can unduly constrain students' thinking and creativity, and can stifle an instructor's ability really to hear the students and focus on their learning. Instead the class becomes an exercise in filling in the instructor's blanks rather than discovering new things. Naturally, we suggest a balanced approach: careful thought on the ideal chalkboard end result and lots of flexibility in the board plan to allow for deviations in the discussion.

The objective of balanced board use is for students to be able to see a pattern of logical analysis unfolding as the discussion carries on during the course of the class, see clear connections between major points and follow transitions from one part of the discussion to another, and to see key arguments that arise in the discussion.

In addition to the ongoing clarification of the discussion that it can convey, good board work can also provide a powerful visual summary at the end of class. This visual picture makes an excellent basis for summary comments by instructor or students. In the problem-first case method structure mentioned in Chapter 9, for example, and in a situation where there are three boards available, it works well to write the problems on the foremost board, raise it, work through the analysis on the second board, raise it, and then complete the class with a summary of the action alternatives on the last board. Then, when class is over, a student can refer to the boards and point out how the analysis on the second board addressed the problems shown at the top on the first board and led into the action plans summarized on the third board at the bottom. Finally, if general principles or conclusions reached during the class have been collected on the side board, the class summary can end with a quick review of the points listed there.

Another key benefit is that the chalkboards can help students see and think more deeply about their own arguments, to provide a "mirror" to their comments. If a student's line of reasoning is written on the chalkboard and the class looks at it, they may begin to see weaknesses and points of discussion more readily than if the words were just left on the air. It is important, therefore, to write the same words that students use. If an instructor edits what students have said or changes the words they used, they often begin to feel as though words are being putting into their mouths. Sometimes, even when the exact words a student spoke are put on the board, a student will feel misquoted. If the instructor has been accurate, the rest of the class will often confirm what was recorded if the speaker, realizing the weaknesses in his or her argument, says something like, "Wait a minute! I didn't say that!" Then the discussion can continue as the speaker and the rest of the class sort out what was really meant.

Perhaps unfortunately, the key instrument for using a chalkboard is chalk. It's messy. It gets all over your clothing, and it often breaks or squeaks at the wrong time. When instructors turn around to write on the board and hear chuckles because there is a chalk line across their bottoms from leaning up against the chalk tray, or when they wipe their face and get chalk dust all over, or when they erase a board and begin coughing from the dust (is "white lung disease" an occupational hazard for instructors?), the class is diverted from the primary learning task at hand. These problems can be diminished by using dustless chalk (no small task to acquire in our experience).

To make a powerful visual impression, use colored chalk to highlight and draw attention to certain points or connections. In our experience, Omega and Myocolor colored chalks are much more colorful, durable, and dustless than Crayola, the usual supplier. If reds, yellows, and oranges are used to highlight key points along the way, the final visual summary of the class as recorded on the boards will reinforce the learning for the students.

Overhead projectors

After chalkboards, overhead projectors are probably the most widely used AV tool. Depending on your skill in using them, overhead projectors can be an effective and transparent tool that enhances learning or a source of confusion and irritation that inhibits learning. As with the other AV tools, the goal is to make the tool relatively transparent except for the information that it adds to the learning environment. If the tool becomes obvious and disconnected from the information it was supposed to bring, it becomes a distraction and then a hindrance to classroom goals. Overhead projectors have great potential for both outcomes.

Instructors who do not learn, in advance, where the switches are, how to focus the machine, how their slides appear on the screen to various parts of the room, and any other detail associated with that particular unit (like where the extra bulb is stored) are inviting a breakdown in classroom concentration. Most of the problems can be avoided by simply going to the classroom early. Make sure there is a side tray or table to place transparencies on. The space should be big enough for both the used and unused transparencies. Make sure there's an extra bulb in the projector and practice changing it. Find the "on" switch. Practice focusing the transparencies. Find out where the machine has to be to project the size and clarity of information that is needed for people in the back to see clearly. Check to make sure that this location doesn't block the participation of some students. Learn where the margins of projection are and perhaps mark them with a water-soluble pen on the projector's surface. This is important; we have probably all watched instructors talk for 10 minutes without realizing that the part of the transparency they were referring to was out of the projection window! What good is an AV tool if it doesn't show students what it was intended to show? Actually, it is worse than no good; it becomes a major distraction from the learning process.

Some instructors like to cover part of a transparency with a sheet of paper while they talk. The paper creates on the projection window an opaque cover which they then slide down to reveal the next item, and the next, and so on. Most audience members we've talked with find this practice very irritating. We even know of one *Fortune* 10 company chairman in a similar situation who demanded that the speaker remove the cover sheet; it was an infuriating child's game for him, and he wanted to be able to read as fast as he could without playing some guessing game as to what the next point was. Our recommendation is to put on each transparency only what people are intended to see at one time. If a list is being built, make a new transparency for each new addition. Put each one up and let people look at it without playing with covering sheets.

Flip charts

Flip charts are a commonly available visual tool. They are a mixed bag of advantages and disadvantages, however. Most students find flip charts a comfortable medium since they are just an enlarged version of the paper and pen that everyone uses. The contrast between the white background and colored marking pens also makes it easier for many people to read flip charts than chalkboards.

In contrast to the chalkboard, flip charts are more permanent. This means the pages written in class can be saved for analysis or summarizing after class, and for later transcription and distribution to students. This is particularly useful when working with problem-solving groups or in team building sessions with people from different working groups (for example, a session designed to improve relations between marketing and manufacturing).

On the other hand, flip charts can be frustrating. They are of a standard size, much smaller than the usual chalkboard, which limits what can be displayed to the students at one time.

If there is a need to refer to what has gone on earlier in the class, or a desire to present a visual summary of the class, flip charts just don't work very well. A common way of dealing with the need to refer to what has been done earlier in the class is to tear off each sheet and tape or pin it to the wall for all to see. That activity, in itself, can be distracting to students. First, the instructor must tear the sheet cleanly without ripping it in half. We have seen this disrupt the thinking of a roomful of students; everyone focuses on the instructor and how he or she is going to recreate this important chart that now exists partly in one hand and partly still affixed to the flip chart pad.

Even with practice at getting the right angle and tug to tear off the sheet cleanly, there is still the time it takes to cut tape and hang the sheet on the wall. Each page that has to be torn off and taped up is a disruption to the flow of the class. If you must post flip chart paper, you can shorten the process by precutting tape before class and by having a student designated in advance to come up, get the sheet, and tape it up. Of course, this interrupts that student's ability to stick with the class. Nevertheless, flip charts used in this latter way function almost like dynamic chalkboards. Handled properly, flip chart sheets can be used effectively to paint a gradually unfolding picture that is portrayed like a mural around the room.

So, flip charts are a mixed blessing. Be specific about what is needed regarding them: extra pads, extra easels – sturdy ones – extra marking pens of specific colors, and the arrangement of the pads, especially if they are used in conjunction with an overhead screen or stationary chalkboard. Plan on checking to make sure that these instructions have been followed; leave plenty of time to ask and get additional materials if things aren't right.

Props

Props can help bring a class alive. For instance, discussing the new product development policies of the Plus Development Corporation, a maker of hard disk drives for personal computers, can be a confusing experience for those not familiar with the industry. Get and bring a copy of the company's first major product, the HardCard (a 20-megabyte hard disk mounted on an expansion board that simply plugs into a personal computer expansion slot), on hand and pass it around, and the class suddenly becomes much more engaging to the students. We know one group of faculty that regularly brings Stihl chain saws to class and cuts old chairs in half as a way of focusing student attention on the products and issues in an analysis of Stihl's position in the chain saw industry.

Well-chosen props can set a supportive tone for a class. In marketing, finance, organizational behavior, and production, numerous props could be used to good advantage. We know one professor who brings two telephones to a certain organizational behavior class because he knows that someone will suggest that a particularly key conversation take place by phone. Rather than having the student talk about the conversation, he hands the student one of the phones and they actually *have* the conversation. He turns his back on the student, picks up the receiver and says, "Hello?" Immediately the realization that you cannot use body language and facial expressions as a means of communication over the phone registers with the student. Then, everyone in the room recognizes that talking about a key persuading conversation and finding the right words to implement that conversation are two very different things. Without the prop, these two significant insights are lost.

Props can be used in most classes. They provide a sense of reality, that the situation being discussed in the classroom is not just an abstract one, but one that reflects real people, real products, and real events. In cost accounting, for instance, pass around a sub-assembly so students can get a feel for the number and variety of parts and the time to assemble them. In discussing financial instruments, bring copies of the instrument in question. In quality control, bring a box of product (like computer chips) and take samples from the box to give students a visual view of what a 2 percent failure rate looks like. And so on. Thinking about how to enliven a class with a relevant prop can produce new insights into how to introduce the case or subject and how to get students to engage in it more readily and powerfully.

Slide-and-audiotape programs

These programs are useful albeit less attractive now in the age of first-class video cameras, videotapes, and DVDs. Slides, pictures, charts, and photos set to a narrative or to music to tell a story or to make a point is an entertaining and memorable teaching technique. I used this technique to create an audiovisual companion to the case, "The Life and Career of a Chief Executive Officer." I took my 35-mm camera and close-up lens to the retired executive's house and photographed selections out of his lifelong collection of clippings and photos. Setting these shots to the man's favorite music using a Wollensak slide-tape synchronizer was a simple but rewarding task. The result was a teaching package that almost invariably has brought classes to tears and deep personal insight for over a decade.

A word of caution on music, however. The copyright laws for use of films and commercial music are strict and have been increasingly enforced. On one project, it took two years to track down and secure permissions for a two-minute segment of music. We had to get written permission from the record producer, the artist, the musicians' guild that supplied the backup, and a parent company that had bought rights to the music. Under guidelines issued by ASCAP, however, clips and segments can be used for educational, non-profit purposes in limited circumstances. Write to ASCAP, the American Society of Composers, Authors, and Publishers at One Lincoln Plaza, New York City, New York 10023 USA (telephone [212] 595-3050) for further information on current policies.

Tape recordings

Audio recordings alone can also be powerful tools in the classroom. We have used recordings of characters in a case, of famous speakers, and of previous class discussions of a topic to add variety, flavor, and emphasis in a teaching session. In connection with "The Life and Career of a Chief Executive Officer," for instance, it is one thing to read the wife's comment, "Sometimes I don't think he even *sees* my needs"; it is quite another to hear the words in her own tender, concerned, thoughtful, and a bit tremulous voice. We know of a colleague who has had one class record a conversation taken directly out of a case and then used that recorded reading in the next iteration of the class. Although it was not the real characters' voices, the effect was similarly dramatic and compelling.

Films and video

Like cases, film and video can provide rich data for class debriefing and discussion. Indeed, many cases nowadays are accompanied by videos. Some may be simply talking-head versions of the protagonist explaining what happened; others are more elaborate tours of facilities and interviews with various key people that add substantially to the data available to the students. It is even increasingly popular to use a film or video as the basic material for a class without accompanying material.

Films and videotapes are sometimes criticized in professorial ranks as entertainment, a waste of time, and a substitute for substance. While some instructors may have overused films in the classroom, don't throw the baby out with the bath water! Many films are able to make certain points or convey certain concepts much more powerfully than reading or listening to lectures. Films can also provide variety in the classroom, reinforce certain principles, convey the personalities of people, and heighten student involvement in a topic. For instance, there is a scene in the film *Shogun* in which the marooned English pilot, Blackthorne, is negotiating with his Japanese war-lord host about whether or not his teachers should be killed if he doesn't learn Japanese fast enough. Blackthorne realizes that his English assumptions about how to persuade his host are useless, and he threatens to commit suicide by *hara-kiri* unless the war-lord relents on his threat to behead the villagers assigned to teach him. The scene portrays powerfully the importance of exchange in negotiations and the importance of understanding what others value in the currencies of exchange.[2]

In a course module on managing change, we have often used the films *Tunes of Glory* and *Brubaker*. The former is historical fiction, and the latter is a true story. The emotion and realism that these films can bring to a discussion of what organizational culture is or how to manage change in an organization far exceeds what can be elicited from students reading a text. When students engage a phenomenon either by work experience or by approximations of it in film, they have more than words and imagination to work with, they have images, sounds, and emotional involvement that bring the discussion alive.

Complete films, or tapes, or short clips, can be shown in advance of the class or in the class itself. Using *Brubaker*, for example, we show only part of the film the night before class, stopping it at a point when the protagonist must make a major decision about how to proceed. The next day in class, we talk about what the students have seen, what they would do, and why. Then, we show the rest of the film, in segments, stopping periodically to discuss what has happened and what the students see as relevant to managing change in a culture-rich organization. Following the film, we talk about how the students'

---

[2] See Allan Cohen and David Bradford, *Influence without Authority* (New York: John Wiley and Sons, 1991) for more information about exchange-based management.

plans varied from the protagonist's and what the underlying principles of managing change might be.[3]

As with experiential methods and action learning, the debriefing session of a class revolving around a film or video is very important. Sufficient time needs to be scheduled to work through the key issues and to allow students to examine, formulate, and present their views of the situation. This scheduling, the choice of materials, and the way the assignment is structured are the main areas where the instructor makes a big difference in the learning effectiveness of films and videos used in the classroom.

One caveat. Many commercially available instructional films present particular techniques and approaches as portrayed by actors. When we have used these commercially produced, somewhat glossy instructional films that employ actors to portray a situation, they often come across to the students as unbelievable. They are too slick, too polished, and too clearly scripted. Less technically polished videos of real managers doing what they do have had a bigger impact on the students we have worked with.

This implies that we should feel free to make our own tapes, a challenging and rewarding activity. With the equipment reasonably available today, it is easy to make good quality videotapes of meetings, conversations, plant tours, and any number of topics in business or other fields with little investment and high promise of educational payback. We have taped company visits for a course on career management, plant tours for a case on manufacturing policy, interviews for epilogs to cases, and executive meetings considering fundamental organizational questions. Although our tapes are not "professional," they serve nicely in the classroom and add realism to our discussions. When making tapes, remember that it is easy to move the camera too much and to switch from one topic to another too quickly. Good lighting is critical as are backup systems and power supplies.

Computer projections

Modern classrooms are increasingly using machines that will project computer displays on large screens. Projectors that are mounted on the

---

[3] See "Brubaker: A Guide for Viewing, Understanding, and Applying the Film," UVA-OB-354, and its accompanying teaching note for more information on this particular film.

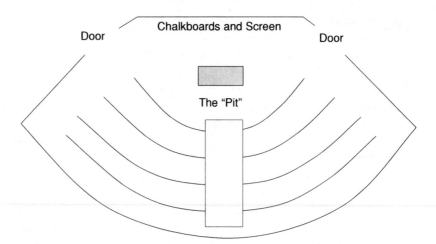

Figure 14.1 Classroom shape

ceiling (and are therefore out of the way) and have high resolution are becoming increasingly powerful and affordable. With the presentation feature of many software programs, one can prepare a series of "slides" or charts ahead of time and then simply project them in class as desired with very little attention to the computer keyboard.

One excellent pedagogical feature of these systems is that an entire class can prepare an analysis or presentation on disk. Then, in class, the instructor can call on different people to come down to the host computer or, if the classrooms are wired sufficiently, hook into the network from their desks and display their results and analysis.

A dilemma with this kind of technology is how to meld it smoothly with other AV aids such as the chalkboard. At our school, for instance, a large wall-size screen is mounted behind the three chalkboards. This is a space saving and very workable system, but it means that use of the screen eliminates the use of the chalkboards and vice versa. A better arrangement would be to have a dedicated space for projections, including overhead projections that could be left showing while the instructor writes or makes notes on the chalkboard. If the classroom were shaped like a truncated fan as shown in Figure 14.1, then this arrangement would be feasible, but the students on the side nearest the screen would be a bit close to the screen. This is, in fact, the design incorporated into our new building. There is a design tradeoff here between central positioning for all to see and availability of multiple media. Unfortunately, most classrooms are square, have lots of windows (the light from which washes out the projections), have the chairs arranged in elementary school fashion, and are designed for using one medium at a time.

Another newly emerging opportunity comes from CD-ROM technology. We have now developed compact disks that contain video clips from several sources including field-based case research. Using these disks we can show video clips in an order of our choosing through computer based hookups to a ceiling-mounted projection unit. This approach allows us to avoid the fast forwarding and rewinding often necessary in using many video clips and old-style VHS tape cassettes.

Conclusion

Audiovisual tools provide wonderful options for the classroom. They help people with different learning modes grasp and retain the content of the class. Managed well, they can be seamlessly and transparently incorporated in the classroom. Managed poorly, they can become major distractions and hindrances to effective learning. We encourage new and old instructors to practice with and use the various tools outlined here to add variety, impact, and power to their teaching.

Further reading

Champoux, Joseph E., *Using Film to Visualize Principles and Practices of Management*, Cincinnati: Southwestern College Publishing, 2001.

Gelb, Michael, *Present Yourself!* Torrance, CA: Jalmar Press, 1988.

Marx, Robert, Todd Jick, and Peter Frost, *Management Live!* Englewood Cliffs, NJ: Prentice-Hall, 1991.

Meisner, Sanford, and Dennis Longwell, *On Acting*, New York: Vintage Books, 1987.

Stanislavski, Constantin, *An Actor Prepares*, New York: Routledge/Theatre Arts Books, 1964.

Timpson, William M. and Suzanne Burgoyne, *Teaching and Performing: Ideas for Energizing Your Classes*, 2nd edn, Madison, WI: Artwood Publishing, 2002.

Vance, Charles M., *Mastering Management Education*, Newbury Park, CA: Sage Publications, 1993.

15 | *Executive education: contributing to organizational competitive advantage*

MARK E. HASKINS AND
JAMES G. S. CLAWSON

I am not young enough to know everything.
– Oscar Wilde

At the dawn of the twenty-first century, Conger and Xin (2000, p. 73) opined that companies should consider the possibility that, "Executive education has the potential to become a truly strategic tool [and it] has the potential to play an even greater role as an essential lever to facilitate strategic transitions." In an even more provocative sense, Watling et al. (2003, p. 225) noted that employee learning "is an increasingly recognized source of competitive advantage" for companies that seek to excel. For those and other reasons, corporate demand for executive education is large and growing. General Electric is often posited as a prototype company committed to education, spending $1 billion annually on training and education (Craven, 2004). On an individual basis, one recent survey found that executives spend, on average, about six days a year in some sort of executive education program and those surveyed asserted that that was "too little" (Farris et al., 2003). And hear this: "Executives do not believe their people have the skills needed to compete effectively" (Cheese, 2003, p. 12). To address the ever-growing corporate demand for executive education, "the number and quality of non-degree executive education providers has grown dramatically in recent years [to include] business schools, private and public companies, corporate universities, trade associations, foundations, consulting firms, and freelance educators" (Lippert, 2001, p. 6). Chances are, if you are (or will soon be) a university business school professor or a corporate trainer, you will have the opportunity to participate in designing, developing, and/or delivering an executive education program.

In this chapter, we explore some of the challenges, nuances, and excitement offered those who teach in executive education programs. By "executive education (EE)" we limit our discussion to any

242

non-degree granting learning experience designed for employed adults and delivered, at least in part, by business school faculty and/or corporate training professionals.

A variety of types

Executive education programs are varied along many dimensions. Some programs may last only a half-day, others several months, and others everything in between. Programs may be centered around a very specialized topic or they may be broadly focused on general management issues and skills. Some programs are targeted to a very narrowly defined target market (e.g., engineers) while others are open to managers from any number of functional jobs or backgrounds. Participants in an EE program may all be from one sponsoring company or the program may be open to managers from any company. For some company-sponsored programs, the focus is consciously on learning materials and examples not rooted in the company itself, while others exclusively embrace their own circumstances, while still others employ a blended focus. Some programs are hosted by a university, other programs are delivered at a company's facilities, while others are delivered at a hotel or conference center. Many programs use only university business school faculty, while others use only company personnel, while others use faculty, consultants, and executives as instructors. And, as you might expect, some programs are very expensive while others are not. All told, the various combinations and permutations of these features, along with even additional ones, constitute the spectrum of EE possibilities currently in the marketplace and potentially available to instructors interested in such opportunities. The next few sections of this chapter expand on some of these dimensions in greater detail, affording you the chance to envision where and how you might plug into EE as a part of your long-term professional development agenda.

Open enrollment versus single-company programs

Open enrollment (OE) programs are those that include participants from numerous companies. Those programs are usually created around a theme that is deemed marketable and a cadre of instructors who are knowledgeable in the subject area(s). Such programs often carry titles such as Power and Leadership, Finance for Non-financial Managers, Service Excellence, and Managing Critical Resources. In those programs, a team of instructors designs a program according to their interests and expertise and perceptions of what will be most appealing to an intended target audience of executives. With the anticipation that the attendees are likely to represent a cross-section of organizations, and perhaps even functions, instructors select materials that portray service-sector as well as manufacturing settings, domestic as well as international settings, and that provide multiple levels of potential learning.

This latter point is key for three reasons. First, registrants for an OE program are not generally screened in terms of admissions criteria, so it is likely that attendees represent a spectrum of skills and experiences that necessitates the choosing of materials that provide learning opportunities for all in attendance. Second, the fact that attendees come from a variety of organizations presents the opportunity for instructors to acquaint themselves with those organizations a day or two before the program starts and to then link in-class discussions and examples to some of those organizations. Finally, OE program instructors should facilitate classroom discussions that leverage the diversity of organizations represented so that learning takes place through the cross-conversations among the participants themselves.

Single-company (SC) programs are just as the name suggests – one company engages someone to design and deliver a program that will be populated by only executives from that sponsoring company. The "someone" might be a business school, an individual, or a professional services firm, any one of which might approach you to solicit your involvement. Generally, the sponsors of such programs have an intended audience and an intended content theme. Instructors are wise to work with clients to flesh out the specifics of the intended content area. Instructors can interview a number of executives and intended attendees to see if the needs they point to align with the needs the primary company contact has described. We believe that instructors have a duty to professionally and gently push back on a client with suggestions and ideas born of their own due diligence. We have, on more than one occasion, done so on subject matter content and instructional formats. In any such instance, the burden is on you to make the case for why the client's preconceived notions of subject matter content or formats are not the best route to go. And, making your case is best done by having researched the company, talked to a number of folks in the organization, listened very carefully to them, probed them with poignant questions, and challenged some of their key assumptions and mindsets. Recently, we had a corporate client that sought to enhance the financial savvy of its management team. They wanted a one week course that explored state-of-the-art financial thinking and practices, along with contemporary leadership insights. After spending a day and half at their main facility and interviewing a number of their executives there, we proposed a program that contained a session on ethics as it pertained to financial performance and reporting. They pushed back, saying they did not want or need such a session. They proudly, and rightly, declared that they had had 30 consecutive quarters of 6 percent growth and were financially a very conservative company. We pushed back saying that that is exactly why they needed the session. In particular, we saw that as the quarters mounted for meeting such impressive goals, the pressure was building on the business unit managers to not be the one whose business unit was the cause of breaking that string. The client listened, we debated a bit, they agreed, we included it in the program design, and it ended up being an important, well-received part of the program.

One other aspect of SC programs that differentiates them from OE programs is the onus placed on instructors to become very familiar with the sponsoring company. As an outsider, you will never be as familiar with the workings of the company, its history, and all of its inside mindsets as those sitting in your class. You do need to know, however: the main historical facts of the company; its current strategy and circumstances; its main competitors, customers, and suppliers; as well as the business leaders within the company. Learning as much as you can about the company not only helps in the due diligence needed for crafting the best program design possible, it also bestows credibility on you when you are in the classroom speaking to 30 of that company's best and brightest. Take care to ensure that you never give cause for the participants to conclude that you do not know anything about their company.

A learning opportunity that presents itself most readily in an SC program is for participants to work in groups on real company problems or opportunities. In such an instance, the program design can include workshops that: build on the classroom learning; utilize teams of participants from different functions and/or different business units and/or different geographies; involve formal presentations to the other participants; and result in some sort of commitment to begin the specified initiative upon their return to work. This latter point is often hard to garner in the absence of a senior executive's sanctioning and support for it, both of which are best made in person by the CEO being present for the workshop report-outs. When a senior executive has agreed to be present for such report-outs, you should prep him or her as to the nature of the task given to the participants, the scaling and scoping of the inquiry the participants were asked to undertake prior to reporting out, and the need for his/her probing dialog to be positive in tone and considerate of the possibilities being raised. When such report-out sessions work well, with a CEO in attendance, the payoff to the company, the participants, and to the program, can be huge.

Another unique aspect of SC programs that instructors need to be aware of pertains to an expanded role for at least one member of the teaching team. In an SC program, we have come to believe that there is a relationship manager role that one of the instructors can take on, in part or in full. That role requires a non-traditional faculty mindset – that is, customer service, administrative details, staying in touch with the key company contact, being proactive on issues with the client, anticipating client needs and wants, taking direction from a client, coordinating a faculty team, evaluating members of a faculty team vis-à-vis client perspectives, and selling different or expanded program offerings. To be honest, some of our colleagues are neither willing nor able to assume such a role, while others are very good at it. There is no doubt, however, that excellence in this relationship manager role is nearly as critical to a successful SC program as the quality of instruction, the materials used, and program design.

Teaching in executive programs

Is executive education any different from, for example, teaching MBAs? Our colleagues take two fundamentally different positions on this issue. The first group says that there is no difference. They assign the same materials, ask the same questions, press the participants just as they do their MBA students. The argument is that, especially with cases, the participants set the level of the discussion by the level of their understanding and so you can teach the materials in largely the same way. Those instructors vary their preparation for executive programs little, if at all.

The second position is that executives are very different from MBAs and therefore must be taught quite differently. Colleagues in this camp cite the following 13 aspects of executive programs as significantly different from MBA programs. Proponents of these points assert that each factor impacts the materials chosen, the assignments given, the questions asked, the way the discussion is conducted, and the way the classes are summarized and completed. The ways in which the impact is manifested is program- and instructor-specific:

1. Executives are not used to being in school and studying, so the way you introduce them to a program can make a big difference.
2. They are not used to studying for long periods of time, so you cannot assign the same volume of materials.
3. Since executive programs are usually much shorter than degree program courses, you cannot take as much time to develop a topic or explore its nuances.
4. Executives are much more focused on the bottom line. They want to know the fundamental principles involved and how to apply them. Because they are still employed and still fresh with work problems in their minds, they have less tolerance for long presentations or poor classes. They expect excellence immediately.
5. People of widely different intelligence, age, and experience will come to seminars and work together in the same room. This places an additional burden on instructors to find ways to bridge those gaps and conduct classes that speak to all the people in class.
6. By and large, executive participants are more experienced than MBAs. This means that they are better able to sift out what will work in business and what won't. There is less room for error, naïveté, and silo-thinking in that environment for instructors.
7. Because executive program participants are more experienced, they tend to have less tolerance for abstractions that have little clear application to their work or their companies.
8. You don't grade executives. They may get feedback on their behavior from peers or from you, but in executive programs you don't give them a report card. Consequently, the burden on the faculty to provide interesting classes is heightened. Indeed, the press of evaluation is usually reversed in executive education classes – since participants have paid a lot of money to be there and are forgoing

valuable work time, they expect to get high-quality experiences and are quite willing and able to make noise if they don't think they are.

9. There usually is no test at the end of executive education classes. That is significant because it leaves both instructor and participant more fuzzy on what the value of the seminar was. What did they learn? How were they stretched? Can they really use the tools we introduced in the seminar? Each class (or module of classes) needs to have clear takeaways.

10. Executives have a much stronger tendency than MBAs to search for frameworks or tools that address problems they face back at work. It requires some skill and effort to get them to see that broad principles that apply to several situations are more powerful in the long run than giving them one specific set of steps to take home with them for today's problem.

11. Executives are more critical of audiovisual materials and handouts than MBAs. Executives are used to having and preparing high-quality audiovisual presentations. They like colored slides and clear drawings and easily understood charts. That expectation should be welcome, because it can force instructors to sharpen and upgrade presentations.

12. Since executives are in session for a short period, they don't have as much time to learn how to learn together or how to manage their own process for productive classroom discussions. Thus, instructors must generally be a bit more overt in steering and encouraging them in ways that make the most of those classroom discussions.

13. Finally, executives may have less experience with extracting principles from discussions than MBAs so it is important to present them with more clear summaries of what has happened and what the key points of the class were.

Our view is a mixture of these two viewpoints. To us, executives, as learners, are quite different from MBAs, even experienced ones. This demands that we prepare differently. We still embrace the case method as our dominant classroom methodology but we modify it for an executive audience. We frequently choose cases that are shorter and that look at situations from a more experienced and expanded viewpoint. We use more handouts, overhead transparencies, and Power Point slides. We often are more directive in assignment questions and we summarize at the end of class more extensively. Moreover, we often combine several learning venues (e.g., case discussions, lectures, role-plays, action learning, team assignments, etc.) in a short period of time to provide variety in a multiday program's pace, to fuel participants' energy levels, and to tap the learning channels and styles of as many people as possible.

Having acknowledged such differences in our approach to an executive education class, we don't shy away from pressing executives or putting them into role-plays. If anything, their experience helps fuel a richer set of class conversations than we would see from MBA students. You have to be cautious, though, since executives are not being graded. Where you might be able to press an MBA because you are the teacher, you might have an executive program participant get up and walk out on you if you press them too hard. They can get defensive more easily since they are not in that kind of arena all the time. You also have to be more cautious with examples in executive programs as well so as to not generate offense via an off-hand comment about one's functional area, senior executives, and/or company.

Some special considerations for EE programs

Identifying program learning objectives. One of the classic ways EE programs are designed is with the objective of addressing executives' perceived competency gaps. In an OE program, the sponsoring organization's marketing plan is constructed to highlight the ways in which a prospective attendee's current shortcomings will be rectified. It is not uncommon, for example, to position a Finance for Non-Financial Managers OE program as providing basic financial savvy to those who need to: have a better understanding of published financial statements; become more adept at product costing; and/or to be more effective designers of performance measurement systems. In many SC programs, the client company will often use their own competency model and diagnostic tool to identify the gaps in people's skills and knowledge that they want addressed in the design of the EE program. In either the OE or the SC program setting, the intent is to fill a gap in participants' knowledge and skill base. In some sense, this approach is a form of "ignorance management" (Galvin, 2004) – an undertaking with merit but one that also needs to be complemented by programs designed to enhance, accelerate, and leverage the resident skills and knowledge that participants already possess.

In designing either an OE or a SC program, one of the key instructor skills needed is an understanding of, and a framework for thinking about, the learning needs to be addressed by the program design and content. As mentioned above, generalized competency models can be found in the literature (e.g., Abraham et al., 2001). Many, if not most, large companies have their own in-house versions, and almost any consulting firm stands ready to help a company develop one. In the next section, we identify some of the high potential EE program subject matter areas that spring from many such competency models. It is, however, important to note that for an executive audience, knowledge and skills that are decoupled from the challenges and roles they face at work are abstract, not readily embraced, and have a shelf life of days, if not hours. Our experience points to the need for anchoring a program's learning objectives in the context of executives making current decisions. Some useful decision contexts to consider are:

1. How to foster better and more collaboration within the organization.
2. How to become an employer of choice.
3. How to stimulate profitable growth.
4. How to nurture creativity and reasonable risk taking.
5. How to create more shareholder value.
6. How to improve customer service.
7. How to manage for enhanced operational excellence.
8. How to develop an effective performance management system.
9. How to craft better supply chain relationships.
10. How to lead in a multinational context.
11. How to best exploit the possibilities presented by the internet.
12. How to most effectively approach post-merger integration.

The value in setting a program's learning objectives into one or more of these (or other) decision contexts is the ready-made relevance that is created for the theories, tools, techniques, frameworks, and ideas that spring from the course materials and the classroom discussions. As we noted earlier, executives, more so than MBA students, are prone to wanting immediate relevancy from the learning experience they are undertaking.

Senior executives. We have sensed a very positive trend in our EE programs over the past several years – more top level executives are attending and/or championing the programs. This is a very positive trend for two reasons. First, engagement at the top of an organization (e.g., CEOs, COOs, CFOs, Executive VPs, CIOs, etc.) means that the program is likely to have a larger, longer-lasting impact. In essence, successfully designed and delivered programs with such participants implicitly, and often explicitly, means that you become a part of a company's strategic thinking process as well as the change management process initiatives that are undertaken. For an instructor, we would assert there is nothing more interesting and rewarding than being a part of a company's work at that level. Second, such involvement by the most senior executives in the company provides a powerfully positive signal to other participants from that organization that this program is important. For many years, we heard midlevel managers rave about a program they had just taken, and then they would ask us if their senior executives had attended. All too often our answer was no and you could see the manager's energy and enthusiasm for heading back to work to make a difference literally drain from his or her face and posture. But now, to be able to answer that question with "yes, they have" tends to turbocharge their enthusiasm for going back and stretching their wings, taking initiative, and putting into practice the insights, ideas, and initiatives they have upon leaving the program. This makes such a difference in the value of a program to the participants and to the sponsoring company that when we are now contacted for designing and developing a new program, we routinely push for, make the case for, and more often than not, get the involvement of senior executives.

When senior executives attend an EE program, two additional, not necessarily negative, issues arise. First, the stakes are raised when a CEO and his or her peers are sitting in your classroom. Perhaps like a veteran Broadway actor who acknowledges some butterflies in the stomach just before going on stage, an instructor may admit that having CEOs and their peers in the classroom can be butterfly-inducing. It is not an overstatement to note that the whole program rests on those people's approval and for an SC program, in particular, the financial stakes at risk for your institution and yourself can be huge. Indeed, Jackson et al. (2003, p. 255) report that, "When senior managers can see how their development can help the performance of the company, the likelihood of buy-in to any executive development scheme is increased." To mitigate the possibility that the program design is not well received at the time of delivery, an SC program's CEO (and peers) should be involved in reviewing the preliminary program designs. Such reviews do not negate the risk that they will not like the materials chosen (you do not usually ask them to review those prior to the program) or the style of the instructors in the classroom – those risks remain during program delivery. The only way to reduce those delivery risks is to pre-pare, prepare, and prepare! And, we would also say, not all instructors are capable of excelling in a classroom full of CEOs and their peers. Thus, it is important for you to know what you can and cannot do in the way of connecting with, providing insights for, and captivating the interests of senior-level executives. We have colleagues who are not interested in such classroom experiences and others that we simply do not invite to join our EE program teams if it is to be offered to CEOs and their peers.

It is this latter point that leads to the next issue. Senior executives are not bashful in stating their opinions and desires when it comes to instructors. We have had to replace instructors on SC programs because a senior executive or two did not feel that instructor was up to the task for one reason or another. If you are leading the delivery team, it is a role you will not often experience and one that you would never relish: breaking the news that you are replacing a team member. Yet it is sometimes necessary, as Jackson et al. (2003, p. 189) note, "companies are becoming more demanding customers."

Coaching. One of the growing opportunities for instructors in EE is executive coaching. In one survey, 70 percent of the executives sur-veyed "believed that coaching is actually more effective than training courses as a means of changing and improving the performance of senior executives and high-flyers" (Anonymous, 2003, p. 17). Such a relationship may run the gamut from becoming friends with, and a trusted confidant of, an executive through a prior EE program who gives you a call once in a while to being recruited by a company to join their team of vetted, trained coaches assigned to one or more execu-tives with regularly scheduled meetings. As you might surmise, such a relationship works only if the executive desires (or is willing to try) a coach and then experiences value-added insights and ideas from the relationship. The key is to remember that the coaching relationship is fundamentally to benefit the executive. That requires coaches to hold in abeyance their own temptations to fulfill personal learning agendas. Strict confidentiality is key in such an endeavor and instructors should not view their time with the coached executive as research-information-gathering time. As noted earlier in another vein, it is critical for instructors to know the limits of their expertise, making it clear in the advice given as to what is opinion versus empirically-based knowledge versus well-formulated theories/frameworks.

Coaching is a means for making a big impact on an organization (Johnson, 2004) and the individuals leading it. There are a number of companies and associations that specialize in executive coaching and for interested instructors making contact with them to explore opportunities for affiliation is a viable means of discovering what is possible. Those organizations include, but are not limited to, the International Coach Federation, Ken Blanchard Companies, Development Dimensions International, Executive Development Group, Corporate Psychological Management.

High impact directions for EE[1]

How do executives perceive their EE experiences, and what does that portend for instructors and providers of EE programs? Several of our Darden School colleagues recently explored some important EE questions in this regard by surveying more than 100 corporate executives. Insights were sought on these specific questions:

1. Do executives believe they are spending too much time in EE programs?
2. What would cause them to spend more time?
3. What are their general motivations for attending EE programs?
4. Why do they choose the programs they attend?
5. What type of program venue do they most often seek?
6. Will this venue preference continue?
7. What is the role of e-learning for future EE programs for executive-level attendees?

The results suggest some directions that instructors, interested in EE, should be ready to exploit.

In general, survey respondents spent six days per year in some sort of professional development program and they were interested in more, not less, EE program opportunities. Those who felt they spent too little time in EE outnumbered those who felt they spent too much time by more than 2 to 1. Thus, a latent demand exists for more EE programs and the challenge is to ascertain and address the issues constraining the

---

[1] Much of this section is reprinted from P. Farris, M. Haskins, and G. Yemen, "Executive Education Programs Go Back to School," *Journal of Management Development*, 22, 9 (2003), 784–95, © MCB University Press. Reprinted with permission.

full exploitation of this demand. Time, money, and relevancy of programs were all about equally important factors in limiting the number of EE programs executives attended. The largest obstacle to spending more days in EE programs was simply an expressed need for more programs of interest. This response suggests a somewhat pervasive "missing of the mark" in the EE programs providers currently offer. Indeed, there seems to be a feeling among executives with whom we have spoken, that they are looking for programs which address the issues they have on their desk now. Thus, EE may need to move more substantively to a "just-in-time" consultancy/coaching orientation.

Survey results also indicated a clear dominance of three factors as to why executives attend EE programs. Those factors are to further functional specialization; to enhance understanding of their company's strategic challenges; and to prepare for a new position or assignment. These findings underscore the immediacy and direct applicability of EE programs that potential attendees want.

The results also suggest opportunities for EE program providers to develop:
- thematic and in-depth functionally oriented EE programs
- customized EE programs that highlight, explore, and work on company-specific strategic challenges, opportunities, and actionable initiatives
- EE programs that explicitly posit and address issues pertaining to career transitions.

Once an executive decided to attend an EE program with a desired content, what factors influenced the choice of whose program to go to? From the survey responses our colleagues received, reputation of the host institution was the most important non-content-related factor in executives' program choice. "Presenter reputation" was also key. The implication for EE programs is to devote resources to:
- building a recognizable and highly reputable brand for the host institution
- investing in faculty thought leadership to create a faculty-based market "pull."

Also of note is that, once busy executives had decided to go to a program, the "amount of time away from work" was the least important factor in deciding which program to attend. Thus, the duration of a course delivered by well-regarded instructors and hosted by an esteemed institution is not as constraining a factor as some think. On the other hand, program costs were moderately important, suggesting that EE providers do need to be mindful of pertinent pricing.

Once an executive finds the time to address a specific developmental need by attending an EE program offered by a reputable institution, what makes that experience most worthwhile? Besides the expected importance of the learning acquired, chief among the key factors was the timeliness of the learning experience and the interactions with instructors. As to the "timeliness" result, this suggests the need for:

- Single-company, customized EE program designers to shorten program development time
- open-enrollment business school EE program providers to develop means for assisting companies in matching current executive needs to appropriate open enrollment EE program offerings.

As to the "interactions with instructors" result, that issue highlights the importance of an EE program's delivery team being not only thought leaders in their fields but ones with an interest in, and capacity to, interact with executives in and out of the classroom. A second tier of factors that make an EE program experience worthwhile for attendees pertains to the opportunity for personal reflection and interaction with other program attendees. These two variables point to the importance of providing slack in an EE program schedule, and creating opportunities at the educational site, for such pursuits. Unfortunately, the desire for slack in the daily schedule of an EE program often runs headlong into the reality of corporate sponsors pushing for EE program designs that leave very little, if any, unscheduled time for the program attendees.

The preferred venue for single-company programs was also explored. In a general sense, single-company programs may use one of four venues: offer the program in-house with or without outside instructors and offer it off-site with or without outside instructors. The survey results depicted that, although there may be a trend toward corporation-sited EE programs and "inside" instructors, the majority of EE program offerings attended are still off-site and taught by non-host-company instructors and this is expected to continue. This is potentially good news for business school faculty as potential instructors for the delivery of EE learning experiences. The bad news is that executives may not be as willing to leave home. Indeed, participants anticipated more use of in-house facilities (as opposed to off-site facilities) regardless of the presenters.

In their survey, our colleagues explored the possibility that the merits of online learning are not as applicable to executives as to other potential audiences (e.g. college students and/or non-managerial corporate personnel). Results indicated that nine out of 10 respondents were interested in online learning (a rather broad-based level of interest) but the level of interest was not very strong – only one out of three was "very" interested. What attributes of such offerings make them a more appealing option as compared with traditional classroom-based EE programs? Respondent perspectives clustered in three tiers. First, travel cost savings, convenience of time and location, and the just-in-time use of online programs were the most attractive features inherent in online learning options. A second tier of attractive features, not quite as important in executives' thinking as the first, were tuition cost savings and the more advantageous use of available time during the day for learning. Rated relatively low as key features for online EE programs and as a driver for substituting it for traditional classroom instruction, were relevance of subject matter and instructional style fitting one's background. In this regard, respondents did not perceive online learning as any more likely to present content of greater relevance than traditional delivery mechanisms, nor did they see online EE as more congruent with their learning styles. In fact, on both accounts, they saw online venues as less attractive than traditional classroom settings. Survey respondents took the initiative to also detail a number of negative factors accompanying online EE programs. In particular, they noted the inability to interact with instructors and other participants, both important EE program desires as noted earlier. Moreover, they expressed concern that online programs might be a "one size fits all" design that does not allow for real-time modifications according to the backgrounds of the participants. It appears that the state of online EE for executives is a mixed bag – that is, it poses attractive benefits but current versions possess shortcomings that preclude its high appeal to executives as an option for them. The first online EE program provider that effectively overcomes (or effectively minimizes) these shortcomings, while preserving the plusses, will be in a position to exploit a heretofore untapped market.

Having considered an array of potential advantages and disadvantages of online learning our colleagues proceeded to ask participants the question: "To what extent, if any, would the learning potential of an online program need to differ from that experienced in a traditional classroom setting for you to prefer the online option?" Underlying this question is an exploration of the tradeoffs executives make in valuing the online versus traditional classroom EE program options. In the aggregate, 29 percent of the respondents believed that online learning could pose up to 25 percent, or even 50 percent, *less* learning potential than that provided by the traditional classroom model. Thus, and somewhat unexpectedly, a substantial percentage of respondents were willing to accept less learning via an online EE program option in exchange for a bundle of other benefits (e.g., lower cost and time-liness). On the other hand, 71 percent of respondents asserted that online learning would actually need to offer at least as much learning potential (48 percent), if not more (23 percent), than a traditional classroom setting before they would prefer it – and thus be willing to encounter the negatives (e.g., lack of participant–instructor inter-actions) associated with that venue. As the technology for, and the designs of, online programs alleviate the historical disadvantages of such a venue, a further shift is likely from the 71 percent camp to the 29 percent camp due to a perceived decrease in loss of learning. This means traditional EE program providers need to embrace the attrac-tive aspects of online learning (e.g. lower cost and just-in-time) in their classroom-based programs because the online providers are pursuing the traditional providers' historical advantages (e.g., providing inter-personal connections). In consideration of the extent to which each of these two approaches must move to capture the ground currently held by the other, it is unlikely that the future portends an either/or outcome. It appears that the obvious is true – customized, blended approaches are likely to be most successful.

To explore future program content, our colleagues asked survey participants to look ahead several years and identify three topical areas in which they were most interested to pursue additional learn-ing. There were four distinct clusters of topics revealed from their responses. Dominating the landscape were finance-related and gen-eral management topics. In the former group, areas for study specif-ically noted by participants included general finance, mergers and acquisitions, derivatives, divestitures, financial reporting, and project finance. In the general management category, a variety of topics were identified including: negotiations, organizational dynamics, strategic alliances/joint ventures, contract administration, making effective pre-sentations, and career development. A second category of interests, not too far behind the first, was a category of interests pertaining to strategy and leadership. In regards to strategy, participants identified such needs as planning, strategies for lean times, strategic thinking, revenue enhancement; and strategy implementation. Concerning leadership, participants noted specifics such as managing change, advanced leadership skills and creativity. The third tier of future needs was marketing- and technology-related topics. In the marketing arena, such topics as sales management, new products, general marketing savvy and positioning were noted. The technology category captured interests related to e-commerce, turning data into knowledge, and enhanced computer skills. All three of these tiers represent EE program content opportunities. The least anticipated areas for these executives' future learning endeavors related to operations and international topics.

While acknowledging it is difficult to draw conclusions based on just these results, our colleagues did confirm that EE is changing. Their survey respondents expressed a desire for more, not less, EE opportunities aligned with their needs. Latent demand exists for the right kind of program – especially those more geared toward finance and leadership. Although those programs may be able to draw large audiences, they may not be the ones that are targets for online learning technologies. The amount of time executives can afford to be away from work and program costs are concerns of some importance. New EE program offerings via online means have potential for executives who have specific, immediate, information-only needs that must be addressed in the context of short, episodic, irregular exposures due to varied work schedules.

High-impact EE program design considerations

From the survey results noted above, based on our own interactions with EE clients, and based on the work of others (see, in particular Conger and Xin (2000), Ready (2004), Mintzberg (2004), and Longenecker and Ariss (2002), several macro-level program design considerations for future EE programs take center stage. First, between 2002 and 2006, we have seen a substantial number of EE program queries from prospective clients in four particular areas – financial acumen, strategic enterprise thinking, leading change, and ethics. It is not clear whether such interests are temporary or long-term, but for the moment, they do appear widespread. Instructors who can brand themselves with thought-leadership in one of these areas, and who can deliver excellent

EE experiences for participants, will have more work than they can possibly do.

Second, we are also finding that in SC programs, executives have an interest in and a willingness to either share the stage with an instructor or to lead a session themselves. This is generally a welcomed and potentially valuable addition to a program design. It does, however, place a burden on instructors to fully brief an executive, who has typically just flown in for the day, on where the participants' learning, thinking, and emotions are at that time in the program. This briefing is important so that the executive can build on, as opposed to undo, the positive progress the program has made in delivering learning and generating participants' enthusiasm for making a difference.

Third, SC clients are very involved in the program design decisions. For one recent client, we went through seven iterations of a one-week program design before they signed off on it. Among other things, they raised issues focused on the relative emphases placed on the program subject matter, our choice of case materials, the amount of time we had scheduled for study groups, as well as the pre- and post-program actions we had proposed. Such hands-on involvement by the client can be frustrating. The challenge for instructors is to listen carefully, process the client comments conscientiously, propose venues that represent high-potential learning, and only make changes that honor each of these aspects of the design process. For OE programs, the parallel is to know the needs of an intended target audience really well. It is not enough to simply design a program that is the manifestation of all that you know on a certain subject or captures all the interesting design features you want to try – the program design must couch such desires in the larger context of what a target audience wants and is willing to pay for.

Fourth, executive participants, in both OE and SC programs, want unadulterated relevancy in the program content and the takeaways it provides. In fact, the bar is rising in this regard as many of our program attendees have MBA degrees and have 15 to 25 years of work experience. Gone are the days when an instructor could simply replay his or her MBA class for executive audience. The best way to provide relevancy is to be intimately familiar with the contemporary challenges, concerns, thinking, practices, and trends at play in the business community. Such knowledge and awareness cannot be achieved by staying in one's office or reading academic journals. Instructors who want to be effective in the EE classroom must be in regular contact with practitioners, visiting companies, attending practitioner and/or industry conferences, reading practitioner papers and journals, all fueled by a genuine interest in the world of applied business.

Fifth, executives are not quite like the video generation (i.e., our teenage kids) but their attention spans are limited and their learning channels varied. Thus, an EE program needs to have a varied rhythm and pace and multiple learning vehicles (e.g., cases, role-plays, videos, readings, workshops, etc.).

Sixth, an integration of the program parts should create a *gestalt* for the whole. This latter point underscores the opportunity and challenge for an EE program delivery team to coordinate and integrate their various content streams. There is value added to a program and to participants' learning, when a business unit financial performance analysis class (taught by an accounting instructor) is integrated with a performance appraisal class (taught by an organizational behavior instructor). To do so, both instructors must know what the other is doing, how the other posits their respective subject matter, and the frameworks he or she employs. A common, nonintegrated EE program format is often referred to as the "dog and pony show" arrangement. In these programs, individual presenters come to a seminar for a day, do their "thing" as it were, presenting their focus and material to the participants, and then leave. The next day, another person comes in and does the same thing. These arrangements are most convenient for faculty who have limited consulting time and who wish to use their time most efficiently and for program sponsors who do not want to pay to have instructors waiting to teach. On the other hand, this format makes it difficult to organize an integrated experience for the participants. A more integrated approach is more costly in time and money, but it generally gives participants a better experience and more lasting learning. In well-integrated programs, instructors meet to plan a seminar and carefully select a sequence of class topics to match the educational needs of the program objectives. Thus, each instructor may only teach one or two classes on a given day and be required to be on-site with participants for several days rather than one. This approach allows participants the opportunity to engage the instructors outside of class and allows them to attend other classes and build on what goes on there.

Last, as noted earlier, the EE program participants that we have been involved with of late are more senior, have more education and business experience, and are generally more financially successful than those we saw 10 or 15 years ago. These people are not only wrestling with a fast-paced, ever-changing, highly competitive business landscape, they are also dealing with questions of life such as: "What's it all about?" "What will my legacy be?" and, "Do I want to keep doing what I am currently doing at work?" These are nontrivial questions that most of us ask in the safe confines of our thoughts. With skilled facilitation, however, an instructor can make the exploration of these questions an important part of an EE program. In some significant ways, avoiding these individual issues in an EE program is not only a lost opportunity but only addressing half the equation. For example, all the frameworks and strategic tools in the world will not enable a business unit leader to lead a business unit turnaround if he/she does not have the energy or passion to do so. Moreover, a lack of energy and passion may be rooted in a desire to be in a different setting, working with different people, spending more time with one's family, stretching one's wings into another field, or any number of other exogenous factors. To the extent those factors can be identified, explored, fleshed out, and considered in the context of one's work agenda, an EE program can be a valuable experience for participants.

With many of these macro-level design issues in mind, instructors are better able to tackle the task of designing a specific program, whether that be an OE or SC program. The Appendix to this chapter presents a discussion and description of a fairly robust, yet specific, EE program design that we have effectively used. It is important to note that just like any program design, the one contained in the Appendix went through an evolutionary process. Indeed, after delivering any program once or twice, you will want to make adjustments to it. Even the best pre-program thinking is often in need of tweaks after having experienced all the nuanced details of program delivery.

Suggestions for "making it stick"

A recurring challenge that instructors face in any EE program is helping participants transfer their program insights back to their work environment. Anything an instructor can do to make the learning "sticky" is a valuable part of program design, and one that those who are paying for the executive program are increasingly seeking. Some of the mechanisms we use to, at the very least, remind program alumni of their time with us, and better yet, spur them on to apply their learning to their work world, include:

1. Inviting participants to write a letter to themselves the evening before a program ends, which we collect and mail to them 90 days later. We ask participants to include in the letter the TO DOs they have made a commitment to themselves to do as a result of their program learning and reflections. The receipt of a letter, written in one's own hand, is a powerful reminder of program insights.
2. At the end of a program, we have also asked EE participants to write a personal charter of actions to be taken when they get back to work. We ask them to note in that charter the things they commit to doing the first day they are back at work as well as the things they commit to doing within one week, one month, one quarter, and within one year from the program's end date.
3. Another useful approach to transferring EE program lessons back to the participants' work environment involves action learning projects (refer back to Chapter 12 for more details).[2]

One final note – there is no administrative detail too small

Presenting an EE program involves a host of administrative details. These include, but unfortunately are not limited to: participant registration, billing, collection of payments, ordering materials, sorting and distributing materials, arranging for cabs and buses, and making sure the class room is properly equipped and arranged for the seminar. At our institution, full-time EE program assistants are assigned to each seminar to take care of these myriad details. They also oversee the logistics pertaining to coffee breaks, meals, and off-campus sight-seeing trips. They deliver messages to participants, track down lost luggage, send faxes for attendees, troubleshoot computer connections, arrange for car rentals, and do many other tasks associated with making a participant's stay pleasant and focused on the seminar. In the absence of a dedicated resource person to deal with all such administrative issues, instructors need to anticipate some distractions for the participants and, to the extent possible, strive to help mitigate those distractions so that program learning for the participants is maximized.

---

[2] For an expanded discussion of the ideas for making executive education program experiences stick, see M. E. Haskins and J. G. S. Clawson, "Making it Stick: Transferring Executive Education Experiences Back to the Workplace," *Journal of Management Development*, in press.

Conclusion

Having now each been involved in EE for more than 20 years, we can say it truly has been one of the most rewarding instructional experiences we have had. Almost without fail, the program participants we have had were bright, respectful, energized, experienced, and interested, and they brought a wealth of knowledge to the discussions. It is worth noting that one of the side benefits from your EE program involvement is the real-time business stories and examples that you can use to enrich the MBA classroom and other EE program classrooms. If given the chance to be involved in an EE program, we whole-heartedly say, "Go for it!"

References for additional learning

Abraham, S. E., L. A., Karns, K., Shaw, and M.A. Mena, "Managerial Competencies and the Managerial Performance Appraisal Process," *Journal of Management Development* 20, 10 (2001), 842–52.

Anonymous, "When Executive Coaching Fails to Deliver," *Development and Learning in Organizations* 17, 2 (2003), 17–20.

Cheese, P., "Keys to a High-Performance Workforce," *Learning & Training Innovations* (July/August, 2003), 12.

Conger, J. and K. Xin. "Executive Education in the 21st Century," *Journal of Management Education*, 24, 1 (2000), pp. 73–101.

Craven, A., "Embracing Learning at GE," *Development and Learning in Organizations* 18, 2 (2004), 22–24.

Galvin, T., "Ignorance Management," *Training* (June 2004), 4.

Jackson, S., E. Farndale, and A. Kakabadse, "Executive Development: Meeting the Needs of Top Teams and Boards," *Journal of Management Development*, 22, 3 (2004), 185–265.

Johnson, H., "The Ins and Outs of Executive Coaching," *Training* (May 2004), 36–41.

Lippert, R.L., "Whither Executive Education?" *Business & Economic Review* (April–June 2001), 3–9.

Longenecker, C. O., and S. S. Ariss, "Creating Competitive Advantage Through Effective Management Education," *Journal of Management Development*, 21, 9 (2002), 640–54.

Longenecker, C. O., "Maximizing Transfer of Learning from Management Education Programs," *Development and Learning in Organizations*, 18, 4 (2004) 4–6.

Mintzberg, H., "Third-Generation Management Development," $T + D$ (March 2004), 28–38.

Ready, D. A., "Leading at the Enterprise Level," *MIT Sloan Management Review* (Spring 2004), 87–91.

Watling, D., C. Prince, and G. Beaver, "University Business Schools 2 Business: The Changing Dynamics of the Corporate Education Market," *Strategic Change* (June/July 2003), 223–34.

APPENDIX[3]

"A 'ROSE + 6' architecture for customized, single-company management development seminars"

The general architecture presented here has evolved through our involvement in a number of significant, single-company programs for a variety of well-known corporate clients. Each of the programs dealt with a particular organizational capability such as creating high-performance teams, partnering for greater client/customer benefit, generating creative solutions, leveraging diversity, and being an employer of choice. Moreover, all the program participants were mid- or upper-level managers who each had significant business unit responsibilities and were viewed by their organizations as today's and/or tomorrow's corporate leaders. Each program was unique, but the macro architecture used in each of them is what we have come to term "ROSE +6" and its key elements are presented in Figure 15.1. It is our belief that the ROSE +6 seminar architecture can be effectively used to provide a provocative, valuable learning experience for managers seeking to become, what Prahalad (1997) terms, the "new age manager", wherein:

the capacity to conceptualize and synthesize the whole, see the connections between parts and be able to imagine the future, can be crucial [as are the abilities to] harmonize the hard and soft information, combine analysis and intuition and balance private and public interest.

---

[3] This appendix is a shortened, excerpted version of an article by M. Haskins, J. Liedtka, J. Rosenblum, and J. Weber that appeared in *Journal of Management Development* 17, 7 (1998), 503–15, © MCB University Press. Reprinted here with permission.

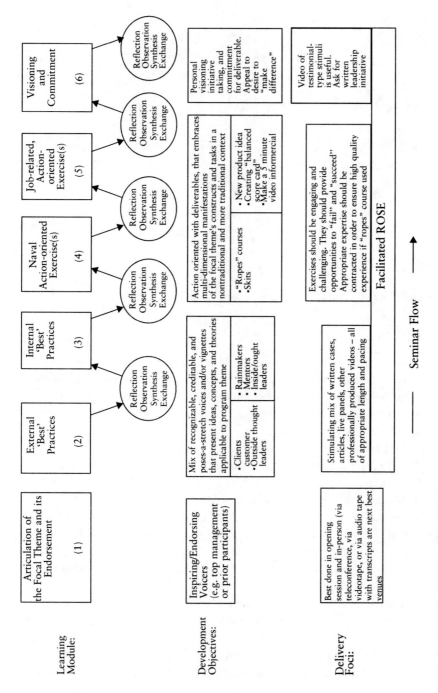

Figure 15.1 The ROSE + 6 Architecture

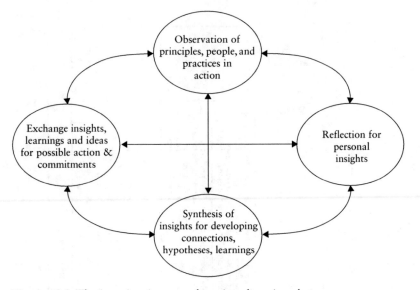

Figure 15.2 The iterative, integrated seminar learning elements

ROSE + 6

At the heart of this architecture is ROSE: *r*eflection, *o*bservation, *s*ynthesis and *e*xchange. True understanding, and the internalization of that understanding, requires engagement in an iterative, integrated seminar learning process (see Figure 15.2) that continuously embraces each of these four elements:

(1) *Reflecting* on the essence, elements, and implications of one's prior and present experiences and observations is an important learning element.

(2) The focused, heightened *observing* of a principle, point of view, person, or process in action. Mediums from which observations may be drawn include video and/or audio material, readings, role-plays, action learning, conversations, and recall.

(3) From an array of observations that catalyze a number of reflective, tentative insights, it is important for managers to *synthesize* their reflections in concert with their own unique view of possibilities, resources, work, self, and others.

(4) A final seminar learning element leverages the synthesis process through *exchanging*, the sharing with others, one's own synthesis. Within the exchange process, program participants are again

engaged in the learning elements of observation, reflection, and synthesis. The exchange process broadens and deepens a personal set of takeaway learnings because it sharpens perceptions regarding key points/issues and helps crystallize and contextualize their meaning through the exercise of serious, focused thought and public discussion.

Module 1 of the "+ 6": articulating a focal theme

Whether it is a one-and-a-half day retreat, or a one-week seminar, an effective program has a primary, provocatively stated, central theme. For example, the articulation of a program's central theme as, "Being an employer of choice" allows for the more eager, energized exploration of such a desired goal than perhaps otherwise possible with a more mundane theme such as, "Contemporary hiring and retention practices." Clearly, "Being an employer of choice" subsumes issues about hiring and retention but it poses a more provocative context for their exploration that, in the end, results in a greater sense of mission. In essence, the statement of a core theme is an opportunity to crystallize and dramatize the objective to be pursued by managers after the program. It can also serve as a platform for top management's assertion of an organizational value and important goal. Last, the core theme statement can be used to powerfully link the organization to an important constituency. Embedded in the "Being an employer of choice" theme, for example, is the fact that talented people have a choice of employers and in order to attract and retain those people, an organization must understand the elements of their choice-making. In contrast, a theme of "Contemporary hiring and retention practices" places a primary focus on an organization's processes and systems, not the prospective employees' active choice processes.

Modules 2 and 3 of the "+ 6": best practices

As depicted in Figure 15.1, those two modules represent the part of the program where provocative, "best" ideas, practices, and principles are presented. This part of the architecture initiates the start of a program-content flow that begins here with outsiders' voices and perspectives and, in the final phases of the program, ends with a participant listening to his or her own voice.

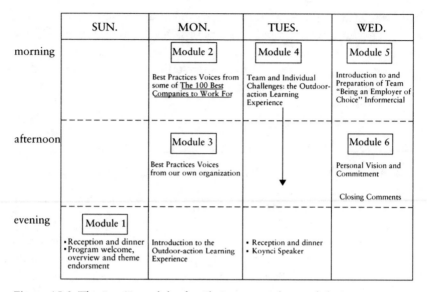

	SUN.	MON.	TUES.	WED.
morning		Module 2 Best Practices Voices from some of <u>The 100 Best Companies to Work For</u>	Module 4 Team and Individual Challenges: the Outdoor-action Learning Experience	Module 5 Introduction to and Preparation of Team "Being an Employer of Choice" Informercial
afternoon		Module 3 Best Practices Voices from our own organization		Module 6 Personal Vision and Commitment Closing Comments
evening	Module 1 • Reception and dinner • Program welcome, overview and theme endorsment	Introduction to the Outdoor-action Learning Experience	• Reception and dinner • Koynci Speaker	

Figure 15.3 The "+ 6" modules for "being an employer of choice" seminar

In Module 2, the views of recognizable and creditable outsiders are presented. Such a start is non-threatening to program participants because the potentially contentious and/or strategically important program content and discussion is, in the beginning, safely about "them" not "us." In addition, such a start is broadening in that outside voices encourage participants to consider ideas and thoughts not of their own making. The involvement of companies touted for their world-class approach to the program's core theme and/or use of acknowledged outside thought leaders (e.g. appropriate authors), also sends a message to participants that they warrant the best assistance possible in their quest to become better or best at the program's core theme. For example, in a program on "Being an employer of choice" (see Figure 15.3), with the support of our client, we designed and produced a video wherein senior management from three other highly touted companies discussed their employee perspectives.

In Module 3 of the architecture, the design is to bring the best practices focus "closer to home." In presenting "others" as the sole source of best practices, there is the danger of creating the impression that the participants' organization must not be doing anything right. Thus, a set of internal voices, on audio or video tape, CD-ROM, or in person, can be an effective step when positioned following the outside voices.[4] This complementary positioning fosters the sharing of internal success stories that are a testimony to the fact that "best" practices can be part of the participants' own setting and it raises the specter that as a firm, and as an individual in this firm, we have some gaps to address between what might be termed "best practices and philosophies" and what appears to transpire on a daily basis at work. Thus, participants gain a sense of some collective and perhaps individual accomplishment as well as an awareness of the need for and direction of some change. Moreover, with an eye to the program's ending focus on "making a difference," attention to success prompts an appetite for possibilities, an energizing catalyst for exploring possibilities and seizing initiative.

Between, during, and after Modules 2 and 3, ROSE plays an important part. Through the use of personal journals or customized workbooks, participants should be encouraged to record words or phrases descriptive of the provocative aspects of what they observe or hear during each module's program content. Such notes serve to capture the essence of an intriguing thought, perspective, question, idea, or insight that will subsequently serve as a gateway to various paths for reflection. After each of these two program modules, participants should be given a few minutes to reflect on the individually perceived stimuli to begin to fashion it into some work-in-process synthesis for discussion. In the privacy of a journal or in dyads, participants may be asked to identify two or three key perspectives presented in the "voices" that pose a new and intriguing way to view a task, a relationship, and/or a possibility for action. After 5–10 minutes of such synthesis and refinement of one's initial insights, participants may then be asked to share the key messages they heard with the larger class. Various personal responses should be facilitated so as to energize a conversation among the participants as ideas and insights are enhanced and enlarged. During the class-wide, open exchange after both Modules 2 and 3, facilitators should capture the participants' comments in order to generate an "outside voices" summary and an "inside voices" summary that can be saved and juxtaposed for a later reflection to occur after Module 5.

---

[4] When the featured internal voices are likely to be organizational members known to the program participants, we prefer audio-only tape to minimize the likelihood of recognition. We do so to avoid the possible discounting of the message by a participant who believes the video messenger does not "walk the talk."

Module 2 and Module 3, in turn, may be closed with an invitation to, and the time for, the participants to again summarize/synthesize in their journals the personally appealing insights and ideas they gleaned from the larger group's discussion.

Modules 4 and 5 of the "+ 6": action-oriented exercises

At the end of Module 3, program participants have begun to fashion some personal and collective ideas about the possibilities that exist for action in pursuing the program's core theme. Such a state of mind is a perfect time to present them with fuel for further introspection and insights as well as an opportunity to "experience" the challenges inherent in, and the requirements for, tackling those possibilities.

We have found outdoor-action-learning formats extremely effective in creating a novel, engrossing experience wherein participants stretch themselves along multiple dimensions (e.g. trusting, listening, teaming, and challenging assumptions, etc.) and find themselves unfettered by preexisting roles or hierarchies. Drawing on the expertise of any number of excellent vendors in this market (e.g. Falls River Center, Impact), a half-day or one-day series of challenges may be designed that provide rich opportunities for experiencing individual and team capabilities. These are not strength or endurance challenges but rather challenges that foster reliance on trust and teamwork, that require communication and creativity, and involve the facing of fears and limitations.

Clearly, time spent in non-work-related tasks is enjoyable because it is a change of pace and engages a variety of senses in different ways from a normal work day. It is, however, conducive to heightened learning because the tasks provide a fresh, uplifting venue for a ROSE that pushes participants to highlight the learnings from the experience and then to relate them to the overall program theme. For example, if the theme is "Being an employer of choice", one of the issues sure to surface in the Module 2 and 3 discussions is "valuing the distinctive abilities that individuals bring to the organization." Such a statement is a provocative set of words that warrant a deeper understanding and internalization than the intellectual embracing they likely garnered during Module 2 and 3's discussion. Thus, an appropriately crafted action-oriented, Module, team exercise, and ROSE on that exercise, will highlight specific examples where one team member's novel way of seeing the challenge provided the breakthrough insight that allowed the team to push ahead to success.

For a half-day afternoon or for a full-day set of outdoor-learning exercises, we engage in a brief ROSE after each event, with a fuller ROSE first thing the next morning. The next morning's ROSE tends to provide additional value because participants' reflections have benefited from an evening's rumination and continued conversations. Participants should be given the time and prodding to reflect on, synthesize, and exchange observations and learnings regarding the thoughts, roles, anxieties, frustrations, and euphorias they experienced prior to, during, and after each event, as well as for the overall experience.

Again with an eye toward the program's attention to personal action plans and commitments in Module 6, a second action-oriented challenge, closer to the participants' work world, provides a vehicle for linking the normative discussions of Modules 2 and 3, and the non-traditional experiences in Module 4, with the pending Module 6 agenda. Generally, the job-related, action-oriented experience presented to the participants in Module 5 should be one that poses a stretch for them, calls on collaboration, and requires a deliverable to be presented to the rest of the program participants. As examples, in an employer-of-choice program, we have asked participants to produce a five-minute infomercial video, set five years in the future, on why their company was identified by *Business Week* as an employer of choice. In a program focused on high-performance partnering, we have asked participants to construct a team charter that details agreed operating norms and team-based performance metrics. In a program on generating creative solutions, we have provided participants with some ordinary household objects and challenged them to use them to spark and flesh out five new service or product ideas that their company could reasonably consider.

For this second action-oriented challenge, it is not the end product that is of particular importance, it is the envisioning of the elements of success or excellence that are reflected in the end product as well as the process by which it is created. A facilitated ROSE, following this endeavor, serves to underscore the portability and validity of many of the themes that surfaced in the Module 4 events. Again through the use of journals, participants may be asked to make explicit what they observed in the way of enabling vs. constraining assumptions, creativity catalysts, and means of individual vs. collective contribution. In the reflective mode, program participants may be asked to recall and relive the flush of success, and the frustration of failure. We actually have participants describe those feelings and make attributions as to their root cause. With the juxtaposition of Module 2 and 3's insights in front of them, and with the Module 4 and 5 reflections still fresh, participants may then be asked to synthesize, to identify, the one or two things they have learned about themselves that they want to change and/or nurture as they pertain to striving for a "best practices" condition in the part of the business they influence. In dyads and/or group discussions, participants may be asked to exchange their observations, reflections, and syntheses. This serves to vocalize one's thinking that is possible only after having engaged in purposeful thought, a form of thinking easily avoided if there is no public at-stakeness to the task (e.g., public or dyadic discussion).

Module 6 of the "+ 6": visioning and commitment

This final module of the architecture is intended to draw on Module 1's call to action; the ideas prompted by the Module 2 and 3 exemplars; and the personal experiencing of some of the core theme's principles at play in the Module 4 and 5 tasks. Module 6 is the culmination of the program and it is intended to foster a sense of wanting to make it happen when back at the office.

There are two important design elements in Module 6 that warrant attention in the pursuit of the program's ending where each participant crafts and publicly commits to a personal leadership initiative. First, intellectually and emotionally, participants' sense of wanting to and being able to "make a difference" is greatly elevated via a real-world story that depicts the power and purposefulness of having a vision, a mind's-eye image if you will, of the arena and means for a dedicated effort to "make a difference." Second, the Module 6 conversations and foci should be at the personal level, not at the level of what the organization should do. The language of "I commit to" provides an important sense of seriousness, purposefulness, and ownership.

Building on an individual's sense of contribution to the collaborative tasks of Modules 4 and 5 and what he/she learned about themselves during those tasks, the careful choreography of Module 6 can begin with an assignment to write a one-page leadership initiative that furthers the ideals, principles, and/or practices made meaningful in one's learnings during the prior sessions and that further the program's core theme. (It is important to note that this task should be highlighted at various points during the program as forthcoming.) We ask program participants to take about 5–10 minutes to organize a few thoughts. We then invite them to watch a video excerpt from Joel Barker's *Power of Vision* (1992). We do so with the intent of elevating participants' sense of boldly envisioning how and where they can make a difference. The vignettes contained in this particular video dramatize the power of having a vision in creating desired outcomes. Without any discussion, after this video ends, participants are asked to then detail their leadership initiative in writing.

As a means of starting the process of public declaration and collegial support for these initiatives, participants are asked to share their leadership initiative with one other participant whose role it is to: listen for and highlight the initiative's potential; offer ideas for synergies with resources and/or initiatives currently in existence that they are privy to; and to look for concrete ways to support his/her colleague in their initiative. After one last opportunity to refine individual initiatives based on these dyadic conversations, the facilitator can then invite session-wide sharing, comparing, and offering of support to other colleagues' initiatives.

A useful framework for participants to use in articulating their initiative is to speak in terms of concrete actions that he/she is committed to doing within one day, one week, one month, and within one year of going back to the office. Facilitators can ask for participants to listen for ways they can support a colleague's initiative by such simple declarations as: committing to call a colleague in one week to see if he/she took step 1 and find out how it went; or committing to introduce a colleague to a key person they know; or committing to partner with a colleague in certain ways to meet stated milestones. The end result of this Module 6 activity is that individuals have personally synthesized their learnings from the prior modules of the program and have fashioned them into a personal agenda for action that they have articulated a public commitment to doing and, second, in most instances, gained a colleague's commitment for support.

A benediction

If at all possible, it is an empowering gesture for one or two members of top management to participate in the entire program. If this is not possible, at a minimum their attendance during Module 6 is important. In either instance, they should be invited to respond to what they have just witnessed in Module 6. There is clearly the potential for them to endorse the initiatives they have just seen being shared, acknowledging them as important contributions along the path toward the organizational challenge spelled out in the opening session. It is particularly powerful if the top executive shares his or her own pertinent leadership initiative and how he or she, too, is committed to supporting others in their initiative.

The ROSE + 6 architecture described in the preceding pages is intended to facilitate introspection, create interpersonal connections, uncover fresh ideas, and catalyze personal leadership initiatives around a core theme. To celebrate such outcomes; to signal the collective potential for the participants to "make a difference" when they return to their workplace; to evoke a feeling of focus and enthusiasm for a key organizational capability; and to provide a symbol for carrying the program's ideas forward, we place a program icon at participants' seats during the last seminar break. For example, in a program focused on continuous learning we have given participants one bookend, signaling the belief that one's learnings are not complete. In punctuating the theme of "making a difference" as presented in the final scene of the Joel Barker video that we use in Module 6, we have presented pewter starfish to participants. Such tangible takeaways can serve as a gentle reminder of lessons learned, commitments made, and a vision of the future shared.

Further reading

Barker, J., *The Power of Vision* (video), Burnsville, TN: ChartHouse, 1992.
Prahalad, C.K., "The Work of New-Age Managers in the Emerging Competitive Landscape," in F. Hesselbein, M. Goldsmith, and R. Beckhard, (eds.), *The Organization of the Future*, San Francisco: Jossey-Bass, 1997, 159–68.

16 | *Using technology to teach management*

RANDY SMITH

> Man is a tool-using animal.
> – Thomas Carlyle

In this chapter, we examine the best practices for the use of technology to enrich the learning experience. The students who are now arriving in our management programs have been using computers for most of their careers. Today's typical MBA students and young managers have been computer-literate since childhood, and are capable of playing a multi-user, online game with global challengers while they listen to digital music and use Instant Messaging to interact with their friends. Some will even say they can add homework preparation to this extreme multitasking lifestyle.

Through the following perspectives, we will examine the use of technology to engage this technologically proficient generation of students in a rich learning experience:
1. Pre-class preparation and exercises
2. In-class technology use
3. Post-class reflection and exercises
4. Assignment submission tools
5. Team project technology support
6. Orchestrating the total experience.

Numerous examples of technology innovators from the leading business schools are presented in this chapter. Many thanks for their contributions to this work and to the profession.

Pre-class preparation and exercises

The use of technology to support a student's preparation for class often provides the most benefit relative to the level of instructor effort involved. School-, university-, or corporate-level resources can be leveraged without a unique development effort for a single course, if such tools are available. If not, simple-to-use tools may be implemented to enable a motivated instructor to accomplish much of what is discussed in this chapter.

Pre-class support: Technology infrastructure

Portals. A student portal, as the name implies, provides a doorway to many of the resources that support a student's educational experience. The well-designed portal will provide a launching pad into the various resources necessary to succeed in the educational endeavor. The following are often one click away from the initial page:
1. Class registration and course information: registration system
2. Class materials, assignments and evaluation: learning management system
3. Recruiting and interview information: career services system
4. School events and speakers: school-wide calendar system
5. Research tools: library system
6. Announcements and online discussion: Web forum system
7. School, university, and corporate information: links to relevant Web sites.

Instructor and staff portals should provide access to the necessary resources to support research, instruction and administrative functions.

Examples:

Wharton: *SPIKE*®
Wharton's *SPIKE* – originally developed in conjunction with Wharton MBA students during the 1994–95 school year – was one of the first enterprisewide education portals. Working closely with Wharton students, the school enhances *SPIKE* each academic year, which, according to Wharton, is key to the product's success. "*SPIKE* is as much about process as it is technology," states Wharton's CIO and Associate Dean Deirdre Woods. "*SPIKE* is successful because it is constantly evolving to address the needs of Wharton's students."

As of this writing, *SPIKE* is in its tenth annual incarnation, and brings together all the resources and information from around the school into a single, integrated interface.

In recent years Wharton's *SPIKE* has expanded beyond the Web to include content delivered to video displays throughout the Wharton campus and to students' handheld devices. According to CIO Woods,

SPIKE is "more than just a Web site, [it's] now an essential information management tool for both students and administrators at Wharton."

Darden: *myDarden*

The two-tier strategy for the Darden portal, *myDarden*, is document management and student/instructor information delivery. "Basing an academic portal on document management is highly effective and marries course assignments, faculty collaboration, and case editing directly to our daily information tool," says Lauren Moriarty, who was for many years director of Web services at Darden.

In its third version at the time of this writing, *myDarden* is both learning-management and document-management based on the Microsoft SharePoint portal server. The collaborative tools in Share-Point facilitate collaboration and teamwork.

Students are directly involved in the evolution and improvement of *myDarden* through feedback mechanisms built into the structure. In addition to continuous minor improvements, the technology team solicits feedback via survey twice each year, and implements upgrades in January and July.

Duke/Fuqua: *FuquaWorld*

Fuqua's dynamic intranet and portal environment, *FuquaWorld*, was originally deployed in 1998 and is now in its third generation of technology and design. The Fuqua portal has evolved to provide constituent-specific information and capabilities to faculty, staff, and students. Fuqua has led Duke in the leverage of Web services and portal technology, and provided leadership and participation in the both the visioning and design process that helped develop the new undergraduate student portal, *DukePass*. This new environment is the first step toward a broader portal environment across Duke, linking Web spaces and information.

FuquaWorld has recently been expanded to include the now-popular *CMC Channel* subportal. This powerful extension aggregates all career-related communications and events for MBA students. The portal environment at Fuqua is constituent-specific and provides filters to tailor information for users (announcements, events, etc.) and includes tight coupling between event and personal calendars. In addition, *FuquaWorld*'s Team Tools subsystem provides students and faculty with a collaborative environment that fits the team-based approaches to management education for which the school has become known.

Learning management systems (LMS)

There are numerous LMS products that can be implemented for storage and presentation of class materials and assignments. Typically, Web-based templates are available to assist the instructor in creating an online syllabus and class description. The instructor can usually submit documents prepared with MS Office. These can be downloaded by students as links from the syllabus or from a personalized student-assignment page. Links can also be made to multimedia cases, simulations, and online collaboration tools.

Blackboard and WebCT are two commercially available LMS products. Prepackaged modules that plug into the products are available from major book publishers. These course-specific modules provide a template for the presentation of the packaged class materials and assignments. Some institutions have created custom LMS systems based upon MS SharePoint or other content-management systems. MIT and several partner schools are working on an open-source portal and LMS product called *SAKAI*. This open-source platform can be customized and extended to meet local needs. A moderately technical support team is necessary to assist with local implementation of this platform. Improvements must be submitted back to the open-source community as part of the platform-use agreement.

Individual class support can also be accomplished by use of Web sites and e-mail if an LMS is not available. E-mail and individual class Web sites can also be used to complement portal and LMS support environments.

Example:

Wharton: *webCafé*[TM]
In lieu of a traditional course management system, the Wharton School of the University of Pennsylvania implemented a customized version of Documentum's eRoom collaboration environment. A major revamp of Wharton's curriculum in the early 1990s emphasized collaboration and teamwork as key components of the learning process. When Wharton deployed an online learning platform school-wide in 1998, it selected a software platform geared to support these goals.

"A key part of the Wharton education is interaction between faculty and students, and students with each other," says Wharton Senior IT Director Kendall Whitehouse. "[Wharton implemented] a technology that enables that interaction to continue any time, any place. It doesn't replace [traditional classroom] interaction; it is a supplement for the other 22 hours of the day."

Having observed students meeting around tables in the school's cafés and lounge areas, Wharton chose "webCafé" as the brand name for the school's implementation of eRoom. Wharton has subsequently added customized extensions to the eRoom platform for education-specific functionality, which enables resources such as an on-line grade book, and "drop boxes" for submitting homework assignments.

Class Web site

An individual class Web site can be hosted at either the school/ university level or at a publisher-hosted site. Tools such as MS Front-Page make Web-page creation no more difficult than word processing. Many instructors can construct their own class sites, and most instructors are capable of maintaining a site created by a technology-support person. Publisher sites provide tools to support editing of the course-site templates provided in the package. Discussions and survey creation are within the reach of more technology-oriented faculty with the new generation of self-service oriented Web-authoring tools, or through publisher sites.

E-mail

E-mail systems are a low-cost and highly flexible means of distributing materials. The University of Phoenix uses an e-mail venue for both the distribution of materials and online discussion. Users can also e-mail links to Web-based resources such as surveys or company Web sites. The appeal of using e-mail is the low level of technology investment, as well as the participant accessibility from slow-dialup Internet access.

Pre-class materials and exercises

Class preparation materials for students are available commercially from book publishers as well as from Darden and Harvard business publishing enterprises. Both Darden and Harvard produce and market multimedia cases, while Darden and Wharton create and market business simulations. E-learning tutorials that focus on core skills are now coming to market from book publishers and business schools with publishing units. Distribution to other schools helps to offset the expense of producing these dynamic tools; they are much too expensive to produce for use in a single school.

Some media materials, however, can be economically produced for a single class. Slide presentations with voice only – or possibly slides that are video-synched to the proper progression – can be created. Technically oriented faculty can achieve this from their offices with only a Web-camera and a self-service product such as MacroMedia Breeze. Making class-lecture slides available before class is another way to help students prepare. Pre-class surveys and online discussions are also a possibility for pre-class work.

E-books

Several book publishers are experimenting with non-business electronic books hosted at the publisher's site.

Multimedia cases

The traditional paper-based text case can be enhanced significantly by using video, animation, and non-linear means of accessing content. When students are experiencing a multimedia case, they can actually see and hear the protagonist tell the story. The nuances of nonverbal communication, the appearance of the office or factory floor, and the intensity of the conversation are difficult to convey in prose, but are easily detailed through video. And while complex topics are hard to describe in text format, animation can be quite effective at illustrating concepts. "Future case development will continue to integrate multiple digital formats to find the best way to tell the story," says Christian Lehmbeck, co-director of Darden Media. "The learning experience is just so powerful. Next-generation students (and instructors) will be increasingly attracted to a multimedia case."

Examples:

Jim Clawson (Darden)
Baltimore Police Department – case description
Mayor Martin O'Malley made reducing the city's annual murder rate an important part of his mayoral election platform. Baltimore's annual murder rate registered more than 300 deaths for the better part of a

decade. O'Malley called Edward Norris, chief strategist for the New York City Police Department's crime reduction model, and asked him to consider signing on with the Baltimore Police Department during the fall of 1999. Now Norris must decide to either leave the home where he grew up and accept a promotion in Baltimore, or stay the course with the NYPD. The case features video interviews with Norris, members of the Baltimore Police Force, and leaders of the Baltimore community as students consider the issues surrounding this important decision.

Robert Bruner (Darden)
Hugh McColl and NationsBank

When Hugh McColl became CEO of North Carolina National Bank (NCNB) in 1983, he set out to transform an institution that operated in just two states into the biggest bank in the country. McColl achieved that vision 15 years and more than 50 acquisitions later when his bank, then called NationsBank, merged with BankAmerica. A dynamic leader who took big risks, McColl's leadership and negotiation styles are legendary and an interesting study. Through excerpts of video interviews with McColl and three of his key officers, along with press clippings, this multimedia case tells the compelling story of McColl the person and his tactics. The case also contains text and charts outlining terms of key acquisitions and company growth data.

Gregory Fairchild (Darden)
Black Entertainment Television

BET is a multimedia case about the evolution of corporate strategy over time. The historical account of founder Bob Johnson's and BET's growth illustrates the role of a leader's vision and persistence in the face of considerable barriers. Insightful interview commentary from BET's founder, Bob Johnson, is interspersed with senior management interviews and relevant contextual background to provide the student with an exciting and interactive case experience.

"The story of BET's development and company strategy is rich in technical, market, and sociological detail," Greg Fairchild says. "The breadth and depth of content in a multimedia case allows students to explore this story from many vantage points, and allows for teaching from multiple functional perspectives."

"Given that BET is a company that produces media content," Fairchild says, "students are able to experience the distinctiveness of the product through actual content clips from the station. In addition, another case objective was to expose students to the managers of color in executive positions in a way that diminishes stereotypes. Film is often able to capture nuances that the written word is not able to, including communicating professional competence and demeanor."

Simulations and courseware

Business simulations and courseware are online experiences that can be played individually or in a multiplayer environment. The assignment can last from several minutes to the entire length of the course. Simulations will be discussed in more detail in the in-class section.

Examples:

Paul Farris (Darden)
Management by the Numbers

The Management by the Numbers application is designed to give students an opportunity to practice and improve their skills in a variety of mathematical concepts. The program is accessible online over low-bandwidth connections, and it does not require the students or instructors to install the application on their computers. This application has an easy-to-use interface and is integrated with a database, allowing for detailed analysis of the questions and the quiz results. Instructors can create questions, use existing questions, modify question variables, and set parameters according to the student's level.

"The application really allows the instructors to focus on more advanced topics as students are building their core skills at their own pace outside the classroom," Paul Farris observes. "Since the program can push a large number of variations on questions related to a specific formula, each student can tailor their own learning experience to focus on material that addresses areas of weakness. Further, they can continue to practice solving problems until they reach their desired level of competence."

Wharton's Learning Lab

The Alfred West Jr. Learning Lab at the Wharton School of the University of Pennsylvania has created nearly two dozen learning simulations used at Wharton and elsewhere. Several specific examples are discussed below in the section on in-class use of simulations.

Purdue's Synthetic Environment for Analysis and Simulation (SEAS) Laboratory

SEAS™ is a business and an economic war-gaming environment developed at Purdue University's Krannert School of Management in association with the Department of Defense. SEAS is built on agent-based modeling. Agent-based modeling allows for scalable, realistic group behavior and evolution of individual agent characteristics and trends. Collection of data at the individual agent level allows for various different views of the same data for analysis in a wide range of disciplines – including, but not limited to, psychology, economics, business, engineering, and sciences.

SEAS replicates the real world in its most crucial dimensions, including competition, regulation, decision variables, and interaction dynamics. It consists of inter-linked goods, stocks, bonds, labor, and currency markets. In these markets there are two types of agents that interact: LIVE, where people act as buyers, sellers, regulators, and intermediaries; and VIRTUAL, where artificially intelligent software agents mimic human consumers in a narrow domain.

Using the SEAS, environment models and theories can be tested in a realistic, safe, controlled synthetic environment. SEAS also creates virtual reality environments using 3-D technology with the Envision Center of Purdue University to provide sophisticated data visualizations. The products from SEAS support both research and teaching at Purdue and have been exclusively licensed to Simulex Inc.

Gerry McCartney, assistant dean for technology at Krannert, notes: "The ability to create a robust, yet rich, model-generating engine allows SEAS to quickly produce a wide variety of sophisticated modeling products usable in many inter-disciplinary activities."

Examples of SEAS projects:
Food Bio-Security Simulation

The Food Bio-Security Simulation is an agent-based simulation used by Purdue's engagement partners in government and business to prepare and train for terrorist events in the food-supply-chain industry.

Fire, Structure, Agent Simulation

This is a simulation that bridges three heterogeneous models (the spread of fire, the mechanical engineering of a building, and individual behavior) and uses the data from each model to generate a 3-D view of a building on fire. The main purpose of the simulation is to facilitate researchers in combining and reusing preexisting building design and evacuation models.

Layered Information Propagation Model

In any simulation, information is exchanged between multiple homogeneous and heterogeneous nodes. This simulation mimics the layered behavior by implementing different types of node behavior, as well as different information-propagation strategies.

SEAS Terrorist Attack Tracker

SEAS Terrorist Attack Tracker is an integrated database of terrorism-related information. The tracker is used in Political Science courses to provide the students detailed information of terrorist organizational models and activities. It also aids them in understanding the proliferation of international terrorism.

Interactive e-learning tutorials

The student's preparation for class can be greatly enhanced through the use of tutorials on technical topics. More advanced tutorials can include diagnostic testing. This method can dynamically present the materials that the student has not understood, and bypass those areas the student has mastered.

Example:

Janice Hammond (Harvard)
Quantitative Analysis – An Introductory Course

Published by Harvard Business School Press, this online course provides a thorough introduction to analyzing quantitative information. Originally designed for first-year MBA students and class tested on more than 1,000 HBS students, the course is in fact suitable for a variety of graduate school and executive education audiences both on site or in distance learning situations. According to the HBSP Web site (http//:www.harvardbusinessonline.hbsp.Harvard.edu), the course offers a simulated setting in which the student "is situated as a consultant to a multifaceted resort hotel businesss. Step by step, this multimedia program gives the learner the knowledge and tools needed to satisfy the hotel manager's demands for information and analysis."

With 2,000 screens to enrich the student experience, the course provides a memorable introduction to business statistics. It includes mastery tests, with technology to help the instructor to assess the results so as to identify both individual and group comprehension of quantitative analysis.

"The learner builds knowledge partly by working through a sequence of increasingly sophisticated challenges from the resort manager. From the basics of describing and summarizing data to the complexities of risk analysis, the program systematically guides students as they learn to use the tools of quantitative analysis," the course description states.[1]

Synched slide presentations

Audio can be synched to PowerPoint and posted to the LMS or the class Web site to create learning modules that make difficult concepts much easier to follow. Recently, inexpensive commercial software has made production of synched slide content quite simple. Presentations using such tools as Microsoft Producer or Macromedia Breeze can be created by instructors on their own with a PC and a microphone. With both, the production steps are as follows:

1) Create an MS PowerPoint presentation of the lecture;
2) Record either voice or video from your desk as you talk through the slides;
3) Transcribe each slide's lecture segment in the note section for that slide – this makes the lecture searchable by topic (Breeze);
4) Direct the tool to generate a final product, which, for Breeze, is a compact, downloadable flash component. It employs broadband access for video-synched slides, and dialup access for voice-synched slides. Load the lecture into the LMS, class Web site, or even e-mail the component.

Example:

Phil Pfeifer (Darden)
Anatomy of a Regression Model
This low-bandwidth multimedia presentation covers the basics of simple linear regression. Some of the topics discussed include how to build a regression model, how well the model fits the data, and the passing

---

[1] For more information, visit http://www.harvardbusinessonline.hbsp.harvard.edn.

of the Four Assumptions. The piece is a conversation between student Todd Riggs and Professor Phil Pfeifer with humorous "fast facts" and flash animation that makes the presentation interesting.

"I was shocked at how well this piece was received by our students," Pfeifer said. "They loved it. I'm still trying to figure out exactly why. Part of it is that students identify with Riggs – a student – as he pushes the prof – me – to keep things simple. Another is the fact that the animation in this piece serves a purpose."

Flash animation is part of what makes the case engaging. "We were lucky to have Matt Shields, an engineer, create the Flash animations, and he nailed them," Pfeifer says. "So many times you see animation for the sake of animation. Because Matt understood what we were trying to accomplish, he was able to create animation that enhanced the concepts we were talking about. Finally, I have to admit I was wrong about the 'fast facts' included in this piece. I thought they'd be a distraction, but students report that they made the presentation more interesting and viewable."

Streaming video presentations

Lectures can be recorded either in a studio or from the office with an affordable Web-cam. The lecture should be segmented in 5–10 minute vignettes that are easily viewed among other activities. Short, topical segments are accessed from a Web-based menu. They can be rearranged and updated easily as the product is enhanced, then asynchronously streamed to students with broadband access. If you have students with only dialup access, you may want to create a version with a still photograph and your voice streamed to the students.

If the video is recorded in an analog format, it will need to be digitized into a video format compatible with the school or university's streaming server. Video streaming at 300K bits per second performs quite well on broadband access through DSL or cable modem. Streaming video cannot be supported through dialup access with current technologies.

Example:

Richard McKenzie (UC Irvine)
Richard McKenzie teaches microeconomics for executive and fully employed MBA students, a 10-week course in the Graduate School of Management at the University of California, Irvine. He has

produced 55 video modules on core microeconomic concepts that are posted on the Internet in downloadable and streaming form (http://www.gsm.uci.edu/ ~mckenzie/module.htm). The modules are also distributed on DVD at the start of his fall classes. They range in length from 4 minutes to 20, with a sizable majority of them in the 8- to 12-minute range. The modules are not intended to replace course lectures. Rather, they are designed to supplement traditional course materials.

Modules are designed to accomplish three goals. First, the modules provide a means by which students who have never had a course in microeconomics can study basic economic concepts (which all MBA students should know on starting their programs) before class begins. Second, the modules provide a means by which students can review key components of lectures, as well as sections of the course textbook (which McKenzie also wrote). Finally, the modules provide a means by which students can repeatedly go over concepts and lines of analyses that are often difficult for students to absorb the first time they are covered in class. Each quarter, McKenzie adds eight to 12 additional modules that provide answers to tests and assigned papers, thus freeing up greater class time for coverage of more course material in greater depth.

Andrew Hill, a member of the computer group at GSM, has developed the McKenzie video system so that it is a one-person operation. That is, McKenzie can record, edit, and post the modules on the Web without anyone else being involved. McKenzie reports that the introduction of the video modules has enabled him to increase his coverage of course material by 25 percent. He also reports that student performance and course evaluations have also jumped. Given that students report spending an average of four hours a week going through the modules, McKenzie has effectively increased his lecture "time" by 40 percent. Students report that they regularly take the modules along with them on their cross-country and international business trips. McKenzie estimates that he saved more time the first year the video modules were available – dealing with repetitive students' questions outside of class – than he spent producing the modules.

Pre-class polls, surveys, and study questions

A good way to ensure that students both read and think about their homework assignments is to have them complete a pre-class survey.

The responses are helpful in orchestrating the class. You can call on students to defend their pre-class positions and conduct a post-class poll to see if positions shifted based on class discussion.

Example:

Greg Fairchild (Darden)
Entrepreneurship: An Introduction
Using Macromedia Breeze, Fairchild has created a series of presentations that include polling and PowerPoint slides with audio. The online surveys track the students' results from a negotiations assignment, and also capture their thoughts about a business case to be discussed together the next day.

"In thinking of new ways to engage students in cases and content, I've been using online surveys with students prior to class meetings that encourage and challenge their assumptions about various topics in the field," Fairchild explains. "These surveys are an opportunity to gauge base knowledge and progress, and to provide an introduction to the day's material prior to class meeting. It also subtly points out to students what they do not know, yet will know by the close of the session."

Automation makes the process easier. "One of my class exercises requires students to negotiate in dyad teams prior to class. Macromedia Breeze allows me to collect their negotiation results in a nonintrusive, asynchronous fashion," Fairchild says. "I simply forward students the assignment, and I don't have to manage their completion, or the tally of results. Breeze does this for me."

In-class technology use

Actually using technology in the classroom can provide both the most benefit and the most damage to the educational experience. Given the short attention span and multitasking nature of today's students, the class period needs to be phased into different delivery/experience modes to encourage active participation. Moving from a short lecture segment supported by a few slides, to a short video clip, to an online class-brainstorming session can engage a mass lecture class of hundreds of students – or even a globally dispersed e-learning class. The master teacher may be able to keep students on the edge of their seats, but most of us could use a little help in engaging our new multitasking, short-attention-span students.

Negative practices and outcomes

Networking in the classroom

If you sit in the back of a classroom where students use laptops, and those laptops are connected to the Internet, you will probably be surprised – and maybe even outraged – at what is really going on. Asking students not to connect their network cable to the Ethernet port (until you instruct them to do so) will solve that problem. More complex system-level solutions are also possible. Limiting access is much more difficult if the network access is wireless, because the signals are not confined to a single classroom.

Death by PowerPoint

Simply reading slides can result in a very bad class; turning your back on the audience to read the slides is an invitation to disaster. If you have to turn down the lighting to see the slides – and turn your back to the audience to read them – there are no words to describe how miserable the classroom experience becomes. The best practices for using PowerPoint are covered in the positive-aspect discussion.

Best practices and outcomes

Networking in the classroom

When necessary, ask students to connect with the network to research a point of interest from the class discussion. When the network is not needed, just say no – have the students disconnect and close their laptops. It is almost impossible to compete for the students' attention against all of the temptations of e-mail and the Internet – it's a high-risk mission.

PowerPoint

If the class is a lecture, create summary slides by using bullet points of major topics and subtopics only. Don't create 60 slides for a 60-minute class – 10 to 15 may be plenty. And avoid busy slides – particularly avoid selecting a cluttered-background template. Make use of large, dark fonts on light backgrounds. A good way to bring the presentation to life is to insert short video clips or screen shots of Web sites that illustrate the point.

If the class is a case discussion, fewer slides are necessary. The minimum deck could be composed of study questions, with one slide per question. Following each question, it may be appropriate to present a slide or two in support of any points needing discussion. Digitized video of a topical expert may be helpful for use in the class summation "takeaway" segment of the class.

If your presentation is very technical and requires numerous slides to cover the material, you may want to create an initial slide that outlines the presentation with links back to specific topics. The last slide in each section should link to the initial outline page.

In-class support: technology infrastructure

The standard, high-end classroom configuration will include the following:

- **Projection**

  Projectors are now available at a price point under $5,000. They feature enough lumens to be seen without dimming the classroom lighting.

- **Controls**

  A control panel can either be wall-mounted or incorporated into a console or podium. The panel operates the screens, sound control, classroom lighting, and the control of various inputs, including VCR, DVD, computer, and document camera.

- **Podiums and consoles**

  Many schools design podiums to contain control panels, while other schools have elected to house most of the equipment in an AV closet, with the controls built into a podium or console. The podium designs can be quite large, however, and may become a psychological barrier between the professor and the students.

- **Smart boards**

  Several vendors market smart-board devices. These are essentially white boards that record the movement of colored markers on their surface, and save the data into a file archive for post-class review. Some schools are experimenting with tablet PCs, using Lotus One-Note, which projects the instructor's work onto the PC. It then archives the class work created thereon for post-class review. The One-Note product can also store a sound file of the instructor's comments about each tablet PC screen. One-Note allows slides, notation on a blank screen, and the other documents from both tablet PCs and conventional PCs.

- **Videoconferencing and digital video capture**
  High-end classrooms may be equipped with video-conferencing cameras and push-to-talk microphones at each seat. Lighting and sound quality are important considerations in the design of these rooms. Classroom sessions can also be recorded for archival use.

Examples:

Darden: Consulting 8407
Cooperative course with Darden, Michigan, and UC Berkeley
Darden's Jeanne Liedtka wanted a fresh idea for teaching a consulting course in the fall of 2002. Designed by Liedtka to put into practice the very processes students would need to utilize in their own consulting careers, the electronically delivered course was taught simultaneously to three campuses across the United States by way of live videoconferencing, the Internet, virtual collaborative management tools, audio-conferencing, and virtual consulting teams.

Once a week, all three business schools were linked via videoconferencing and Web collaboration software for classroom instruction to review case studies and to build consulting strategies. Outside class time, the virtual teams planned presentations using telephone conferences and group Web sites. Class syllabi, team notes, and collaborative tools were available at all times through a community Web site, and streaming video of each class session was posted weekly.

Participation was lively and students quickly learned to adjust to the new pedagogy. Guest speakers and participating school alumni also contributed to the experience. At the end of the 13-week program, student groups conducted their virtual presentations using all collaborative tools, and responded to a course evaluation, facilitated and tabulated through the Web-based collaborative program.

Videoconferencing to connect all three schools was possible using conferencing systems standardized to the capability of the lowest common denominator. A third-party bridging service facilitated stable connections and provided image control and immediate technical assistance as necessary. Each school drew upon their classroom technology groups for coordination and operation of each video session. Selection and implementation of collaborative Web tools was initiated by Darden, which also provided training and support.

This collaborative class was the second in a series of courses presented to this group of business schools and was built on the technical successes of its forerunners. As the collaborative tools, both videoconferencing and virtual Web-based applications have, gradually become more sophisticated, they have been better accepted as legitimate instructional devices in technology-critical business school environments. As well as underscoring the importance of such collaboration in a consulting career, this course examined common difficulties, and gave students a hands-on look at real-world solutions.

Wharton: the Wharton Video Network

With the opening of Jon M. Huntsman Hall in 2001, the Wharton School of the University of Pennsylvania undertook a major step in integrating digital video into the classroom experience. The Wharton Video Network – part of the school's *SPIKE* student intranet (see Pre-class support: technology infrastructure) – delivers digital video of recorded class sessions, a special events and speaker series, and course materials such as examples of television advertising campaigns.

The centerpiece of the Wharton Video Network is a custom-designed system to automate digital video capture in any Wharton classroom and deliver it over the school's intranet.

All 48 classrooms in Wharton's Jon M. Huntsman Hall, as well as the classrooms in the school's San Francisco facility, include a digital video capture-and-playback system. These classrooms contain three video cameras controlled by the instructor from a touch panel in a custom-designed lectern. The video is digitized (as an MPEG2 file) in real time, and then transferred to transcoding stations where it is automatically converted into a streaming format for Web delivery. Data about the class – such as the course number, instructor, date, and time – is automatically sent to a database, which then generates a Web-based interface to the online video content.

"Our goal," states Wharton Senior IT Director Beverly Coulson, "is to make digital video as readily available as the chalkboards and overhead projectors in Wharton classrooms."

Electronic content for in-class use

Simulations and content for the instructor's version of multimedia cases provide some of the best enhancements to the classroom experience.

Simulations

Simulations enhance learning by creating live, multiuser, interactive environments. Students learn by experience to apply concepts to real-world situations. The dynamic nature of simulations makes learning exciting, and helps generate lively group discussions.

Examples:

Paul Farris and Phil Pfeifer (Darden)
The Beer Game
The Beer Game is a fun, competitive simulation designed to elicit behaviors that are characteristic of many product-supply chains. This game has been highly successful in business schools, and in executive education programs around the world. Students learn firsthand about the bullwhip effect and the benefits of systems thinking. Managing supply chains is a complex task involving the coordination of companies involved in the manufacturing, distribution, and retailing of a product. Managers within each firm in the supply chain make decisions that impact their own company's success, as well as the success of other firms in the supply chain.

"Our implementation of the famous Beer Game is very slick," Pfeifer observes. "I remember playing it using chips and note cards, and relying on the students to stay in step and keep accurate records." With this Web version, all the boring details are handled automatically, so that students can concentrate on their decisions. As a consequence, the messages are clearer, and the learning is more efficient.

Phil Pfeifer (Darden)
Prisoner's Dilemma
This simulation allows anyone with a Web browser to participate in an interactive Prisoner's Dilemma tournament. The simulation provides an excellent forum to explore the tendencies of individuals/companies in competitive situations. In Prisoner's Dilemma, participants must choose between cooperating and defecting in a situation where defection is always in an individual's best interest, but mutual cooperation is better than mutual defection. Students are paired anonymously by the application with other students, and they compete in a series of rounds. The students are then linked again, and play another game. This process continues until the instructor ends the tournament, and the results are posted to the class.

"We wanted a way to create a rich Prisoner's Dilemma experience for our students," Pfeifer recalls. "Using the web, we can accomplish this quickly with a very small amount of administrative overhead. It takes about five minutes to explain the interface and get the tournament started. The random pairing of students and the anonymous play are important features of this tournament . . . as is the fact that the number or rounds per match is random. With a random number of rounds, cooperation is more likely to emerge."

Erika James (Darden)
Crisis Management
The Crisis Management simulation allows instructors to set up a series of scenarios that guides a user through a crisis. The user makes choices based on text information, video information, and information from teammates that affects the next scenario they receive. The simulation tracks the path of the user, and shows the results at the end of the session.

"Everyone with the opportunity to participate in the Confronting Crisis simulation is able to engage in 'real-world' experiences that capture the challenges they may face in management positions," James says. "The application brings to life complex situations that force you to respond and make decisions in real time. With print cases, you have the luxury of time, and weighing pros and cons before deciding. That's not how a real crisis works; the simulation mirrors a real-life crisis."

Wharton: On-line Trading and Investment Simulator (OTIS^{TM})

With a portfolio containing billions of dollars, Wharton's On-line Trading and Investment Simulator (OTIS) provides an experiential way to learn about the impact of equities market fluctuations. The application helps to illustrate key concepts such as portfolio balancing and management, benchmarking, and the effect of large-scale fund "buys and sells" on market positions.

Using actual data from today's financial markets (supplied by a feed from *Financial Times*' FT Interactive Data), OTIS permits student "fund-managers" to buy and sell equities and to compete against the actual market. OTIS tracks equities in the Standard & Poors 500, and stores real-world data on positions, values, histories, and dividends. OTIS includes a set of analytical tools that students can use to evaluate their own performance, such as the S&P 500 benchmark, and the achievement level of their fellow students.

OTIS is the first product from Wharton's Learning Lab to come to market under the Wharton Addison-Wesley Business Series imprint.

Wharton: Oil Pricing Equilibrium (OPEQ^{TM})

Unlike OTIS, which often runs throughout an entire course, Wharton's Oil Pricing Equilibrium (OPEQ) typically occupies a single class session. Instructors in negotiations courses use OPEQ to teach issues involving shared resources and incomplete information. The oil-pricing simulation demonstrates principles of individual versus overall profit levels, and the behavior of competitors in a closed market.

OPEQ is a round-based simulation tool that combines computer-enabled game play with face-to-face interaction. Students break into teams of roughly three players each, and compete in a three-way contest. Each team represents the oil production board for one country. Three competing "countries" play against each other in a single "world." In a typical simulation, each student team sets production levels for each year, with the goal of maximizing the country's profits. OPEQ can simultaneously run games for multiple worlds. This keeps team sizes manageable, and also provides data for comparative analysis on team strategy and performance across worlds.

All teams receive the same information, such as the equations that predict the market price of oil and the resulting profit margins. However, teams are not informed of the production levels set by the other countries until they have set their own. Periodic unexpected "events" further complicate the picture, forcing the teams to make decisions in an uncertain and changing environment. After production levels have been set, the application computes and displays both individual country profits and total world profits. It is then time for the next round.

In the early rounds, students interact through the computer simulation only. In later rounds, the instructor tells each team to choose a representative. These players go into the hallway and attempt to make a deal regarding future production levels. They then return to try to persuade their teammates to follow (or not follow) the agreement.

Later, a fourth country enters the competition. This country does not consist of actual student players, but is a collection of computer-based actions. If one country now reneges on its agreements and overproduces, it is difficult to identify the source of the increased production. The game and its outcome become the basis of an interesting instructor-led conversation on the nature of negotiation.

Wharton: Virtual Interactive Bond Engine (VIBE^{TM})

The Virtual Interactive Bond Engine (VIBE) was originally developed by Professor Michael Gibbons for his finance class in "Fixed Income Securities." VIBE forms the basis for an entire semester's work in bond-portfolio management, and presents a series of progressively complex assignments on managing a portfolio of fixed-income securities. Each semester consists of a series of simulations – typically between three and six per semester – each of which runs for a week or two. Unlike OTIS, which uses real-world data, VIBE consists of a series of carefully constructed scenarios. It is configurable by the instructor to fit various trading scenarios and is suitable for individual or team-based learning.

Taking long or short positions, students build portfolios from a universe of bonds created by the instructor. Students design each portfolio to perform in certain ways, depending on changes in the interest rate. As virtual time passes, VIBE automatically calculates the effects of the changes and reveals them to the players.

Students can view the performance of their portfolios relative to those of their classmates. Based on a player's performance, he or she may be hired to join someone else's team, and allotted a salary in play money. The final semester grade is based on several game components – including a student's individual and team earnings, and the salary a student receives for signing with a team. (The assumption here is that performance and salary are directly correlated.)

Another feature allows students to assess their progress throughout the semester. VIBE includes metrics that students can use to gauge their own performance, and see how it compares to that of their classmates. As Professor Gibbons states, "It doesn't help the students if they find out they're doing poorly once the class is over. It's too late then. In order to learn, they need to receive feedback throughout the class."

Multimedia cases
Multimedia cases are beginning to include an instructor version that features video and other materials not offered to students. That content can be used to support the epiphanies of the case discussion – or be used to lead the students to those epiphanies. Material in the student version can set the stage for discussion and case review.

Polling
In large lecture environments or in synchronous e-learning classes, polling may be a very useful tool for engaging students in the class. This assumes that a collaborative product to support polling is available, and that the students have computers.

Video-conferencing guest speakers
Bringing industry leaders into the classroom through video conferencing is an excellent way to provide a rich class experience with a minimum time investment from the speaker. These classes function best when the classroom has two-way audio and video. Successful sessions can be accomplished, however, with a good conference phone and an Internet connection to support slide-sharing products such as WebX or NetMeeting.

Video materials
If an instructor uses a lot of video, it may be useful to get it digitized and link the various elements to a navigation menu. The DVD format holds a good deal of video, and the menu system allows direct access to clips as necessary to support the discussion. A good example of this is to digitize commercials and organize them by topic for use in a marketing class.

Example:

Jack Weber (Darden)
DVD materials
Personal Leadership Professor Jack Weber makes extensive use of video and audio files for spontaneous use in his Darden Executive Education classes.

Historically, Jack maintained a repertoire of tape-based video and audio content – and playback equipment – at the ready on a portable cart that was wheeled into his classroom every day. At any given moment, Jack could quickly dive into the relevant content, and produce a recording in one of four or five different media formats. Playback equipment supporting those formats was stacked high on the cart, and all video and audio outputs mixed down to one tether which was connected to wall inputs. While this method indeed produced results, format playback was not consistent, tapes failed or got lost, equipment developed problems, and selecting and cueing tapes to their desired play points was cumbersome at best.

The solution to this retrieval and playback dilemma was to digitize and categorize the segments Jack needed for his various classes. With the help of personal editing and digitizing software, and the now-pervasive use of DVD playback equipment, Jack was able to segment and catalog his clips onto home-made DVD media. This once voluminous collection of tapes and CDs was now reduced to a mere handful of disks. Playback equipment was virtually eliminated and replaced with a portable DVD player to allow Jack subtle cueing ability during class interaction, as well as the ability to search, cue, and play in a matter of seconds.

Playback to the newly upgraded ceiling-mounted DLP projector and surround speakers is impressive and consistent. The result is a more spontaneous and enriched classroom experience.

Post-class reflection and exercises
Archive the in-class experience
In-class materials and even the board work (if a smart-board device is used in class) should be archived in the LMS or the class Web site. This will support post-class reflection and examination review.

Post-class discussion
Either e-mail or a collaboration tool can be used to continue "take-away" discussion, or to further probe issues not reaching closure in class. The preparation can be used as a lead-in for pre-class discussion in the next session.

Post-class polls
If a polling tool is available, a post-class poll can be given to bring closure to the in-class discussion. If you performed a pre-class poll, then comparing the results (regarding change in perspective and opinion) can provide an interesting capstone for the class.

Class community
The LMS or the class Web site can be made available to alumni who have completed the class. This helps them keep up with advances in the class's body of knowledge. You may even allow alumni of the class to participate in post-class discussion, particularly encouraging them to share their real-world experiences.

Assignment submission tools

Assignment submission tools can automate the workflow between students and instructors, freeing up time and reducing mistakes.

Example:

Fuqua
Fuqua's assignment submission tool was originally designed for the school's executive MBA programs in which distance learning makes up a large component of the program designs. Additionally, as the tool has proved its flexibility, it has been adopted for use in many daytime MBA courses.

Like the functionality available in many Learning Management Systems, Fuqua's assignment submission tool handles the fundamentals of allowing students to download assignments from instructors and then submit these completed assignments online. Fuqua's tool incorporates metadata, which allows numerous behaviors not available in many other assignment systems.

At its most basic, this metadata allows instructors a high degree of control over the distribution of their documents. Instructors can manage the release dates of materials as well as their due dates. These dates set up a window during which students can access the materials and/or return assignments for grading. Due dates can be applied as hard or soft due dates. Submissions made after a soft due date are marked as late. Hard due dates disallow any submissions after the date has passed.

Reporting tools provide instructors with up-to-the-minute reports on the status of assignment downloads and submissions by students. The tool's metadata also incorporates the concept of teams. This enables assignments to be delivered to and managed as team assignments with the same functionality as individual assignments.

"Routing" is another example of a behavior facilitated by the assignment submission tool's metadata. Instructors can predetermine to whom submissions are made available. At its simplest, this allows instructors to route specific submissions to specific support staff and/or TAs for assistance with review and grading. Another more complex application of submission routing is used for peer reviews. Instructors can structure assignments in which one student's or team's submission is made available to another student or team for review and comment. Once reviewed, comments are returned via the assignment submission tool.

Team project technology support

Using collaborative technology for team support helps alleviate the difficulties of scheduling same-time, same-place meetings for busy students. It also helps students prepare for working in geographically dispersed virtual teams.

Several commercial collaboration tools are available that provide a feature set to support team projects. If a commercial tool is not supplied, many of the features can be provided in separate products, and integrated through the LMS or the class Web site.

In addition, some schools have embedded these capabilities into their portal environment. Fuqua's Team Tools within *FuquaWorld* is the best example of this approach. The environment includes IM with presence sensing, a team Task List for projects and group efforts, e-mail distribution lists, team discussion boards, team scheduling, and shared network documents. Fuqua's extensive team meeting space with large shared displays further supports team-based collaboration and interaction.

E-mail and calendar

Although some collaborative products may provide their own e-mail functionality, it is best to use the school/university e-mail and calendar systems. The ability to check schedules and to send meeting invitations is a mandatory feature for support of physical meetings, but these functions are best delivered through the primary mail and calendar system.

Instant messaging (IM)

Although there are some security issues that must be mitigated, IM is beginning to be accepted for teamwork at the corporate level. The students arriving in our programs have been using IM most of their lives, so they will want to use the medium for their project teams. Most of these products support a feature called Presence, which tells a team member who else is currently online – and may even detail who is available for interaction.

Shared-file storage

Another important feature is shared-file storage. A very helpful component of that capacity is version control, which archives previous versions and provides check-in and check-out, so that only one person edits the document at a time. The Track Changes function in Microsoft Word is one way of reviewing one another's edits and comments.

Screen sharing and collaborative editing

Many tools can share a team member's screen with the rest of the team. Some products even allow the entire team simultaneous, real-time editing for a document.

Project planning

A project-planning tool is very useful for laying out the milestones in the project and for documenting responsibilities.

Brainstorming
Some commercial products provide the ability to have the team explore a topic in a parallel mode, and may allow the contributions to be anonymous. A less sophisticated, threaded-discussion tool or e-mail can also provide support for brainstorming exercises.

Polling
Many products allow the creation of polls that can be used to document team decisions and move the discussion through team impasses.

Conclusion
In this chapter, we have covered many possibilities for the use of technology in teaching management. The optimum combination of those methods depends on your teaching style, your audience, and the course. The following best practices will help mitigate the risk in using new technologies for any phase of the educational experience:
- You should experiment with only one new technology at a time.
- Tell your students when you are trying something new, and make them part of the prototyping process.
- Ask students for feedback about how the new element could be improved.
- If the class is being delivered in an e-learning format, much more technology is necessary for a good on-site experience.
- Always practice new technology several times – both in your office and, if it is to be an in-class exercise, in the classroom. Perform a final test just before the classroom or online experience. If you have technology support staff, always make sure they are on call or physically present the first time you use a new technology in class.

You should remember that using technology in some phases of the educational experience will help you connect with and engage new students who have a technology-based lifestyle. We can't go back – we have to move forward with students if we want to continue to be relevant and effective in preparing them for a productive career. Technology can indeed be a bridge between current instructors and the new generation of students.

Further reading

Anonymous, "Less Classroom, More Technology," *T + D*, 59, 5 (May 2005), 24.

Bauer, Chris, "Virtual Classrooms," *Printing Impressions,* 47, 12 (May 2005), 54, 56.

Bersin, Josh, "Evaluating LMSs? Buyer Beware," *Training,* 42, 4 (April 2005), 26–31.

Darbyshire, Paul, "Instructional Technologies: Cognitive Aspects of Online Programs," *Information Management,* 18, 1/2 (Spring 2005), 19–20.

Domermuth, David, "Creating a Smart Classroom," *Tech Directions,"* 64, 6 (January 2005), 21–2.

Peluchette, Joy V., and Kathleen A. Rust, "Technology Use in the Classroom: Preferences of Management Faculty Members," *Journal of Education for Business,* 80, 4 (March/April 2005), 200–05.

Wallace, Raven M., "A Framework for Understanding Teaching with the Internet," *American Educational Research Journal,* 41, 2 (Summer 2004), 447.

17 | *Counseling students*

JAMES G. S. CLAWSON

"Be yourself!" is about the worst advice
you can give to some people.

– Tom Masson

No matter how well credentialed and
trained psychotherapists may be, if they
cannot extend themselves through love to
their patients, the results of their
psychotherapeutic practice will be generally
unsuccessful. Conversely, a totally
uncredentialed and minimally trained lay
therapist who exercises a great capacity to
love will achieve psychotherapeutic results
that equal those of the very best
psychiatrists.

– M. Scott Peck, M.D.,
The Road Less Traveled

You're sitting in your office when a student nearing graduation comes in with the news that his best friend and classmate has just been killed in an automobile accident. He seems confused, on the verge of tears, and not sure what to do. He obviously wants to talk.

A student enters your office in tears; the probable grade of C in your course would mean failing out of graduate school and severe shame before family members.

Citing "personal problems" and "pressure" as her reasons, a bright, promising student in your class comes to your office and announces her intentions to leave school midway through the first year.

A student who has hardly talked at all during the semester comes in to your office, sits down, and says, "I'm not sure why I'm here, but you seem like the person to tell. I've just learned that my fiancé has cancer."

An executive education program participant says he can't stand his boss, but can't quit his job.

A female student comes in and says that she knows of a male student who is cheating companies out of recruiting funds and that he has threatened her with bodily harm if she tells anyone.

A newly promoted company manager confides in you that he doesn't feel up to the task and wonders if he can do it.

At one level, it is easy to forget that students (including executive education program attendees) have lives and issues beyond our classroom. At another level, we should feel honored when they share those aspects of their lives with us as potentially having something worthwhile to offer in return. At another level, HELP! What do we do now?

Students will seek your counsel: You cannot avoid it. The topics will range from their grades and other school issues to personal and family problems as well as career issues. Some instructors shy away from these situations for one of two reasons: either they don't believe that instructors should be counseling students or they underestimate their own skills in doing so and retreat out of a feeling of inadequacy. Philosophically, our view is that teaching includes the role of counselor. As instructors, we have significant influence on the intellectual, ethical, and psychological natures of those attending our programs. While we tend to focus on Level Two (Conscious Thought), our influence is not so tightly compartmentalized that we can avoid a spillover effect, whether intended or not, on students' emotional and personal lives. The teacher who accepts that reality and is willing to develop skills as a counselor can contribute to the development of students in a wonderfully broadened and rewarding way.

Responding to counseling opportunities

When a student approaches with a counseling concern, instructors can respond in three fundamental ways: Make themselves unavailable physically and emotionally, refer the individual to someone else, or agree to talk with the person further.

Making yourself unavailable. It is easy to do. Signals sent in class and after class – including the formality of an instructor's speech, the non-emotional content of conversations, his or her facial expressions, accessibility as indicated via stated office hours – all send a message to students about a willingness, or lack thereof, to see them. Some instructors choose this alternative to save time for their research and/or consulting activities. To them, student counseling is not a part of a teacher's role. They define the instructor's job as everything but counseling. That viewpoint leads instructors to avoid student contact, in class or out, as a diversion from their primary professional activity.

We disagree with that approach. When a person accepts the responsibility of teaching classes, we think that person accepts the responsibility to provide advice, wisdom, counsel, ideas, and assistance on almost any subject a student might raise. We do not mean that instructors are psychologists or that they should be setting up a quasi-counseling office, only that students often see instructors as authority figures with training, experience, and wisdom in a certain subject area, in business, in dealing with people, in the various demands of life in general. If instructors have developed a learning, open, comfortable relationship with students in class, it is quite natural for some students to project that relationship onto other dimensions of their lives where they are in need of advice. Students are sensitive to an instructor's availability, and how accessible an instructor is sends a powerful signal about the value placed on the role of counselor.

One thing that limits counseling availability and, therefore, effectiveness is the widely used "office hours" system. Office hours can be a tool either encouraging or discouraging students' counseling visits, but in general, this system clearly supports other activities at the expense of student contact. If all hours are "office hours," that is, if instructors are available for students at any time, then that open-door policy sends a message to the students. If instructors are available to meet students only two hours per week, they get a different message. In a university that values research above teaching, office hours may be necessary to meet promotion objectives and expectations, but those objectives are then met at a high cost: the potential loss of positive influence on individuals. The same is true for consultants and corporate trainers who shun their students because of the pressures of prospecting for new clients or coping with looming deadlines.

Most instructors have set office hours. We do not, and certainly corporate trainers do not. When a student has a need to talk, our door is open. The goal of our teaching activity is to help students develop a variety of academic, social, team, interpersonal skills as well as their confidence, curiosity, courage, career, focus, and clarity of purpose. Many instructors from other schools are appalled when they learn of our open door policy. For them, student contact hours are a thing to be minimized, and the best way to do that is to schedule short office hours, usually at times during which students are least likely to come.

Assuming you are among those who schedule office hours, consider how you use the office-hour system. Do you have lots of office hours, scheduled for the convenience of students? Or is the thrust of the institution, and thus your personal emphasis, on protecting personal privacy and time? Think about their relationship to the students' schedules and make a conscious choice about the balance between being alone to "work" and being available to "work with" students.

In ancient and medieval settings, students commonly looked to their teachers for guidance in many aspects of life, not just the professional one. Ulysses instructed his household servant, Mentor, to train his son Telemachus in all aspects of life. The medieval guildmasters were responsible to the community for the social and moral behavior of their protégés as well as their intellectual and professional skills. A teaching role historically calls us to be willing and able to understand and address various aspects of students' lives.

In a counseling capacity, to whatever extent that mantle is taken on, remember that separating aspects of our lives is very difficult. If we are influential in one aspect of a student's life, that influence is likely to spill over into other aspects. Our study habits; our social relationships; our exercise regimen; our attitudes toward money, power, social influence, and the meaning of life – all combine to produce what we are each able to do professionally. Students who see us as successful and thus ascribe to us some level of "having figured it all out," naturally may look to all aspects of our life as contributors to our accomplishment. We teach what we are. And students will learn what we are as they watch us teach and live life. In this sense, we are counseling them anyway. If we define our role to exclude active or face-to-face counseling, we lose some control over what conclusions students reach about how our lives have been composed to create who we are. But since we are "counseling" them anyway by the way they observe our behavior, we may be inadvertently teaching them to be distant from employees if we in fact are behaving that way toward them.

The best approach we believe, is to recognize that we have influence and to use that influence in open, freely given, honest ways. If we distance ourselves from those in our programs, and ignore them as individuals, we teach them that we think they aren't worth our time and energy, and we withhold from them the multidimensional aspects of our lives that just might provide an insight or an encouragement they truly need or want.

Referring to another person. In some business schools, instructors often refer troubled students to their Organizational Behavior (OB) colleagues. The finance, marketing, and operations instructors, for example, may feel that, because the OB instructors are behavioralists, they are the ones best qualified to provide counsel. That conclusion may or may not be true. For the most part, although the OB instructors have studied various aspects of human behavior in organizations, they are not counseling experts.

Passing along students in order to avoid dealing with human problems can be a serious mistake. This practice only further solidifies in the students' minds the common image of the other "hard" discipline-oriented team members as people who poorly understand the human side of business. If your inclination is to send students to the OB instructors because, as a finance, accounting, or other non-OB-area instructor, you don't want to deal with such "soft," human issues, please reconsider that action and its influence on students.

There are, of course, many times when students should be referred to someone else. Such occasions may be most prevalent, paradoxically, when an instructor does feel like giving advice in an area in which he or she is not trained. If an instructor is either utterly ignorant of counseling skills or overly confident of the applicability of his or her advice, students should be advised to get alternative viewpoints. (We will discuss referrals in more detail later.)

Agreeing to talk with the student. If you choose to accept counseling students as part of your teaching role, is there a model of counseling that can be helpful? Yes. Here are some thoughts.

Basic model of student counseling

Student counseling can be seen to entail five basic steps:
1. Assuming some responsibility for responding to students' emotional as well as intellectual growth and well-being;

2. Creating a safe, counseling environment;
3. Active listening;
4. Assessing the seriousness of the situation and your ability to handle it; and
5. Helping each student to reach his or her own conclusions.

Step 1: Assuming some responsibility

We have already considered this step. Yes, we each make a choice philosophically and personally either to be a counselor or not. Our teaching signals to students whether we are approachable, interested, and have any counsel worth seeking. Our teaching can also signal just the opposite.

Instructors cannot avoid this reality, they can choose, however, to manage it. So, our encouragement is for instructors to take some responsibility for the personal aspect of their role, to be willing to engage students one on one and on topics outside subject matter. If they come for help, care enough to listen to them. Be willing to try to help.

How many friends do you have with whom you can talk about anything? We mean *anything*. Usually such conversations are based on years of history, trust-building, and an understanding that your confidant will listen without judgment. We had one colleague who answered that question, "80 percent!" By that, he meant there was 20 percent of his life that he had not yet told his wife, much less other friends. When you need someone to talk to about the deeper things of life, where do you go? Does it cost you $100 an hour?

Developing an interest in others amidst a busy schedule is no easy task. When students come to you for advice or in search of a sounding board, ask yourself the larger question: "What is the impact of my behavior on this human being?" Realize that whether you say, "Come in and sit down," or "I can't see you now, I'm busy," you are "teaching" at that moment.

Step 2: Creating a safe counseling environment

Instructors learn quickly that classrooms as learning environments function best when properly planned and equipped. The same holds true for an environment in which you have candid conversations with students. Specifically, the goal in counseling is to create a setting in which the student feels safe, comfortable, and free to speak candidly.

Creating an effective environment for counseling begins on the first day of class with the attitude you present to the students. When students finally stand at your office door, they will pick up signals that suggest to them where they stand on your personal priority scale. Is the door open? Is there a seat? Is the office comfortable for personal talks? Are there physical barriers between the student and you? If you are interrupted by another instructional team member, do you ask that person to come by later, or is the discussion with the student allowed to be interrupted, or worse yet, is the student asked to leave and come back another time? Do you take phone calls during a student's visit? Do you look students in the eye? Are you constantly checking the time? Do you seem interested in what a student is saying?

The answers to each of these questions either make the "space" between the instructor and student warm and likely to be helpful or cold and less likely to be helpful. When the Japanese refer to the relationship between two individuals, they say, "naka yoi" or "naka warui" meaning "the space between us is good" or "the space between us is bad." As a counselor, the goal is to create good space so that the conversation has the best change of being helpful to the student.

If a student has gone to the trouble to make an appointment or has just walked in and is clearly in distress, turn off the computer hum that invades the counseling atmosphere, turn off the ringer switch on the telephone, clear the desk, and say something like, "I'm all yours. How can I help?" All these things signal to the student that he or she is about to get undivided attention, which creates better space between the two of you. The principles here are to avoid interruptions and to focus attention on the student's concerns.

Many instructors' offices are stacked with books, papers, and other accoutrements of the academic or training lifestyle. We've all been in colleagues' offices where there wasn't even a place to sit down. If counseling is important, consider the impression that the office space makes on someone entering. Go outside and come in; pause at the threshold and ask, "Is this place inviting? Is it conducive to honest, personal conversation? Is there a window or light glaring in the visitor's face? Do the distances between chairs distance the relationships?"

The layout of your office can greatly influence the counseling setting. If the desk faces the door, there is a barrier created. If the desk faces a side wall or back wall it is easy to swivel to face incoming guests, and enter the conversational space. If your office is large enough, divide the room into two parts, an "office" part with desk and computer and a "sitting room" with two chairs. This can be done visually, if not physically, by using a rug, some pictures, or by the arrangement of the chairs or file cabinets. The visitor then will know immediately when you have left the work space and enter the counseling space. We have a colleague who, very sensitive to this use of space, has his work station in the back corner of his office and the counseling space near the door. The room is carpeted and furnished in soft colors – beige, tan, and sand. The counseling space contains two large easy chairs. When you come in and sit down, you feel almost like you are in a living room – relaxed, comfortable, at ease. A great place to have a conversation.

Step 3: Listen actively

When a student comes to you for counsel, begin by letting the student do most of the talking. One of the best ways to listen is to use the listening techniques and attitudes described by Carl Rogers, the psychologist who introduced an effective means of therapy called "reflective listening" or "active listening."

Why listen? Rogers and Farson wrote, "Listening brings about changes in people's attitudes towards themselves and others, and also brings about changes in their basic values and personal philosophy." When people are listened to attentively, they tend also to listen carefully to themselves and clarify what they feel and think. Over time, reflective listening builds trusting, positive, even powerful relationships.

Paradoxically, listening can also constructively alter the attitudes of the speaker as well as those of the listener. The speaker can learn from being with a person who listens well. A person being actively listened to frequently experiences a shift in understanding of the problem. Usually, part of that shift is increased personal responsibility for creating, understanding, and solving the problem. As an instructor cum counselor, this self-teaching effect is something for which one can reasonably strive.

The theory of active listening arose from Rogers's experience as a therapist. He concluded that most people have the answers to their problems within them. Even if they don't, he argued, they are unlikely to implement any outside advice unless they are deeply convinced of the value of and committed to that course of action. Hence, encouraging and facilitating the speaker's attempts to sort out his or her own feelings and thoughts can be much more productive than trying to suggest solutions of your manufacture. Active listening has the pleasant byproduct of being somewhat less demanding of the counselor's wisdom than is giving advice, while at the same time being more helpful to the speaker. Thus, active listening is particularly appropriate for instructors who are not trained therapists but who want to help their students.

Active listening is not simply listening to or parroting the other's comments; it is a skill that is actually quite difficult at first. Active listening requires you to suspend your own interests, values, critical views, and tendency to instruct. We have found that this suspension, for even short periods of time, is taxing, hard work. Moreover, since active listening is a reactive technique more than an active one, it also requires that you gain some skill in knowing when to use it and when not to.

Active listening has four essential components: knowing when to use it, a sincere desire to truly understand the other person's point of view, a non-evaluative acceptance of – although not necessarily agreement with – the other's point of view, and some skill in checking to make sure that what you thought you heard was indeed what the other person was trying to say.

First, active listening is an appropriate technique when you don't understand what the other person is thinking or feeling. Sometimes we assume we know what another is thinking and feeling when we really don't. It is easy to assume that another's experience is similar to our own. Pause when you think you understand another person and ask yourself if you really know what's going on for him or her. If you don't, or if you want to confirm your guesses, you can use active listening to learn more.

Second, you must have a sincere desire to understand the other person's point of view. If you try to use this tool without really believing in its underlying philosophy, that contradiction in your behavior and belief will show through. Consequently, the quality of your relationship will be eroded. Active listening is not something you can do easily unless you understand the principle and subscribe to it.

Active listening is also nonjudgmental. If you are constantly evaluating the other person (that is, using your values to judge whether what they are saying or describing is good or bad), the other person will sense that, and his or her defenses will rise. Judgments, even positive judgments, are dangerous, because they allow the possibility that the speaker will be found wanting, inadequate, or wrong. This realization creates caution in the speaker's communication. When you listen, set aside your judgments. Don't try to determine what is good or bad, just try to determine what is. You can worry later about what needs to be changed and whether or not you can have any influence on that change.

Finally, you need to be able to reflect the substance and feelings that the other person has expressed. You become a mirror or a chalkboard that shows the other person what he or she is saying and feeling. You have to repeat the substance and show the emotions to the speaker. You choose your own words but present, as near as possible, an accurate, mirror reflection of the person's words, thoughts, and emotions. The reflection must be accurate in order for the person to deal with it effectively.

Every spoken message has two components: *content* and *feeling*. Together, these two components give the message meaning. Compare, for example, "I got a B on my finance exam" with, "Yippee! I pulled out a B on my finance exam!" The emotions underlying each statement are very different, but we commonly tend to overlook the emotions of the speaker when we listen. A key active-listening skill is to attend to both the substance and the connected emotions of the student's communications.

How to begin. Common questions students ask can begin a counseling session. For example, the question, "How am I doing in your class?" depending on the way the question is spoken and the relative classroom success of the person asking it, can lead to a private discussion. This may or may not be what the student came in to talk about. The student who asks is likely to have invested some emotion in the occasion. Therefore, a response that is curt or nothing more than a mere letter grade, even if the student is doing reasonably well, is probably not sufficient to address the feeling behind the question. You might ask, before or after giving a grade, "Are you anxious about the quality of your performance?" And add, "I'd like to hear more about that if you want." If the student is bursting out with the desire to talk, of course, you may not even need an opening comment.

Even without the student's prompting, you can begin an active-listening session with a simple "door opener" such as "How are you doing?" As the student speaks, your goal is to put aside your own values and judgments and to try genuinely to see and understand the student's world. You focus on two aspects of the communication: the substance and the emotions attached to the substance. You are not trying to interpret, to reformulate in your own value system, to judge or find solutions; rather, in the active-listening mode, you want to be a nondirective facilitator, one who simply helps the speaker get it all out as easily as possible.

Not all communication is verbal; nonverbal cues play a big part in communicating both substance and emotion. Be aware of the steadiness of the speaker's voice, the facial expressions, body posture, hand movements, eye movements, and breathing, all of which contribute to communication and can aid your understanding of what the student is thinking and feeling.

As you listen, you occasionally signal to the speaker that you understand and are following his or her ideas. You can do this with simple words like, "I see," or "Uh-huh." Frequently you must, however, reflect what you have heard in substance and observed in emotions. This restating of substance and feeling serves two critical purposes. First, it helps both people to understand whether or not you are on the same wavelength, which is important for both you and the student. You need to know that you are not letting your own values cloud your understanding, and the student needs to know that you are willing, for a moment, to see the world as he or she does.

Many people, especially in business, consciously and unconsciously, avoid showing their emotions. They do this so completely that they even have trouble recognizing emotions; they cannot even distinguish between emotions and thoughts. This phenomenon increases the difficulty of understanding a speaker's world. So, we need to test our ability constantly to see the world in the way that the speaker sees it. If you occasionally reflect to the student your understanding of what he or she is saying, you can check the accuracy of your understanding. If the student nods agreement or says, "Yes! That's it!" and continues without interruption, you can assume that you "got it." Anyone who successfully accomplishes this reflection probably has a good idea of what is being communicated.

Second, reflection helps the student to understand his or her own concerns. The benefit is similar to what you gain in the classroom by writing down what students recommend. I have been in many case discussions where I have written verbatim what a student said on the chalkboard and had the student say, "I didn't say that!" I look around the room, and we all agree that he did. Seeing the words, hearing the repeated words, and seeing ourselves in social mirrors in this way *clarifies* for ourselves what we are thinking, feeling, and concluding. Sometimes when we translate thoughts into behavior (speech), we realize that we really don't like the approach or, alternately, that we are more committed to it and its underlying principles than we thought. Active listening, then, can be thought of as a social chalkboard, a conversational mirror in which students can see more clearly how they are, how they think, how they feel, and what needs to be done about their situations. These reflections help a speaker consider the topic more objectively and to see clearly what he or she is thinking and feeling.

We run two risks when we try to restate the feelings that are expressed by another person in our own terms. If we overreach in our retelling, we run the risk of interpreting. Suppose a student says, "I'm always exhausted. I feel like I could drop. I always stay up late and work hard all day to get the work done." An overreach would be an attempt to interpret why the student feels this way; it goes beyond what she has said. "It sounds like you don't think you'll be able to keep up with the work" is an overreach and may activate her defense mechanisms.

On the other extreme, if we say only, "It sounds like you're working long hours," we run the risk of merely parroting the speaker and seeming to her to be ridiculously simple. We need to strive for the ground between parroting and interpreting where we can, in our own words, reflect to the person what she was saying and feeling: "It sounds like you're feeling a little overwhelmed right now."

Some other common listening techniques are also useful. Good listeners maintain direct eye contact. You can also lean forward or in some other way let your position indicate your interest in what the speaker is saying. Resist the temptation to talk about your own views and experiences until after the speaker has expressed his or her own.

By listening actively, you release the student from fears and inabilities to consider his or her problems. Your simple act of focused listening communicates an acceptance of the worth of the person (although not necessarily of the worth of the person's solutions, opinions, etc.). Note Rogers' and Farson's explanation:

This releasing of the individual is made possible first of all by listening, with respect and understanding. Listening is a beginning toward making the individual feel himself worthy of making contributions, and this could result in a very dynamic and productive organization. (p. 21)

Behaviors that limit counseling effectiveness. Beware: You can do things that will limit your ability to listen and be a helpful counselor. Criticisms, judgments, and evaluations are perhaps the most dangerous. A threatening atmosphere makes effective communication much more difficult. As a counselor, your job is to create an atmosphere of trust and safety where the student can speak candidly. Criticism will destroy this atmosphere in a heartbeat.

When you are actively listening, avoid positive evaluations as well as critical ones. Rogers and Farson wrote that "it is a difficult lesson to learn that *positive evaluations* are sometimes as blocking as negative ones... To evaluate [an individual] positively may make it more difficult for him to tell of the faults that distress him or the ways in which he believes he is not competent." Note that Rogers and Farson were writing for a wide audience, and the special role of instructors as evaluators and graders makes the suggestion to withhold positive evaluations especially difficult to follow. A student who insists that he is hopelessly lost in a subject may be searching for simple reassurance. Yet, in some cases, simple reassurance could stifle discussion of an underlying issue of far greater importance. When in doubt, listen to the student talk out his or her own concerns.

The active listener, when speaking reflectively must be conscious of the language he or she uses to avoid doing more harm than good. Language should be geared to the audience. A student may come to you for personal or professional help. In the latter case, instructors sometimes tend to speak down to the students, perhaps inadvertently embarrassing them by assuming that they know more about the professor's subject area than they do. At times like this, you should remember that you were a novice once yourself and try to respond to the student with language and a level of detail that matches the student's understanding. Matching language to audience is always sound advice in teaching, but in counseling it can mean the difference between humiliating and helping a student.

Nor is it wise to listen at the wrong time or in the wrong place or about the wrong subject. "Wrong" in each of these cases is difficult to evaluate and is largely determined by the instructor's judgment. As an example, you might want to appear approachable and respectful in and after class in order to encourage students to come to your office. Don't try to be in a counseling mode after class in the front of the room or standing in the hallway. This signals a lack of propriety that may drive students away.

Step 4: Assess the seriousness of the situation

In counseling sessions, you should always be considering the question, "Does this person need to see a professional counselor?" You need to have a healthy sense of your own limitations as a counselor. You may be able to listen to and provide some advice to basically healthy, functioning adults who may be going through periods of minor depression or stress, but most instructors are neither trained nor equipped to handle serious cases in which therapy may be required.

What do you look for in your assessment? Perhaps the first thing is any indication that the student in contemplating suicide or self-abuse. If a student talks about taking her own life or the life of another, do not assume that this is a passing exaggeration; most will turn out not to be serious, but do not make that assumption. In many cases, the mentioning of suicide can be interpreted as a request for help and not really based in a desire to do oneself harm, but do not assume this. Always treat these cases as potentially true and encourage the person to see a professional counselor.

In the same way that mentioning suicide may be a call for help, not mentioning it may indicate a deeper willingness to actually hurt oneself. In the relatively rare instances when a student appears extremely distressed or depressed, you might ask at an appropriate time, "Do you feel like hurting yourself?" or "Have you been thinking at all about hurting yourself?" If the answer is positive or if you sense a deeper trouble, refer the student to a counselor.

Other signals you can look for are situations in which a student hasn't been able to function for several days, seems to be neglecting personal hygiene or dress, is not eating properly, cannot sleep for extended periods of time, or is constantly morose and depressed of spirit. These cases, too, you should refer to a professional. The sources of these problems are probably more deep-seated than what is happening in school and should be treated medically.

You should know what you can recommend from the range of services that are available at your institution and in the community. You may wish to visit the university's counseling office to become familiar with it and the counselors. Getting to know some of the professionals in the community gives you additional resources to turn to. Then, when you conclude that you are confronted with a situation that goes beyond your ability to counsel, a situation that is potentially dangerous, long-term, or deep-seated, you can gently refer the student to someone with whom you have some experience.

You could keep handy a list of the qualified, local psychological counselors that you know and trust. Simply saying, "Why don't you go to the student counseling center?" may not be enough. I referred a troubled student to the campus counseling office once and learned later that the counselor had broken all professional rules by having an affair with her, which in turn caused major problems for the woman and her marriage over several years. I never sent anyone there again and learned a hard lesson: you cannot assume that a phone listing on campus or in the community qualifies counselors to see your students. Since that experience, I determined to refer my students only to people that I have met and developed some confidence in.

Making a referral is a skill. Vague encouragements are often useless to stressed or depressed people. Sometimes they feel a stigma is attached to counseling and will resist gentle suggestions. Faced with this reaction, implicit or explicit, I usually explain that, in the same way that we go to a physician when our bodies are overstressed, we can reasonably go to a psychologist when our minds are overstressed. That kind of reassurance may reduce the stigma the student sees.

Stressed by other pressures, a student may not even have the strength of mind to pursue a vague referral; it may seem like too much to do. Instead, suggest that the individual contact a specific name at a specific location and phone number. You should also try to achieve some sense of commitment from the individual that he or she will take action, especially if the situation is serious. You might simply, gently, ask, "Will you call this person?" And add, "Please let me know when you've done this. I'm concerned about you and want to make sure you get some help." In rare cases, you may wish to contact the office yourself and ask them to contact the individual. You must consider in cases like this, however, whether this step violates the confidence with which you were approached in the first place.

In short, as you listen, assess the person's condition to see if you feel reasonably prepared to handle the problem. If you have any doubts, refer the person to a professional and follow up. If the person seems reasonably stable and mature, you will probably venture some advice. When you do, here are a couple of things to remember.

Step 5: Help the student find good answers

Advice, especially from an amateur, is dangerous. Remember that the students may do whatever you tell them. If you know, as I do, colleagues who make off-hand, passing comments to students who then change their lives dramatically, you will be sensitive to the importance of considering carefully what you advise them to do. The fact that they come to you indicates that they are open to your input, respect your advice, and may well act on it. Treat the encounter with similar seriousness and attention.

That's why we suggest the reflective approach; you don't have to give much advice at all for it to work. Most counseling sessions, however, will come to a point when listening is no longer appropriate. The student will expect you to say something new, to suggest some action, or to interpret what the student has said. At this point, there are a couple of conservative things you can do. First, you can describe similar experiences of your own. The goal here is not to say, "Do it the way I did"; rather it is to share a little and thus signal the student that you too are human and that people can work through these situations and carry on productively. Your method of handling situations in the past may suggest something to the student that he or she can do, but I think you ought to let the student glean those ideas from your comments rather than give them specific advice. The reason for this is that your decisions, no matter how similar to the student's, were made in a different context with a different background and a different set of underlying personal values.

Discussing the possible consequences of various action plans, preferably those suggested by the student, may also be more productive than giving specific advice. Your advice may add to the student's burden rather than relieve it. It may be another example, in the student's mind, of how the rest of the world is trying to control him or her. Rogers (1942) had this to say about the giving of advice:

The individual who has a good deal of independence necessarily rejects such suggestions in order to return to his own integrity. On the other hand, the person who already has a tendency to be dependent and to allow others to make his decisions is driven deeper into his dependency.

Remember these consequences as you give counsel. Give advice sparingly, if at all, and always in the context of what you would do, not necessarily what the student should do. Talk about alternative actions and what the consequences of each are, so that, in the end, the student can choose the alternative with its associated consequences.

Avoid responding to demands for decisions, judgments, and evaluations; don't let students push you into accepting responsibility for their lives by answering such questions. If you give advice, and they try it, and for whatever reason it doesn't work, they will blame you, not themselves. Help them to see that each individual makes choices in life and then must live with those choices. Resist the temptation to increase their dependency by giving answers. Answering a question with another, well-chosen, question is often a ploy that can leave the way open for students to express, explore, and evaluate their real concerns. By asking good questions, you, the listener, can participate in a helpful way without assuming any responsibility for the student's decision-making or action.

Avoid extracting heavy promises from students. Under pressure, a student will at times promise anything just to escape the unpleasantness of force, particularly if the visit has been anticipated by the instructor, who has prepared a good plan for the student to follow. The cure of forced commitment could be worse than the disease. If you give advice, give it freely without demanding that the individual do exactly as you say.

If some action is imperative, a good question to ask is, "What are you going to *do*?" This approach can take the discussion out of the potentially suffocating realm of speculation and abstractions and encourage the student to find an outlet in action. When the student then chooses an action plan, it will be his or hers, not yours.

When moving from listening to other forms of communication, most untrained instructors are tempted to use the *directive* approach characterized by "You should...," "I think that...," or "Don't you think that you ought to..." The *nondirective* method of responding asks questions that are sincere questions, not veiled statements of opinion: "Are you ready to make a change?" instead of "Don't you think you're ready to make a change?" And the nondirective makes no use of the advice-giving "you shoulds" and "I thinks." The nondirective is the method of speaking that is consistent with the principles of reflective listening, and as such, it is the method of communicating that I recommend.

Not giving advice may be hard for you. You may think that your experience gives you the insight necessary to guide the student. At times like this, remember that you cannot live students' lives for them and that you really don't understand more than the tip of the iceberg of their experience and why they are now behaving the way they are. If you do, you will see that the quality of your advice and experience to them may be negative rather than positive. The more we focus on our own experiences and in so doing attend to our own needs, the less able we are to attend to the needs of others.

If you decide to give advice, don't be shocked if the student resists it. Even if it is the right thing for that student to do, he or she may respond with anger. Just because you are trying to help someone does not mean that person, in a distressed state, is going to treat you kindly. The student may resent what he or she sees as an attempt to have greater control over their lives, and get angry. Students may lash out at you. In counseling sessions, you should guard against feelings of defensiveness and resentment of opposition to your views; your goal in a counseling session is not to defend yourself but to help the student.

Be aware that the listener's emotions can also pose a barrier to receiving your advice. The more involved people are in a problem, the less likely they are to listen to the feelings and suggestions of others. In the same way that it will be difficult for you to counsel effectively if you are wrapped up in your problems, it is difficult for troubled students to listen to your feelings and suggestions. This is another reason why reflective listening is usually more powerful than directive counsel.

Conclusion

All instructors, ready or not, will be called on to counsel students. As in any aspect of the job of teaching, reflection and preparation before the fact can help you face the unexpected. In thinking about your role of counselor, you have important decisions to make about how available you will be, how your time will be structured, and how open to others' personal concerns you will present yourself. Having either consciously or unconsciously chosen a level of availability and focus, your effectiveness as a counselor (and I believe, therefore, in part as a teacher) will hinge on your desire and ability to develop some of the skills discussed here.

You can do many things to practice. You can begin by asking yourself how you would handle the students' concerns with which this chapter began. You can also practice reflective listening in conversations with colleagues, in meetings, in negotiations, in conversations with your spouse or friends, and even in the classroom. If you use active listening when students are presenting their materials in the classroom, you may well find your understanding of their views can make your plans to teach them much more powerful than they have ever been before.

Further reading

Britsch, R. Lanier, and Terrance D. Olson, *Counseling: A Guide to Helping Others*, volumes 1 and 2, Salt Lake City: Deseret Book Company, 1983.

Egan, Gerard, *The Skilled Helper: A Model for Systematic Helping and Interpersonal Relating*, 7th edn, Belmont, CA: Wadsworth Publishing, 2001.

Keefe, William F., *Listen, Management! Creative Listening for Better Managing*, New York: McGraw-Hill Book Co., 1971.

Miller, Alice, *The Drama of the Gifted Child*, New York: Basic Books, 1981.

Peck, M. Scott, MD, *The Road Less Traveled*, New York: Simon and Schuster, 1978.

Rogers, Carl R., *Counseling and Psychotherapy*, Boston: Houghton Mifflin Company, 1942.

Rogers, Carl R., *On Becoming a Person*, Boston: Houghton Mifflin Company, 1961.

Rogers, Carl R., and Richard E., Farson, *Active Listening*, Chicago: University of Chicago Industrial Relations Center.

Viorst, Judith, *Necessary Losses*, New York: Ballantine, 1986.

18 | *Evaluating students: the twin tasks of certification and development*

MARK E. HASKINS AND
JAMES G. S. CLAWSON

> In school you get the lesson first and then
> the test. In life you get the test and then the
> lesson.
>
> — Tom Groneberg,
> *The Secret Life of Cowboys*

Grading students is an established part of university education. Few professors find this task a particularly pleasant one. Most bemoan the tedium and time required to read exams, correct papers, and to determine final grades, especially the lower ones. In some ways this is similar to the attitude regarding performance appraisals in business. Many managers shrink from giving performance appraisals as they do not have the right information to make an evaluation, and they do not feel comfortable judging another person's life. Yet, periodic assessments of performance are critically important. This chapter introduces some principles and techniques for evaluating students.

Why evaluate students?

The two primary reasons for evaluating students are (1) to provide feedback that contributes to their learning (i.e., the developmental objective) and (2) to render a judgment regarding their mastery of a body of knowledge (i.e., the certification objective). In the former, the evaluative signals we send to students (i.e., grades, comments, debriefs, etc.) can and should be given in such a way as to foster a student's "double-looped learning" (Chris Argyris's term as used in Korth, 2000). That is, assessment feedback is a second-order input into the cues and content that students receive, process, assimilate, and adopt as part of their "sense making" (Weick, 1979) of the world within which they reside or strive to enter. It helps students answer such questions as: "Do I have what it takes to have a career in that field? Where do I need to devote more of my study time? I thought I understood that... how could I have been so mistaken? I seem to be able to do the analytics well enough, why aren't I able to interpret the results and apply them to different decision contexts?"

The certification objective, at the level of receiving a degree from a school, is primarily an attestation to third parties that the graduate has met the school's minimal standards. Some schools refine their degree-signaling message by adding levels of achievement such as "with distinction," or "magna cum laude." Those descriptors assert that the student was in a distinguished group of graduates from that institution. The certification objective is also achieved at the individual course level where each professor assigns grades commensurate with some absolute or relative standard of student performance. The information content of these grades is vested in their relative positioning and scarcity (e.g., receipt of one of a few As signals much better performance than receipt of one of many Bs). Certification requires assessment and assessment, by its very nature, is evaluative – as instructors we cannot, nor should we, downplay or divest ourselves of that responsibility.

We believe that both the developmental and the certification objectives can be met with similar assignments/tests, approaches to grading, and evaluative standards. The main difference, however, between these two objectives is found in the nature of the feedback delivered to students, the frequency of the feedback, and the consequences springing from the feedback.

Feedback frequency. In general, frequent developmental feedback is much better than infrequent feedback. In our courses, we provide developmental feedback on two dimensions – students' class contributions and their subject-matter proficiency. During a semester-long course, we have found it useful to provide two or three interim evaluations of a student's contributions to the class discussions. Thus, if the course meets 30 times, this timing creates an interim class contribution evaluation after about every 10 classes. This timing for class contribution feedback does not necessarily require the assignment of a formal grade but it does require some sort of substantive professor evaluation.

As a formal but unintrusive mechanism for providing regular developmental feedback on subject-matter proficiency, unannounced quizzes or case write-ups are quite useful. We frequently do this at least once a semester, if not twice. The purpose of such a quiz or case write-up, whose grade we often announce will not be recorded, is to provide students with a brutally honest moment, on a very specific issue, technique, or theory. The first-hand realizations springing from poor performance on such a quiz or case write-up are often a powerful motivator for improved study or the seeking of help – two very positive outcomes.

The frequency and timing of certification-type feedback is less frequent than for developmental feedback. Generally, graded exams, problem sets, and papers are intended to assess mastery of a body of knowledge, tools, and/or frameworks. As such, we are comfortable with, during a semester-long course, a mid-term paper or exam along with an end-of-course exam or paper.

The nature of feedback. Clearly, the very intent of developmental feedback is that it be as extensive and as specific as possible in order to be actionable. Whether in a memo or in person, stating to a student that, for example, their classroom comments are merely "not valuable" is unhelpful to a student who is conscientiously striving to do well. Rather, the feedback should note specific examples where the student's comments caused the class discussion to have to unproductively backtrack or slowdown. Likewise, if a student's comments exhibited that he or she had not been paying attention because the answer to their question had just been discussed or someone else had just made the very same point, they need to be told that. If, on the other hand, their classroom comments and questions are not disruptive or otherwise inappropriate but they simply depict too low a level of understanding of the issues being discussed, they need to be told that also – with specific examples. On the flip side, we all like to receive positive feedback. As instructors, we should look for opportunities to provide positive developmental feedback of the sort, "Sue, that was a great observation you made in today's class," or, "Thanks for the case analysis you provided today. It showed some rigorous analysis and creative insight." When possible, offer a positive remark before moving into constructive criticism.

Even the grading of exams and papers for certification purposes should clearly depict what the gaps are between what the student did versus what was expected. There is nothing more unhelpful to a student, and frankly more of an abdication of an instructor's professional responsibilities, than for exams and papers to be returned with no comments, no corrections, or no clues as to why the assigned grade was what it was. Thus, certification events can, and should, morph into developmental events. To fully achieve such an extended purpose, graded exams and papers, with comments, should be returned to students in a timely manner. At our school, we have a policy of three weeks or less.

Feedback action plans. Whether it is purely developmental or whether it is certification-oriented, performance feedback received prior to the end of a course presents time for action plans targeted at achieving the best possible performance during the remainder of the course. It is our belief that good interim performance warrants positive and encouraging feedback. Instructors should also take the opportunity to suggest several things to those receiving positive feedback. First, suggest to your students that they seek ways to stretch themselves. This might include suggestions such as: in class discussions they should look to integrate the topic of the day with other topics from prior days or from other courses; in their preparation of the daily assignments they should explicitly contemplate why a manager, or a banker, or a shareholder, or a customer would find the issue important; become a teacher to a friend, classmate, or study group member who is having difficulty with the topic; and/or peruse the business press for contemporary examples of the course topics. Second, it is important to communicate to students receiving positive feedback that they not rest on their laurels – that is, with several weeks left in a term and with additional topics to be covered, without continued hard work there is still the possibility of undoing their current good standing. Last, it is sometimes quite enjoyable and productive to invite students in good standing into a conversation about related elective courses they might enjoy; career options they may not have considered; and/or collaborative research opportunities you can extend to them.

For those students receiving less than positive interim course performance feedback, instructors should suggest a meeting wherein several ideas for action can be suggested. One suggestion that students frequently respond favorably to is to invite them to have a half-hour weekly meeting with you. The purpose of such a meeting is for the student to: (1) verbally summarize that week's lessons and important takeaways and (2) to pose questions they had wrestled with but were not sure they had properly addressed. As you listen to both of these discussion points, you can offer suggestions, clarifications, further queries, and confirmatory comments as appropriate. Another action idea is to suggest that students avail themselves of the school's tutoring program (this assumes, of course, that the school has one). If you judge that additional readings or exercises might be a productive course of action for a student, make specific suggestions in that regard. Last, sometimes students just need an instructor's suggestions regarding: a better approach to studying the material; how to best prepare for a quiz or an exam; and/or how to manage their time better. Sometimes they need to simply hear that an instructor has confidence in them and that all is not lost.

At the end of a course, action plans are, for the most part, unrealistic as students move on to other courses and commitments. If students did not do well in a course, it may be important to advise them to take a second course in the same general area so that they can ultimately improve their mastery of an important subject. Instructors should always be open to students wishing to speak with them about their final exam or paper – such a conversation is one last opportunity for encouragement, clarity, and specificity regarding areas of a student's strengths and weaknesses.

Methods of evaluation

The ideal evaluation method gives the evaluator a clear, accurate, and unequivocal assessment of a person's knowledge, skills, and attitudes, and critical thinking as they relate to the ultimate objective of a course. There are two links that are important here: (1) the accuracy and comprehensiveness of the evaluation method; and (2) the closeness with which the course objectives match the skills and knowledge that a person is intended to acquire as they leave the course.

With regard to the latter, some instructors appear to forget (or ignore) that what a student may need in the "real world" may or may not match the objectives that they have set for their courses. This has been an ongoing criticism of management education courses for several decades and has perhaps been most prominently leveled by Henry Mintzberg (2004). Too often, instructors design a course to transmit knowledge related to their own research or some abstract theoretical framework and pay little attention to how that knowledge might be applied and used in the students' careers.

Students function at, and learn at, three levels: knowledge (thoughts), skills (behavior), and attitudes (motivations). If instructors recognize these when planning a course, it becomes clear that planning for students' growth in knowledge alone is insufficient. To effectively educate students for their post-school work experiences, it is important to also consider their motivations and their behavioral abilities as a course of instruction is planned. In other words, it is not enough that students know something, but they must also learn how to apply that knowledge about something at the right time and place and be able to do so with an attitude and awareness that fosters its successful application. With these three levels of student learning in mind, evaluation methods can be devised that address them all.

There are many types of evaluation-oriented exercises. The most common are exams, term papers, team reports, quizzes, class participation, 180–degree assessments, class presentations, intern projects, and one-on-one interviews or oral examinations. Let's consider each briefly.

Final exams. Final written examinations are fairly effective at providing information for assessing students' knowledge and even self-descriptions of what they think they would do in certain settings. Remember, though, that just because a student writes that he/she would do a certain thing or take a certain course of action, there is no way to be sure that they would actually do it, let alone be able to do it. Pfeffer and Sutton (2000) refer to this as the "talk (even written talk) substitutes for action" gap. Moreover, written exams, which provide no opportunity for an instructor to probe, in real time and in varied directions, a student's underlying perspectives, are limited vehicles for assessing student attitudes.

Written exams vary widely in style and content. Multiple choice and short-answer exams are common, much easier to grade than case exams, and do a good job of testing awareness of concepts. Case analysis exams are more lengthy and difficult to assess. Case exams do a much better job, however, of getting students to identify problems, analyze their causes, think about which tools to apply, how to apply them, and what actions to then pursue than more objective-type (e.g., multiple choice) tests.

We generally give case exams or exams that require a tripartite blend of short-answer qualitative analysis along with fill-in-the-blank numerical answer along with extended written interpretations/action plans/evaluations. Indeed, an argument can be made for exams that embrace a variety of approaches (see, for example, Krieg and Uyar,

2001). Before reading students' case analyses, we prepare an evaluation sheet that outlines the key principles and insights that their analysis ought to include. This sheet includes sections where we can rate (usually on a five-point scale ranging from poor, below average, average, above average, and outstanding) such things as: problem identification (mentioning the major ones); analysis and use of the relevant analytical tools; various criteria for the action plan (including timing, technique, contingencies, etc.); and a final section on readability and presentation. Next, we quickly read several students' case analyses. We often read five or so and then reflect on whether the grading sheet needs recalibrating. "Am I too harsh or too lenient?" Once grading begins, we suggest using a set of editorial marks on the student's written analysis. A check mark, for instance, means "Good point" or "Yes, that should be here." A double check mark means "Extra good point." A question mark means "I don't agree with you" or "I question this." A minus sign means "This just isn't true" or "You've misapplied this concept." A wavy line suggests "Maybe so, maybe not. This is fuzzy thinking here." When finished, the students can see the places where they have made good, bad, interesting, and questionable comments. We will always make a few marginal notations on the exams to augment this evaluative shorthand.

It is also a good idea for an instructor to keep a separate sheet noting common mistakes or, conversely, nifty insights that students have made. Thus, by the time all of the exams have been read, a list of the best and worst points for each section from the entire exam will have been created. It is useful to compile these notes into a single feedback sheet, highlighting the elements that constitute an excellent exam. Few, if any, actual exams will contain all of the necessary elements, so students reading this compilation can simply see what others did that they did not do. Another approach for communicating expectations about the content of a well-answered exam is to photocopy the best one or two exams and put them on reserve in the library (with the students' names blacked out) so students can see them and compare their papers. Some instructors simply put a copy of their grading key on reserve in the library.

Term paper projects. Term papers are another commonly used device for evaluating students. Like written exams, term papers focus more heavily on student knowledge than on skills or attitudes. Most term papers contain an inherent dilemma: they are often assigned early in a course so students can get started on them and yet students often need to experience at least half to two-thirds of the course in order to prepare a high-quality paper. It is also a challenge to frame the term paper assignment in such a way as to require the right level of effort and the appropriate amount of student-specific inquiry and insight. We are careful to make it clear that we do not want a doctoral thesis (thus we set page limits) nor a mere regurgitation of the content of the course. Care in these assignment arenas warrants conscientious thought. It is important not to cannibalize students' preparation time for your class or others. The term paper should provide students enough freedom to demonstrate their best, most rigorous thinking.

In regard to the feedback related to term papers, students appreciate an advance copy of the grading sheet likely to be used to evaluate their papers. It helps them gauge their effort to be most congruent with an instructor's expectations. If the paper's readability and grammar form a part of the grade, it is important to note that in advance. It is also important to be specific about any calendar milestones, with deliverables, along with the consequences of failing to meet those milestones. Once the papers are turned in, it is important for an instructor to commit to two things: timely turnaround (i.e., two to three weeks maximum) and substantive comments. In this latter regard, remember that more marginal notations are better than fewer, both positive and negative comments constitute robust feedback, and be perceptive regarding both errors of omission (e.g., the student did not push his or her argument far enough or did not use all the facts at hand) and commission (e.g., the student wrongly interpreted the data or incorrectly applied a statistical technique). It is often time-consuming to render detailed, paper-specific comments on term papers and it is tempting to avoid doing so. In general, reading and commenting on an average quality paper takes about one minute per page – thus, a 20-page paper normally takes about 20 minutes to read, evaluate, and write some pertinent comments. We cannot imagine it taking any less time. Remember though, do not assign a term paper if you are not willing to give it the grading time it deserves. To preserve adequate time to do this, we recommend that instructors schedule "grading" on their calendars so that other commitments are not allowed to preempt the time this important endeavor warrants.

Team reports. Team reports provide an opportunity to assess a variety of students' abilities especially if peer evaluations are a part of the assessment. Reading team term papers or observing team presentations provides an opportunity to not only evaluate students' knowledge but also their abilities to work together. It is fairly easy to tell whether a project was managed and integrated or unmanaged and thrown together at the last minute with little thought for how the whole would appear. Of course, an instructor is not generally able to see the team-work that transpired or not, but it is possible to get a sense of it from the quality of the output.

Team projects can be graded individually or uniformly. In the former, the instructor needs to be told, by the team members, who did what. Team members' peer evaluations can also be used to assess individual contributions to team projects. In such an instance it is important for the instructor to identify which aspects of teamwork the team members should assess. This makes the team's efforts highly galvanized since each team member knows that each teammate will be submitting an evaluation of their contribution. Chen and Lou (2004) report that students actually prefer that peer evaluations be used as a part of a team project assessment. Moreover, Kruck and Reif (2001) opine as to the importance of a proper implementation of the peer evaluation process and provide several suggestions, including: (1) give students a total number of points, not evenly divisible by the number of peers to be evaluated, to allocate across their colleagues; (2) carefully craft an option and procedure for a team to "fire" a non-contributing peer; and (3) use an intranet web site for soliciting and garnering the evaluation data so as to facilitate when and how the peer assessments are submitted as well as how the data is then accumulated and analyzed by the instructor.

Let's admit it – in a group project setting, it is much easier to give every student the same grade. Although this option might be adopted to encourage teamwork and seeks to smooth out the effects of individual contributions, it also makes it easy for the stronger members of the team to give up on proactively facilitating the team process and simply do all of the work themselves, submitting the finished project with everyone's name. Even in such a situation, we still assert that it is important for there to be some sort of mechanism for individual feedback assessment. An approach that can be used is to have each team member submit to the instructor a brief memo commenting on the contributions of, and what it was like working with, each of the other team members. The instructor can then codify these comments, by assessed student, and distribute them to the assessed student. The comments should not identify the author and instructors may want to add their own additional comments. Such an approach is worth undertaking because team skills are an important competency (see Ellis, 2003, for a provocative discussion in this regard) for students to develop, even if they are not the focal topic of the course in which the team project was assigned. Thus, instructors should not let such an opportunity go by without some sort of feedback on that dimension attached to students' completion of a team project.

Quizzes. Quizzes are often used to remind students of the importance of keeping up and for giving them a brutally honest assessment of their course content mastery to date. This is especially true for unannounced quizzes. Scheduled quizzes are more useful for making sure that key foundational course concepts are in place before moving on to more difficult topics. A scheduled quiz has the effect of encouraging students to study early and not procrastinate till the end the term. Scheduled, or unscheduled, quizzes can either be done during a brief 10–15 minute window in a class or they can be posted online where students are asked to complete it in their own time prior to a specified date. Likewise, quiz grades can be recorded as a component of the student's overall course grade or they can be graded but not recorded, thus purely serving as an intermediate feedback mechanism. We have used both scheduled and unscheduled quizzes and find that they are very useful devices for getting students' attention regarding their knowledge and skills development on a very specific aspect of a course. Embedded in the usefulness of such a device is the need for the quiz to be graded promptly (preferably within 24 hours) after it has been taken. Any prolonged delay in getting the assessment back to students undermines the value of the quiz as either a developmental or certification device.

Class discussion contribution. Many instructors grade students' class discussion contributions. This is particularly true in case courses where what students contribute to the class discussion and learning process may be as important as written papers or exams. We regularly give class contribution grades (accounting for 33 percent to 50 percent of a student's final course grade) to classes of 60 or more students and find it quite manageable. And it can be done without excessive demands on the instructor. There are, however, three aspects of such an endeavor that are important: quickly getting to know one's students; making it clear what counts as valued class contributions; and developing an easy-to-use process for recording contributions.

To assess student class contributions, instructors must know their students. A key aid in learning a bit about them and putting a face to a name is the class card. This is a card with basic demographic information on the student: a picture, the student name (along with a phonetic spelling), some brief biographical data, and space for making daily class contribution marks. Some instructors take pride in memorizing much of this information before classes begin. They enjoy being able to call students by name and refer to their undergraduate majors or previous work experience in the first or second class. This clearly leaves a favorable impression on the students in that they are dumbfounded that an instructor (1) is that conscientious and (2) could keep all of this information in his or her head before even meeting the class.

A second aid to learning who the students are is name tents with the students' names printed in large letters front and back and placed in front of the students during class. There are a variety of commercial products available for making name tents, but the simplest is an ordinary 8½-by-11-inch piece of paper folded into thirds and taped. Name tents greatly help link the student's face and name in the mind of the instructor. Likewise, name tents help the other students to quickly learn classmates' names, which is conducive to fostering a classroom environment where student discussions are epitomized by students addressing their comments to one another, not necessarily to the instructor.

Finally, if possible, an instructor can require students to sit in the same seat each time the class meets. With this simple rule, a seating chart is possible that will serve to accelerate an instructor's learning student names and faces. With digital photography capabilities at the ready, we now create seating charts with student pictures and names placed on a diagram of our actual classroom.

Research has shown a recency effect at play in people's ability to recall information. Consequently, in grading students' class contributions it is imperative that instructors mark class grades as soon after each class as possible. If several days pass, or even several hours, it is impossible to accurately recall all of the students who contributed to a class discussion.

So, armed with class cards, name tents, and a seating chart, how might you record student class contributions? We have seen a variety of systems, but one that works well and makes it difficult for students to discount is a seven-point scale from −3 to +3. In this scheme, the instructor gives each student a mark after each class. A zero stands for "said nothing" or "excused absence." The awarding of a +1 is given for a reasonable comment, some small contribution that moved the class along modestly. On the other hand, a +2 denotes an excellent comment that generated new insights for the class or stimulated a substantive, purposeful debate. The awarding of a +3, for us, is a rare event, given when someone really cracks a case so thoroughly that there is not much left to say. Assigning a −1 indicates that a student's comment represented a modest diversion from the class's focus, repeating what someone else already said, or coming in late and creating a mild disturbance. A −2 records the fact that the student was not prepared when called on, was stubborn on a point already refuted, or absent without advance notice. We do not recall ever awarding a student with a −3. Such a score would, however, indicate overt classroom insubordination and/or totally unprofessional behavior. In a baseball analogy, a +1 is like a single, a +2 is like a double or a triple, and a +3 is like a home run. Likewise, a −1 is a strikeout, a −2 is hitting into a double play, and a −3 is akin to throwing the game. With this scoring system, students have considerable control over their contribution grade. Students often bemoan the existence of "chip shots" (i.e., brief, nonsubstantive, fairly obvious comments) and how grading class contribution encourages such comments from classmates. But, in this scoring scheme, merely speaking in class to get "air time" is no guarantee of positive marks.

These daily data can be entered into a class contribution spreadsheet (see Figure 18.1). (Instructors should also keep the raw scores on the original cards in case the computer file is not functional for some reason.) From this file, we calculate the number of times a person has talked, the simple sum of their scores, and the percentage of +2s and +3s compared with the number of times talked. The first is a measure of the frequency of their comments, the second provides a composite of quantity and quality, and the third is a quality ratio. It is also possible, if desired, to ascertain the minimums and maximums, the averages, the standard deviations, and normalized Z-scores across the class population. In this spreadsheet, it is a good idea to also leave columns for other assignments like term papers or exams – in this way, all of your grading data is in a single computer spreadsheet.

Figure 18.1
EXAMPLE OF RAW SCORES FOR CLASS CONTRIBUTIONS

(from a semester-long, 37-student course)

CONFIDENTIAL CLASS PARTICIPATION RAW CLASS SCORES DATE:

Session	1	2	3	4	5	6	7	8	9	10	11	12	13	14	15	16	17	18	19	20	21	22	23	24	25	26	27
STUDENT																											
1 Stud. A	1	1	1	1	1		1	1	1	1		1	1	1		1	1		1	1		2		1	1		
2 B	1	2	1	1		1	1	1	2			2	1	1			2	1		1		1					
3 C	2	1	1	1	1	1	1	1	1	1	1	2	1	1	1	1	1	1		1			1	1		1	
4 D	1	1	1	1	1	1	1	1	1	1	1	1	1	1				2		2		1	1	1			
5 E	2	1	1	1	2	1	1	1	1	1	1	1	2	1	1	1	1	1	1	1	1	1	1	1			
6 F	2		1	1	2		1	1	2		1		2			1		1	1		1	1					
7 G	1	1	1	1	1	1	1	1	1		1	2	1	1	1	2	2		2								
8 H	2	2	1	1	1	1	1	2	1		1		1	1	1	1	1	1	1	1	1	1	1	1	1	1	1
9 I	2		1	1	1		1	1			2		1		1				-1			1					
10 J	1	1	1		1	2	2	1		2	2	1			1			1	1	1							
11 K	1	1	2	1	1	1	1	1	1	1	1	1	2	1	1			1	1	1	1	2		1		1	
12 L	1	1	1	2	1	1	1	1	1	1	1	1		1	1	1		1	2	1	1		2				
13 M	1		1	1		1	1	1	1	1		1			1	1	1		2	1	1	1		1			
14 N	1	1	1	1		1	1	1		2		1			1		1	1	1	1	1						
15 O	2	1	1	1	1	1	1	1	2		2	1	1	1	1	1	1	1	1	2		1	1		1		1
16 P	1	1	2	1	1	1	1	1	1	1		1	1	1	1	1	1		1	2	1	1	-1	1	1	1	1
17 Q	1	1	1	1	1	1	1	1	1	1		2	1	1	2	1	1		1	1	1	1	1		1		

Figure 18.1
(contd.)

Session	1	2	3	4	5	6	7	8	9	10	11	12	13	14	15	16	17	18	19	20	21	22	23	24	25	26	27
18 R		1	1	2	1	1		1	1	1		2	1	1	1	1	1	1	1		2	1	1	1	1	1	
19 S	1	1	1	2	2				2	−1	2	2	2	2				1	1	−1	2	2	1	1	1		
20 T	1	1		1	1	1	1	1	1	1	1			1	1	1	1	1		1	1	1	1	1	1	1	
21 U	2	1	2	1	1	1	1	1	1		1		2	2	2	2	2		1	−1			1		1		
22 V	1	1	2		1	1	2	1	2	1	1	1	1	1	1	1	2	2	1	1	1	1		1	1		
23 W	1	1	1		1				1	1	1	1	1	1	1	1		2		2	1	1	1				
24 X	1	1		1	1	1	2	1	1	1		2	2	1	1			1		1	1	1	1		1		

ETC.

Studs. = 37

	1	2	3	4	5	6	7	8	9	10	11	12	13	14	15	16	17	18	19	20	21	22	23	24	25	26	27
# Talking =	29	28	29	23	24	27	18	27	16	25	24	22	26	24	11	25	18	21	29	16	19	19	27	12	28	25	
% Talking =	78	76	78	62	65	73	49	73	43	68	65	59	70	65	30	68	49	57	78	43	51	73	32	76	68		
# of 3's =	0	0	0	0	0	0	0	0	0	0	0	0	0	0	0	0	0	0	0	0	0	0	0	0	0	0	
# of 2's =	7	3	5	1	3	6	2	5	0	6	5	9	3	5	3	3	3	3	1	6	3	5	7	0	1	5	
# of −1's =	0	0	0	0	0	0	0	0	0	1	0	0	0	0	0	0	0	0	1	0	1	0	1	0	0	2	
# of −2's =	0	0	0	0	0	0	0	0	0	0	0	0	0	0	0	0	0	0	0	0	0	0	0	0	0	0	
# of −3's =	0	0	0	0	0	0	0	0	0	0	0	0	0	0	0	0	0	0	0	0	0	0	0	0	0	0	

NOTE: Totals are not accurate since this is an excerpt from an actual spreadsheet and does not include all students in that file.

During the progression of a semester course, we believe it is a good idea to distribute mid-term evaluations of class contribution to each student to (1) provide an opportunity for discussions regarding the congruency of the instructor's point of view and the student's; (2) allow for students to gain further clarity, if needed, regarding an instructor's expectations about class contributions; (3) to do all this at a point where substantial time remains in the course during which students can take action on the feedback. These mid-term evaluations can take the form of reporting a letter grade that would be assigned if class contributions were to end as of a certain date or they can be a simple memo that communicates to students whether the instructor's current assessment of their contributions places them in the bottom, middle, or top third of the class. A more extensive approach that fits in between these two and that incorporates students' own reflections, is conveyed in Figures 18.2 and 18.3. No matter the approach taken for interim class contribution feedback/assessment, instructors should invite students to come speak with them if they have questions or concerns; and/or provide some encouragement and suggestions for improvement.

One final aspect of assessing students' class contributions involves making it clear to them what constitutes a valuable contribution. In the absence of specificity and clarity in that regard, students often think that the only thing that counts is correct answers to assigned questions or to the questions an instructor poses in class. It is our belief that a rich and robust class discussion involves more than just answers. Among other things, it involves asking thoughtful questions, rendering eye-opening analogies, making linkages to other courses and work experiences, and the courageous defense of a point of view. In order to codify and clarify our expectations regarding how students can make valuable class contributions, we often hand out (or post on the course Web site) a memo like that presented in Figure 18.4.

180° Assessments. Recently, we have experimented with an on-line, 180° feedback system for students to receive developmental feedback on their class discussion contributions at the mid-term point of a course. Students initiate the Peer Feedback Process by:
1. completing an online self-assessment (see Figure 18.5); and
2. naming five fellow students in the class from whom they want feedback.

We suggest that students select peers who they believe will give honest and helpful feedback. Once a student has logged in the five peers they

Figure 18.2
A SAMPLE MID-TERM CLASS CONTRIBUTION
FEEDBACK SHEET

TO: COURSE:_____

FR: Professor _____   DATE:_____

SUBJ.: Organizational Behavior (OB) Mid-term Class Contribution Feedback

This mid-term class contribution feedback exercise is intended to give us both an idea of how we are doing while we still have some time to make some mid-course corrections. BEFORE you turn the sheet over to see my present view on your contributions to the class, please fill out this side of the sheet with your view. When you have finished, you can turn the sheet over and see my perspective and compare the two.

OB MID-TERM CLASS CONTRIBUTION: YOUR PERSPECTIVE
Mark a single "X" where you think you are performing in the section.

		QUALITY QUARTILE			
		1st	2nd	3rd	4th
	1st				
QUANTITY	2nd				
QUARTILE	3rd				
	4th				

.... tear off here ....

FEEDBACK TO INSTRUCTOR
I believe that feedback is a two-way street, so here's a chance for you to comment on my teaching style and approach. Would you also please note here a couple of things that you think are going well or that need to be improved in the way I am conducting the class and return it to my box? Thanks.

would like to receive feedback from, the online system sends automatic e-mails to the instructor and those five peers, soliciting their assessments. The questions posed to those six people are the same questions that the student filled out on the self-assessment questionnaire. The system gives everyone five days to complete the assessment. At the end of the five days, the initiating student receives an automated report summarizing the feedback rendered. We shut the survey process down

Figure 18.3
A SAMPLE MID-TERM CLASS CONTRIBUTION FEEDBACK SHEET

FEEDBACK TO STUDENT FROM INSTRUCTOR

TO:

COURSE:_____

FROM: Professor _____

DATE:_____

So far, I see your contribution, in relation to the rest of the class, about this way:

      Quantity percentile _____ %
      Quality percentile _____ %

The quantity score is a simple sum of your daily marks, and the quality score is the ratio of outstanding comments to the number of times you have talked, a home-run hit rate if you will. (NOTE that a 0% does not necessarily mean that I don't value what you say.) These scores will be weighted .75 and .25 and combined to get your final class contribution score. You may wish to mark the point defined by the two numbers above on the chart on the preceding page and compare your perception with mine. With regard to the specifics of your class participation, I have checked below some areas that you may wish to work on from here on out.

SUGGESTIONS FOR IMPROVEMENT:

___ Contribute MORE frequently; you have a lot to offer.
___ PREPARATION is not evident; do it or present it better.
___ Take a position, be more DECISIVE.
___ Emphasize QUALITY by being more incisive.
___ Support your conclusions with more data and LOGIC.
___ Practice being more ASSERTIVE; use voice, words, pauses.
___ FOCUS more on your classmates than me; convince them.
___ Try to be more CONCISE; distill/present points succinctly.
___ Use FIRST PERSON SINGULAR; avoid rhetorical questions.
___ Consider CONSEQUENCES of your suggestions. Force yourself to think about "If I do that, what will happen?" for at least two steps of your action plan.
___ LISTEN more carefully. Sometimes your comments do not follow from what has been said.
___ Be more of a LEADER; others respect you, step up to it.

In addition to this list, I encourage you to **write down** one or two things that you observe others doing effectively or that you want to do more effectively and PRACTICE incorporating them into your contributions.

Figure 18.3
(contd.)

Finally, may I repeat that I think good preparation consists of bringing at least three pages of notes to class: one with your list of the problems and questions that we should address, one with your analysis/diagnosis of the causes of those problems and their interrelationships, and one with a carefully thought-out action plan that addresses who, what, how, when, where, why, and what the consequences will be. In this way, you can be prepared for each major chunk of each class.

Figure 18.4
"WAYS TO MAKE VALUED CLASS CONTRIBUTIONS" MEMO

At Darden, students are expected to participate regularly in class discussions. Indeed, class discussions are a central element of the Darden pedagogy and classroom covenant. Student contributions to class discussions are evaluated by faculty and form a significant part of each student's course grade.

Students and faculty should view several types of class-discussion contributions as positive. Ideally, individual students should exhibit, at different times, the ability to make all of the following contributions.

- Responding to an instructor's cold call or offering a coherent recommendation and thorough supporting analysis
- Responding to a professor's question or a classmate's question in such a way as to provide insight or clarity on an issue
- Asking a thought-provoking question that focuses the class discussion on a key issue
- Making an insightful comment or asking a probing question that rejuvenates a listless discussion or redirects a conversation headed down an unproductive path
- Building on previous comments in such a way as to broaden and deepen the learning potential
- Where appropriate, offering work-experience insights or making explicit connections to other courses so that the focus of the discussion is enriched, elaborated, and emphasized
- Challenging assumptions and ideas constructively.

Figure 18.5
DARDEN SCHOOL 180° FEEDBACK QUESTIONS

Self-Assessment Questionnaire

Please answer the following questions. For questions 1–7, use the following scale:

5 = Excellent, 4 = Above Average, 3 = Average, 2 = Below Average, 1 = Poor

1. Comes to class prepared to discuss the case having read the case and the accompanying material ☐ 1 ☐ 2 ☐ 3 ☐ 4 ☐ 5 ☐ N/ A

2. Participates in class with meaningful useful comments ☐ 1 ☐ 2 ☐ 3 ☐ 4 ☐ 5 ☐ N/ A

3. Listens well to others ☐ 1 ☐ 2 ☐ 3 ☐ 4 ☐ 5 ☐ N/ A

4. Is engaged in the class ☐ 1 ☐ 2 ☐ 3 ☐ 4 ☐ 5 ☐ N/ A

5. Is willing to debate all sides of an issue ☐ 1 ☐ 2 ☐ 3 ☐ 4 ☐ 5 ☐ N/ A

6. Speaks to classmates rather than instructor ☐ 1 ☐ 2 ☐ 3 ☐ 4 ☐ 5 ☐ N/ A

7. Respects others' opinions ☐ 1 ☐ 2 ☐ 3 ☐ 4 ☐ 5 ☐ N/ A

8. What would you recommend I CONTINUE doing?

9. What would you recommend I STOP doing?

10. What would you recommend I BEGIN doing?

Submit

---

after five days so that everyone is rendering an opinion generally based on the same set of possible observations. Since students are soliciting feedback from their peers, the tendency, when asked to provide feedback on a classmate, is to think seriously, constructively, and honestly about one's responses. We stress that the goal of the feedback is to be helpful and developmental.

When students receive their summarized feedback, we ask them to take a few minutes to review the data. They know who the five peers are whom they asked to render an assessment and the data they get back is a composite of those responses so the identity of an individual peer's comments is not knowable. If there are gaps between a student's self-assessment and their peers' assessments, we encourage the student to think about what can be done to narrow those gaps. As always, we invite them to have a conversation with their instructor if they desire to obtain further insights and/or ideas.

Class presentations. If the truth be told, a lengthy lineup of student in-class presentations gets boring pretty fast. The first several may be interesting and insightful, but sitting and listening to report after report can numb a class. The presenters, to be sure, are motivated, eager for their chance, and no doubt learn a lot from those who went before them. There is a cost to be paid in the motivation of the listeners, though, especially those who have already presented. This phenomenon highlights the value of participative learning. Passive listeners find it difficult to tune in and concentrate.

If in-class presentations are a part of a course's graded requirement, it is best to keep them short, let students pick their topic, and to provide plenty of time for the rest of the class to ask questions and make observations. When the class is invited into the post-presentation discussion, they are more likely to pay attention. With the thought of trying to structure the course to maximize the novelty of and interest in the presentations, one idea is to schedule only a few on any given day and spread them over a term. This may be difficult, though, since the later presentations may have a distinct advantage over the earlier ones. Another idea is to require a one-page memo from the listeners that identifies what they thought was the most interesting presentation; why they found that one so interesting; and what sort of follow-up conversation would they like to have with the presenter. These memos can be collected and redistributed to the appropriate presenters.

Class presentations can be excellent practice for giving management presentations. Consider inviting other faculty to sit in to add an edge of tension that more closely approximates what students will encounter on their jobs. Even better, have presentations on real companies and arrange for managers of the companies to attend and ask their own questions. Be careful here, though, and make sure that both the students and the managers understand what is going on, lest the presentations be weak or out of line with the managers' expectations and the school's reputation damaged by the experience.

If class presentations are used, communicate to the students in advance about the criteria for evaluation. Be explicit about the kinds of background information, analysis, and presentation skills expected. A grading sheet distributed in advance can be a big help in this regard. During the presentations, give copies of these forms to the entire class and ask them to hand the completed forms to the presenting team or person when they finish. This is a quick way of getting specific peer feedback from a large audience with a minimum of logistic difficulty.

One-on-one interviews. This is an excellent way to assess students' capability, but it is quite costly in terms of time. In general, students like and appreciate one-on-one interviews with an instructor because they provide an opportunity for student-specific instruction and interaction. On the other hand, such an approach is often disliked because there is no place to hide – students must come face-to-face with what they do and don't know and all in the presence of their instructor. From the instructor's point of view, interviews can be an excellent way to learn more about one's students and to get a much better sense of how the course is going.

Such interviews can be formalized or informal. In the former, instructors post a blank schedule and ask students to sign up for a time slot. In the latter, instructors simply invite students to come by their office if they want the opportunity for such an experience. Obviously, in the latter case the conversation is purely developmental in nature whereas in the former case it can be both developmental and a graded assessment.

Principles of feedback

No matter the catalyst or focus for giving students feedback on their performance, there are some principles to keep in mind:
1. Feedback should be timely so that the student can connect the feedback to his or her performance. This is especially true of mid-term papers or class-contribution feedback. As the elapsed time from task to feedback lengthens, the instructional value of the feedback declines.

2. Feedback should specifically describe both what the individual does well and what needs to be done better. Avoid a single letter grade as the only form of feedback offered.
3. Feedback should encourage the individual, no matter what level of achievement, to continue to grow and learn.
4. Feedback should clearly describe an instructor's expectations.
5. Feedback should offer some specific suggestions on what a student might do to improve.
6. Feedback should provide an opportunity for students to respond if they have questions, are confused, and/or unsure what to do next.
7. Feedback should strongly signal an instructor's willingness to help a student learn.

Some other issues relating to evaluating students

Grades. There may not be a more controversial topic among degree-granting institutions than that of grades. Among the issues of concern and debate are standards, inflation, definitions, and autonomy. We have the luxury, at our school, to have all course grades posted for all instructors to see and to have colleagues that are willing to engage in discussions around such questions as: Why are our course grade distributions so different? What does an A mean and a B mean? Why are there so few C grades awarded in that course and so many in another course? Doesn't anyone ever fail a course? Should we have a forced curve or a forced course GPA? Such discussions are not particularly easy to have when a teaching team is mostly composed of "lone ranger" instructors who invoke the mantra "it's my classroom, you can't tell me how to grade my students." But it is a fallacy that students are students of the instructor, not the school. Second, what one instructor does with his or her grades does impact, at least indirectly, the grades of other instructors. In particular, grades have value much like a currency does. The relative supply of a particular grade, in part, determines it value along with what can be "purchased" with it. If everyone gets an A, it is relatively meaningless. If those receiving an A have access to the best jobs, then an A has more value than a B. Thus, we believe that the supply and value of a school's grades should be closely monitored and managed for the good of the students, recruiters, and the school's reputation; think of it as akin the US Federal Reserve System. We invite instructors to contribute to the common good of their institutions by engaging in grade conversations and searching for a grading policy and practice that contributes to a schoolwide set of standards, clarity for all those affected, and that truly differentiates students' relative achievements.

In any discussion about grades, one of the first issues to address is what grade categories will be in play and what each means. At our institution, and as we write this chapter, we use the following categories and related definitions:

A   Excellent
B+   Very good
B   Good or satisfactory graduate work
B−   Minimum no-penalty grade
C   Not satisfactory as a general level of work
     but passing for a particular course
F   Failure

It is important to note that all six categories are in play and used (although not, unfortunately, by all instructors) by the school's portfolio of courses.

Of particular note is the role of Cs and Fs. One grade of F and a student is dismissed from school. He or she may petition our Academic Standards Committee (ASC) for readmission and in so doing, the committee must assess three things: (1) whether there were there extenuating circumstances contributing to the grade of F and if so, (2) whether the student is able to adequately address those extenuating circumstances, and (3) whether the student successfully completed the rest of the program. Note that at our institution, an F cannot be compensated for with an offsetting higher grade in another course. The role of C grades is similar. Any student who at the end of the first year of our two-year program has three or more C grades (out of 10 grades) is dismissed from school. (At the end of a student's third semester, it is four or more grades of C, and at the end of the fourth semester, it is five or more grades of C.) Now, any student falling into these categories may petition the ASC for readmission and that committee's deliberative concerns are invoked. Again, our school has chosen not to allow a C grade to be offset by a higher grade – we do not use a GPA in our academic standards. Rather, we have chosen to require a certain minimum level of mastery across the portfolio of courses that a student takes. Other schools, choose different means of setting and enforcing standards. Whatever the nature and means of an institution's

academic standards, it is important, we believe, for instructors to re-
affirm, from time to time, that they support and believe the standards
are accomplishing their intended purpose.

Of course, grade inflation exists! It is the case at our
school and it has been documented more broadly elsewhere (see
www.gradeinflation.com; Johnson, 2003). May we make a personal
appeal to you, the reader, right now: Fight and resist any unmerited
tendency for rising grades in your courses and at your school. As two
letter writers to the *Wall Street Journal* put it, and we cannot state
it any better, when "students are called customers, [schools] fret over
providing the best customer service. What's the very best way to keep
customers happy? Give them what they want. Well, they want As.
Getting Bs, Cs, and especially Fs are likely to cause customer attrition"
(Duffy, 2002, p. A13). But yet, "the cruelest thing a teacher can do to
his or her students is to mislead them as to their true abilities" (Huxley,
2003, p. A9). In the end, that is what it is about – helping students learn
and then assessing the extent to which they did.

Recently at least one of us has become convinced that we need to
simplify our grading systems and find ways to make them connect the
four principal constituencies of the system: students, faculty, recruiters,
and the material. We have come to believe that a mixed model with a
forced curve on the top and an absolute scale on the bottom with an
unusual set of grading categories represents a better way to grade. The
forced curve on the top avoids grade inflation by making the top half
of the system relative to each cohort. Each class, for example, could be
graded with 15 per cent in the top category and 25 per cent in the next
category. The bottom half of the scale would be absolute in that it is
the faculty's responsibility to attest that the students who pass have a
minimal understanding of their subject matter.

But what about the categories? The letter system, A, B, C, etc., has
been a traditional meme passed down for generations. When faculty
assign these grades, what do they mean? Probably different things for
different graders. I propose a set of definitions that will connect all four
constituencies, namely the degree to which the faculty member *endorses*
each student with respect to his or her subject matter *to the recruiter.*
In this system, the instructor answers a simple question as he or she
grades each student: to what degree would I endorse this student to a
recruiter with respect to my subject matter? "Enthusiastically endorse"
(EE) is the highest category, "positively endorse" (PE) would be second,

"endorse" (E) would be third, "hesitantly endorse" (HE) would be fourth, and "cannot endorse" (CE) would be last. Any one of the three people involved would see such a grade and know immediately what it means. Every instructor can tell whether and to what degree they would, face-to-face, endorse a student to a recruiter.

Cheating and honor systems. "Today's business students have grown up in a society where distinctions between right and wrong have become blurred and where unethical behavior is observed and even expected in high-profile leaders" (Kidwell, 2001, p. 45). Indeed, "business students are among those with the worst attitudes toward cheating and those most likely to bring lax ethics into their professional lives" (Callahan, 2004, p. 219). To some extent, and it is debatable to what extent, this is the reality within which we teach. How does an instructor know if an assessment of a student is based on that student's own insights and work? We do not think that we can ever be 100 percent sure that it is.

The two common approaches to deal with this concern are: honor systems and policing systems. In the former, instructors generally agree to allow take-home exams or unproctored exams when students have agreed to, and signed up for, managing their own, and their classmates', academic integrity. As a result, student organizations are formed to deal with violations and instructors and/or administrators are asked to keep at arm's length. These systems can have both positive and negative effects.

The potential of student sanctions for other students' behavior can keep students much more honest than instructor policing. But, let's not be naïve. Performance anxiety, the pressure of a job search, a desire to excel, all can push students to be tempted to, and to actually, cheat. Indeed, the University of Virginia has a long history of a student-run honor system and yet, within the recent past, a physics course made national headlines when more than 100 of the students enrolled in it were accused (and most found guilty by their student peers) of cheating. Now, you could say that the honor system worked in that so many students were accused, tried, given the chance to defend their actions, found guilty, and sanctioned. How many students had done the exact same things for years before? Does it still go on today? No one knows for sure. Even in our own classes, when students have been confronted with cheating, some admit to it and quietly leave school while others pursue the due process of the student-run honor system and end up not being expelled, much to the chagrin of the instructor who firmly believed the student had cheated.

As an instructor, it is always a good idea to clearly state the ground rules for a graded project, paper, presentation, or exam (see Figure 18.6 as it relates to one set of guidelines given to students for studying and taking a Darden School exam). Define for your students terms such as "fair use," "plagiarism," and "academic integrity," and remind them that just because something is available online does not mean that it is in the public domain; it is too easy these days to cut and paste text and figures from Web sites. Proper attribution is simple to learn, and reference books such as the *Chicago Manual of Style* provide ample models to follow. In addition, graded tasks should be carefully crafted to give students the best possible opportunity to demonstrate what they have learned and they should be constructed in such a way as to make it awkward and effort-laden to cheat on them.

The alternative to honor systems, what we call policing systems, are perhaps more common. For exams, this means that they are proctored, in-class, and perhaps even varied from student to student. In regard to papers, this may mean that students are required to submit them via an online mechanism (e.g., www.plagiarism.org) where they can be screened for plagiarism.

Conclusion

Evaluating students is an important part of an instructor's role. For many, it is a distasteful task. It is, however, a task that can be a part of helping students learn (the developmental role), and one that is ultimately a certification signal to the student and his/her potential employer. Most would agree that proper certifications of the surgeons who will perform surgery on us, the engineers that design and build the bridges over which we pass, the architects who build the buildings that tower over us, and the teachers to whom we send our children are core societal expectations that we have and that enable us to live without having to be fearful and worried about every aspect of our lives. Shouldn't we also expect the same regarding those to whom we entrust the management of our retirement accounts, the making of the products we eat and use, the creation of the jobs that provide us with economic means, and those who lead the organizations that play a powerful role in the communities wherein we reside?

Figure 18.6
EXAM CHECKLIST

This checklist will identify what materials can and cannot be used while **STUDYING** for the Accounting exam on Thursday, December 9, 2004.

	Can Use	Cannot Use
1. Materials from prior years' students		x
2. Materials prepared by first year students **not** in your learning team without your help	ok*	
3. Materials prepared by your learning team without your help	ok*	
4. Materials you prepared with other first years	x	
5. Materials you prepared with your learning team	x	
6. Materials you prepared on your own	x	
7. Materials from others that you consolidate into your own notes	ok*	
8. Templates (pre-prepared spreadsheets)	x	
9. Outside sources (e.g. Web sites, articles, books other than those from the course, etc.)	x	
10. Use of prior ACC exams.		x

This checklist will identify what materials can and cannot be used while **TAKING** the Accounting exam on Thursday, December 9, 2004.

	Can Use	Cannot Use
1. Materials from prior years' students		x
2. Materials prepared by first year students **not** in your learning team without your help	ok*	
3. Materials prepared by your learning team without your help	ok*	
4. Materials you prepared with other first years	x	
5. Materials you prepared with your learning team	x	
6. Materials you prepared on your own	x	
7. Materials from others that you consolidate into your own notes	ok*	
8. Templates (pre-prepared spreadsheets)		x
9. Outside sources (e.g. websites, articles, books other than those from the course, etc.)		x
10. Use of prior ACC exams.		x

*Note: It has been our experience that too much reliance on materials that you have not had a part in creating is often not as helpful to you as relying on those materials that you have participated in creating. Trust your own learning. Good luck on all your exams.

Further reading

Brookfield, S., *Developing Critical Thinkers*, San Francisco: Jossey-Bass Publishers, 1987.

Callahan, D., *The Cheating Culture*, Orlando, FL: Harcourt, Inc., 2004.

Chen, Y., and H. Lou, "Students' Perceptions of Peer Evaluation: An Expectancy Perspective," *Journal of Education for Business* (May/June 2004), 275–82.

Duffy, M. E., "Grade Inflation: Who is to Blame," *Wall Street Journal* (4 January 2002), A13.

Ellis, L., *Leading Talents, Leading Teams*, Chicago, IL: Northfield Publishing, 2003.

Huxley, S. J., "'Soft' Graders Dilute Trust in Education," *Wall Street Journal*, (1 August 2003), A9.

Johnson, V. E., *Grade Inflation: A Crisis in College Education*, New York: Springer-Verlag, 2003.

Kidwell, L. A., "Student Honor Codes as Tool for Teaching Professional Ethics," *Journal of Business Ethics* (January 2001), 45–49.

Korth, S.J., "Single and Double-loop Learning: Exploring Potential Influence of Cognitive Style," *Organization Development Journal* (Fall 2000), 87–98.

Krieg, R. G., and B. Uyar, "Student Performance in Business and Economic Statistics: Does Exam Structure Matter?" *Journal of Economics and Finance* (Summer 2001), 229–41.

Kruck, S. E., and H. L. Reif, "Assessing Individual Student Performance in Collaborative Projects: A Case Study," *Information Technology, Learning, and Performance Journal* (Fall 2001), 37–47.

Mintzberg, H., "The MBA Menace," *Fast Company* (June 2004), 31–32.

Pfeffer, J., and R. I. Sutton, *The Knowing-Doing Gap*, Boston: HBS Press, 2000.

Weick, K., *The Social Psychology of Organizing*, Reading, MA: Addison-Wesley Publishing, 1979.

19 | Teaching evaluations: feedback that can help and hurt

MARK E. HASKINS AND
JAMES G. S. CLAWSON

> It is a serious thing to interfere with another
> man's life.
>
> – Gilbert Arthur Highet

Teaching evaluations may be a school's or a training department's most controversial subject. Many instructors shy away from giving and getting potentially painful feedback no matter how helpful it might possibly be. Perhaps this is true for the very reason most of us have chosen to be instructors – the autonomy it provides and the understandable knee jerk thought of, "Who are you (they) to tell me what to do and how to do it?" Yet, if we are to continue to improve our teaching skills and to grow in our craft, we need ways of collecting constructive feedback and of acting on it (Newble and Cannon, 2000; Fry et al., 2003; Seldin et al., 1999). Our desire is that instructors craft potentially useful means of getting and giving feedback on teaching, have the courage to receive and give that information, and find the discipline and determination to follow up on the feedback. Indeed, assessing, judging, and taking action based on teaching evaluations is a serious endeavor because it impacts lives.

Why evaluate instructors?

Let's face it, many, if not most, teaching evaluations are done because school administrators require it. Ostensibly, such a requirement is for instructor performance evaluations to determine salary raises, teaching assignments, promotion, tenure, and/or professional development plans. Our experience is that, unless your teaching evaluations are outside the norm, either on the high side or the low side, they have little differential impact on any of those decisions. Setting aside this mildly cynical view (yes, we acknowledge that), a conscientious instructor can and should use teaching evaluations to assess teaching effectiveness and for identifying ways to improve it. The trigger for such an evaluation, besides an instructor's requirement that there be one, may be one's own reflections or the comments of colleagues or students. Perhaps you observe too many students not really engaged in your course. Perhaps over lunch, a colleague who has just sat in on your class offers some feedback. Or you may have solicited comments from students either informally in conversation or more formally on some sort of mid-term feedback form. Any of these should prompt an instructor to stop and think about how he or she teaches and how that teaching might be improved.

Teaching evaluations can also be helpful for finding ways to enjoy teaching more. Sometimes, after several years at the same institution teaching the same course, classes can seem to run together, students begin to all sound alike, the material seems elementary and boring, and you are in a rut. At times like these, it is important to reassess one's teaching to see if it can be rejuvenated and made more uplifting for all concerned. Teaching evaluation information can point to, and prompt ideas regarding, new directions for honing the craft and for course design (Forsyth et al., 1999).

Instructor evaluations can also give students more information for choosing courses. This kind of evaluation is usually, but not necessarily, run by student organizations. The objective here is to provide students, prior to taking a course, an inside look at the nature of a course, the style and effectiveness of the instructor, the weight of the assignments, and other pertinent information that help students plan their term and workload.

Teaching evaluations also come into play when an instructor applies for an instructor position at another institution. Departments seeking to hire an experienced instructor often ask for a longitudinal sample of teaching evaluations, along with course syllabi and published works. The teaching evaluations are, if in the mainstream, not a critical variable. If, however, they are abnormally low, they are a disqualifier and if unusually high, a tie-breaker if two candidates are otherwise equally qualified. It is unfortunate, in our opinion, that they do not seem to carry more sway. This could be due to the twin facts that at most institutions, scholarship is valued more highly and profession-wide, teaching evaluations (especially student evaluations) are frequently discounted and viewed as a necessary evil (more on this later). We do not believe excellent scholarship and excellent teaching are mutually exclusive, nor compensatory.

What to Assess When Conducting a Peer Evaluation

What should be looked at when assessing a peer's teaching abilities? The answer, of course, depends on several contextual factors such as: the purpose of the evaluation; the type class being observed; and how the assessment is going to be performed. No assessment technique or instrument is likely to capture the kinds of information required in all of the variations possible in these settings. That complexity, however, can leave the observer overwhelmed and therefore more likely to fall back on an overly simplistic approach: sitting in on a colleague's class with no structured observational method, perhaps not even making notes, and then casually reflecting on the experience as required by the purpose of the evaluation. Sometimes instructors who would never be so cavalier in their research use this approach in assessing colleagues. On the other extreme, one could easily devise a peer evaluation protocol so complex that the user would have a difficult time observing their colleague because of having to focus so heavily on the requirements of the observation protocol.

Recognizing the dangers of watching for things that do not match the purpose of the evaluation and of easily becoming overly complex, we suggest several dimensions that can be used when making a peer (or even a self) evaluation. These dimensions include: preparation, assignments and materials, openings, style and technique, sensing students' understanding, clarity, mannerisms, quality of questions, enthusiasm, use of time, transitions, closing, and student rapport. A sample evaluation/observation guide, incorporating these factors, is presented in Figure 19.1.

Preparation. Instructors must be prepared for class. The multifaceted nature of many instructors' lives that includes administrative, committee, consulting, research, writing, counseling, and other responsibilities can easily relegate class preparation time to last on one's list of priorities. Yet nothing is more distressing to a student than to face an instructor who is not prepared. Newer instructors may have to prepare longer to meet classes, while more experienced instructors may find it easier to face the class with less preparation time. Remember though, that even though you may be experienced with the subject matter, the task at hand in each class is to facilitate the learning of a group of students who have not mastered, nor perhaps even ever heard of, the topical content for the class. You are teaching people not material. In that sense, careful consideration as to how to position, present, and probe

Figure 19.1
A sample peer-evaluation guide

Instructor name: _____ Course: _____
Observer: _____ Date: _/_/_ Place: _____

<u>Assignments and Materials</u>
   Clarity:

   Appropriateness:

<u>Chronological Log of Key Class Questions and/or Transitions</u>
<u>Instructor Attributes</u>

Style:
   Mannerisms:
   Physical presence:
   Use of humor, stories, examples:
   Clarity:
   Enthusiasm:
   Listening:
   Rapport with students:

<u>Opening</u>
<u>Closing</u>
<u>Key Questions/Transitions</u>
<u>Use of Facility and/or Audiovisual Materials</u>

a subject for the benefit of a particular group of students is warranted prior to each and every class.

As you observe a colleague, ask, "Does the instructor appear prepared for this class?" Positive signals, in this regard, include: having overheads and handouts laid out and ready to go when the bell rings; knowing clearly what the assignments are; displaying the ready use of well-thought-out examples to emphasize/elucidate a point; and having a sense of the students' readiness for learning. Instructors may not refer explicitly to a set of notes (which is actually a good thing if their plan is thoroughly internalized), but the mere presence of notes signals preparation as does the use of contemporary examples, references to current events, linkages to other courses the students may be taking, and an organized chalkboard plan that unfolds during the class.

Assignments and materials. Instructors who are serving as observers should read the assignment for any class they are going to observe. This will help in gauging the clarity of the assignments, the appropriateness of the materials, and for contextualizing the students' responses in the class. Are the assignment questions clear? Do the students know what they should do in preparation for the class? Do the materials fit the assignment and are they at an appropriate level for the students? Does the assignment create enthusiasm for the class? Is class time devoted, at least in part, to the assignment students were given? Are the students' comments in class indicative of an assignment that was confusing, unclear, or too lengthy?

Openings. Openings are important. They can propel a class down the right path or create confusion and dispirited engagement on the day's materials. Does the instructor provide a connection with the previous class? Does the introduction prepare the students adequately for the day's work? Is the opening abrupt, overly lengthy, or appropriate for the mood, activity, and attention of the students in the room? Does the class begin on a sour note or a positive, "Let's learn something today!" note? How long does the impact of the opening last into the class? Did it set up a discussion or lecture that flowed naturally and smoothly? Did the opening establish a basis for the topic or merely assume the class knew why the day's topic was important?

Style and technique. This is a broad category that can capture a number of aspects of an instructor's behavior in the classroom. Was the instructor animated and clearly interested in the subject matter? Was the instructor's style attractive to the students or off-putting? Did the instructor seem skilled in the use of various teaching techniques (as described earlier in the book) or was the instructor ill-at-ease? Knowing that different students have different learning channels, did the instructor invoke a variety of channels: words, analytics, pictures, diagrams, discussion, examples, and connective linkages? Did the instructor present him- or herself as open to student questions and comments? Did the instructor talk to the chalkboard as opposed to the students? Did he or she appear hurried, hassled, and hollow, or the opposite? In the end, different styles and techniques can be effective and the best way to gauge a colleague's approach is to assess the classroom atmosphere. If, as the observer, you were bored, turned off, disappointed, or unenergized by the class, and did not come away having learned something new, chances are the same is true for the students.

Attention to students' level of understanding. Did the instructor pay attention to the students' grasp of the material, occasionally checking that understanding with them by asking questions or asking a student to explain, in their own words, the point, the principle, or the practice just discussed. Was the instructor trying to understand student questions or assuming the needed response before the questions were asked? Was the instructor concerned about the students learning or his or her own covering of the material? (You have to be careful here, because your understanding of a subject matter may bias your assessment of the instructor's focus of attention. The goal on this dimension is to watch how the students are responding.) Like any leadership situation, leading a class does necessitate checking, once in a while, if the followers (students) are following.

Clarity. This is a dimension that cuts across several of the other observational categories. Was the opening clear? Were the transitions, explanations, questions, use of various teaching techniques all clear? Let's posit teaching as striving to make clear, to those who may not see yet or well, how various phenomena work, how theories apply, how ideas can be implemented, and/or how rigorous analyses can be applied. In this sense, clarity is a critical feature of the effective classroom. Good teaching helps make things clear to students. This is not tantamount to giving answers, since we can be striving to either clarify more general frameworks, debates, and points of view, or to have students discover (with our assistance) their own answer. Specific, single answers are not always the objective nor desirable. Be careful not to confuse lack of clarity with an appropriate, purposeful wrestling with difficult problems. Certainly, clarity must ultimately come about but a course design may position that clarity as the objective for the next day's class or as a process dependent on student reflection.

Mannerisms and tendencies. We all have idiosyncratic mannerisms – the issue is whether or not they add to, or detract from, the teaching effectiveness of our classes. As one watches another instructor, consider whether their mannerisms detract from your attention to the subject matter. If so, could they be changed? What would it take to change them? What alternative use of hands, catch phrases, or physical positioning could one choose to avoid such distraction? What mannerisms of speech are used that are annoying? Is the instructor using "Uhh . . . " or some other time-seeking mannerism to collect thoughts or buy time? Does the instructor sound condescending in response to questions? Does he or she ridicule (even in an attempt at humor) people or other disciplines (accounting is a frequent target in this regard)? Does the instructor make eye contact with all parts of the room? Is the instructor "nailed to the floor," never moving around? If students are called on during the class, is it a representative mix of the students in the class? Does the instructor achieve an engaging balance between an informal versus formal persona while conducting the class?

Quality of questions. One of the most important parts of a class is the questions that an instructor asks. In observing and evaluating a teaching colleague, it is often useful to keep a running log of all the questions he or she asks during a class to review together, later. This sequence, a kind of time lapse view of his or her intellectual probings, is often very revealing. By reviewing this log, you can see how the intellectual development of the class went and how skillful questions were or were not used in that development process. Note how long each question took to answer. Better questions tend to stimulate more discussion, multiple insights, and open the door to another discussion and level of learning. When the instructor asks a question, was the class able to carry on for several minutes and do so in a flowing, natural way or were the questions phrased in ways that prompted one-word answers or created jerky, confused, convoluted discussions? Notice, too, what kinds of questions the students ask and how they are answered. Are the student questions in sync with the instructor or is there a large gap, indicating perhaps that the instructor has moved too fast or presumed too much on the part of the students? Does the instructor encourage students to respond to classmates' questions and comments?

Use of time. Time management is a challenge for many professors. Does the instructor use time wisely? How does he or she handle diversions? Is he or she able to get students back on track? Does he or she allow too much time to be spent on trivial issues? Do the students seem bored with too much time spent on particular subjects? Conversely, do the students seem overly rushed to get through a topic? Is the end of class rushed? Why? How could more effective use of time, earlier in the class, have prevented that end-of-class rush? What topics got too much attention, and which ones got too little? Did the instructor seem preoccupied with, and therefore spend too much time on, a personal story? Did the class run past its designated end time? Think of the class as needing to pose a pace akin to a comfortable jog as opposed to a walk or sprint. Having said that, there are points where it can speed up (e.g., reviews of prior lessons) and slow down (particularly difficult or complex points).

Transitions. Transitions move the class from one topic to another. Openings and endings are big transitions wherein the instructor shepherds students into and out of the subject matter quickly and efficiently. During class, transitions are the bridges from one lesson learned to the next one to be learned. Is the instructor able to recognize leverageable transition points? Does the instructor make sure that all of the students are aware of the transitions that are occurring or does he or she allow a few students to make the progression and leave the rest to fend for themselves? Is it clear in the class when the students are to move from one arena to the next? How does the instructor handle attempts by students to jump back to an old topic or students who did not make the transition and are therefore holding the class back? Transitions serve to integrate the learning points planned for a particular class and for a course, overall. In effect, transitions are the mortar between the tiles, ensuring that the learning mosaic is well cemented, connected, and long-lasting.

Closing. Closings are, like openings, major transitions. Ideally, a closing should leave students with a sense of progress from having attended the class and a sense of anticipation for the next class. This progress/anticipation duality strengthens their learning and gives them an appreciation for the value of the time just spent. Case instructors often leave a class, to some extent, "hanging in the air." Case students, especially new ones, often express frustration at not having more closure and completion in each and every class. Although some classes are designed to create such an effect in anticipation of the next class, continued frustration, class after class, for lack of clear closings and carefully constructed bridges to subsequent classes, can be demoralizing and counter-productive to learning. Strong closings do not necessarily give all the answers nor provide discrete takeaways for each class, but they should provide a clear context for the class and how it fits with the next one. For example, an instructor may choose to leave some questions unanswered at the end of a class, recognizing the difficulty of the topic and placing the current class in a broader context. This can be done by stating:

We have wrestled in this class with the way matrix organizations are implemented in the aerospace industry. That discussion has left several questions in the air for us. Questions like how to train managers and technicians alike to handle multiple lines of authority and how to manage the uncertainty a matrix organization creates in responsibilities and task definition. In our next class, we will continue this exploration of matrix organizations and examine the case of matrix management in a large service organization. Many of these same questions will arise there, and we will be able to continue sorting out the advantages and disadvantages of matrix organizations that have arisen today.

This kind of comment can help students see, not only the specifics of the day's discussions, but also how the next discussion will continue to address their concerns about higher level techniques and questions. Did the instructor pay attention to the closing comments or did he or she move too quickly through it? Were the students involved in the summary and closing? (Often this is an excellent way to get a good summary and to reassess students' mental grasp of the topic as you leave the classroom.) Did the closing relate to where most of the class time was spent? Did it appear powerful or trivial, confirmatory or controversial, and was it helpful or confusing?

Student rapport. Before and after class, observe how the instructor interacts with the students. Do students stop and speak with him or her? Does the instructor initiate a connection via one-on-one greetings? Is there a set of signals being sent that say, "I am interested in your learning today and I want to further it," or signals that say, "Teaching this class is a necessary evil. I cannot wait until it is done and I can get back to more important things"? Instructors do not have to be friends with students, but they do have to be friendly to them. And, since the instructor is the authority figure and perhaps a number of years older than the students, it is appropriate and positive for the instructor to take the initiative in being friendly and personable.

We acknowledge that even this relatively short overview of the things that one can look at when observing a colleague is somewhat lengthy and complex. Even attempting to attend to these many criteria during a single class period is a significant task. Perhaps it is useful to simply posit all of the foregoing as the backdrop to, and the cues for, answering just two questions:

• What does the instructor do well?
• What could the instructor do better?

Remember that instructors (i.e., you as an observer of a colleague and the colleagues who observe you) are generally trained to be critical observers, and by default, observe colleagues in that mindset. If you are called on to evaluate a colleague's class, it is important to look for what goes well, along with what did not work so well.

Most colleague observations have to do with administrative evaluations. Their presence therefore can significantly raise the tension everyone feels in the classroom. There are some conventions of courtesy around visiting colleagues' classes that can be used to mitigate this potential "tension in the air." First, always ask permission to sit in on a colleague's class, preferably well in advance. Second, read the materials for the class. Third, be as inconspicuous in the class as possible (e.g., do not sit in the front row or fidget). Fourth, don't talk in the class. Fifth, do not walk out of the class before it is over. If you cannot be there for the whole time, don't go. Last, after the class is over, seek out the colleague and thank him or her for letting you sit in and offer to provide a few observations, if they are interested, later at their convenience.

Self-assessments

The focus of a self-assessment can be as varied as the field of teaching. It is possible to reflect on your own preparation for class, knowledge of recent developments in a subject area, the quality of tests and other graded tasks, and the content and organization of the course. Indeed, humans have a unique quality of being able to behave and to observe their own behavior. In some ways, you may be more qualified to assess your teaching skills than anyone else. We each understand the goals of our course, the mental decisions made on the spot in class, the intentions of our behavior in class, and the nature of our field.

We all want to think well of ourselves. We all, however, have emotional defense mechanisms that protect us and filter out some negative, but potentially important data that we could use if we could see it. You can use video tapes to review classes. Invite student comments formally and informally, and even invite colleagues to come to your classes if for no other reason than to give feedback. You can simply reflect on a class and ask questions such as those posed in the prior section of this chapter to identify areas for improvement. Disciplined instructors often make notes on things to improve after each class session, and over a term, develop an agenda for improvement for the following term.

Here are some additional self-reflection questions. As you think about each, and perhaps others that you craft, be honest with yourself. It is very easy to succumb to the "tyranny of the good enough," as one of our colleagues puts it. If "good enough" is good enough, at least admit it and then ask yourself two more questions: *"Why is it OK?"* and *"Is that an acceptable level of performance for me for the next 15 or 20 years (whatever the number of years remaining in your career is)?"* We would opine that if the answer to the second question is yes, you are either near retirement or you should seriously consider an alternative focus for your career endeavors.

- What was I trying to accomplish in this course and what techniques or strategies did I use?
- What didn't I accomplish that I wanted to, and why?
- Were the methods of instruction appropriately varied and interesting?
- Did I link the discussion to students' work experiences?
- Was I interesting, making full use of voice, gesture, and expression?
- How well did I open and close each class, and the semester?
- How well did I conduct class, by listening, explaining, questioning, and answering?
- Were the textbooks, handouts, reading and reference lists current and relevant?
- In hindsight, how well was the syllabus designed, and how closely did I follow it?
- If grades were involved, did I grade the way I said I would, and was the grading consistent?
- Were my class notes well organized and logically sequenced?
- Did the assignments and projects fit well into the course?
- Did the exams assess a representative range of skills and knowledge?
- Did I make full use of the facilities?
- Did students seek me out for counsel, and if so, how well did I respond?

Videotapes are a great way to facilitate a self-assessment. A review of a videotape of your own class, with the aid of a peer or a teaching counselor, is likely to produce positive changes. Viewing the videotape alone, however, is far less threatening and it, too, can produce desirable changes. As you review a videotape, all the questions and cues posed earlier remain germane. Moreover, simply ask yourself if you would have, as a student, found the class interesting, energizing, and worth your time. Be honest. If, in any way, you have to justify, explain, or rationalize a yes answer, chances are, you could have done better.

Student evaluations

Student evaluations of instructors' teaching are highly controversial (see for example: Morgan et al., 2003; Yunker and Yunker, 2003; and Dunegan and Hrivnak, 2003). Some instructors discount student evaluations altogether, using the rationale that the students do not have the maturity, experience, or judgment to know whether the instructor's behavior is effective or not. Many instructors also argue that the use of student evaluations turns instructor evaluations into a popularity contest in which each professor tries to outdo others in entertaining the students at the expense, it is implied, of rigor and learning.

Despite these arguments, students are the only people with the instructor in each of his or her sessions, and they are the ones most familiar with an instructor's behavior. Moreover, if students are the focus of our teaching efforts and if they do not learn in, or from, our course, in what sense can we say that we have taught them? Students seem to us, therefore, a very legitimate source for feedback on teaching.

We do not need to, nor should we, let students push us into an entertainment mode. In fact, our experience is that students see through this very quickly and lose respect for such instruction. Students value instructors who understand them, who work hard to teach them well, who exhibit a willingness and capability to make subject matter relevant and interesting, and who stretch them and appreciate their efforts and exploratory thinking. Most students want to learn. Most want to be challenged intellectually. We must be vigilant to not blame students for our own weaknesses in providing interesting and stimulating classes. Asking for student feedback does not obligate us to accept all suggestions – it does obligate us, however, to carefully consider them.

Beware, there will come a time when at least some of the feedback you receive from students is negative, perhaps strongly negative. We have all experienced at least one student coming into the office and saying, or sending an anonymous note, or submitting one formal feedback comment that goes something like, "This is the worst course I have ever taken. I cannot see how you can be called a teacher or how they let you stay here."

It is important to place such comments in the midst of the rest of the comments one receives. If this is a representative example of a number of comments, then some serious soul-searching is in order. If it is one student in three years, discount it and move on. We have seen instructors, ourselves included, read a generally excellent set of student evaluations and then agonize over two or three negative comments. Usually this is more common early in a career. Older, wizened instructors do not let isolated, nasty comments like the example above bother them.

When asked to evaluate instructor performance, students comment most often on three areas: the organization, structure, and clarity of the course; teacher–student interaction or rapport; and teacher communication skills and subject-matter expertise. Other items sometimes considered in student evaluations are workload and difficulty, grading, method of examinations, and some global assessment of the success of the course. Of course, the purpose of an evaluation influences the questions asked. Evaluations for administrative purposes will often be constructed like standardized tests, with some allowance for the instructor to insert five to ten optional questions that relate directly to his or her course. Some institutions have developed questionnaires which include questions on such dimensions as helpfulness for students with difficulty, sensitivity to students' feelings, flexibility, tolerance of student ideas, fairness in evaluating students, clarity of speech, respect for students, praise, triteness, and interest in the subject matter.

Here is a list of common topics included on student evaluations that we find most germane and helpful:
- communication skills
- favorable attitude toward students
- knowledge of subject
- good organization of subject matter and course
- enthusiasm about subject
- fairness in evaluation and distribution of discussons
- willingness to experiment
- encouragement of students to think for themselves
- makes the subject matter interesting

What should you do when a bundle of student evaluations shows up in your mailbox? It had been a pretty good week till you saw that familiar package waiting for you. Honestly, after 25 years of teaching, we still pick and choose when to open that package. If there is something important pending, or even something just plain enjoyable going on, at the time the evaluations arrive, we hold off opening them. We wait for a quiet time, generally near the end of the week, and at the end of the day, to open them. This is not because we expect them to be bad, we just know that if there are two or three negative reviews, it will sting. Like a garlic taste that lingers after lunch well into the afternoon, negative teaching evaluation comments are the strongest and get replayed in our mind for a while. No matter, the packet of evaluations must eventually be opened and read. Our colleague Bob Bruner (2002, p. 2) suggests the following (please note that we only provide key excerpts here):

Read the evaluations twice, the first time quickly to gain a sense of the whole. If the feedback is worse than you expected, catch your breath; put it aside for a while until you can re-read it more objectively. If the feedback is complimentary, you have a different challenge, though no less important: find the humility to look for genuine opportunities for improvement. Re-read the evaluations slowly, and consider the following:
- Cross-sectional patterns. *Sort students' [evaluations] into two piles, positive and negative. Make separate inventories of each.*
- Command and connection. *Look for these critically important qualities. Their absence is a showstopper. "Command" is shorthand for confidence, authority in the subject, apparent mastery. Command also has an interpersonal dimension: the ability to gain attention, respect, and following of students. "Connection" is shorthand for attending to the students: to know who they are, to listen well in and out of class, to understand the learning opportunities and challenges they face, to sense where they might be struggling, and simply to be available.*
- Look at the details. *To a large extent the overall evaluation of your teaching is the least useful information in the feedback, because it says little about what you might do differently next time. The results are built up from the details of your teaching. In this regard, the qualitative comments offered by students are valuable.*
- Your norms or theirs. *Many community norms are not discovered until violated (e.g., a heavy workload, requiring team projects). A close reading of the evaluations can help crystallize an understanding of school norms, your own philosophy of teaching, and where they collide.*

- Trends over time. *How does the most recent evaluation compare to earlier evaluations? Do the same comments tend to reappear?*

The challenge is to step back and entertain the possibility that the evaluations are really saying something valid. If, as many of us tend to do, you find yourself reacting to negative feedback through the denial, then anger, then depression cycle, accelerate through that process as quickly as you can to get to the "let's do something about it" stage. Do not, however, embrace more than you can deliver. Identify the one or two most important things to work on the next time around, making sure those issues get your full and conscientious effort. Striving to do too many things differently than you are accustomed to doing is a recipe for failure. View your development as a process. Positive improvement each and every year is more doable and sustainable than going from the bottom rankings to the upper rankings in one short academic cycle. If there are negative comments that you are baffled by, consider meeting with a student or two to ask them to help you flesh out the noted concern so that it becomes an actionable item.

Effectiveness of evaluations

Self-evaluations are of limited use for administrative purposes (i.e., decisions on promotion and pay raises). But discrepancies between self-evaluations and other evaluations, such as student ratings, can be important catalysts for change. If you see differences between what you think you are doing and what your students say, pause to carefully consider them. The areas most likely to surface in this regard are things such as effective use of class time, summarization of main points in lectures and discussions, openness to other viewpoints, and making helpful comments on papers or exams.

As we have discussed, peer evaluations are quite valuable indeed, yet are not all that frequent. We believe they should be a more regular, recurring part of one's career leading up to, and even after, tenure. If such evaluations are not part of an institution's normal practices, ask a colleague to sit in on a class or two. In addition, if you have the opportunity to team-teach with a colleague, do so, and then make sure a post-class debrief takes place. When it is you who have observed another colleague, prior to the post-class meeting with him or her, write up your notes, editing them as need be, and plan on giving them to your colleague. If you are observing a colleague in an official capacity for performance evaluation purposes, it is still a good idea to posit developmental ideas/opportunities, along with your evaluative judgments.

As we noted earlier, student evaluations are an object of much debate. On balance, and as we have assumed in our earlier discussion, we believe they can be very helpful in one's professional development. They should, however, be used judiciously in school performance evaluation decisions due to several documented, problematic issues. First, the goals a student brings to the rating/evaluation task have been shown to be strongly related to the ratings given (Murphy et al., 2004). One implication of this is to collect data regarding the students' objectives (e.g., "improve my instructor's confidence," "motivate the instructor") in doing the rating, along with the ratings themselves.

Second, the results reported by Yunker and Yunker (2003) also suggest the need for linking students' course performance to their teacher ratings. This suggestion is the result of their empirical finding of "a statistically significant *negative* relationship between student evaluations and student achievement" (p. 313). This counterintuitive result warrants more research. Even so, it does pose, at a general level, the basis for a linkage between student performance and their ratings of an instructor. At our institution, in the MBA program, we do not report, for analysis purposes, this sort of paired data. However, in some of our one- and two-week executive education programs, we have begun pairing, in the codified feedback reports to instructors, individual participants' numeric instructor ratings with their qualitative comments. We find this pairing informative.

Third, Morgan et al. (2003, p. 25) find that, "although administrators believe that student evaluations are good indicators of teacher effectiveness, instructors do not share this belief. Further, instructors recognize that factors exist which bias the evaluations to a greater degree than their administrative counterparts." This suggests the need for administrators and instructors to collaborate on designing the process for gathering, and the weighting of, student evaluations so that both parties can establish some shared bases for the evaluation ratings.

Last, and perhaps most troubling, are the research results reported by Dunegan and Hrivnak (2003). They report that, "As long as images of the instructor were consistent with expectations, students were inclined to conserve cognitive energies by completing the student evaluation mindlessly. It was only when images of the instructor were not consistent with expectations that a mindfully completed student evaluation was forthcoming" (p. 292). No one should rely on, nor even bother to gather, *mindlessly* completed instructor evaluations! Therefore, care must be taken to deroutinize the student evaluation process. Ideas in that regard, presented by these authors, include:

- Decouple the time for the evaluation process from other, high-responsibility, high-anxiety-producing points in the calendar.
- Signal to students, in substantive ways, the importance of their inputs (e.g., give them class time, and plenty of it, to do their evaluation).
- Make transparent how the feedback from students is used.
- Publish, in aggregate form, the student feedback results.

Implications of Assessment for Instructor Development

We once had a dean who, when the business school rankings came and our school had dropped in the poll, made contact with the appropriate people who had conducted and prepared the ratings report. His explicit words to the instructors were that he was going to view "the data as our friends" rather than the enemy. He wanted to preempt our natural tendency to find fault with it to rationalize or excuse our drop in the rankings. His oddly constructed phrase conveyed a positive, proactive attitude that many of us might not have chosen to embrace, left to our own accord. His attitude was simply that these are the results, let's understand them, and then let's figure out what we can and can't do in response to what we learn from them. The same should be true with the teaching evaluations we receive. Bruner (2002, p. 3) notes six arenas for response:

- Crystallize your priorities. *Not all requests must be granted. One good criterion for assessing the implied requests [for change] is to consider whether the change will promote better [student] learning.*
- Manage the feedback process. *Consider collecting other points of reference . . . [triangulate the process and the information].*
- Get an attitude – the right attitude. *The capacity to teach very well can be learned.*
- Be student-centered, and trust that decent evaluations will follow. *The straightest path to positive evaluations is to focus on [student] learning and the delivery of an intellectually valuable experience.*
- Accept variance. *Uncomplimentary feedback is the occasional companion of any instructor who takes risks with new material, tries*

new teaching styles, gets a poor draw of students, or believes that challenging [your] students is good.

- Be action-oriented. *[Develop] action steps beginning soon: reading on teaching techniques; asking to observe a successful colleague's class; asking a colleague to observe you at a few points in your course; searching for more suitable course materials; tinkering with the course design. Above all, don't shrink from the task.*

  Like it or not, a reputation as a poor, good, okay, great, super, boring, or entertaining classroom teacher is often a label that we acquire early and one that sticks. Clearly, early success can create space for an instructor to experiment and even slack off a bit. We would definitely encourage the former and discourage the latter. An early, unfavorable or unwanted label serves to raise the bar in future courses to overcome or alter that label. The formal and informal grapevines, around most universities and corporate training centers, are alive and well. Thus, students enrolling in your course will come with a preconceived notion of what you are going to be like and the burden is on you to change preconceptions into new realities. Generally, that is not done with small, minor, insignificant tweaks in one's approach. As we have said elsewhere, it is unwise to make wholesale, broad changes. It is best to make a very strategic, significant, visible change that bears on both students' learning and perceptions. We had one colleague who very early in his teaching career got very bad student evaluations – the common complaint was that he was never available outside the classroom. He finally internalized that message, committed to addressing it, and reworked his research and consulting schedules to be more available for students. His ratings improved markedly simply because of one strategic, significant action item.

  One last suggestion: Put into writing your own personal teaching philosophy. The chapter on professional portfolios will give you an idea of how to do that. Such an endeavor will force you to confront your specific goals, processes, desires, and attitudes about the craft. If you find it difficult to be crisply concrete in, and energized from writing and then reading such a document, that is a cue for some serious reflection. As you step back from the completed document, is there one thing about your teaching that you would like to be known favorably for amongst the students? Amongst your peers? Identify what that is and what it would take to achieve that. Go for it.

Conclusion

Feedback is an essential part of learning. As instructors, we return exams and give grades to our students and look to reinforce executives' insightful class comments, so that they might have an objective assessment of what they do well and what needs improvement. In short, we use feedback to students to help them learn. Yet, we often eschew feedback on our own performance. Various means of evaluating instructors' teaching should be considered as avenues of strengthening an educational system and of helping individual instructors be better teachers.

We have briefly described several sources of feedback data. No one of the three sources of teacher evaluations should be considered by itself; rankings from one group alone may not be sufficient basis for an evaluation. Yet taken together, self-assessment data, student evaluations, and peer assessments can supply a reasonably accurate evaluation of teacher performance. If we approach the evaluation process as a means to better performance, then "interfering with another's life" via this endeavor makes evaluation a positive, purposeful, and hopefully, welcomed effort.

Further reading

Aylett, Robert, and Kenneth Gregory, eds., *Evaluating Teacher Quality in Higher Education*, London: Falmer Press, 1986.

Beerens, Daniel R., *Evaluating Teachers for Professional Growth: Creating a Culture of Motivation and Learning*, Thousand Oaks, CA: Corwin Press, 1999.

Bruner, R.F., "Taking Stock: Evaluations from Students," *Teaching Concerns* (newsletter of the Teaching Resource Center at the University of Virginia) (Fall 2002), 1–3.

Cannon, R. and D. Newble, *A Handbook for Teachers in Universities & Colleges*, London: Kogan Page Ltd., 2000.

Dunegan, K.J. and M.W. Hrivnak, "Characteristics of Mindless Teaching Evaluations and the Moderating Effects of Image Compatibility," *Journal of Management Education* (June 2003), 280–303.

Forsyth, I., A. Jolliffe, and D. Stevens *Evaluating a Course: Practical Strategies for Teachers, Lecturers, and Trainers*, London: Kogan Page Ltd., 1999.

Fry, H., S. Ketteridge, and S. Marshall. *A Handbook for Teaching & Learning in Higher Education*, London: Kogan Page Ltd., 2003.

Margulus, Lisabeth S., and Jacquelyn Ann Melin, *Performance Appraisals Made Easy: Tools for Evaluating Teachers and Support Staff*, Thousand Oaks, CA: Corwin Press, 2004. (Includes CD-ROM)

Morgan, D.A., J. Sneed, and L. Swinney "Are Student Evaluations a Valid Measure of Teaching Effectiveness: Perceptions of Accounting Faculty Members and Administrators," *Management Research News*, 26, 7 (2003), 17–32.

Murphy, K.R., J.N. Cleveland, A.L. Skattebo, and T. B. Kinney. "Raters Who Pursue Different Goals Give Different Ratings," *Journal of Applied Psychology*, 89, 1 (2004), 158–64.

O'Leary, Kimberly, *Evaluating Clinical Law Teaching: Suggestions for Law Professors Who Have Never Used the Clinical Teaching Method*, Highland Heights, KY: Salmon P. Chase College of Law, Northern Kentucky University, 2002.

Seldin, Peter, *How Colleges Evaluate Professors: Current Policies and Practices in Evaluating Classroom Teaching Performance in Liberal Arts Colleges*, Croton-on-Hudson, NY: Blythe-Pennington, 1975.

Seldin, Peter, et al., *Changing Practices in Evaluating Teaching*, Boston: Anker Publishing Co., Inc., 1999.

Yunker, P. J., and J. A. Yunker, "Are Student Evaluations of Teaching Valid? Evidence from an Analytical Business Core Course," *Journal of Education for Business* (July/August 2003), 313–17.

20 | *Research presentations*

JAMES G. S. CLAWSON

One stereotype of research is that it is a
dispassionate process. The investigator is
depicted as detached from the ideas, the
methods, and the findings of the study he or
she is conducting, as a neutral, unemotional
actor in the scientific enterprise. We think
the original dictum that gave rise to this
distortion was intended to help minimize
bias in the way a study was run, to steer the
researcher away from forcing data to go the
way he or she felt they should go to fulfill a
preference. We believe that, over time, this
has been translated, in some research
method texts, seminars, and symposia, into
an admonition against feelings as a
component of the mature researcher's
repertoire. If this were true, research would
be a rather mechanistic and unimaginative
endeavor.

– Peter Frost and Ralph Stablein,
Doing Exemplary Research, p. 249

Teaching professionals in a variety of roles often are called on to give
presentations of their research. Whether as a scholar visiting another
institution, making a presentation at the Academy of Management or
another professional conference, or as a new graduate searching for
a job, you can rest assured that the quality of your presentation can
have a significant impact on your career. Many of us have sat through
dry, dull, boring presentations about what ostensibly is the pride and
passion of the presenter's professional life. It needn't be so. There are
many things you can do to bring your research to life and make it more

memorable and powerful in the minds of the listeners. If you clarify your purpose in giving the presentation, you will likely have a stronger foundation for beginning.

The purpose of the presentation

Research presentations have at least three purposes: showcasing your research skills, presenting important and interesting insight, and practicing or demonstrating one's communication and teaching skills. As you plan a presentation, each of these purposes, pursued in concert, can contribute to an excellent experience for everyone.

A fourth purpose – one that is nonetheless important to acknowledge – is that of learning from the audience to whom one is presenting. Approaching your presentation with an overt awareness of this objective will help you to avoid becoming defensive when people ask difficult questions. The natural human tendency is for the presenter to assume and act as if he should know everything with regard to the topic – but this all-knowing façade in settings like these can be destructive. No matter how well trained and expert you may be, there is always more to learn, different perspectives, competing hypotheses, and additional or alternative lines of inquiry. Excellent preparation, rigorous study, and provocative thinking, combined with a sense of humility and curiosity is a wonderful persona to present – and likely to be well received by all.

Preparing to present

Research presentations occur in a variety of settings. Anticipating this variety can help you avoid being caught off guard. First, consider when and where the presentation will be given. Will you be speaking after lunch? During lunch? Late in the day? Each of these time slots has their own opportunities and challenges. If you're speaking during lunch, plan for extra noise and people getting up and moving back and forth to the drink table. Don't take these potential distractions as personal affronts or signs of discourtesy or disinterest. If you're speaking after lunch, you may have to be extra energetic in order to hold their attention. What you eat for lunch can make a difference here, too. In our experience, it's better to go in a little hungry than overstuffed from a lavish meal with your hosts.

What about the location? Do you know the setting? If you can, arrange some time to walk around the place, looking for cords that might trip you, where the seating is, and how the scene looks from the audience's point of view. Do you have a sense of the atmosphere of the place? Try to see the presentation room in advance and become mentally more accustomed to the idea of speaking there. As senior faculty, we have hosted dozens and dozens of visitors over the years. We are delighted when the rare individual actually asks in advance about the nature of the research presentation setting and circumstances. These questions belie a sensitivity to instructional issues and an interest in managing as much as one can to make a positive impression and a productive learning experience.

Gauge the audience

The nature of your audience should inform your preparations for speaking. Remember to focus on working with the audience as much as possible. Know something about the audience and be flexible enough to adjust your presentation to match their interests. That is not to say that you give over control of the session to the audience, for in this of all sessions, you want to make sure that you can present enough to establish the three basic objectives outlined earlier.

Assess in advance not only the group's research skills and focus, but also their common teaching style. If you are visiting a case-oriented school and give a solid monologue the whole time, it is likely that the audience will be turned off. If you are case-trained and visiting a lecture-oriented school, efforts to engage the faculty may be viewed with skepticism. This does not mean, necessarily, that you must abandon the approach that you are best at – just "fit" with the audience. You have to balance your knowledge of the audience with your preferred style and make some adjustments for the sake of communication effectiveness.

Avoid "Why you chose this topic"

A common failing among doctoral research presentations, in particular, is an initial, long, drawn-out discussion justifying the topic. A lengthy intellectual genealogy of how your interest in a topic came to be is time consuming and boring. A simple and clear statement of the research question or main thesis is much more effective at the outset than a long lead in. You can make no more than three or four comments as to why the topic is important, give some indication that you are familiar with the other researchers in that area and any major competing points of view, and then get to the heart of your presentation. We have all seen presentations get totally derailed by long ideological genealogies that, in the end, accomplished nothing. We believe it best to get to the heart of your research effort quickly.

It is important to be able to phrase the driving research questions early in the presentation and allow them to provide the fundamental focus of the presentation for the audience. Frequently, research questions can be framed as hypotheses, but our experience is that a clear, lay language statement that then points toward an operationalization procedure that produces hypotheses is more effective. Of course, this depends on the nature of your audience. If your listeners are mainstream empirical researchers, the hypothesis approach may be best.

Limit the number and complexity of your overhead transparencies

Research indicates that human short-term memory can retain about five to seven items at a time. Too many overhead transparencies can ruin a presentation. So can too much complexity in those slides. Winnow down a set of slides to those that are clear, easily read and understood, and which, when taken together in sequence, tell a clear, logical, and believable story.

Too many presenters use stacks of slides typed with tiny typefaces that show enormous tables of numbers or convoluted, complex diagrams. The volume of slides means that the individual has to flip through them quickly, making even the simpler ones difficult to catch and follow. Remember, no one in the room is likely to be as deeply engrossed in the subject as you. Even if your audience is familiar with the area, they will not be able to follow in 60 to 90 minutes every step you've taken over several months. The message is clear: choose a minimal number of slides. Make them simple and easy to read. Have a second file of backup slides that show the details if asked. Don't try to drag the audience through every detail of your work. If they see holes, they will ask and you can respond directly.

We believe that the basics of a research presentation can be presented on about seven slides. The first is an overview of the talk and the sequence of the presentation. This gives the audience a little road map of where they are headed. The second is a clear statement of research question(s). From this slide the presenter can discuss the current literature and research findings without showing slide after slide summarizing the literature. The third is an outline of methodology. You don't have to show examples of questionnaires (although have some handy in case people want to see them). The structure of the study should be clear from this slide.

The fourth slide outlines the qualities of your data. Where did it come from? How was it chosen? What are its strengths and weaknesses? What are the demographics of the sample? This can be done on one or two slides. The fifth slide outlines the analytical approach taken. What tools were used? What steps taken? Why were these the right tools and steps to take? The sixth slide then summarizes the findings of the study. What was learned?

Finally, the last slide answers the "So what?" question – that is, the implications of the findings for management or for further research. On this page, the presenter can diagram his or her own anticipated plan of follow-on study after the thesis is done; faculty are interested in the likelihood of ongoing research productivity in a prospective faculty member.

Of course, each of these seven slides can be expanded to include more than one slide. Do so cautiously. It is a good rule of thumb to plan on three to eight minutes per slide. Plan to present a basic core and have backup materials for each section in case there are questions about the details.

Gene Zelazny (1999) has produced several excellent summaries of tips for "making the most of your presentation." He suggests using the story board technique to lay out your concepts in sequence and check the logical and visual flows. He also shows many things you can do to prepare simple but informative charts and transparencies. A key point is that there is a "data-to-chart" process. Simply making an overhead of a computer printout is insufficient. Think of the message that each transparency is intended to convey, identify the key comparison involved in that message, and then organize the data for that chart in a way to convey that message clearly and unambiguously. Percentage comparisons, for instance, are best shown by pie charts where the relationship to the whole (the concept of percentage) is most clearly and graphically displayed. Do not, for example, use tables of percentages to convey that message.

Zelazny recommends writing out the introduction, transitions between sections, and the conclusions for a presentation. This discipline teaches one to find the right words for these key moments and helps the presenter get into and out of the presentation smoothly. Notice that in this respect, presentations are similar to the teaching classroom. Zelazny uses a story board form for each slide that has three sections: spaces for a mock up of the slide, for the key concepts of the text to accompany the slide – what he calls the "so what" of the slide, and for the transition statement that leads into the next slide.

What about audience involvement?

A major theme of this book is that people learn best when they are actively involved. We believe this is also true of an audience – with a caveat or two. If they are involved too soon, there may not be enough time to finish the presentation in a timely, conclusive manner. Furthermore, efforts to use involvement techniques may be seen by an audience as just that, the use of techniques, rather than a genuine interest in engaging them.

It is a good idea to state at the outset a preference for questions to be held off to the end or, if preferred, let the audience know that questions along the way are fine. In either instance, be judicious in the number of questions you allow, gauge the audience interest in any one particular question to then assess the breadth and depth of your response, and always assume a shorter answer is better than a longer one.

Conclusion

Research presentations are important events in an instructor's career – whether you are a faculty candidate, a conference presenter, or a visiting professional. There is much one can do to plan for and execute them more effectively. Most of these steps involve fitting a presentation to an audience and the setting. Research presentations, however, are not classroom teaching situations. The more experienced nature of the audience requires more considerations. Respect their experience, present your topic and methodology concisely, and be willing to learn from their comments. Learn to gently manage the audience's participation. Be excited, prepared, concise, and clear. Demonstrate a command of the subject matter as well as an openness to learning and a curiosity for the possibilities that spring from the discussion.

Further reading

Alley, Michael, *The Craft of Scientific Presentations: Critical Steps to Succeed and Critical Errors to Avoid*, New York: Springer Publishing, 2005.

Baker, Glenn, "Lasting Impressions," *New Zealand Management,* 48, 6 (July 2001), 74, 76.

Denny, Bob, "Organizing Content Requires the Ability to Think Backward," *Presentations*, 17, 9 (September 2003), 58.

Englund, Randall, "Cater to the Learning Styles and Senses of Your Audience," *Presentations*, 15, 2 (February 2001), 88.

Friedman, Karen, "Give Your Audience a Reason to Listen by Cutting the Clutter," *Presentations*, 19, 3 (March 2005), 50.

Frost, P. and R. Stablein, *Doing Exemplary Research*, Newbury Park, CA: Sage Publications, 1992.

Harper, Jacqui, "Presentation Skills," *Industrial and Commercial Training,* 36, 2/3 (2004), 125–27.

Matthews, Carmen, "Nine Ways to Keep an Audience Mesmerized and Motivated," *Presentations*, 19, 4 (April 2005), 42.

Zelazny, Gene, "Say It with Presentations: How to design and deliver successful business presentations," McGraw Hill, 1999.

21 | Managing a degree program: behind the "Glory"

MARK E. HASKINS

> I find the three major administrative
> problems on a campus are sex for the
> students, athletics for the alumni, and
> parking for the faculty.
>
> – Clark Kerr (former President,
> University of California)

In this book, we discuss many issues, opportunities, and challenges that arise in connection with an instructor's course, classroom, and career. This chapter speaks briefly to the opportunity that an instructor may have to lead a school's academic program, or some significant part thereof. Contrary to the opening quote above, there are a number of issues that must be addressed in the design and delivery of an academic program. As but one significant example of the issues to be tackled in this regard, this chapter presents a generalized planning framework for designing and delivering that part of an MBA program during which students take the bulk of, if not all of, their required courses. This framework is also applicable, in large measure, to the electives part of an MBA program and to undergraduate business programs. We find that an organizing framework, such as the one discussed here, facilitates the planning process, the communication of a shared vision, and the galvanizing of purposeful action. This chapter also highlights some of the other dimensions of managing a school and its programs that some instructors may aspire to address and may be uniquely qualified to tackle at some point in their career.

Overview of an academic program planning framework[1]

Let's focus for a bit on the required curriculum part of a residential MBA program as a context for developing a generalized framework for managing an academic program. We begin with the premise that within an MBA program, a non-integrated, independently designed bundle of required courses is efficient to plan, but it leaves a lot of potential for student learning untapped. Moreover, a required curriculum's content, and the timing of that content during the year, often compete for the time, energy, effort, and share-of-mind that students devote to other school-related activities such as clubs, speaker series, and career-related searches. At the Darden School, where our required curriculum constitutes the entire first year of our two-year residential MBA program, we ask, "How can the required-curriculum phase (RCP) of our MBA program be designed to: model the integrative nature of business; leverage the varied stimuli to which students are exposed during the school year; and create a memorable, valuable learning experience for students?" We believe that those responsible for designing and administering the best possible RCP of an MBA program, or any educational program for that matter, can benefit from thinking of themselves as architects of a multidimensional student *experience* as opposed to the more common view of deliverers of discrete, isolated parts.

It is important to identify a program's objectives. At its core, our MBA program, and the RCP contained therein, is designed to deliver experiences that maximize students' learning in ways, and with outcomes, that create an affection for and a loyalty to the institution. These three overarching objectives are intended to envelop a number of specific goals. In particular, we strive to provide an RCP experience wherein students develop subject-matter expertise as well as learn how to: insightfully analyze business situations and create appropriate action plans; be tough-minded but not tough-hearted decision-makers; be effective leaders and contributing team members; and learn how to assess themselves and their desired career paths. We strive to do this via a program design that: stretches students while providing them with support; is rooted in a pervasive commitment to all opportunities for

---

[1] An earlier version of this section appeared as, "A Planning Framework for Crafting the Required-Curriculum Phase of an MBA Program," in the *Journal of Management Education* (February 2005), 82–110, by Mark E. Haskins, © 2005, Organizational Behavior Teaching Society. Used here with permission.

student learning; embraces a real concern for students' circumstances; and that meets or exceeds student expectations. It is important to us that students learn and grow as a result of their RCP experience and that the experience itself is viewed by them as distinctive, high value added, and exceedingly positive – so much so that we want each student to become unabashed ambassadors for the Darden School experience and committed supporters of the school. For students to have learned a lot and hated the experience, for any number of reasons, is not want we want. To have enjoyed their time at our school and not learned lessons that will serve them well, is not what we want either. These three objectives are inseparable and in our opinion, the essence of almost any educational program – who would choose one and not the others?

In the way of an analogy to introduce this chapter's program-planning framework, consider nuclear power. Nuclear energy can be created by fission (the process widely used today) where power is produced by splitting the nuclei of atoms. A solid RCP experience can be crafted by isolating, and separately managing, it's various components. On the other hand, a more powerful potential for nuclear energy is possible from fusion. This is the process of combining the nuclei of atoms. This is harder to do and not as widely used. It is the potential fusion-like interactions of an RCP's components that are ripe for careful and creative design attention and that can enhance students' RCP experiences. In particular, connecting the affinity groups students are a part of, the career-related searches they pursue, and the required curriculum they take through an RCP design focus on balance, integration, and standards is what gives rise to the framework presented here. Through the use of an easily remembered mnemonic device, BASICS, these six elements (balance, affinity groups, searches, integration, curriculum, and standards) are codified. Figure 21.1's portrayal of the BASICS framework succinctly highlights the three RCP design foci that can be fused with the three student venues to craft an RCP that: enhances student learning; fosters affection for their shared RCP experience; and results in a loyal cadre of supportive alumni.

Three student venues

Note that Figure 21.1 brings to the RCP-planning forefront the three primary venues within which students experience the RCP of an MBA program. These venues are givens, in some form or another, regardless of the school. Specifically, these student venues are a required

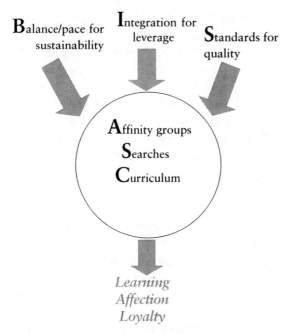

Figure 21.1 The BASICS framework

curriculum, various affinity groups, and their career-related searches.
A general word on each follows.

In regard to the **curriculum,** a concern for how adults learn and what
they need to learn is important. In considering the "how," research
shows that adult learners build on, and leverage, such factors as life
experiences, an explicit "need to know," and a preference for self-
directed learning (see Knowles, 1990, especially chapters 3 and 5;
Zemke and Zemke, 1988). Thus, in our required courses, we: (1) continually look for opportunities to tap into students' prior work experience; (2) use real business cases to depict important managerial tasks
and challenges; and (3) strive to foster classroom discussions based on
where students' real-time comments and questions lead. In regards to
the "what" is learned, we embrace a multidimensional learning agenda
within, and across, the required courses. This agenda seeks to provide
opportunities for learning about not only foundational concepts (e.g.,
net present value techniques) and contemporary practices (e.g., real
options analysis) connected to actual business situations, but also about
working with others, learning to express one's self boldly and clearly,

working under pressure, managing one's time, thinking critically and constructively, and leading.

Not only is individual learning a focus and expectation of our RCP, so too is learning through, and within, various **affinity groups**. Knowles (1990, p. 172) asserts that, "[adult] learning is enhanced by interaction with other learners" and yet Boyatzis et al. (1995a) note that one of the long-standing criticisms of MBA graduates is an inability to work well in groups. Together, these two points simply underscore the importance of RCP designers and administrators explicitly seeking to foster group learning experiences. During their Darden School RCP, students experience three key affinity groups: (1) an unchanging, assigned, demographically and experientially diverse 60-student, classroom section; (2) an assigned, diverse, 6-person learning team (i.e., study groups) that meets daily; and (3) self-formed and self-led interest groups. Within these affinity groups, students are expected to be both beneficiaries from, and contributors to, the potential learning latent in each group's interactions. The BASICS framework explicitly embraces this expectation.

The third student venue posited by the BASICS framework pertains to their career-related **searches**. At the Darden School, and with only the RCP in mind for purposes of this discussion, this involves the activities students pursue in forming a career objective, obtaining a summer internship after their year of required course work, or participating in other career-related activities such as soliciting venture capital for a business start-up idea. From our students' perspective, the outcome of these search activities is an important indicator of the quality of their RCP experience and it serves to signal the "correctness" of their institutional choice and the "rewards" of their efforts. From the Darden faculty's perspective, however, these student searches are often viewed as an intrusion on the RCP's academic component. The RCP opportunity to seize though is to meld student search agendas with classroom agendas and affinity group activities so that each is leveraged. The BASICS framework prominently positions this opportunity.

Three program design foci

In pursuit of the RCP objectives noted earlier, all in the context of the student venues just presented, the framework highlights three program design foci that occupy most of our RCP discussions: **integration** for leverage, **standards** for quality, and **balance or pace** for sustaining student interest and effort. Alone, these design foci warrant careful, creative stewardship. But, it is their potentially positive connections to each of the student venues that contribute most to the framework's stated objectives. Such connections can produce a program-enhancing gestalt because of: the more efficient, synergistic use of students' time; the multidimensional learning opportunities crafted from previously isolated or independent events/tasks; and the closer linkage of learning agendas to the realities of students' lives. Each of these design foci is discussed below, first in general terms, and then in more specific ways with several Darden School RCP examples as to how we connect them to the student venues.

Balance and pace

Nutritionists extol the merits of a balanced diet in order to attain a healthy physiology and distance runners emphasize pace in order to sustain steady progress in a marathon. Likewise, conscientious architects and stewards of an academic program should strive to provide a healthy **balance** to, and create a sustainable **pace** for, their programs. It is useful to think of balance in two complementary ways. First, there is the need for balance amongst a program's components. This is not "to say that system components... must all be expressed equally. [Rather,] the components [should] exist in a balance that fluctuates *according to circumstances*" (emphasis added) (Conner, 1998, pp. 70 and 69). Indeed, those who design and manage an academic program may find it useful to take into consideration the varied demands encountered by students from a number of on-going and seasonal contexts (e.g., summer-internship interviewing, popular school social events, interesting speaker series, due dates for course papers, the daily, weekly, and semester blend of quantitative and qualitative courses and topics). Like instruments in a symphony, different program contexts are in the fore at different times, yet all need to blend to create a harmonic whole.

A second kind of balance for program managers to consider is the "dynamic balance [that] occurs when expectations about a situation favorably compare to what we perceive to be happening" (Conner, 1998, p. 33; Zemke and Zemke, 1988). Key to achieving dynamic balance is a sense of preparedness. "The feeling of being prepared... is a function of having confidence that the various impending challenges have been accurately anticipated, or having the competence needed to effectively resolve whatever does happen. [Such an alliance of competence and confidence] significantly advances the chances of succeeding in a new environment" (Conner, 1998, p. 35). At the Darden School, we have found that building such confidence and competence requires the delicate management of the pace with which the RCP of the MBA program unfolds for students. "A pace that matches the scale and complexity of the various dimensions of the [program] ... is important [because] ideally, it builds momentum over time, and the momentum creates a sense of *pull* where [the program's learning agendas do] not feel forced. Rather, it should coincide with the [students'] growing interest to participate" (Wenger et al., 2002, p. 195). Indeed, an appropriate pace allows students to master today's RCP demands so that a dynamic balance is achieved – i.e., a confidence and competence is established that anticipates tomorrow's RCP demands. Too fast a pace interferes with the building of competence and confidence and it can accentuate the slightest imbalance in the demands of the RCP venues. Too slow a pace increases the probability that students become bored, distracted, or dissatisfied, thereby diffusing their energies and undermining the pursuit of RCP goals. Examples of Darden School RCP design elements that seek to achieve an appropriate balance and pace in the contexts of students' required curriculum, career-related searches, and affinity groups, are discussed below.

Curriculum – balance and pace

Consider the reality that students can only digest so much information in preparing for any given day's classes. With this thought in mind, Darden's RCP planning/oversight committee periodically has had a staff assistant conduct a reading study – that is, that person reviews all the required course assignments and tallies the number of case, text, and article pages assigned to students by week, by day, by course. If a course is too high (a collective judgment made by the RCP planning/oversight committee) *vis-à-vis* other courses or if a particular day or week is too high in relation to others or in juxtaposition to what else is going on in the life of the school at that time, adjustments to assignments are noted for next year. Inevitably, we have found the number of pages assigned tends to grow over time as instructors add article reprints and text chapters to supplement their primary case studies. This fact, in concert with daily course alignments that get modified over time as instructors change their requests for teaching different days of the week and an ever-expanding array of other sanctioned school activities, can create some real "ouch points" (as one colleague calls them) in the calendar. We find that too many and too frequent "ouch points" undermine student learning and lead to student dissatisfaction.

Affinity groups – balance and pace

Every year, there seems to be a growing number of student affinity groups (besides their assigned classroom sections and learning teams mentioned earlier) in which students get involved. There are career-interest groups, hobby clubs, support groups, social clubs, and community-service groups. Every week these groups seem to be in full swing. If there is not a group fitting student interests, enterprising students start one. There is value in students pursuing such activities and there is value in those activities enhancing, rather than impinging on, a student's academic learning and career-related search. Because of the potential RCP value latent in such activities and because language is important in framing our thinking, we refer to these sorts of activities as "co-curricular activities" not "extra-curricular activities." This small change in terminology provides a significant reminder to instructors of the relevance of these activities to our design efforts and to students' overall RCP experience – they are not extraneous activities. To this end, our Director of Student Affairs works with student co-curricular leaders to be: (1) good stewards of their members' time; (2) creative agenda builders that benefit members' academic and career-related search needs; and (3) astute schedulers of group activities in concert with other parts of the RCP.

Student learning teams (i.e., study groups) are another important affinity group that plays an important role in students' lives during the RCP phase of their studies. As we design the RCP, we have found it necessary to frequently remind ourselves of not only the importance of the informal student-to-student tutoring that goes on in learning teams but also of: the operating modes they explore and employ; the amount of time they spend meeting; and the challenge their members face in balancing roles as both teachers and learners within their teams. Historically, we viewed learning teams as self-managed teams, subject only to the purview of team members. We learned, however, that the teams had few tools and little skill to effectively operate. To address this, we created the position of Learning Team Director, and an instructor is assigned to that position as part of his or her academic load. This instructor is knowledgeable about teams, develops and delivers a program of interventions and information for fostering effective teams, and is a member of the RCP planning/oversight committee where an informed, explicit learning-team perspective is valued and a communications link back to the teams is established.

Searches – balance and pace

With an eye to improving the balance and pace related to students' career-related searches, we have introduced into the curriculum a professional development series. This series of eight to 14 sessions, led by Career Services professionals and held during regularly scheduled class periods, is introduced in some of our pre-matriculation activities and then spread across the academic year although it is most heavily loaded in the fall semester in order to prepare students for the January start of on-campus, corporate summer internship recruiting. It is scheduled (i.e., paced) in such a way as to provide students with the elapsed time and appropriate milestones that foster steady progress toward, and a well-thought-out focus on, maximum preparedness for all aspects of their internship search. Allocating class periods for the professional development sessions also provides balance between academic class preparation and summer-internship search preparation. As a rule of thumb, we assume each class period has attached to it two to three hours of student preparation time. Thus, for a professional development session with a final resume deliverable or a short list of researched company interview possibilities, students do not have to do that work on top of, or in lieu of, a nonaccommodating class schedule – it is assumed that preparation time is available for that work.

Integration for leverage

To create maximum value from an academic program, "organizations must reach beyond synthesis [i.e., the mere combining of parts] to synergy" (Brown and Duguid, 1998, p. 98). Thus, program designers and managers should search for leverageable connections within and across program components and venues that increase student learning, facilitate more effective/efficient student searches, and provides students with a richer array of affinity groups from which to draw. In particular, and as reported by Friedman et al. (1998), there are "three conceptually distinct dimensions of strategic integration:

1. external integration [e.g., linking the various components of a program to the school's overall strategy and mission];
2. institutional integration [e.g., linking the components of a program to each other]; and
3. internal integration [e.g., creating connections within a single program component (e.g., the required curriculum)]."

The conscientious and creative pursuit of all three types of integration can enhance students' program experiences. A few Darden School examples of integration are posed below, again in the contexts of a required curriculum, student affinity groups, and career-related searches.

Curriculum – integration

From a required-curriculum perspective, integrative planning is the conscientious designing of an enhanced learning environment through the leveraged use of materials, time, lessons, and topics. Specifically, required-curriculum integration can occur in at least three ways. At one level, integration is the RCP-wide, coordinated sequencing of topics, across courses, whereby the principles learned in one facilitate those taught in another. For example, the leader of our required accounting course connects with the leader of the required marketing course to make sure accounting covers the topic of cost behaviors (e.g., fixed versus variable) before marketing's use of breakeven analysis. Similarly, the leaders of our required finance and organizational behavior courses meet to dovetail the mergers and acquisitions topic with that of corporate culture. Integration also occurs when faculty are willing and able to facilitate a linkage of their classroom discussions to those in other courses. Indeed, the more familiar faculty are with the frameworks and topics covered in the various required courses, the more natural and frequent those course-spanning classroom discussions can be, and thus, the more integrative the lessons and insights achieved. For example, it is useful for our accounting instructors to be familiar with the ethics course's stakeholder model so that when accounting covers budgeting, and the games people often play during that process, they can embrace the use of such a model. Classes that use the same materials (e.g., a particular case study) are another powerful form of integrative leverage. In the recent past, our RCP accounting course has used a case also used in the quantitative analysis course, as well ones used in the ethics and operations courses.

Likewise, our RCP economics course has shared a case with the finance course.

Required-curriculum innovations and improvements are developed through integrative mechanisms (Boyatzis et al., 1995b) but "integrative devices are unnatural in academia [and] the maintenance of integrative mechanisms is difficult" (Boyatzis et al., 1995c, pp. 222 and 221). Such a reality underscores the importance of identifying simple and sustainable mechanisms for developing the instructors' understanding of the entire required curriculum in order to design its integration. In this regard, four specific Darden School examples of the mechanisms we use follow. First, instructors teaching in the required curriculum receive the same weekly packet of materials and assignments that students receive, thus enabling instructors to easily see the day-by-day specifics of the other courses their students are currently taking. Second, during the RCP planning/oversight committee's yearly planning activities, course leaders (i.e., 10 instructors who each design one of our 10 required courses and then coordinate its delivery across five student sections) provide detailed overviews of their tentative course designs for the explicit purpose of other course leaders identifying integration possibilities. Based on the possibilities identified and the energy they galvanize, course leaders then decide which five courses should coexist in each of our four, eight-week terms. Third, each term's five course leaders review the daily class schedule of course content in order to capture these integration opportunities. Last, instructors periodically sit in on each other's classes, team-teach, or take a teaching assignment in another course, all of which fosters an awareness of the content in other required courses.

Affinity groups – integration
Instruction in the classroom is not the only, nor may it even be the primary, source of student learning. Students learn from their peers during: in-class discussions, the class preparation that takes place in daily learning team meetings; schoolwide, student-run tutorials; and in a host of informal settings. In presenting a case analysis and related action plan, students learn how to communicate clearly and more persuasively. In responding to classmates' or learning-team members' ideas, they learn the value of listening for possibilities and constructive, critical thinking. In managing their learning-team process and cocurricular activities, they learn to follow and to lead. Lessons of this sort are the richest

when students have a varied array of colleagues from which to draw, interact, and observe. With this in mind, we do not randomly assign students to their classroom sections or to their learning teams. Our director of student affairs personally assigns students to both with the objective of maximizing the diversity within a section and within a learning team, along at least five dimensions (home country, type of prior work experience, undergraduate major, gender, and ethnicity).

In another vein, we encourage student clubs to integrate their activities with what is going on in the rest of the program. For example, if the summer internship-recruiting season is eminent, club leaders are actively encouraged by the director of student affairs and the director of career services to offer career-oriented activities for their memberships. If a special required curriculum event on e-business is upcoming, club leaders are made aware of the schedule and encouraged to tie their agendas (e.g., topics for their outside speakers), during that time, to that event. If a student group is interested in initiating a values-based leadership conference, they are encouraged by instructors and administrators to integrate it with the organizational behavior and ethics courses by inviting instructors from those areas to participate – those course instructors, in turn, are expected to provide a meaningful link from their courses to the conference. If student groups sponsor notable outside speakers, we strive to alert an RCP course leader in advance so that those speeches might be videotaped for future editing and classroom use.

Searches – integration

Students typically enrol in MBA programs to change careers, enhance their current career prospects, or to develop the skills and contacts necessary to go into business for themselves (GMAC, 2003). Such pursuits require time and know-how in order to be successful. The reality is that for many students, the process begins with the start of school. After years of trying to hold back the earlier and earlier encroachment of students' career-related search activities in the calendar, we have finally gravitated to the position of striving to integrate and leverage it. For example, and specifically in regards to the RCP, we try to avoid situations where students must choose between preparing for a class and preparing for the next step in their internship-search process. With this in mind, and as noted earlier, we introduced the professional development series into the regular RCP academic class schedule several years ago, with each session getting its share of student preparation time the day before. Moreover, whenever possible, the required courses strive to align their requirements with concurrent student search activities. For example, students are free to analyze an industry and a company that is congruent with the direction of their planned company interviews, for a required paper in our strategy course. Likewise, the required ethics course has devoted a class or two to common recruiting dilemmas in order to eliminate the need for a separate Career Services department briefing on how to recognize, avoid, or handle problematic recruiting situations (e.g., Should a female student tell her classmates and/or the Career Services department about advances from a male recruiter? Should students wanting interviewing practice take one of a limited number of interviewing slots with a company they are not really interested in?).

Standards for Quality

We think of the RCP of our MBA program as a learning delivery system. In that regard then, "An ideal delivery system provides quality practices, tools, and templates needed to ensure the organization is yielding [its] service at a standard" that pleases constituents and achieves organizational objectives while "also providing for the integration of the entire system and processes" (Adams et al., 1999, pp. 108–09). Quality at the RCP level is not a function of the aggregated quality of the RCP's individual component parts – it is a function of that PLUS the quality of the components' interfaces since none of the components are experienced in isolation by students (Smith, 1996). This expanded view means that those who design, manage, and deliver the RCP cannot operate as free agents. Indeed, free agent tendencies must be subrogated to RCP-wide concerns, hallmarked by a "constancy [in the] reliable set of standards of behavior" (Bennis, 1999, p. 32). The most effective means for communicating and implementing an agreed set of standards is through shared practices, tools, and templates. Below, several BASICS-inspired practices conducive to the pursuit of quality in our RCP are discussed.

Curriculum – standards

A school's admissions staff should not be the de facto awarders of degrees. Students develop academic insights and mastery not by being admitted into a program or by the mere passage of the academic calendar. Since we cannot read the minds of students to see what they have learned, students are asked to demonstrate their learning to us. If we ask them to demonstrate it via class contributions, exams, and papers, we have an equal obligation to render a meaningful assessment and certification. Reinforcing that point, it is our experience that adult students want and respect an honest evaluation of their performance and they want differential performance to be reflected in differential grades. As noted in this book's chapter on evaluating students, at our school: the entire grade distribution of A through F is in play and used; the school's academic-good-standing threshold is not a minimal GPA (where one good grade can offset one bad grade), but rather, students must achieve a B− or better in at least eight of their ten required courses, and achieve at least a C in the other two; teaching teams (usually three to five instructors deliver a required course across the five RCP student sections) deliver a shared and coordinated course and they use a common exam, enabling instructors within a course to call grades in a collaborative, peer-reviewed manner; distributions of final course grades are made available to all instructors for their review and discussion; and students receive interim course grades and those projected to not meet the RCP-ending academic standards are put on notice.

Affinity groups – standards
The two primary affinity groups within which students interact on a daily basis are their classroom sections and their learning teams. To expedite the development of these groups to become high-quality, high-performing teams, we have found it useful to share with them some of the lessons learned over the years regarding pitfalls to avoid and processes that help. This can be done through panel discussions, role plays presented during orientation week and at various points throughout the year, and through written communications. For such sessions held after school starts, we find it is best to schedule them within the confines of the regular class schedule in order to maximize student attendance and to avoid conflicts with other events. We also schedule these sorts of sessions a couple of times throughout the year when the timing is projected to be most beneficial (e.g., when learning teams tend to break up and when classroom sections are reconstituted at the start of a new term).

Because we believe the quality of the student learning teams to be so vital to their RCP experience, it was noted earlier that we have a team member who serves as a learning team director. This instructor is a resource, along with the director of student affairs, to teams having difficulty. In addition, this director is a proactive steward of various learning team activities during the year designed to enhance the quality of their experience and performance (e.g., a team building day on a ropes course and use of a learning team process diagnostic survey). Under the guidance of the learning team director, students may also be asked to create a learning team charter that articulates a code of conduct the team members commit to in pursuing their shared vision of high-quality performance. As the year progresses, learning teams are asked to revisit and revise their charters, if needed.

Searches – standards

A key concept in achieving high quality student searches for their summer internship, pertains to having high standards of professional conduct. A host of issues are embedded in this notion, not the least of which concerns students wisely investing time and thought in preparing for their searches so that: (a) other people's time and assistance is efficiently used, and (b) other parts of the program are not neglected due to an inordinate amount of time spent on an unfocused, ill-prepared search. Professionalism also pertains to students being realistic and pragmatic in their searches. Preparation and pragmatism necessitate planning with clear priorities. Our Career Services personnel play a critical role in this through the advice and assistance they offer students. Thus, the standards used in hiring and training these professionals is a key factor in the quality of service they provide as are the policies in place governing student access to these professionals. In addition, student searches have become so varied that the quality of professional assistance is also a function of Career Services personnel bringing to bear specializations in such areas as oversees placement, foreign students seeking employment in the United States, specific industries, and non-traditional job searches.

Professionalism also pertains to how students present themselves to recruiters and the consistency and care with which the Career Services personnel deal with companies. Information about suitable attire, appropriate correspondence, as well as interviewing do's and don'ts, all represent sound advice for students. Career Services personnel must also communicate, and consistently enforce, a school's recruiting policies to all constituencies.

Key success factors

The various features of our RCP, a few of which were highlighted above, are the result of years of trial and error, incremental tweaks, and the adaptation of ideas borrowed from elsewhere. They are, in our opinion however, the result of at least four, absolutely crucial factors. The important point to note for academic program leaders/managers is the need to be explicit about the foundational underpinnings that are absolutely necessary for the design and delivery of a program that meets its stipulated objectives. The following four factors may not be key at other institutions, but they are at ours.

Factor no. 1

The cornerstone to crafting our RCP lies in a shared, conscientiously talked about set of **explicitly stated faculty values** centered on the priority of a programwide learning experience for students. We believe that responsibility resides with the faculty, not the administration, to make our BASICS-inspired RCP effective and sustainable. Whatever the unique values of an institution, they should under gird faculty hiring practices, promotion and tenure deliberations, and they should be a vibrant part of the institution's culture. When personal or course-specific agendas seemingly clash with program needs/goals, those values should galvanize course leaders to open, honest debate with one another where "what's best for the program" becomes an often-used phrase and touchstone. There should be a discernible sense of stewardship amongst instructors.

Factor no. 2

From a set of shared values, instructors should forge a **shared vision** for their program. Faculty conversations, sparked by questions such as those presented here, are useful in fueling the constant articulation of a shared program vision. What would be the hallmarks of a program at our institution if it were successfully implemented? In what ways can we integrate program components better? Are our program components balanced across the courses, across the calendar, across cocurricular events, and across student's career-related search activities? Are we fanatically dedicated to high standards in all aspects of the program? Where can standards be improved and/or clarified? Have we brainstormed lately about some BASICS-inspired, program-planning possibilities? What resources and processes are needed to bring about the successful implementation and operation of a more balanced, integrated program? What contextual factors must be considered? What are the implications for faculty, staff, and administrators if this path is pursued? Can appropriate commitments be garnered and sustained? Who should lead this effort?

Factor no. 3

Together with Smith (1996), we believe it is important that program managers periodically design and execute **an assumptions audit** in order to expose and examine the assumptions embedded in the design of a school's existing program. Over time, unchallenged assumptions can inhibit change and the exploration of new possibilities. Exposing and debating embedded assumptions facilitates the development of shared understanding, communication, vision, and actions to be taken. Several years ago, through a series of e-mail queries and small-group brainstorming sessions, we executed such a study and identified close to 40 collective RCP assumptions. After refining the language describing each assumption, members of our RCP planning/oversight committee were asked: "For each assumption, should we (a) keep it, or (b) modify it as a planning/design element? Why?" From the initial inventory of assumptions, we discovered that several long-held assumptions could and should be modified. We also found several of the assumptions were core to what the mission of the school was and we were renewed in our dedication to those. Establishing such clarity regarding the underpinnings of an existing program's design is an invaluable step because it creates the basis for comparing answers to "what do we want?" with "what do we have?". The "want-versus-have" gaps then become foci for possible program change.

Factor no. 4

Our standing **RCP planning and oversight committee** is critical in that it "brings people together across the academic disciplines to discuss the learning processes" (Smith, 1996, p. 26). At the Darden School, this committee is faculty-led, with a focus on "both content and process" (Boyatzis et al., 1995a, p. 9) in striving to nurture an ever-better

BASICS-inspired approach to our RCP. It comprises carefully selected course leaders from all 10 required courses, the registrar, the director of student affairs, the associate dean for the MBA program, the director of Career Services, the learning team director, and the coordinators from our RCP's five classroom sections, all of whom are committed to doing what it takes to create a required-curriculum *program*. The chair of this committee is an instructor and is, for all practical purposes, the RCP manager.

Managing the electives part of an MBA program

The foregoing discussion has focused on managing the required-curriculum phase of an MBA program. We believe the framework introduced is also applicable to an electives curriculum setting, undergraduate settings, and even to part-time programs. What would differ across these settings are the operational implications of the framework.

In the electives part of a full-time MBA program, those responsible for managing that program should still be concerned with integration, balance/pace, and standards. In an electives context, the issue of integration takes on the added dimension of developing a robust, non-duplicative portfolio of electives available to students. The concern for balance and pace raises questions about when electives are scheduled across the year, and in what time slots during the day, so that potential conflicts and imbalanced course loads are minimized. The issue of standards remains virtually the same as for our RCP with the additional need for a set of guidelines that govern the approval of new elective proposals.

In this latter regard, our school has an instructor designated as the Second-Year Coordinator whose main task is to oversee the school's portfolio of elective courses. Our Second-Year Coordinator works with the proponent of a new elective to make sure proposals meet the standards laid out for them. Proposals are evaluated to make sure that (these criteria are from the Darden School's 2004 P&P manual):

- course objectives and content are consistent with the objectives of the electives program, which are
  - to enable students to individualize their experience by providing opportunities to pursue chosen areas of interest in greater depth,
  - to offer an innovative and relevant leading-edge MBA elective curriculum,

- o to provide the further opportunity to explore global business issues,
- o to develop further leadership capabilities in students,
- o to support and encourage activities outside the classroom that serve to enhance the Darden Community, develop individual relationships, and foster a sense of social responsibility,
- o to support and facilitate the transition of students from the academic to the business community, and
- o to foster the exploration of ideas, concepts, and themes that prepare students for lifelong learning and continued professional development.
- • course pedagogy and delivery, including teaching materials, are effective in achieving the objectives of the course; and
- • student performance, evaluation, grading, and feedback standards are consistent with standards of the school.

The broader context within which programs exist

In a report titled, "Management Education at Risk" (AACSB, 2002, p. 5), the AACSB identified three critical issues facing those who administer and lead management education programs: "a shortage of doctoral faculty, a need to ensure the relevance of curricula to the global business world, and a convergence of degree and non-degree education." To this list, we would add: governance; third-party rankings; differentiating one's programs; and using an appropriate set of program performance metrics. Indeed, as we administer the programs at our school and as we hear of others' concerns in managing parts or all of their programs, these items appear to be the pervasive, overarching issues.

Instructors. In regard to instructors, not only are there fewer doctoral business graduates, there is an ever-larger cadre of existing business school instructors drawing nearer to retirement. Thus, related questions emerge: Who will teach in the business schools of tomorrow? Will there be a great use of adjunct instructors and other non-traditional faculty? Will there need to be a greater reliance on technology-based instruction? Must class sizes be enlarged to achieve some additional economies of scale? Yes – to all of those questions.

The real question then becomes how to best manage a program under these inevitable circumstances. The only answer we can foresee is to vest ultimate program responsibility in a core group of instructors who are devoutly passionate, committed, creative, educational stewards. They will need to be both: champions of an educational vision and savvy about operational details; exemplars of instructional excellence and embracers of new ideas; appreciators of scholarly research and the world of practical business affairs; and they will also need to be able to balance and placate the oft-competing preferences of a school's varied constituencies. Do such folks exist? We believe so. We do, however, believe that prevalent instructor incentive systems dissuade prime candidates from stepping forward and for those who do step forward, the systems actually punish them with lost raises equal to those colleagues publishing one more article in a peer review journal. We cannot continue to ask instructors to take leadership roles in administering programs, designing world-class curricula, being readily accessible to students, and to publish at the level their comparable cloistered colleagues do.

Globally relevant curricula. Managing a significant part of a school's academic program presents, among other things, one on-going challenge – to what extent and in what way(s) can/should students' learning be globally focused? Embedded in such a question are a myriad of others, not the least of which include:

- Is the achievement of a globally relevant curriculum a matter of simply using nondomestic course materials or having instructors with a real, current, working knowledge of international settings?
- Do more international students in a discussion-based classroom make for more globally oriented learning?
- Should students spend some of their program time overseas? If so, how much is enough time? What are the costs? Who bears them? What is the liability exposure of the school for such trips?
- Is it imperative that a school have overseas alliances? If so, what is the best way to structure them and utilize them?

These are but a sampling of the thorny issues that surface and that, as best we can deduce, have no tried and true answers. Our school has exchange programs with overseas schools for a semester but less than five or six students take advantage of them every year. Our school has a one-week overseas trip that many students do register for and yet we wonder what can be learned, of consequence, in a mere five days? Our instructors are encouraged to spend a semester or a year overseas teaching with any number of schools with whom our school has an affiliation, yet no more than one colleague every three or four years takes advantage of such an opportunity. We look to hire people who were born and raised outside the United States and everyone else is looking to hire virtually the same folks. About 20 percent of our students are from outside the United States and in classroom discussions, it is spotty at best whether they are able and inclined to participate in ways that provide global learning for the rest of their classmates – it happens, but not nearly as frequently or substantively as we strive to make it.

For sure, almost every business topic lends itself to something worth learning when posed in a nondomestic setting. We have concluded the best way to bring this about is through widening the instructors' experience base and through preplanned, choreographed involvement of the international students in one's class. Moreover, it is also worthwhile to periodically take an inventory of the program materials in use by sampling some (or all) of the school's courses. The last time we performed such an analysis, about 25 percent of all the classes in our required curriculum had some sort of globally oriented material assigned. We would subjectively opine that somewhere between 25 percent to 50 percent might be a relevant percentage to seek. We do know, however, that in the absence of a program manager, committed to being a good steward of a globally oriented curriculum, it will not happen of its own accord.

Degree and Nondegree Programs. In the AACSB (2002, p. 25) report mentioned earlier, one of the questions posed in regards to the existence of both degree and nondegree programs at the same institution was, "Is the quality of instruction in degree programs enhanced by involvement with leading-edge executives participating in nondegree programs?" From reading the report, it appears that the authors conclude yes and yet they seem to equivocate on that answer elsewhere in the report. Our answer to the question is, "absolutely yes!" We encourage schools to create as many opportunities as possible for such involvement and we encourage instructors to take regular advantage of such opportunities. The bottom line is that whether it is teaching on a team in a three-day or three-week, nondegree executive education program, once a year or three times a year, there are a number of immediate and tangible benefits to instructors and, in turn, to their degree-seeking students. Indeed, we spend about half of our yearly class time with executives in nondegree education programs and would not want to alter that mix at all.

One of first benefits is the experience of working with a small team of colleagues to design and integrate a powerful learning experience for the executives who will attend the nondegree program. Executives live and experience the integration of business concepts and educational programs designed for them must present content in an integrated fashion. Such a self-contained, well-defined learning context allows for instructors to directly learn the content and styles of their colleagues as they seek to discover the leverageable connections across their disciplines that executives expect. The development of such a capability is important and transferable back to the degree program planning process.

A second benefit is that interactions with executives greatly facilitate instructors staying informed in regard to contemporary business challenges/concerns/opportunities. Yes, we can read about business concerns in the journals and the press, but that information is often old, sanitized, and/or biased when it gets reported for public consumption. Listening to executives discuss, in your own class and at the lunch table and at the receptions, the issues of importance to them is a wonderful way for instructors to stay abreast of contemporary business issues. Such insights and information are invaluable as we craft our own thinking about business; consider interesting and important lines of inquiry for our research endeavors; and as we strive to make our degree program courses most relevant and fresh with contemporary examples. (It is important to note that it is paramount that instructors, taken into the confidences of the executives they interact with, always respect, when warranted, the confidentiality of the information and perspectives shared.)

A third benefit flows in the other direction. We have found that executives like to "cut to the chase" and therefore appreciate the frameworks and syntheses that instructors have generally developed over the years in their degree program courses. In addition, executives like exploring the best ideas an instructor can bring to them from the hundreds of degree-seeking students they have instructed who have studied the very same topic the executives are exploring.

In general, the more varied, the more authentic, the more current the perspectives that we can garner and bring to our roles as program architects and stewards, the better. In our minds, this reason alone is sufficient to warrant the involvement of instructors in executive, non-degree educational programs.

Governance. To some instructors, an intriguing and important part of their larger role as a university instructor is getting involved in, and/or interacting with, their school and university governance structures. There is some debate as to when an instructor should do this. Some would say not until after receiving tenure as it can be a distraction from the task of honing one's teaching and furthering one's research program. Others argue that there is no better way for an instructor to get fully enmeshed in the lifeblood of their academic setting than to eagerly serve on task forces, or advisory councils with alumni or trustees, or to even chair a standing committee. We embraced for ourselves, and continue to recommend for our junior colleagues, the latter approach. We certainly found the time to become involved in such ways and to do the other things that were expected of us. Clearly, such a pre-tenure career strategy does not lend itself to a 30-hour work week. As we think back over our pre-tenure years, and we can even remember having this very conversation with one another, when a typical work week was closer to 50-plus hours, 48 weeks out of the year. There is ample time to do more than many university faculty members do.

One of the cherished parts of an academic career is having the freedom that comes with it. Perhaps the most succinct way to describe our job is to note that we have many of the benefits of being self-employed with none of the headaches. To a large measure, that is true. The quid pro quo, however, is protecting and honoring a program governance structure by contributing to it. In the absence of instructors' being willing to conscientiously devote their time and talents to the governance of a program, a school, or even their university, professional administrators will fill the void and then instructors will find themselves marginalized when important strategic and operational decisions are being made.

The most common way of becoming involved in a pertinent piece of governance that interests you is to be a member of a committee. Now, whether you are a committee member or a committee chair, such an endeavor poses a unique challenge and opportunity – how to operate as an assembly of peers who have no real authority over, or to, one another and who are all bright and generally strong-willed? It is a fascinating experience to observe colleagues in these arenas – there clearly are those who do it well and those who do not. There seem to be five traits of those instructors who make valuable committee contributions and who are enjoyable to work with in the process. Those colleague traits are: they are enthused about the task at hand; they always come prepared for the task at hand; they possess and practice an ability and a willingness to really listen for the possibilities posed by their colleagues; they are patient; and they clearly and boldly share their suggestions and assessments.

There is no doubt that instructors can leave a mark on the students they teach by being the best they can be in the classroom. There is, however, an additional calling that we invite you to consider – leave a positive mark on the institution that has chosen to employ you. For us, being an instructor is a rare and wonderful way to live a life and make a living. Those that preceded us left a legacy that we benefit from and that we must steward for those who follow. All schools and programs have governance systems and processes. Such systems and processes built on the premise of program governance require that there be qualified, eager, committed instructors to step forward and take on the appropriate roles. These are not roles that should be left to those nearing the end of their careers or to those who cannot teach very well or to those who have no research programs. There is an inextricable link between the governance of a school and what goes on in the classroom and what goes on with research agendas. This is manifested in a number of ways, not the least of which are: the allocation of scarce monies; perspective toward faculty hiring; the academic standards in place; a curriculum portfolio; connections to outside constituencies; quality of students; and direction for the future. To not be a part of the governance process debating and deciding issues in these arenas is to abdicate an a priori influence on the overarching forces impacting one's classroom and research.

Business School Rankings. Yes, before you even ask, business school rankings are here to stay . . . unfortunately. We must confess to Friday afternoon daydreams of a world where all business schools refused to cooperate with the rankings publications in an attempt to bring them to an end. Alas, that won't happen in our lifetimes. Therefore, any business school program manager, and committed group of instructors, must be aware of the means by which the key rankings are constructed. For example, if a particular ranking values an ever-higher proportion of international students amongst the study body, that fact alone has implications for the dominant instructional methods a school can use (i.e., it is quite difficult to have discussion-oriented classes when many or most of the class does not share a common first language). Likewise, if a particular ranking values ever-higher GMAT scores, a focus on higher GMAT scores may increase the need for a school that prizes team work to have its students, instructors, and/or admissions staff interview prospective applicants in order to identify those bright students who are most inclined to teamwork as opposed to working alone.

Currently, as we write this chapter, MBA program rankings are constructed and published by *Business Week*, *The Economist*, the *Wall Street Journal*, the *Financial Times*, *Forbes*, and *US News & World Report*. There are just as many, or more, sources for rankings of universities/colleges in general as well as for undergraduate business programs. In total, when we Google™ the phrase "business school and rankings," 1,890,000 Web sites are listed! Not only do the myriad of rankings surface from such a search but so too do the many articles and editorials debunking/criticizing the rankings along with all the various schools' promotional announcements that embrace their particularly positive ranking. Thus, rankings are, if not an important part of a schools' management concerns, a very visible part of the public image of a school that must be managed. Indeed, what gets measured is what gets done and as long as the rankings are used in some fashion by prospective students and recruiters and cheered or bemoaned by a school's alumni, they remain pertinent to the managing of any program.

With a bit of tongue in cheek, and admitting our own predisposition against the current trend for rankings, we refer the reader to Policano (2001). Professor Policano is the former dean of the business school at the University of Wisconsin–Madison. His article, titled "Ten Easy Steps to a Top-25 MBA Program," provides just that. For example, schools should "increase services to recruiters, including valet parking, free meals, and gift baskets in hotel rooms." Likewise, because some rankings rely on the starting salaries of a school's MBAs, schools should "eliminate not-for-profit programs" of study. When it comes to fostering student satisfaction, another key metric used in many of the rankings, schools should "provide a wide variety of student services for MBAs including free breakfast and luncheons, free parking, and a physical fitness center exclusively for MBAs." In fact, he opines that "the least expensive way to a higher ranking is to [simply] fudge the data." It is clear that he is frustrated by the existence of the rankings. He concludes, and we concur, that "Were it not for the media [rankings], the vast majority of business schools would continue to fill their niche in the market and continue to innovate and do what they do best. Instead, chasing the rankings continues to divert significant resources that could otherwise be allocated to hiring additional faculty and staff, improving classroom technology, keeping the curriculum innovative, and providing more opportunities for students. The business school industry is definitely worse off as a result. In the end, it is the students who suffer" (p. 40).

Don't forget to differentiate your program.[2] Are we in danger of commoditizing the 100,000 MBA degrees awarded (including those from my own institution) each year? We think so. Are we in danger of commoditizing other degrees and programs of study? Probably. Why is that the case? The GHP – the Great Homogenization Process – is at work.

We are most familiar with MBA programs and we see evidence of the GHP every day as a result of a number of forces taking root. For instance, we cannot think of a single MBA program that does not espouse, to some extent, the goals of: globalization, more human diversity, leverageable alliances, the incubation of business start-ups, action-learning agendas, and state-of-the-art technologies and facilities. It should come as no surprise that such overlap exists because school representatives visit each other's campuses and Web sites to "borrow" good ideas. They conduct benchmarking studies of other institutions' programs, comparing them to their own. Consortia are formed to provide face-to-face opportunities, and institutional commitments, for sharing information. Accrediting agencies impose similar templates and criteria on the schools they visit. Last but not least, deans devour the latest business-press rankings and find themselves driven to, and motivated by, an identical set of scorecard metrics.

But the GHP doesn't stop there. Schools compete for many of the same type (if not the very same) of faculty, students, and corporate friends. Instructors select course materials from the same directory of publishers and frequently exchange course syllabi. Peer review processes for tenure and promotion reinforce similar developmental foci.

---

[2] An earlier version of this section first appeared as "The GHP," in *BizEd* (January/February 2003), pp. 54–55, by Mark E. Haskins, © 2003 by AACSB International and used here with permission.

Case-oriented programs introduce lectures to clarify concepts while lecture-oriented programs introduce cases to exemplify practice. Such forces are beginning to create, not a robust and vibrant distinctiveness across MBA programs, but rather a widespread, indistinguishable sameness.

Now, none of these factors, taken alone, is necessarily unsound or to be avoided. It's natural to trade ideas with colleagues in seeking to improve one's program. But when stacked one atop the other, such forces create an ever-expanding arena of similar practices, philosophies, purposes, and programs. It's not as if we are adapting ideas from other industries to our business as Ford might do with lessons learned from Wal-Mart. The "borrowing" and the "mimicking" of ideas when we are all in the same business, promotes commoditization and preempts differentiation.

At one level, the GHP may appear to be inevitable. After all, the risks and rewards of crafting distinctive program features are problematic. Even modestly successful differentiations have historically been hard to defend, and often do not contribute to the quest for valued, sustainable, comparative advantage. For the bulk of MBA programs, an unexplored challenge exists: courageously differentiate the boundaries within which an MBA program operates.

In the context of these thoughts and in the spirit of provocatively inviting instructors and administrators to contemplate ideas for MBA program differentiation, we offer three suggestions. Admittedly, these ideas would require significant and fundamental changes in the incentives to, behaviors of, and rewards for faculty and administrators. Even so, we believe such changes are possible and perhaps even essential for the MBA's continued growth and success.

First, let's focus on student profiles. What if schools admitted students with only one, two, or no more than three very specific profiles and crafted programs of study tailored for that profile instead of assembling a class of students with an intentionally broad array of attributes as is most commonly done? Under this approach, schools would gear admissions processes to identify and select students according to a few, specific profiles. A school's entire program (if only one student body profile is pursued), or the program crafted for each different student section within a school (if more than one profile is pursued), could be designed and delivered in a way that understood and leveraged that student profile. For example, at the course level, we could design a very different accounting course for a classroom comprised of visual-type learners, with humanities backgrounds and substantial non-US life experiences, versus a classroom comprised of kinesthetic-type learners, with science backgrounds, whose life experiences were US-centric.

Programs might need to be different lengths for different student profiles. Course content would need to be crafted so as to most powerfully connect to, build on, and compliment a chosen student profile. Class sizes might have to be smaller in order to achieve tailored learning objectives and the same courses might have to move at different speeds for different groups of students. Such differentiation, of course, poses many challenges. But, with so many potentially interesting student body profiles from which to choose, a school has numerous potential niches within which to establish a reputation for excellence.

Second, we can change our educational philosophy. What if we provided just-in-time (JIT) learning rather than just-in-case (JIC) learning? MBA programs are largely, if not totally, JIC oriented – that is, we say, "We think you will need to be able to calculate (or at least understand) the capital lease liability figure reported for a publicly traded company in the United States." Then, the student goes to work for a large, privately held company, in the human resources area, never again giving one moment's thought to such a calculation.

On the other hand, a JIT design assumes students' learning agendas are based on a "need to know" which springs from their affiliation with an employer who requires certain skills and knowledge. In a JIT model, recruiters would hire students upon their admittance to an MBA program rather than after graduation. It would not be necessary for students to be on the hiring organization's payroll immediately, but their educational program would, in large part, be determined through the collaboration of the student, faculty, and the employing organization.

This model integrates a student's real-time work experience with his or her learning needs, necessitating an educational calendar periodically punctuated by students spending time with an employer. Moreover, the time from course design to delivery would need to be shortened in order to respond to students' emergent learning needs. Schools would need to develop a process for identifying, from within their student ranks, similar JIT needs so that a critical number of students could come together in a shared course experience. A certain number of JIT courses would likely span different amounts of calendar time for different groups of students. But the types of employers that hire a school's students under such an arrangement, the mix of JIT and JIC courses, and the customization of course content, all present dimensions for further MBA program differentiation.

Finally, what if we differentiated the degree itself? If an entire program's targeted student profile (or a section of students within a program) is comprised of undergraduate liberal arts majors, going through a program of study tailored to them (à la the first suggestion above), we could prominently differentiate their degree as something like MBA*LA*. We might award an MBA*EN* to students with an engineering background for whom we also tailored their MBA program experiences. Similarly, the same could be done for any number of targeted, pooled undergraduate profiles for which we customized an MBA experience. Such differentiated designations could serve to signal an MBA program's intentionally selected student body and specifically tailored program.

We do not advocate differentiation merely for the sake of differentiation. We do believe that constituent-oriented, high-quality, substantive, thoughtful differentiation is possible and would rejuvenate and enhance the overall MBA landscape. The siren call of the GHP is luring us in the opposite direction – to a land of commoditized programs, degrees, and graduates. It is time to acknowledge the existence of the GHP at work in MBA programs and others before commodity-like attributes become firmly entrenched (if they haven't already).

Put together a balanced scorecard.[3] The purpose of a balanced scorecard initiative is to identify measures that can help in monitoring, steering, and evaluating a school's and/or a program's progress on its strategic goals. It provides a great litmus test of, "if it is important, find a way to measure it or you will never know if you are where you sought to be." It all starts with a clear statement of a vision that is then translated into a set of goals. At the Darden School, we strive to have:

- The world's best teaching faculty known for case method and experiential learning;
- The world's best graduate business education programs (MBA and Executive Ed.) for developing results-oriented leaders with a general management perspective;
- An alumni network unmatched for its effectiveness and integration in the life of our school; and

---

[3] We want to acknowledge our colleagues Ming-Jer Chin, Lynn Isabella, and Alan Beckenstein for their assistance on this Darden School project.

- International recognition for shaping management practice and business education through managerially relevant research and curriculum materials.

Performance measures add rigor and discipline to the process of strategic management and vision directedness – they should never be the "ends" nor should they be static. Adjusting strategy to fit what is measurable instead of what is most effective is a temptation and a risk that is important to acknowledge and we caution any program manager against doing that. Some of the measures we proposed posed challenges in obtaining the necessary data. Even so, measures should be carefully considered as to their relevancy, validity, and importance – if deemed to meet all three criteria, they (or a substitute surrogate) should be pursued, not abandoned due to the difficulty inherent in obtaining the data.

Refinement of a set of performance metrics for a particular program should be a constant part of the strategic process. Collectively, it is best to think of a selected set of metrics as merely helping to illuminate performance. No set of metrics can be comprehensive or perfectly congruent with all aspects of the efforts, resources, inputs, and tradeoffs embedded in the stretch goals one often seeks to pursue. The specificity with which metrics are described is conducive to their implementation while also prompting discussions for the creation of cascaded metrics suitable for subsidiary parts of a focal program. As an example of attempting to translate a vision stated as a goal into measurable results, here is an excerpt from a draft of our scorecard report to the Darden School dean that proposes several measures pertaining to the school's first strategic goal.

GOAL NO. 1

"World's best teaching faculty known for case method and experiential learning"

The Darden School is dedicated to assembling a world-class cadre of instructors who create engaging and stimulating learning environments through interactive activities and materials crafted around contemporary business situations. Our faculty is sensitive to the learning needs and goals of our students, whether they are MBA students preparing for their new careers or seasoned managers wishing to expand horizons or sharpen skills and perspectives. For Darden faculty, teaching is a joy and their passion, not an activity that must be endured.

Measures

General teaching indicators
1. *Combine the two ratings below into one composite rating*
   - mean teaching ratings for all of First Year courses (source: FY survey)
   - mean teaching ratings for all of Second Year courses (source: SY survey)
2. *Combine the two ratings below into one composite rating*
   - mean teaching ratings for Executive Education's custom programs (source: program-ending survey)
   - mean teaching ratings for Executive Education's open enrollment programs (source: program-ending survey)
3. Query faculty once a year, asking: *On a scale of 1 (not enjoyable at all) to 10 (the most enjoyable year ever), how enjoyable was teaching at the Darden School this year?*

"Best"
Add question on First Year, Second Year, and Executive Education (EE) program-ending surveys like...

On average, the collective faculty line up I experienced this year (or in this EE program), was _____ compared to all those I have ever had elsewhere (track the distribution % of those responding year to year)

The Best	_____
In the top 10 percent	_____
In the top 25 percent	_____
Average	_____
Below average	_____

"Known for"

A simple, straightforward approach to assess the level of Darden's "known for" the case method [experiential learning] construct, could involve asking three questions, to three constituencies, to get at each of their: (a) understanding of the construct, (b) the value (or importance) they place on the construct, and (c) their perceptions regarding Darden's "known-ness" for the construct. The questions could be posed to the following three constituencies prior to their attendance at Darden:

- MBA applicants on their applications or at some other appropriately earlier point in their inquiry to Darden
- corporate recruiters on a registration form prior to them coming to recruit
- EE program participants when they enroll for a program

The three potential questions, to each of these three constituencies, might be:

(assume: 1 = not at all, 5 = moderately, and 10 = very much)

(a) *On a 1 to 10 scale, and for each of the following five bullet queries, to what extent do you understand that case method learning...*

- *relies on real-world based stories?*
- *relies on students for the quality and direction of class discussion?*
- *involves the task of students identifying a managerial problem?*
- *involves the students recommending an action plan?*
- *requires students to be deal with ambiguity in the learning process?*

(b) *On a 1 to 10 scale, how important is case method learning to you for the purpose you are exploring at Darden?*

(c) *On a 1 to 10 scale, when you think of the Darden School, to what extent do you perceive it to be a case method school?*

We have found it very worthwhile to undertake the challenge and the exercise of translating vibrant, galvanizing vision statements into concrete goals with measurable attributes. Such an undertaking can often surface some of the latent constructs and levers available to a program manager to more effectively manage the program.

―――――――――

Conclusion

As we all know, the half-life of change and renewal is short. Changing circumstances and new program leaders often prompt new ideas and new ways of doing things. What has not changed for us over the years, however, is a commitment to, and on-going conversations about: a program's **balance** in creating a sustainable pace for students throughout the calendar; the **integration** of program components for leveraged learning and the efficient use of student time and school resources; clear, concise, and frequently communicated **standards** to promote high quality in each and every detail of the students' experience; how **best** to embrace global perspectives in our programs; the critical nature of **faculty** staffing, development, renewal, and shared values; the relation of our **degree and nondegree** programs; **governance** of the school; the business press **rankings** and their impact on us; **performance metrics**; and how to excel and **differentiate**. As an instructor, you should expect, and dare we say, you should want to be involved in these sorts of on-going discussions and decisions at your institution. To not be involved is to be disconnected. To not be involved is to have diminished input into the future of your programs and school. To not be involved is to abdicate some stewardship responsibilities you have in regards to those who will come after you. One simple, yet highly valuable, way to be involved is to be an active proponent of managing one's school and programs using the concepts, principles, and ideas we all teach – if we did just that, who knows how much better our programs might be.

Further reading

AACSB (2002). *Management Education at Risk*, www.aacsb.edu/publications/metf/default.asp.

Adams, W.A., C. Adams, and M. Bowker, *The Whole Systems Approach*, Provo, UT: Executive Excellence Publishing, 1999.

Bennis, W., *Old Dog, New Tricks*, Provo, UT: Executive Excellence Publishing, 1999.

Boyatzis, R.E., S.S. Cowen, and D.A. Kolb, "Taking the Path Toward Learning." In R. E. Boyatzis, S. S. Cowen, and D.A. Kolb (eds.), *Innovation in Professional Education* (pp. 1–11), San Francisco: Jossey-Bass Publishers, 1995a.

Boyatzis, R.E., S.S. Cowen, and D.A. Kolb, "Management of Knowledge: Redesigning the Weatherhead MBA Program." In R.E. Boyatzis, S. S. Cowen, and D. A. Kolb (eds.), *Innovation in Professional Education* (pp. 32–49), San Francisco: Jossey-Bass Publishers, 1995b.

Boyatzis, R.E., S.S. Cowen, and D.A. Kolb, "Reactions from the Stakeholders: The Trials and Tribulations of Implementing a New Program." In R. E. Boyatzis, S. S. Cowen, and D.A. Kolb (eds.), *Innovation in*

Professional Education (pp. 205–27), San Francisco: Jossey-Bass Publishers, 1995c.

Brown, J.S., and P. Duguid, "Organizing Knowledge," *California Management Review,* 40, 3 (1998), 90–111.

Conner, D.R., *Leading at the Edge of Chaos,* New York: John Wiley & Sons, 1998.

Friedman, B., J. Hatch, and D.M. Walker, *Delivering on the Promise,* New York: The Free Press, 1998.

GMAC, "MBA Expectations," *USA Today* (24 February 2003), B1.

Knowles, M., *The Adult Learner: A Neglected Species*, Houston: Gulf Publishing, 1990.

Policano, A.J., "Ten Easy Steps to a Top-25 MBA Program," *Selections*, 1, 2 (2001), 39–40.

Smith, K. R., Faculty leadership and change in higher education. *Selections*, 13, 2 (1996), 19–27.

Wenger, E., R. McDermott, and W.M. Snyder, *Cultivating Communities of Practice*, Boston: Harvard Business School Press, 2002.

Zemke, R., and S. Zemke (1988). "30 Things We Know for Sure About Adult Learning," *Training*, 25, 7 (1998), 57–61.

22 Managing a nondegree client program: an overview

MARK E. HASKINS

> To improve a company fast, develop people fast.
>
> – Andrall E. Pearson
> (past president, PepsiCo)

Many instructors find themselves with the opportunity to manage an educational experience outside the realm of a traditional degree program, managing educational experiences for major trade associations, single companies, and corporate consortiums, government agencies, and philanthropic organizations. All such settings pose challenges and opportunities that stretch instructors in ways akin to, as well as dissimilar from, those rooted in managing a degree program. In this chapter we will focus on some of the unique aspects of managing a major educational relationship with a *Fortune* 500 client. It is fair to say that our institution essentially serves as the corporate university for this client, taking on a multifaceted set of responsibilities around the issue of people development.

Issues similar to degree programs

A number of nondegree educational program concerns have counterparts in typical degree programs. Program design issues that address integration, pace, balance, and quality continue to be of critical importance in nondegree educational programs – whether the program lasts two days, or spans several months. Similarly, students in nondegree programs are a part of a classroom affinity group and, in our environment, small-group learning teams. Developing the connections and cohesiveness of those groups is another priority. The principles discussed in the prior chapter regarding those themes, though tailored to the nondegree client, apply here as well.

Issues dissimilar to degree programs

What are the unique challenges related to managing a major nondegree client relationship centered on the education and development of a varied number of their people? There are many, both big and small. We will focus on just a few of the more significant aspects of such endeavors. Namely, we will discuss the following issues: needs analysis, establishing a sound basis for the relationship, the program design process, expanding the relationship, calendar issues, and we will end with ten reminders.

Several premises undergird the process of working with clients on nondegree educational programs. First, we strive to design, develop, and deliver programs that *make a difference*. That may sound trite, but it is key. We have plenty of opportunities to simply "pull off the shelf" a nondegree educational program design that we have employed 69 times before. We call that approach "teaching for dollars." Eventually, an instructor grows weary of such performances, clients quickly become disenchanted with the generic quality of the experience, and both parties fail to develop a meaningful personal and professional relationship – instead, it is merely a one- or two-time transaction that ends. We are not excited by such endeavors.

Second, instructors must find the learning potential presented by the client to be intriguing and worthy of their time. A curiosity must fuel their interest and they must be willing to learn about the client. Such learning must be a driving force – not a means for piling up chargeable hours: in fact, it is not likely that all the time you spend learning about a client, staying current on client issues/initiatives, and managing the relationship is time for which you will be paid.

Last, for university instructors, managing a large-client nondegree educational program often casts an instructor in a role quite different from a strictly academic one. More specifically, if you are an instructor at an academic institution, you probably experience a fair amount of autonomy and independence. Indeed, we have often described our life as professors, when limited to the traditional context, as having all the benefits of being self-employed with none of the headaches. That is not true when managing a large-client nondegree educational program, however. In such a context, you are likely to have clients that expect you to be available at their behest, totally responsive to their requests, and deferent to their processes and approvals. When such relationships involve hundreds of thousands, if not millions of dollars over extended periods of time, you are at worst merely a vendor, and at best, a partner, both of which mean you do not have nearly so much autonomy and independence as if you were only a university degree-program instructor. Learning how to operate in this vendor- or partner-like capacity requires a sensitivity to the client that is much better if you develop actual affinity for the client personnel with whom you will be working.

Establishing the basis for a sound relationship[1]

At the outset of a client relationship, it is important to craft a memorandum of understanding (MOU) that narratively describes the nature, timing, and extent of the relationship between the two parties. As an example, we present the MOU, crafted by our colleague George Shaffer, between the Darden School and the *Fortune* 500 client that is the focus of this chapter. This document translates initial conversations regarding the relationship into a cemented, more formalized, recorded understanding. Such clarity, as early in the relationship as possible, is both wise and useful.

Memorandum of Understanding

*The ABC Company (ABC) and the Darden Graduate School of Business Administration, University of Virginia (Darden) agree to join together in an educational relationship to support the ABC goal of strengthening business performance through the creation of "**people-intensive processes.**"*

While the specifics of the relationship (specific program content, number of offerings, intervals between offerings, etc.) will evolve over the next few months, the structure of the agreement is guided by these general principles:
- *Darden will assist ABC in **developing a comprehensive learning model** based on the needs and the overall goals of the company. It is expected this model will consist of a leadership curriculum and*

---

[1] For an additional discussion of this topic, see M. Haskins and G. Shaffer, "Getting an Executive Education Relationship off to a Great Start," *Development and Learning in Organizations: An International Journal*, 20, 1 (2006), 10–12.

a functional curriculum. Darden may work with ABC to develop processes and tools (such as the identification and utilization of corporate key experiences) **to strengthen ABC's decision-making associated with the development of people and to reinforce accountability for their behaviors.**

- *The parties intend* **to develop and implement a comprehensive Leadership Curriculum** *featuring state-of-the-practice leadership and management programs. The Darden School will design and deliver educational initiatives to support ABC's desire to establish people-intensive processes throughout its organization. This curriculum* **will be centered on a series of three interrelated programs,** *each designed to enhance individual performance and accountability. It will be* **linked to the ABC Behavior Model** *and targeted for ABC's Senior Executives, Executive High Potentials, and Emerging Leaders and the program names will be, respectively, the Senior Executive Program (SEP), the Leadership Development Program (LDP), and the Emerging Leaders Program (ELP). The programs will be delivered at the Darden School, in Charlottesville, Virginia. While specific dates need to be established, it is the intent of the parties to deliver the inaugural program within six months of the date of this MOU.*

- *In assisting with the design of an overall learning model, Darden will help define the* **Functional Curriculum** *and identify programs aimed at developing functional excellence in specific areas such as Finance, Legal, and specific functional skills required to support the roles of the business units. Darden will assist in the definition and content of the programs, and will design and deliver programs in the functional curriculum, unless otherwise agreed to by both parties.*

- *In addition, the relationship* **will foster research opportunities** *on key business issues which will benefit both ABC and the Darden School. With mutual consent, for example, ABC case and teaching materials may be developed by Darden faculty and utilized in educational initiatives, including ABC programs, the Darden MBA program, and other Darden executive education offerings.*

- *By mutual agreement, other educational initiatives – such as action learning projects and/or follow-up workshops – may be developed and implemented by the parties.*

- *ABC and Darden agree they* **will maintain the confidentiality** *of any sensitive, competitive, or proprietary information that either party* *may disclose to the other in the development and implementation of this relationship.*

*While it is important to identify the activities and facilities (the "what") of what we offer, what distinguishes Darden is the **overall level of professionalism** associated with "how" we perform our tasks. The following attributes can be used for this qualitative evaluation: Highly knowledgeable and experienced faculty, with the ability to make sound judgments and informed decisions, to design highly relevant educational experiences and course materials all of which are aligned with customer goals and objectives. In the classroom, Darden faculty are highly engaging facilitators who lead participant-centered discussions focused on individual and organizational growth and development.*

*Should issues arise over the course design, delivery, facilitators, etc., it is important to have **a process for problem resolution**. Long-term relationships with organizations are a goal of the Darden School. Our success is based on our ability to "partner" with clients in all facets of program development and delivery. That is why we use phrases such as "ensure a mutual understanding" ... "to ensure clarity"... "in a very interactive way"... "we greatly value the active involvement and participation from ABC"... "mutual agreement"... "for client review and approval." The process is relatively straightforward: there is mutual respect, willingness to share, and planned and spontaneous opportunities for discussion. In our experience, we are able to converge on the "right answer" as a result of this openness and transparency. This is the nature of the conversation and it applies to everything we do. Together, ABC and Darden discuss the needs analysis, program design, program delivery, the relevance of the material, effectiveness of the faculty, and appropriateness of the pedagogy, as well as accommodations and food service. In the final analysis, it is Darden's responsibility to be in alignment with and supporting ABC's goals and objectives.*

*The **financial arrangements** of the relationship for program development, delivery, and room and board are, as best as can be delineated at this time, judged to be:*

Program development ($x,xxx per day) includes the following activities:
• *Preparation for, and conducting of, needs analysis interviews*
• *Site visits*
• *Program design time*
Program delivery ($xxx,xxx per week) includes the following:

- *Personnel – Senior director (1), faculty leader (1), faculty team (5), program administrator (1). We estimate that a minimum of eight Darden staff and faculty professionals will be active in this relationship.*
- *Facilities – Dedicated classroom, 6–8 dedicated breakout rooms, participant binders, books, and materials*
- *Break services throughout the day*

Room and board ($xxx per person, per night):

- *Individual guest room in the Darden Executive Residence Center with, color TV, private bath, private telephone, separate direct modem access, fitness center, all meals (breakfast, lunch, and dinner) in the Darden Center Dining Room.*

Besides describing the general timing, nature, quality, costs, and extent of the program deliverables, one of the key elements of the MOU is establishing the usage rights of the materials developed for and during the relationship. For example, if instructors develop cases for the ABC Co. programs, it is important for the MOU to specify that those materials could also be used by the Darden School in any of its other educational programs. Unfortunately, we have learned this lesson the hard way. We failed to address this issue in advance with a recent client. The client refused even though the materials we had developed contained no company-specific information. It is still not clear to this day why the company took such a hard-line position. Nevertheless, that experience simply underscores the importance of gaining clarity on that issue at the outset of the relationship.

To formalize the relationship and the "purchase" of the requested educational services, clients frequently issue purchase orders or contracts that are unique to their organizations. The MOU is a vital document in the client's formulation of the contract terms that both parties will sign. Chances are, if an issue has not been discussed and dealt with in a mutually satisfactory manner in the MOU, the more legalistic contract or purchase order undertaking will be a source of problematic negotiation.

The Program Design Process

Needs analysis. One of the most enjoyable aspects of a major nondegree program endeavor is working with the sponsoring organization to define the needs the program should address. The process of

undertaking a needs analysis is really a process of discovery and translation. Discovery involves identifying the portfolio of issues most needing
and amenable to being addressed by the program you have been tasked
to design and deliver. Translation involves operationalizing generalized
needs into specific topics and program content. In this latter regard,
as part of our ABC Co. relationship, they wanted us to improve a
specific cadre of employees' "commercial acumen." Frankly, we spent
a great deal of time with ABC Co. personnel striving to clarify what
that meant. Indeed, clients usually have a preconceived notion of what
they want addressed but it still needs fleshed out to be operational and
validated.

A needs analysis usually involves two foci. The first focus is a series of
on-site or phone interviews of two primary constituencies – senior executives and potential program attendees. Both interviewee groups can
provide perspectives regarding program content emphases and examples to leverage not previously specified by your primary client contact.
The second focus usually involves a review of a client's recent internal
documentation that might exist pertaining to the catalyst for their call
to you. In this regard, we have often reviewed the results of such things
as employee attitude surveys, benchmarking studies, employee competency inventories, and even court orders mandating certain types of
educational programs.

For either focus, we have found the best way to proceed is to have
two colleagues involved in the needs analysis process. We have been
involved in needs analyses with an entire instructor team (containing
as many as 5 or 15 instructors) and we find that model needlessly costly
to the client and needlessly confining to the ultimate choice of the best
delivery team. Whether the duo is two instructors or one instructor and
a senior administrator, it does not matter. It is crucial, however, that
one of the instructors involved in the needs analysis be the on-going
instructor leader for the relationship.

In conducting on-site or phone interviews, it is always a good idea to
craft an interview protocol. Such a protocol should be sent to the interviewees in advance of your interviews so that they have time to develop
their thoughts. The protocol is also a good device for the interviewers
so that they stay on task and develop a set of comparable interviewee
responses. Here is a recent example of a needs analysis interview protocol that we used. Clearly, the duo doing the interviewing and crafting
the protocol should have already become fairly knowledgeable about

the client organization so that an appropriate protocol is developed but, more importantly, so that the interviewee responses are understood in ways that allow for pertinent and prompt follow-up queries.

A Needs Analysis Interview Protocol

The purpose of the Darden School visit and interviews is to learn more about ABC Co. and to find the set of themes, ideas, issues, and business challenges senior management wants included in the Leadership and Functional Curricula. We have found that meeting with senior leaders at their location helps bring the context alive for the faculty, and subsequently, the participants. We also find that after about 8–12 interviews the most critical ideas, issues, and concepts begin to emerge.

A typical interview consists of two Darden School representatives meeting with one ABC senior leader for about 45 minutes. Our interviews are open-ended, wide-ranging, and conversational. The following questions are offered to provide a general sense of the discussion areas:

- *What do you see as the mission/purpose of your organization?*
- *What are the key issues and challenges currently facing the company that should be addressed in this educational partnership? What is the history and context behind those issues?*
- *What are the strategic challenges and opportunities you see as most significant over the next 5 years that the Leadership Curriculum could help you address?*
- *What is it that you like the most about how your management team works? What is it that most frustrates you about how your collective management team works?*
- *Describe the metrics used to measure performance in your organization. Are these the right metrics? What alternatives have been considered?*
- *Describe how your organization has changed over the past 3–5 years? What may have been "lost" that needs to be retained? What is "new" that you don't know how you "lived without it"?*
- *On a scale of 1–10, how "active, involved, engaged, and positive" is your management team? What explains your rating? What proportion of your management team "drains energy"?*
- *What companies do you most admire, other than ABC, and why?*
- *What do your vendors, customers, employees, and investors most often say about ABC?*

- *Overall, what are the 2 or 3 strengths of your management and high potential pool? What are the 2 or 3 weaknesses?*
- *What is the single most important topic the Leadership programs should cover?*

Source: George Shaffer and Mark Haskins

The interviews and the review of any pertinent internal documentation should be performed in as short an elapsed time period as possible in order to facilitate your remembrance of the subtleties of thought and meaning surfacing during the conversations and sparked by what you heard or saw. There will be many such items and we find it impossible to write them all down as they occur. Such a compacted freshness of insight and ideas is most easily captured in the next phase of the needs analysis – a written document synthesizing what you have heard and what you have preliminarily extracted from those insights regarding the most dominant themes and issues to address in your program design. This document, once polished and thoroughly reviewed should be made available to the client for review and discussion. Moreover, once finalized and endorsed by the client, this document will play a vital role in the briefings to be conducted with each instructor that is asked to join the team. The outline of such a document is presented below. It is interesting to note that this short summary is the distillation of over 20 client interviews and nearly 50 pages of hand-written notes recorded during those interviews.

Synthesis of Needs-Analysis Interviews for ABC Co.

1. *Leadership/OB (Headline title: Building, Managing, & Leading for High Performance)*
   - *Culture (Old to new, Values, Cross-cultural)*
   - *Creating a Context for Success (Coaching, Team-building, Networking)*
   - *Rigor in People Planning (Succession Planning, Career Planning, Developing People, Performance Reviews)*
   - *Change and Performance Management (people side), Dealing with Ambiguity*
   - *Emotional Intelligence*

- GE lessons, <u>Good to Great</u>, *survey of current, provocative management theories*
- *Leverage ABC's 360*

2. **Strategy (Headline title: Developing the Enterprise Perspective)**
   - *Strategic Thinking (Identifying value-creating opportunities)*
   - *"Learning organization" and best practices*
   - *Change Management (strategy, systems, growth)*
   - *Inculcating a General Management Mindset (finance, economics, performance, risk)*
   - *Entrepreneurial/Innovation Spirit (in a company that is becoming a bit more centralized – "manage the tension")*
   - *High Performance Teams*
   - *Customer Focus (translate it into ABC environment)*

3. **Financial Acumen – Value and Risk Analysis (Headline title: Valuing the Business)**
   - *Financial Risk Analysis and Management (hedges, commodities, taking positions, foreign exchange)*
   - *Real Options Theory*
   - *Shareholder Value (how to capture it, maximize it, and identify the business drivers of it)*
   - *Portfolio Management/Perspective*
   - *Capital Allocation*
   - *Wall Street Perspective*

4. **Financial Acumen – Financial Statements/Accounting (Headline title: Understanding Key Principles)**
   - *Financial Statement Savvy (US GAAP, EBITDA, Performance measures and their deconstruction)*
   - *Cost Analysis, Cost Structures, Cost Behavior*
   - *Cash Flow, NPV (importance of)*
   - *Ethics in Financial Performance*

5. **Public Policy/Economics (Headline title: Thinking Globally, Acting Locally)**
   - *Macroeconomics*
   - *Global Mindset/Perspective*
   - *Assessing Political/Country Risk*
   - *Business and Government Relations*
   - *Understanding Regulatory Context*
   - *Regional Insights (Latin America, China, Europe, Africa)*

- *Insights from Developed Markets Applicable to Emerging Markets*
6. **Communications (Headline title: Influencing Others)**
   - *Presentation Skills*
   - *Persuasive Writing, Presence, Influence*
   - *Developing a Compelling Story*
   - *Negotiations*
   - *Managing a Crisis*
   - *External Affairs Management*
   - *Media Relations*

Source: George Shaffer and Mark Haskins

This summation of the needs analysis appears to present a portfolio of topics that might involve a program spanning several months as opposed to the two weeks stipulated by the client in this case. Indeed, the summation document is not the venue for winnowing down what you learned during the needs analysis. The document is the vehicle for facilitating conversations with the client to decide on the relative emphases to place on the topics in the confines of the stipulated program duration (e.g., two weeks). In going through this process, the client will often eliminate some of the themes and/or plan for future programs to address the themes that do not make it into the current one.

General program design. Once the needs analysis summation document has been used to facilitate an earnest discussion settling on the program's particular and relative thematic foci, it is best if the instructor team leader prepares a generalized program design. This short document serves to: confirm his/her understanding of the tradeoffs decided on and the important design criteria needed to be kept in mind as an instructor team is assembled and as they are asked to flesh out the macro design; focus everyone's attention; and it provides a first cut at a set of themes that will work in combination and within the program length of time. From the foregoing needs analysis, here is the brief program macro design that resulted.

ABC Co. Senior Executive Program (SEP) General Design
1. *Global Context … 90% of ABC Co. employees are non-US.*

2. *Pedagogy . . . Short cases, vignettes, simulations, and peers to share internal best practices*
3. *Materials . . . Fresh, short, global*
4. *Relevance . . . Case discussions with explicit instructor linkages to ABC Co.*
5. *Key Themes and Relative Weights*
   - *Leading and Managing for Performance Excellence (30% Leadership)*
   - *Developing the Enterprise Perspective (25% Strategy)*
   - *Valuing the Business (25% Financial Acumen/Value and Risk Analysis)*
   - *Thinking Globally, Acting Locally (20% Public Policy/ Economics)*
6. *Specific Content – Includes strategic challenges and their leadership implications; shareholder value maximization; keys to economic development; leadership and world class performance; ABC's value proposition; country development issues; valuation of ABC Co. by parts; creating value – capital investment analysis; working capital management; building capabilities across functions and business units; using real options; leading organizational design; market structure, regulation, and competition; governments and growth/microeconomics and infrastructure; opportunity identification and risk analysis; leaders as strategic visionaries.*
7. *Special Topics – In addition to the above, classes are devoted to: stakeholder management and ethics; the extended enterprise; and a portfolio mindset for entrepreneurial growth.*
8. *Program Duration – 2 consecutive weeks*
9. *Prerequisite – Nomination by Executive Officer*
10. *Target Audience – ABC Co. Executive Officers; Corporate and Business Leaders; selected others*
11. *ABC Co./Darden School Relationship Goal – The goal of the ABC Co./Darden School relationship is to strengthen ABC Co. business performance through the creation of people-centric processes, including the design and delivery of programs in the Leadership Curriculum.*
12. *Program Objectives – The overarching objective of this program is to create a learning environment that allows senior executives to focus on key ABC Co. business issues in the areas of strategy,*

financial acumen, public policy/macro economics and leadership. In addition, there are three specific objectives as follows: to facilitate the development of an ABC Co. enterprise view; to enhance analytical and conceptual skills for value creation; and, to strengthen the leadership capabilities of ABC Co. leaders.

13. *Delivery Methods – The program will engage participants in active discussions on actual, relevant, business problems. Various methods will be used to engage the group including case discussions, small group discussions, group presentations, lecturettes, contemporary articles, videos, guest speakers on special topics, and interactions with the CEO and other senior leaders.*

13. *Delivery Dates – September 6–17, this year; September 11–23, next year*

15. *Delivery Location – Darden School, University of Virginia, Charlottesville, Virginia*

Source: George Shaffer and Mark Haskins

Assembling the team. It is now time to assemble the instructor team. The key to this step is simply knowing what your colleagues specialize in, enjoy doing, the extent to which their instructional styles blend, their willingness to learn about the client, their level of interest in integrating their program streams with those of others on the team, and frankly, their willingness to take guidance from the team leader on such issues as: selection of materials, key connections to make to the client's issues, and requests for program involvement outside the confines of their particular sessions. For high profile, multiprogram clients seeking a multiyear relationship, we prefer to assemble a team of core instructors for whom we have positive, first-hand knowledge. Such clients are not the ones on which to experiment with untested, unknown instructors for one or more of the key program streams. Such clients do pose an opportunity, however, for developing untested, unknown instructors via cameo roles (ideally one, or no more than two sessions) if their expertise is strongly connected to a client issue or need.

A part of the team assembly process requires that the instructor team leader clearly and powerfully articulate the client needs to be addressed by each prospective team member. To do this, the team leader must be so familiar with the client company and its needs that he/she can, in essence, represent the concerns and views of the client to the prospective team member. Inevitably, prospective team members pose questions that do not follow your invitation script and it is important to be able to answer them so that a colleague can make an informed decision whether to accept your invitation to join the team or not. Instructors generally want to know how many sessions they are being asked to design and lead, the themes they are expected to address, the extent of the development effort expected of them, program dates, and the nature of any extra-program activities they will need to do.

Sometimes it is necessary to involve instructors who are not a part of your institution or for whom the client has made a specific request. In the first instance, it is important to have a network of key contacts throughout the world that you can draw upon for suggestions or to invite. In the absence of such a network, or even in addition to such a network, it is important to have maintained a broad exposure to the management literature so that you know who has written some provocative material in a certain area. We have assembled instructor teams comprised entirely of our university colleagues, others have involved all nonpersonally known experts, and others have involved combinations of the two. In either instance, there is a direct correlation between your ability as the team leader to assess the client's needs, the prospective instructor's expertise and professional style, and the fit of the two.

Detailed program design. Once the team is assembled, it is time for the team members to propose specific sessions based on the macro design document, the needs-analysis summary document, and all the briefing insights you can provide. The more information you can provide them with, the more closely you can connect the program needs to the themes and issues you know they have expertise in, and the more client context you can provide, the more likely their detailed proposals will be on target, thus minimizing the number of iterations back and forth between them, you, and the client. As the instructor team leader, your task is to assemble the collective team members' program streams, review them for appropriateness, and forward them to the client for discussion and ultimate approval. The resulting document might involve 10–15 pages for a two-week program. An excerpt of one day's session overview is presented below.

The Darden School/ABC Co. Senior Executive Program (SEP)
Session Overview

Tentative Session Themes and Flow
Note: We will use the Good to Great book by Jim Collins as an overarching context for the program with numerous sessions connecting to it.

Monday, September 6, 200X
  Opening reception, dinner, and welcome

Tuesday, September 7, 200X
1. *STRATEGY AND LEADERSHIP – "Strategic Challenges and their leadership Implications." We develop focus by introducing briefly the connections between leadership, strategic thinking, and organizational design. Then we ask, "What are the key challenges facing you (at the organizational, work group, and personal levels)?" The last half of this discussion focuses on "What are the implications of these challenges for the kind of leadership we (the participants) need to be developing?" This list becomes the developmental focus for the week and is posted on flip charts around the room – challenges on one side, implications on the other. This will be a joint session with Jeanne Liedtka and Jim Clawson.*

   Learning takeaways: set context for rest of program; development of a broad ABC Co. perspective across businesses; understanding of shared challenges; identification of learning partners with similar unique challenges.

2. *STRATEGY – "Why Strategic Thinking?" In this class we will examine the concept of strategic thinking by introducing the concepts of: competitive advantage, value creation and capture, and strategic capabilities. This class will provide a context for many of the ensuing discussions. Jeanne Liedtka.*

   Learning takeaways: understanding of key strategy concepts and development of shared vocabulary; chance to examine a set of different strategic models and their link to sources of competitive advantage; understand dynamics of how strategic choices can be made through default rather than deliberate action.

3. _FINANCIAL ACUMEN – "Shareholder Value Maximization."_
Introduce the context for shareholder value maximization (SVM).
Key things are to see different models and understand how each has
evolved. Finally, lay out implications as a model for the company.
Ken Eades.

Learning takeaways: understand how shareholder value maximization
has emerged as the leading management paradigm in US financial mar-
kets. As part of this, participants will be exposed to different governance
models and how each translates into a framework for aligning stakehold-
ers and management and also how this gets translated into a process for
decision-making. This class establishes the key principle that it is share-
holders that matter which forms the basis of everything that follows in
later sessions.
Source: Mark Haskins

Senior executive preview. We believe it is imperative to have support
for any program we do from the CEO and his or her executive team.
To that end, we either provide an extensive overview to them in person
at their headquarters or, more preferably, we invite them to attend the
initial offering of the program. (We are very careful to not call the
initial offering a pilot program as we have invested substantial effort
and resources into having it be the exact program the client wants from
its very first offering.) A CEO and his/her team are frequently not able
to attend a two week program or many times even a one week program.
Remember, it is our strong preference that they do so because when
future attendees ask, "Do the senior executives buy into what we are
talking about?" we want to be able to say from first-hand knowledge,
"Yes, they do." If they can't attend the program, however, we often
propose that they attend a preview version of the program. We have
done one-day and three-day preview versions of two-week programs
for a CEO and his/her immediate team.

The timing for such a preview program should be such that there is
time between it and the first full-fledged offering of the program for
program changes that might need to be made. From a CEO perspective,
the objectives of such a preview program include: a first-hand engagement with the instructors in the classroom, using some of the materials
that their personnel will be asked to study, and to be briefed on the

entire program content by the instructors who will deliver the various components of the program. We also reformat our class sessions during this preview program, announcing to the CEO and his or her team that they will differ a bit from our usual classes. For the program preview, each class begins as it normally would with the instructor and his or her assigned material but that 'live class' lasts only about an hour – thus, it will be a bit accelerated. In these shortened sessions, instructors still facilitate discussions that are reflective of the type of discussions that will be conducted in the full-fledged versions to be held in the regular rollout of the program. After approximately one hour, instructors depart from the regularly planned class progression and: (1) provide an overview of how that class discussion is likely to progress in the longer, usual class time frame (e.g., 90 minutes), (2) highlight the learning objectives for that class, (3) note the role that any learning team time plays in advance of that class, (4) introduce any instructor-specific frameworks/takeaways pertaining to that class, and (5) provide a general overview of the remainder of their proposed stream of classes. Generally, there is a constructive, positive exchange of ideas between instructors and the preview-program attendees, with an ending clarity as to what the instructor is mandated to do in the regular program rollout.

Listen, iterate, revise, listen. As perhaps you have picked up from the foregoing sections, the design and development of a nondegree program for a client involves astute listening, knowledge of the capabilities of potential instructors, and the mapping of provocative program designs to client needs. Again, it cannot be understated, the better one can accomplish this at the outset of the relationship the more likely the delivered program will be a success and thus the more delighted the client, and the more sought after you and your team and your institution will be as a world-class educational provider. In our experience, we have found clients quite willing to spend the money needed for an instructor leader and his/her team to do the due diligence that makes a program successful. After all, the purpose of the program is, as one corporate president recently stated, "to elevate everyone's game" so that the company will be ever-more successful. If we can be a part of a client's improved performance and enhanced success, what a great outcome for all parties.

Calendar issues

Setting and coordinating a calendar of program-related events and milestones is a nontrivial task. For ABC Co., we had three different, two-week programs, with at least two offerings each in an 18-month period, that needed to be designed and delivered, involving about 12 different instructors. For the client, this program portfolio involved nearly 200 executives coming from all over the world. The client had to establish the criteria for those selected to attend, solicit nominations, consider the company's own cycle of business events, allow non-US participants enough time for visas and passports, and then make all the travel arrangements. Because of all the client and instructor planning and work that was needed, an overall planning schedule was imperative. The working schedule we developed established tentative deadlines, final approval deadlines, and program delivery dates. The planning schedule presented below was a dynamic document, in that it flexed and changed as we went along but it was always current and the mutual focal point for the client and for the instructor team.

ABC Co. /Darden School Planning Calendar

This year...

July 8 – Senior Preview of Relationship and Senior Executive Program (SEP)

July – Learning Model Finalized

August 1 – SEP Design Complete

August 1 – Advance SEP Materials Mailed

September – ABC Co./Darden School Contract Finalized

September 6–17 – First SEP Delivered

September 20 (week of) – Debrief SEP (with emphasis on LDP design)

October 4 (week of) – Program Descriptions Prepared for LDP and ELP

October 4 (week of) – Review SEP Participant Feedback

October 15 – Initial (Fairly Complete) Draft of LDP

October 30 – LDP Design Complete

November – Initial Functional Curriculum Menu Complete

December 6–17 – First LDP Delivered

December 20 – Debrief LDP (with emphasis on ELP design)

Next year...

January – Initial Training and Skill-Building Curriculum Menu Complete

January 10 (week of) – Review LDP Participant Feedback

January 15 – Initial Draft of Emerging Leader Program (ELP) Design

February 15 – ELP Design Complete

March 13–25 – First ELP Delivered

March 28 (week of) – Debrief ELP (with emphasis on Functional Curriculum)

April 11 (week of) – Review ELP Participant Feedback

June – First Functional Curriculum Program (FP) Delivered

June – Debrief FP and Review Participant Feedback

June 19 –July 1 – Second LDP Delivered

Ongoing – Debriefs and Reviews Occur After Each Program Offering

September 11–23 – Second SEP Delivered

September – Second FP Delivered

October 9–21 – Second ELP Delivered

December – Third FP Delivered

Source: George Shaffer and Mark Haskins

Instructors' calendars can be a challenge. Our colleagues need anywhere from six to eight months lead time in order to block off a two-week period of time. Therefore, it is incumbent on the team leader to personally connect with each instructor and find calendar openings, compare the openings across all the team members, check those dates with the client and with local hotel availabilities, and then lock the appropriate dates in with all parties. It is also wise to check with instructors every couple of months to verify that the selected dates are still on their calendars and that your program has priority during those times.

Once a specific program proposal, containing all the class session descriptions, contributed by the entire instructor team, has been approved by the client, it is time to assemble the team for an extended meeting whose purpose is twofold: (1) make sure everyone knows what the others are doing in the program so that connections and integration are captured and embraced, and (2) lock in specific days, and times during the day, when each instructor will teach. We find that developing a succinct block schedule (e.g., see Figure 22.1) on a meeting room

Figure 22.1
Example of program block schedule

Week One – Senior Executive Program (SEP)

Tuesday	Wednesday	Thursday	Friday	Saturday
7 Sep.	8 Sep.	9 Sep.	10 Sep.	11 Sep.
Clawson & Liedtka 8:00–9:30 AM *Strategic Challenges and their Leadership Implications*	Rodriguez (1) 8:00–9:30 AM *Productivity: The key to Economic Development*	Rodriguez (2) 8:00–9:40 AM *Lessons from a World Development Tour:*	Freeman & Liedtka 8:00–10:30 AM *Strategic Stakeholder Management and Ethics*	Eades (5) 8:00–9:30 AM *Creating Value: Capital Investment Analysis II*
Break 9:30–9:45	Break 9:30–9:45	Break 9:40–10:00	Break 10:30–10:45	Break 9:30–9:45
NO LT	LT 9:45–10:30	NO LT	NO LT	LT 9:45–10:30
Liedtka (1)	Clawson (1)	Clawson (2)	Rodriguez (3)	Eades (6)
9:45–11:40 AM *Why Strategic Thinking?*	10:30–12:00 Noon *Leadership and World Class Performance*	10:00–12:00 Noon *Level Three Leadership*	10:45–12:00 Noon *Governments and Growth: Budgets and International Finance*	10:30–12:00 Noon *Managing Working Capital*

Figure 22.1
(contd.)

| LT 11:40–12:30 | Lunch 12:00–1:00 | Lunch 12:00–1:00 | Lunch 12:00–1:00 | Liedtka (2) |
Lunch 12:30–1:30	LT 1:00–2:30	No LT	LT 1:00–2:00	12:00–2:30
Eades (1) 1:30–3:15 PM *Shareholder Value Maximization*	Eades (2) 2:30–4:15 PM *Valuation of Parts: Growth and Value*	Clawson (3) 1:00–2:15 PM *The LPI* Break 2:15–2:30 Eades (3) 2:30–4:15 PM *Workshop Valuation of ABC*	Eades (4) 2:00–3:45 PM *Creating Value: Capital Investment Analysis I*	Working Lunch *Building Capabilities Across Functions & Business Units*
Personal time Reception, Dinner, LT for Rodriguez (1)	Personal time Reception, Dinner, LT for Eades (3)	Personal time Reception, Dinner, LT for Eades (4)	Personal time Reception, Dinner, LT for Eades (5)	*UVA Football 3:30 UVA vs. UNC*

Figure 22.1
(contd.)

Week Two – SEP.

Monday	Tuesday	Wednesday	Thursday	Friday
13 Sep.	14 Sep.	15 Sep.	16 Sep.	17 Sep.
Eades (7)	Eades (9)	Rodriguez (4)	Liedtka & Rodriguez	Liedtka (4)
8:00–10:00 AM	8:00–9:30 AM	8:00–9:30 AM	8:00–10:00 AM	8:00–10:15 AM
Creating Value: Capital Investment Analysis III	*Using Real Options (Part I)*	*Governments and Growth: Microeconomics and Infrastructure*	*Business Unit Workshop: Opportunity Identification and Risk Analysis*	*Workshop: Cross-Business Unit Opportunities (REPORT OUTS)*
Break 10:00–10:15	Break 9:30–10:00	Break 9:30–10:00	Break 10:00–10:15	Break 10:15–10:30
LT 10:15–10:45	NO LT	NO LT	LT 10:15–11:00	NO LT
Clawson (4)	Spekman & Liedtka	Rodriguez (5)	Venkat	Clawson (6)
10:45–12:00 Noon	10:00–Noon	10:00–12:00 Noon	11:00–1:00 Noon	10:30–12:00 Noon
Leading Teams and Task Forces	*Strategic Supply Chain Management*	*Market Structure, Regulation and Competition*	*Portfolio Mindset for Entrepreneurial Growth*	*Leading Strategic Change*

Figure 22.1
(contd.)

Lunch 12:00–1:00	Lunch 12:00–1:00	Lunch 12:00–1:00	Lunch 1:00–2:00	Lunch 12:00–12:45
LT 1:00–1:45	NO LT	LT 1:00–2:00	NO LT	NO LT
Eades (8) 1:45–3:15 PM *Introduction to Options Thinking*	Eades (10) 1:00–3:30 PM *Using Real Options (Part II)*	Clawson (5) 2:00–3:30 PM *Leading by Design*	Liedtka (3) 2:00–4:30 PM *Workshop Introduction*	Clawson 12:45 AM–3:00 PM *Personal Charters*
Break 3:15–3:30				
Liedtka & CEO 3:30–5:00 PM *Linking Corporate and Business Unit Strategy – Part I*				
Personal time Reception, Dinner, LT for Eades(9)	Personal time Reception, Dinner, NO LT	Personal time Reception, Dinner, NO LT	Personal time Reception, Dinner, LT for Liedtka (4)	

Source: Mark Haskins

chalkboard, or projected EXCEL spreadsheet, is an efficient means for crafting a daily and hourly program schedule. Once the pieces of the block schedule are in place, agreed on, double-checked, and evaluated as to program flow, pace, integration, and appeal, instructors are asked, before leaving that meeting, to record their program commitments in their calendars. As you might imagine, if one instructor were to miss a calendar conflict, changing the block schedule has a horrendous domino-effect – it is best to nail it down with everyone still in the room. From the block schedule it is a simple matter to create a more finished-looking schedule that program participants will receive along with the session assignment sheets that the team leaves this meeting tasked to produce.

From this point on to the start of the program, the program administrative assistant (PA) is intensely involved, primarily making sure all the program logistics are taken care of and done well. This person, who reports to the instructor team leader, coordinates the receipt of all the instructor assignments, converts the block schedule to a publishable schedule, arranges audiovisual and technology requests from the instructors, prepares and sends out any advance mailings to the program participants, and responds to any and all queries from participants that can range from suggestions for travel to the type of clothing to bring, and any special dietary needs. This person is critically important and serves as the first point of contact for the program that the participants will interact with and ultimately meet. This person must be detail oriented, very personable, client oriented, and able to interface with instructors who are often demanding, slow to respond, and not prone to remembering details.

A quick word regarding a program's advance materials is warranted. Generally, we obtain a roster of program participants from a client four to six weeks prior to the start of a program. About three to four weeks prior to the program, the PA either sets up a Web portal or ships via some sort of overnight express service the following materials: a welcome letter from the instructor leader; local travel information; local weather information; short bios of the instructor team; a welcome letter from the PA; the first two days' schedule, assignments, and material; as well as information about the Darden School, the University of Virginia, and the Charlottesville, Virginia, area. The importance of those materials is to enable attendees to hit the ground running upon their arrival – indeed, we plan on the first day of any program being a full, fruitful, representative program day.

Program delivery

Each of our nondegree programs begins with a reception and dinner the night before the first day of classes. This is a relaxed, casual time for attendees to get to know one another and for the instructors to circulate and welcome everyone. Then, as dessert and coffee are being served, one of the senior directors of the Darden School's executive education office stands up and formally welcomes everyone and provides a bit of history and overview of the particular program they are attending. Next, the instructor leader stands and adds his or her welcome. In addition, he or she describes the learning/teaching methods the participants will experience and makes it very clear what the participants can expect from the instructors and what the instructors expect from the participants. Finally, the PA stands to add his or her welcome and makes whatever administrative and logistical announcements are needed. We strive very hard to keep the total time for these three speakers to no more than half an hour. Generally, we dismiss participants to their first learning team meeting to discuss the next morning's assignments and, thus, the program begins.

In their hotel room, program participants find a binder of materials pertinent to the first week's sessions. This may include various assignment sheets, cases, reprinted articles, descriptions of simulations, instructions for certain classroom deliverables, any learning team tasks, and that week's schedule. In the schedule they receive, we find it best to account for all their time from breakfast through learning team time following dinner. During that block of time, we also schedule breaks which we point out to the participants that we will honor; therefore, they can plan to conduct any business they may need to deal with during those times. Such an approach greatly reduces, in fact it virtually eliminates, participants being absent from classes and/or having to leave in the middle of a class to conduct some business. The schedule is full and compact as we strive very hard to provide a rich and full day's experience. The one thing we do not want participants to say when they leave is, "It was a great program but they could have done it in less time."

The final dinner for any program is special. All during the program, instructors have shared meal time and break time with the participants, in addition to their classes, so the final dinner is often a warm and enjoyable evening. We often arrange for some special entertainment that evening and/or a very light assignment for the next morning so that folks can socialize into the evening and enjoy themselves.

After the final program class has ended, the instructor team joins the participants in their classroom, along with the PA. The PA hands out the program evaluation (a sample excerpt is presented in Figure 22.2) and the instructor leader makes a few closing comments and thanks all the pertinent people, and then the team hands out the program certificate (nicely framed and suitable for displaying). The PA collects the completed evaluations. There is a final farewell and the program is over.

Expanded relationships

Besides the program-specific tasks and issues discussed above, one of the things we strive to accomplish with our non\degree program clients is a comprehensive connection that extends beyond just the design and delivery of a discrete program (or set of programs). We are interested in a larger relationship. We are privileged to have attained that with the focal company of this chapter and others. In particular, we have been involved in enabling local instructors from around the world adapt and deliver some of our program designs and materials for local use in order to impact those company personnel whose English language skills preclude their attendance at our U.S. venue and us going to their locale to deliver the program. Moreover, we continually listen for opportunities, in all of our discussions with a client, for opportunities to suggest that they connect with one of our colleagues whose expertise might be helpful in the arena they are seeking assistance.

One of the more exciting aspects of client involvement that often emanates from an initial program design and delivery relationship is providing counsel and direction for an organization's overall people-development agenda. Briefly, and just as an example of some of the arenas for our expanded involvement with ABC Co., consider Figure 22.3. As you will note from that exhibit, ripe areas for assisting a client in such an expanded capacity include: the role and crafting of key experiences for certain personnel, executive assessment, coaching relationships in the organization, and succession planning. In addition, we have worked with clients on establishing a broader array of curricula than we can deliver, or for which others are better suited to deliver, all packaged as a constructive, coherent people development plan.

Figure 22.2
Sample program evaluation excerpt

University of Virginia
The Darden Graduate School of Business Administration
ABC Co. Senior Executive Program
September 6–7, 200X

Program Evaluation

We value your comments and will use them in evaluating, improving, and strengthening this course. Please circle your ratings and provide your comments, ideas, and suggestions in the space below each question. (Please explain if any poor ratings.)

1 What is your **overall evaluation** of the program? Comments:

Poor	Fair	Average	Good	Excellent
1	2	3	4	5

2. Did this program **meet your expectations?** Why or why not?

Much Less Than Expected	Less Than Expected	Just What Expected	More Than Expected	Much More Than Expected
1	2	3	4	5

3. We desire to offer the best possible **service** and would appreciate your opinion on the following:

	Poor	Fair	Average	Good	Excellent
Accommodations at Sponsor's Executive Residence Center	1	2	3	4	5

Your Room # _____

Meals at the Abbott Center	1	2	3	4	5
Service by Sponsor's and Abbott Center Staff	1	2	3	4	5

Comments or suggestions for improvements to above accommodations, meals and services:

Figure 22.2
(contd.)

4. Each of our **Marketing/Program Administrators** coordinates all aspects of each program and works with faculty to ensure that program materials, logistics and requests are handled effectively. **How would you rate the Administrator for this program (Jennifer)?**

<u>Poor</u>	<u>Fair</u>	<u>Average</u>	<u>Good</u>	<u>Excellent</u>
1	2	3	4	5

<u>Comments:</u>

5. Individual Class Evaluation – **Please circle your ratings and provide your comments, ideas, and suggestions in the spaces below each question.**

<u>Poor</u>	<u>Fair</u>	<u>Average</u>	<u>Good</u>	<u>Excellent</u>
1	2	3	4	5

WEEK 1		
Tuesday	**Appropriateness of Topic and Material**	**Effectiveness of Faculty in Delivery**
Strategic Challenges and their Leadership Implications Professors Clawson and Liedtka	1 2 3 4 5	1 2 3 4 5
Why Strategic Thinking? Professor Liedtka • Piaggio	1 2 3 4 5	1 2 3 4 5
Shareholder Value Maximization Professor Eades • *Walt Disney Productions, June 1984*	1 2 3 4 5	1 2 3 4 5

Figure 22.2
(contd.)

6. How do you feel about your **workload** during the program?

Far Too Light	Too Light	About Right	Too Heavy	Far Too Heavy
1	2	3	4	5

   a) What topics should be expanded or included?
   b) What topics should be reduced or excluded?

7. What **suggestions** do you have for the instructors?

8. A group of your direct reports will be with us for a 2-week program later this Fall.
   a. Of the subjects you have discussed during the two weeks you have been here, which ones should be a priority for that next group to also explore and discuss? Be as specific as you can be.
   b. What topics not covered in the program you just completed would you like to see covered in the upcoming program for your direct reports?

9. As you think about your own continuing professional development, and the possibility of attending a future 2-day program, what topics would be of most interest to you to concentrate on for two days?

10. If you were asked to give a **quote** on this program, what would you say?

May we use your quote? YES ____ NO ____

       Name: _____
      Title: _____
    Company: _____

11. May we use you as a reference for future participants?
    YES ____ NO ____

Please return this
evaluation to:

               Jennifer, Marketing/Program Administrator
               Executive Education, The Darden School
               P.O. Box 7186
               Charlottesville, VA 229067186

To expand on one aspect of the holistic client relationship model presented in Figure 22.3, let's consider the "key experiences" component for a moment. Now, let it be said right at the outset, we are not in a position to dictate the jobs and secondments that ABC Co. personnel should have as part of a planned set of key experiences involved in their personal and professional development. We are, however, in a position to facilitate the client's overall planning and thinking about such things. Indeed, Figure 22.3 posits key experiences as part of the organization's continuing development dimensions. That basic thinking can be enhanced by creating an overall development framework as depicted in Figure 22.4. Such a framework maps various organizational populations against the various development opportunities that should be a part of their professional development cycle. In essence, this framework identifies who will have what kind of development experience.

In pushing the key experiences dimension a bit further, Figure 22.5 presents a prototype instrument for individual assessment regarding the extent to which certain key experiences have already been a part of their professional path. Clearly, one of the key aspects of this instrument is identifying those critical key experiences. Indeed, those experiences are best delineated against a set of organizational values and desired behavioral capabilities (see Figure 22.6). The discussions leading to the ultimate identification of a codified set of key experiences are ones that are likely to span months if the organization has done no prior work in this regard. On the other hand, if foundational work has been previously laid by the organization, the discussions may constitute no more than an afternoon meeting. In either case, you as a knowledgeable, outside third party can bring great value to these discussions through the perspectives and questions and probing that you do.

Once the organizational population targeted for key experiences as part of their professional development has been established (Figure 22.4), and the most important type of key experiences identified and linked to a set of desired organizational capabilities and individual behaviors (Figure 22.6), and an instrument created to assess the extent to which individuals have had such experiences (Figure 22.5), it is useful to then expand on the objectives of the stated key experiences (Figure 22.7). At the same time, it is important to identify how the various key experiences might best be undertaken and what the intended professional learning is expected to be for the individual.

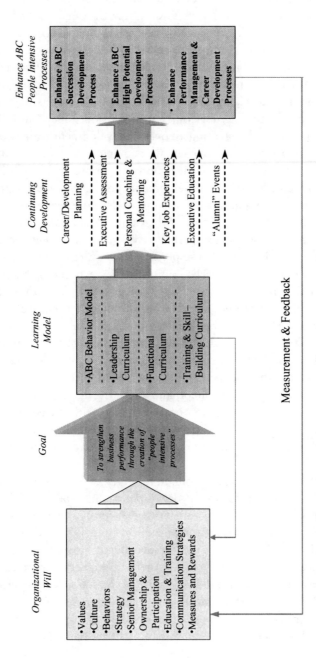

Figure 22.3 Diagrammatic overview of a large client relationship

Figure 22.4
Professional development framework

DEVELOPMENT OPPORTUNITIES					
Leadership Curriculum					
Functional Curriculum					
Core Curriculum					
Regional Learning Center Programs					
Key Experiences					
Development Planning					
People Review Process-Coaching and Feedback					
= Primary Target Audience	All Employees	All Supervisors/ Managers	High Potential Emerging Leaders	Group Managers/ Regional Business Leaders	Executives and Officers

TARGET POPULATION

Source: George Shaffer

We have found these key experiences frameworks, tools, and discussions quite energizing and helpful for our client as they strive to craft comprehensive, coherent, and aligned paths for their key people to pursue. We welcome and envision similar sorts of involvement on any of the other Figure 22.3 "continuing development" dimensions.

Ten reminders

As this chapter concludes, acknowledging that we have merely touched on the high points of managing a nondegree program and client relationship, here are 10 reminders. We offer these as tips and suggestions, not 10 commandments.

Figure 22.5
Key experiences assessment instrument

PARTICIPANT'S NAME	TITLE		BUSINESS UNIT
PARTICIPANT'S SIGNATURE	DATE	SUPERVISOR'S NAME	

Key Experiences Assessment - code the following areas regarding your current degree of experience.

Scale: *1 – Little or no experience; 2 – Moderate experience; 3 – Extensive experience*

KEY EXPERIENCES	1	2	3
	Little or No Experience	*Moderate Experience*	*Extensive Experience*
Working Globally • Living or working outside of one's own country • Interacting with people from other countries	☐	☐	☐
Running a Business • Managing an entire operation, business, or major project • End-to-end responsibility for performance • Profit and loss responsibility	☐	☐	☐
Growing a Business • Leading a start-up	☐	☐	☐
Partnering Externally • Developing strategic relationships with external constituencies	☐	☐	☐
Leading Change • Strategic organizational initiatives • Process management or reengineering initiatives	☐	☐	☐
Working in Partnerships and Alliances • Mergers and acquisitions • Joint ventures	☐	☐	☐

Figure 22.5
(contd.)

Leading People ☐ ☐ ☐

- Lead, supervise, coach, mentor others

- First-line supervision

- Leading large teams

Working in Teams ☐ ☐ ☐

- Member of team, taskforce, work group

Collaborating Across Organizations ☐ ☐ ☐

- Utilize broad network of relationships

- Cross functional perspective

- Gain cooperation toward a common goal

© 2004 George Shaffer, Lecturer in Business Administration, and University of Virginia Darden School Foundation.

---

1. Every client and program is different – approach them that way.
2. Become as knowledgeable of the client and the program-specific clientele as you possibly can.
3. It is not just about content and lessons – it is also about excitement and motivation and possibilities for you, your team, and the client.
4. As the team leader, strive for an integrated, seamless flow of topics and sessions across instructors and across the days.
5. Be thorough and proactive on calendar issues – more anticipation and confirmation is better than less.
6. Cultivate multiple senior level contacts within the client organization – key contacts leave and you want multiple champions/partners within an organization.
7. Avoid glittering generalities – discipline yourself to be precise in articulating the client needs addressed by your program and how each program session contributes.
8. Be thorough and proactive on budget/cost issues with the client – no surprises.

Figure 22.6
Key experiences and leadership attribute matrix

ABC Co. BEHAVIOR MODEL	Working Globally	Running a Business	Growing a Business	Partnering Externally	Leading Change	Leading People	Working in Teams	Collaboration
Exhibits the Highest Personal Standards								
•Acts with the Highest Integrity and Demonstrates Co. Values								
•Seeks to Learn Continuously								
•Shows Initiative and a Strong Bias for Action								
Creates a Climate for Success								
•Actively Communicates								
•Acts as a Change Agent								
•Builds Teams								
•Makes People Better								
Transforms Strategy into Results								
•Displays a Global Mindset								
•Demonstrates Analysis and Judgment Skills								
•Exhibits Business Acumen								
•Demonstrates Technical/Functional Excellence								
•Builds Commitment to Organizational Direction								
•Insists on Accountability and Execution in Self and Others								

KEY EXPERIENCES

Source: George Shaffer

9. Know your limits – if you are not interested or capable of managing a large-scale project and relationship, don't even try!
10. Communicate, communicate, communicate and document your communications so that things do not fall through the cracks, so that action items get done, and to avoid redundancies.

Conclusion

The large-scale program/client relationships that we have managed have provided some of the most enjoyable aspects of our career and some of the best and deepest learning we have had. In all honesty, such endeavors have been a very pleasant and rewarding surprise for

Figure 22.7
Key experiences activities and outcomes

Key experiences are planned developmental experiences or job assignments. THREE EXAMPLES of key experiences, their definitions, suggested developmental activities, and expected learning outcomes:

1. Leading People – Experiences that provide opportunities to lead, supervise, coach, or mentor people for whom one is either directly or indirectly accountable. These may include leading large teams, providing first-line supervision of people, and leading teams representing diverse functional, professional, or demographic background or job levels.
   Suggested Developmental Activity (one example)
   – Jointly create a developmental plan for each person you supervise
   Expected Learning Outcome (one example)
   – Ability to build organizational capability by developing its people
2. Partnering Externally – Experiences that provide opportunities to develop or maintain important collaborative or strategic relationships with groups or individuals external to the company. Examples include business partners, regional and local government relations, contractors, suppliers, investors, the media, community and environmental organizations.
   Suggested Developmental Activity
   – Negotiate with public officials in support of business objectives
   Expected Learning Outcome
   – Ability to influence external constituencies
3. Developing Global Awareness – Experiences that provide opportunities to live or work outside of one's own country, or to work in a function that involves interacting with people from other countries.
   Suggested Developmental Activity
   – Lead a team comprised of both local nationals and international assignees
   Expected Learning Outcome
   – Enhanced understanding of "global" business practices and cultural norms

someone who thought the academic life was a vow of poverty and an extended stay on campus. It must also be said that some of our lowest and least enjoyable moments have been in relation to such programs. But, as in other aspects of life, you learn, you move on, you know what to look for and avoid, and over time you see the ways you can help a client and personally grow.

Further reading

Bachler, C., "The Trainer's Role is Turning Upside Down," *Workforce*, 76, 6, (1997), 93–105.

Bailor, C., C. Beasty, J. Compton, A. DeFelice, M. Lager, and D. Myron, "100 Proven CRM Ideas," *Customer Relationship Management*, 9, 6 (2005), 28–40.

Barrett, N., "A Client's Perception of Business Education," *Executive Development*, 7, 5 (1994), 16–17.

Carneiro, A., "Teaching Management and Management Educators: Some Considerations," *Management Decision*, 42, 3/4 (2004), 430–38.

Elmuti, D., M. Abebe, and M. Nicolosi, "An Overview of Strategic Alliances between Universities and Corporations," *Journal of Workplace Learning*, 17, 1/2, (2005), 115–29.

Ghoshal, S., B. Arnzen, and S. Brownfield, "A Learning Alliance between Business and Business Schools: Executive Education as a Platform for Partnership," *California Management Review*, 35, 1 (1992), 50–67.

Lockee, B., and M. Reece, "Educational Exchange," *Pharmaceutical Executive* (April 2005), 18–21.

Roche, E., "How to Strengthen Customer Exit Barriers," *Customer Relationship Management*, 9, 3 (2005), 26.

Ryan, L., and R. Morriss, "Designing and Managing a Strategic Academic Alliance: An Australian University Experience," *Journal of Workplace Learning*, 17, 1/2 (2005), 79–87.

Weinberger, J., "Customers for Life." *Customer Relationship Management*, 8, 7 (2004), 32–38.

23 | Dealing with the press

JAMES G. S. CLAWSON

> I am unable to understand how a man of
> honor could take a newspaper in his hands
> without a shudder of disgust.
>
> — Charles Baudelaire

It may be a bit surprising to find a chapter on dealing with the press in a book on teaching business management. As it turns out, though, business management instructors are confronted with a surprising number of opportunities to speak with the press. Journalists of all kinds, newspaper, magazine, and freelance, are likely to call one day, sooner than you might expect, to ask your opinion about any number of broad topics that they heard somewhere that *you* had special expertise in. This chapter will present some ideas that may help you deal with these opportunities.

Press contacts usually happen in one of three ways: cold calls, referral calls, and publication follow-ups. In cold calls, an instructor gets a phone call out of the blue and is asked some questions about events taking place in the world or a particular topic on which the writer is developing an article. It may not be you in particular whom they are calling, rather it may be they are simply seeking someone at your company or university who can give them some good insight or pithy quotes.

Referrals typically come from colleagues or from your organization's public relations department. University or corporate press relations offices keep contact with various new wire services in their regions so that when an academic or corporate opinion is called for, the reporter may call the press office which will then refer the writer. If the press office has done its job, it will have contacted you in advance to ask about areas of expertise or research interest. With this information, the university or corporate public relations officer can refer reporters to people who are most likely to know something about the topic in question. The public relations officer may be willing to maintain the middle person role, offering to call the reporter back and explain an instructor's background so that the reporter can call with a knowledge of who they are calling and what their expertise is.

Referrals can also come from colleagues who have been contacted by the media and believe your expertise is more relevant for the topic at hand. Similarly, even if you have had interesting things to say, the reporter may ask you at the end of the interview for referrals to other colleagues around the country who are familiar with the topic.

Publishing articles and books can also lead to media inquiries. With Web-based searches so easily and readily available, reporters can simply type in a few key words and your name may come up.

Why talk to the media?

Talking to the press accomplishes several things. First, it can enhance the reputation of your school or company. Having your name and institution referred to in the *Wall Street Journal* or the *New York Times* and even the local papers can heighten the institution's reputation. The company or school will be seen more as a place that has interesting people with interesting viewpoints.

Talking with the press is also useful feedback for an instructor. Exposure in the press can enhance an individual's reputation. Personally, it is flattering and rewarding to realize that people in society might be interested in your life's work. By itself, this motivation is perhaps not very laudatory, but coupled with your role as a teacher, it can be seen as an opportunity to expand one's sphere of influence. Talking with the media is a chance to influence and teach more people. The questions that reporters ask teach us a lot about the kinds of things that the media are interested in and, in some cases, have stimulated our thinking to do additional reading or research on certain topics.

Some realities of press relations

When a reporter calls, there are a couple of things to remember. First, the person is likely working on a tight deadline. If these people miss a window of interest, their work is worthless, so they are pressing for immediate and insightful commentary. If you have a phone message from a member of the press and don't get back to him or her the same day or, at the latest, the next day, it may be too late. Alternatively, there are those working on articles of general interest for a series that have longer deadlines. With those people, you can make appointments to talk about the subject in person or by phone at a later time. In fact, interviewers will often suggest that. If their topic is not a pressing one, it is to both your benefit and theirs for you to collect your thoughts and to have some ideas clearly in mind.

Understand that reporters are informing their own general knowledge about a field as they conduct an interview, and they are likely to use only a minuscule portion of what you say. Sometimes, this boiling down is so severe as to be very frustrating. We have one colleague who drove two and a half hours each way for a seven-minute interview. He was willing to do this because the show was aired on national television, but still, the whole day was taken, driving, putting on makeup, organizing the shoot, taping, then driving home, all for a seven-minute appearance. Similarly, telephone interviews can go on for an hour and result in a single sentence quote.

Part of the challenge in interviews with reporters is academic language. University faculty, in particular, often become accustomed to speaking in abstract and theoretical terms. In our attempts to be accurate in our research, we tend to try to see and describe all of the nuances of the phenomena we observe. These kinds of discussions are death to popular media articles. Stephen Hawking in his book, *A Brief History of Time*, noted that his publishers told him that every mathematical equation in the book would halve his reading audience. He therefore sought to write a book without any equations in it. As it turned out, there was one, Einstein's well known $e = mc^2$. But the point is well taken.

This observation suggests the importance of finding pithy, insightful, meaningful one-liners at a minimum, and more broadly, developing some skill at clear and concise speech. This, of course, will also help in the classroom, another reason why talking with the press is useful. Practice the skill of boiling key theories and concepts down into language that all can understand. Do the "grandma test": How would you explain your insights to Grandma when she asks? If you find yourself talking on and on during an interview, pause and ask the reporter if you're commenting on what they wanted. If the reporter asks a different question or shifts the topic, know that you need to be more concise for that interview. Save your detailed academic explanations for the appropriate audience. Likewise, have lay explanations ready for your lay audiences.

There are a couple of things you can try to negotiate with reporters. First, you can ask for a copy of the article when it is printed. Asking for a copy of the published article does several things. First, it is a bit of a burden for the interviewer, so it urges them to make sure that this is a worthwhile interview. If you're willing to spend your time on the interview, is the reporter willing to spend a moment sending you the final version? Second, it means the interviewer has to get your name and address. This means spelling it out and making sure he or she gets it right. No matter how often you try to make sure of that kind of detail, strange things are printed in articles. I was once quoted in a local newspaper as being an economics professor at a neighboring school! Reporters talk to many people, and they make mistakes. Finally, getting a copy of the article provides a means to check what was finally printed and whether or not what you thought was important really got through. This is an excellent means of checking the clarity of your communication and of the understandability of your comments. Learn to guide the reporter to the kinds of things you want to make sure are remembered and quoted. Having short, clear, insightful statements ready at hand will aid in this process. Yes, they are merely sound bytes, and yes, they are not as accurate or thorough as your research or papers, but they are what hundreds, thousands, and even millions of people will know of your work, so it pays to be skillful in managing their knowledge. (By the way, we've never met a reporter who would send a copy of an article in *advance* of its publication. They value intensely the freedom of the press. You can request that they read your direct quotes back to you, but even then, deadline pressure may preclude their willingness to do so.)

Ask reporters at the beginning of the interview what they are writing about, what tone they want to set, and why they want to do this article. You can tell by their answers whether they are looking to you as an example of the subject or a counter-example. In the latter case, your comments are not likely to be recorded and presented in a favorable light. Reporters have biases, too, and they write to present those biases. Realize that your comments may be used in the context of an article as the foil that proves the main theme of the article and respond accordingly.

Conclusion

Talking with the press, even over the phone, can be an unnerving experience. If you anticipate that the press may call, if you practice simple summaries of your work in advance, and if you negotiate the terms of the interview up front, you will go into those interviews with much greater confidence. If you also realize that what you say may not be used by the reporter in any volume if at all, your reaction to the finished product will be less frustrated and surprised. The press, in a way, can be seen as a teaching vehicle. If you wish to, and if you see the value of it, manage the press in a way to expand your teaching influence and to let others know about your work and insights. With this attitude in mind, your experiences with the press may be very positive.

Further reading

Bloch, Jeff, "Meet the Press: How to Foolproof Yourself When a Reporter Calls," *Inc.*, 19, 5 (April 1997).

Chanen, Jill Schachner, "How to Treat the Press," *ABA Journal*, 84 (June 1998), 90–91.

Cocheo, Steve, "Getting Along with the Local Media," *American Bankers Association Banking Journal*, 95, 7 (July 2003),16–22; 60.

Fitch, Brad, "Here Comes Trouble," *Association Management*, 56, 10 (October 2004), 61–67.

Marken, G.A., "Following Fundamentals Builds Journalist Relationships," *Public Relations Quarterly*, 48, 1 (Spring 2003), 27–31.

Stern, Gary, "Dealing with a Media Onslaught," *Utility Business*, 3, 2 (February 2000), 30–33.

24 | *Managing yourself and your time*

JAMES G. S. CLAWSON

> I wish I could stand on a busy corner, hat in
> hand, and beg people to throw me all their
> wasted hours.
>
> – Bernard Berenson

Teaching careers have many wonderful features. We get to spend our lives studying things we want to study, working with bright young people whose lives we can influence and edify; we have enormous freedom over the way we spend our time; we often have immediate access to excellent physical fitness facilities at reduced rates, and we have a summer schedule that can be adapted to meet our own needs. The corollary in the corporate world may not have quite as much summertime freedom, nevertheless most of the other benefits still apply. The job of teaching business management has great variety: We alternately act as teachers, researchers, writers, counselors, administrators, consultants, expert witnesses, representatives, and public speakers. Personally, we are hard-pressed to imagine a more rewarding, worthwhile, stimulating profession.

These same features, though, can be overwhelming. The work is never done, it is hard to leave it at the office, students come and go, making it easy to lose sight of their individual growth and development. Pressed by the desire or the demand to publish and/or design the next dynamite class or program, we often work long hours and ignore other dimensions of life. The university tenure system places heavy pressure on young faculty to produce or face the prospect of being let go. Peopled by self-confident and independent individuals, the ranks of academe and corporate training departments are often rife with political battles and unfortunate jealousies of fame and fortune.

In the midst of these swirling and contradictory forces, we all try to sort out a path that will be personally and professionally satisfying. Some institutions become so all-consuming that individuals sacrifice their families, their health, even their lives over incidents and pressures occurring at work. Other instructors seem to manage rather well and to be rounded, well-balanced individuals. How your life unfolds, of course, depends on your choices, and how you respond to the consequences of the choices made.

We think it is useful, therefore, to pause and consider some principles of managing yourself and your time – and perhaps more important, your energy. If you can do these things well, your productivity, the quality of your products, and your experience of your life and career will likely be enhanced. To stimulate your thinking about this issue of balance, we include here an exercise we've used in other settings. We invite you to complete the "Balancing Your Life" exercise that follows, then to reflect carefully on the gradual life structure that you're building. Whether you're in academe or the corporate world, balancing your life in a way that enhances rather than reduces your energy is an important activity – whether you realize it or not!

"Balancing Your Life" exercise

One of the most difficult things about managing life in the modern era is finding the right kind of balance in our lives. The constantly growing and competing demands of life on many fronts push us to make daily behavioral decisions about how we spend our time and talents without being able to think clearly about the consequences of those decisions over time.

Some people naturally seem to find a balance that fits them and their own definition of success over the years. Others have a more difficult job of it. The tragedy is not in missing a common "right" balance. Rather, the tragedy lies in making daily decisions that add up over a lifetime to a balance that one realizes, in retrospect, was not what we would have consciously chosen.

This exercise is designed to help you see your current behavioral allocation of time and how that matches up with your personal definition of success. The exercise is built upon some fundamental assumptions:
1) We all have a limited 168 hours per week of time.
2) We all have some freedom in choosing how we spend that time.
3) We all have some talent to apply to the time we have.
4) We all have various dimensions to our lives that we choose, consciously or unconsciously, to develop or ignore.

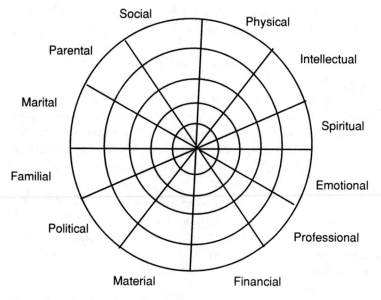

Figure 24.1 Personal profile of development

There are several steps to completing the exercise:

1. Write down your personal definition of success. What does it mean to you now to be "successful?" Research shows that an individual's definition of success may vary over a lifetime, but we need a place to start. What does it mean to you to be "successful?"

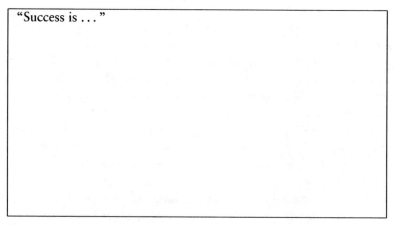

2. On the Balance Wheel diagram in Figure 24.1, assess your current level of personal development on each of the dimensions shown there. Use a scale of 1 to 10, where 1 is completely undeveloped

Figure 24.2
Aspects of adult life

PROFESSIONAL (career and job)

FINANCIAL (money affairs)

MATERIAL (things collected)

RECREATIONAL (time spent in play)

PHYSICAL (exercise, etc.)

SLEEP

INTELLECTUAL (knowledge, thinking)

EMOTIONAL (awareness and control of feelings)

SPIRITUAL/PHILOSOPHICAL

MARITAL (with your spouse)

PARENTAL (with your children)

FAMILIAL (with your parents)

SOCIAL (with your friends)

SOCIETAL (community work)

POLITICAL (political work)

---

and 10 is perfectly developed or "world-class" development. A person who can barely walk around the block without sitting down may be a 1 or a 2 on the *physical* dimension whereas the Olympic champion decathlete may be close to a 10. When you have marked your level of development on each dimension, you can shade in the area of your development across all dimensions. This will produce a profile that summarizes your perception of your life's development, a measure of balance, at this point in time. We have a little Excel spreadsheet that can do this for you automatically if you prefer. You can find this little tool at either www.CareerNextStep.com or http://faculty.darden.virginia.edu/ClawsonJ/.

3. On the Balance Wheel, draw another line around the wheel that notes your *desired* level of development on each dimension. If there's a gap between your current state of development and your desired state, this may suggest to you places where you'd like to focus more time, attention, and energy in the weeks ahead.

4. Consider the list of aspects of life in Figure 24.2. These are the same dimensions that appeared in Figure 24.1. Assess how much *time a*

Figure 24.3
Allocating time over the aspects of adult life

In the spaces below, write the number of hours you spent last week actually doing something in each area.

ASPECT OF LIFE	TIME I SPENT ON IT LAST WEEK
PROFESSIONAL	_____
FINANCIAL	_____
MATERIAL	_____
RECREATIONAL	_____
PHYSICAL	_____
SLEEP	_____
INTELLECTUAL	_____
EMOTIONAL	_____
SPIRITUAL /PHILOSOPHICAL	_____
MARITAL	_____
PARENTAL	_____
FAMILIAL	_____
SOCIAL	_____
SOCIETAL	_____
POLITICAL	_____
TOTAL	_____

There are 168 hours in a week. If your total exceeds 168, then you're multitasking. The number of "shadow hours" or hours above 168 is an indication of how much multitasking you're doing in a week. Some is probably okay. If you have a lot, you may be adding stress to your life.

---

week you spend on each one. If you have the inclination, you may wish to keep track of your time for a week since our memories of how we spend our time do not often match up with the realities. If not, think back on the previous week and try to allocate the time you spent on each dimension. Use the form in Figure 24.3 to write down your assessments of how much time you spent on each dimension last week.

Figure 24.4
STAGES of growth in terms of "maturity"

You can use the definitions here to help you decide what level of development you've reached, or want to reach, in each of the dimensions shown on the Balance Wheel in Figure 24.1.

1. **EMBRYONIC:** Unaware that the dimension exists and therefore pays no attention to it.
2. **YOUTH:** Aware that the dimension exists but does nothing about developing it.
3. **ADOLESCENT:** Aware that the dimension exists but believes that it can be developed later; therefore, does nothing about it now.
4. **YOUNG ADULT:** Aware that the dimension exists and concerned about developing it; has a superficial awareness that a person must work at developing it all along and makes modest efforts to develop it.
5. **MATURE ADULT:** Aware that the dimension exists and concerned about developing it; deeply cognizant of the need to develop the dimension constantly and working hard to develop it.

---

5. The definitions in Figure 24.4 suggest another way of thinking about your development on each aspect of life. You could ask yourself to what extent you have "matured" on each dimension. You may wish to keep these definitions in mind as you shade in your 1–10 development.
6. Now, consider the relationships between your definition of success, your current time allocations, and your level of development. What connections do you see? What disparities? Are there "flat spots" on your wheel diagram that concern you? How do they relate to your definition of success and your allocation of time? Do you want to do anything about them? How much time and talent will it take to make changes? If you make no changes in your time allocations, what will your development profile look like in 10 years? In 20 years?

Managing energy
Instructors burn lots of energy. It takes time and focus to prepare to teach, to manage and facilitate discussions during class, and to counsel students after class. We have come to believe that managing a successful

career in teaching requires not only good time management, but careful management of one's energy. As you look at and reflect on your Balance Wheel exercise, you may conclude that there are areas of your life that you'd like to spend more time and attention on. We'd argue that means spending more *energy*.

We invite you to think about how well you manage your energy. Do you consciously do things to enhance your energy and to minimize the energy drains in your daily schedule? Note below the things that either enhance or detract from your energy levels.

ENERGY INFLUENCERS

ENERGY ENHANCERS	ENERGY DRAINERS

What can you learn from your list above? If you need exercise daily to make sure that you can bring your best faculties to the classroom, perhaps you should figure out how to get that exercise every day. If your diet affects your energy level, perhaps you should figure out how to eat so that you have the highest levels of energy available to you when you enter the classroom. If you know of some people who are "energy suckers," can you manage your relationship and interactions with them so as to minimize the amount of energy they take from you?

Conclusion

Life is largely about choice. You can build the life structure that you wish – if you know what you want and are aware of how your choices thus far in life have contributed to your present state of development. By reflecting on your current developmental profile (the Balance Wheel) and then comparing that with your definition of success, perhaps you can see where you would like to spend more energy and where you'd like to spend less. Further, if you relax your concerns about *time management* a little and focus more on *energy management* perhaps you can do some things that will help you navigate the difficult demands and challenges of the professional instructor. Whether you work in academe or in the corporate world, our belief is that you can make choices that will leave you with a full measure of energy on a daily basis – pumped up and ready to go into the classroom, eager to meet your students, eager to see how they engage your material, and eager to learn with them jointly.

Further reading

Clawson, J. C., and M.E. Haskins, "Beating the Career Blues," *Academy of Management Executives* (August 2000), 91–102.

Csikszentmihalyi, Mihaly, *The Evolving Self: A Psychology for the Third Millennium*, New York: HarperCollins, 1993.

Fassel, Diane, *Working Ourselves to Death, and the Rewards of Recovery*, New York: Harper, 1990.

Glassner, William, *Choice Theory*, New York: Harper Perennial, 1999.

Lakein, Alan, *How to Get Control of Your Time and Your Life*, New York: Signet, 1996.

MacKenzie, R. Alec, *The Time Trap: The Classic Book on Time Management*, 3rd edition, New York: American Management Association, 1997.

Schein, Ed, *Career Dynamics*, Reading, MA: Addison-Wesley, 1978.

25 | Using teaching portfolios and course portfolios

RANDOLPH NEW[1]

> Of course, before we know he is a saint,
> there will have to be miracles.
>
> – Graham Greene

Professionals in fields such as art, photography, and architecture have long used portfolios to document and display their best work (Hutchings, 1998c, p. 13; Seldin, 2004, p. 3). Over the past fifteen years, portfolios have begun to be used more widely in higher education as tools for student, instructor, and institutional development. The portfolio can provide its audience with deeper and more meaningful evidence than simple description will normally allow, as on a résumé for example. In addition, the process of constructing the portfolio can lead to individual reflection and improvement.

This chapter describes *teaching portfolios* and *course portfolios* and provides guidance to individual instructors regarding their development and use. In addition to the individual benefits, teaching and course portfolios respond to calls for business schools and business instructors to take teaching more seriously and to develop the "teacher" role as fully as the "researcher" role (e.g., Frost and Fukami, 1997).

Teaching portfolios

A teaching portfolio is a collection of materials that document an individual's teaching performance, generally over a period of several years (Seldin, 2004, p. 3). It includes work samples and reflective commentary to reveal what was done and the thinking behind the teaching (Braskamp and Ory, 1994, p. 229). It is not an exhaustive compilation of all the documents and materials relevant to an individual's

---

[1] Robins School of Business, University of Richmond, Richmond, Virginia 23173, (804) 287–6497, e-mail rnew@richmond.edu.

teaching performance; rather it presents thoughtfully chosen information on teaching activities along with "indisputable evidence" of their effectiveness (Seldin, 2004, p. 3).

Seldin (2004, p. 3) estimates that as many as 2,000 colleges and universities in the US and Canada (where it is typically called a teaching "dossier") are now using or experimenting with teaching portfolios (up from only 10 or so institutions thought to be using portfolios in 1990). He also reports portfolios being used in Australia, Kenya, England, South Africa, Finland, Israel, and Malaysia.

Why prepare a teaching portfolio?

Teaching portfolios may be prepared for many reasons (Braskamp and Ory, 1994, p. 231; Seldin, 2004, p. 4):
- as part of documentation submitted in a job search
- as part of documentation submitted to a tenure and promotion committee
- as part of documentation submitted in a post-tenure review
- as part of documentation submitted for teaching awards, grants, or released time
- to empower instructors to choose documents and materials that, in their judgment, best reflect their performance as teachers, because it is not limited to items sought by administrators
- to stimulate teaching improvement, by providing a structured approach for self-reflection about teaching effectiveness and areas for potential improvement
- to foster an academic environment where teaching is thoughtfully practiced, assessed, and discussed
- to share teaching expertise and experience with less-experienced instructors
- to provide a written legacy to help future generations of teachers within the department or institution

An instructor might also prepare a teaching portfolio to make their teaching public and available for peer review by posting it on the Web, thereby contributing to the scholarship of teaching (Kahn, 2004, p. 37).[2] This idea has been debated, with those opposed arguing that

---

[2] The idea of portfolios contributing to a scholarship of teaching has been a driving force behind the course portfolio movement, and will be discussed further in the course portfolio section of this chapter.

individual teaching portfolios are too localized and too broad to be considered scholarship, and that innovations and other worthy evidence included in portfolios should be prepared as articles and published in refereed journals (Cox, 2004, p. 66).

The reasons for preparing the teaching portfolio are important to keep in mind as one considers what is to be included and how it is to be arranged.

Preparing the teaching portfolio

Although an individual instructor frequently works alone to prepare his or her teaching portfolio, it is recommended that when possible it be developed with the interaction and mentoring of a department chair, colleague, or instructional development specialist (Rodriquez-Farrar, n.d.; Seldin, 2004, p. 5). This would seem especially important when the portfolio is being developed for major personnel actions such as tenure or promotion.

Seldin (2004, p. 7) suggests following these eight steps to create the portfolio:

Step 1 – Planning: what is your purpose and audience? What evidence will they expect to find, and what types of evidence will be most convincing?

Step 2 – Summarize Teaching Responsibilities: in two or three paragraphs, identify courses taught in the past few years, their status (students taking, elective, etc.), and perhaps ancillary teaching activities (advising students or student organizations, etc.)

Step 3 – Describe your Approach to Teaching: a two to three page reflective statement about your teaching philosophy, objectives, strategies, and methods (why do you do what you do in teaching?). What are your beliefs about teaching? What are your aims for students, and why? How do your actions reflect your beliefs? What evidence will show that your actions reflect your beliefs? Examples? How do you apply your knowledge of pedagogy to your subject area specialization? How have your methods changed? What is your role in fostering critical thinking and life-long learning skills? How do you make decisions about content, resources, methods? What instructional methods have you developed? Innovative activities designed?

Step 4 – Select Items for the Portfolio: Figure 25.1 provides a list of possible items to include. Consider purpose and audience for the

Figure 25.1. *What to include in the teaching portfolio*[3]

1. Materials from Oneself

- statement of teaching roles and responsibilities, including course titles and numbers, enrollments, student status (undergraduate or graduate level), required or elective, and a brief description of the way each course is taught
- personal statement regarding teaching philosophy, strategies, objectives, methods, and procedures for evaluating student learning
- personal statement regarding teaching goals for next several years
- representative course syllabi, including any reflective comments on courses or syllabi
- course and instructional materials developed (for your courses), including study guides, case studies, annotated bibliographies, etc.
- if not included above, description of how any noncourse specific foci have been implemented (computer or other technology, student writing assignments, critical thinking efforts, etc.)

2. Teaching Development Activities

- description of steps taken to improve teaching effectiveness
- description of curricular revisions, including new course projects, materials, and assignments
- participation in programs to sharpen teaching skills
- contributions to programs about teaching effectiveness
- research that directly contributes to teaching
- grants secured for teaching-related activities
- committee work related to teaching and learning
- participation in any other off-campus activities related to teaching (e.g., consulting used to develop classroom cases or examples)

3. Materials from Others

- student course or teaching evaluation data, with professor's analysis and comments
- honors or other recognition from colleagues or students, such as student teaching or advising awards, or departmental statements regarding professor's teaching
- performance data or reviews as a faculty advisor
- statements from colleagues who have reviewed professor's course materials and/or have observed the professor in the classroom

[3] Adapted from Braskamp and Ory (1994: 230–31); Rodriquez-Farrar (n.d.), and Seldin (2004: 10–12).

Figure 25.1. (*cont.*)

- invitations from outside groups to speak about or present research regarding teaching
- videotape of the faculty member teaching a typical class
- evidence of help given to colleagues on course or teaching development

4. Products of Good Teaching

- student scores on pre- and post-course exams
- examples of graded student course work, showing examples of excellent, average, and poor performance (could include exams, essays, case analyses, journals, papers, individual or group projects, videotaped student presentations, etc.)
- evidence of student early semester learning versus end of term performance
- statements from former students and alumni (from exit interviews, surveys, letters, etc.)
- evidence of influence on student career choice, including assistance given (e.g., references) to secure student employment or graduate school admissions
- successive drafts of student work along with professor's feedback
- a record of students who succeed in advanced field of study
- statements from colleague at other schools on how well students have been prepared for graduate school
- record of students taking future courses, independent studies, or internships from the professor
- publications authored by students
- graded appraisal tools showing a clear relationship between appraisal methods and course objectives

portfolio, as well as your particular personal preferences and style of teaching, academic discipline, and particular courses.

Step 5 – Prepare Statements on Each Item: in preparing your statements, consider whether you have a variety of measures of your teaching effectiveness, dates and topics for each, you have provided documentation for each claim made, you have cross-referenced your narrative with the appendices.

Step 6 – Arrange the Items in Order: the sequence of statements about accomplishments in each area is determined by their intended use.

Step 7 – Compile the Supporting Data: evidence supporting all items mentioned in the portfolio is retained by the instructor and made available for review and/or copies placed in the appendix. This would include, for example, letters from colleagues, original student evaluations, samples of student work, etc.

Step 8 – Housing the Portfolio: typically the portfolio material is housed in a single one- to two-inch, three-ring binder, with identification tabs for separate sections.

Seldin (2004) contends that the vast majority of instructors can present an effective teaching portfolio in eight to ten pages plus supporting appendix material (pgs. 12–13). He reports that most instructors can prepare this (or at least reach third draft stage) in 12–15 hours spread over several days, especially if working with a skilled mentor (Seldin, 2004: 13). Is the time and energy required to prepare a teaching portfolio worth the effort? Seldin states that "in the view of the nearly four hundred faculty members I've personally mentored as they prepared their portfolios, the answer is a resounding yes" (2000: 44).

Criticisms

Burns (2000) is highly critical of the claim that teaching portfolios improve teaching, given an absence of supporting empirical studies. Although many who have developed a teaching portfolio report improvement, Burns notes that these claims seldom consider possible extraneous factors such as placebo effects. She expresses other reservations as well: generalizations about their effectiveness may be limited by selection bias; the preparation costs (time, effort) may be significantly understated by proponents; the reliability and validity of instructor or administrative judgments about teaching effectiveness may be no better with portfolios than when based on other measures (such as student ratings); and portfolio preparation may actually be counterproductive, especially for new instructors who might spend too much time developing one at the expense of other priorities and even perhaps to the detriment of their (perceived) teaching effectiveness.

Current teaching portfolio resources

Seldin (2004) includes chapters describing how teaching portfolios are used at seven public and private institutions of various sizes: Drexel University (Lim, 2004), Miami University of Ohio (Cox, 2004), Oxford College of Emory University (Frady, 2004), Pace University

(Anstendig and Knapp, 2004), Rutgers University (Devanas, 2004), Texas A&M University (Simpson and Layne, 2004), and the University of Evansville (Wandel, 2004). He also provides 22 sample portfolios (without appendices) from 16 disciplines (accounting is the only business area included).

Course portfolios

The course portfolio can be considered a subset of the teaching portfolio, designed to accomplish certain purposes more fully (Hutchings, 1998c: 13). While the teaching portfolio provides a somewhat comprehensive account of one's teaching performance over multiple years, the course portfolio focuses on what transpired within a single course. Compared to the teaching portfolio, the course portfolio has developed more recently, is not as widely used, is less well defined in format and content, and is more widely described as contributing to the academic discipline through the scholarship of teaching. This latter point is further discussed below.

Why prepare a course portfolio?

The idea of the course portfolio emerged from an American Association of Higher Education (AAHE) project begun in 1994 to build upon Boyer's (1990) work on the scholarships of discovery, integration, application, and teaching.[4] The project goal was "to create ways to treat teaching as a scholarly activity that can be shared, documented, studied, reviewed, rewarded, and continuously improved – and that leads to learning" (Miller, 1998: v). During the project the course

---

[4] In his widely discussed book, Boyer argues that for many reasons the academy must move beyond its dominant view that scholarship is limited to traditional research, with publication as the primary yardstick by which scholarly productivity is measured. He advocates that we return to the definition used in earlier times, with scholarship referring to a variety of creative work carried on in a variety of places, with its integrity measured by the demonstrated ability to think, communicate and learn. He suggests an enlarged definition that would more realistically reflect the full range of faculty work. This includes four separate, overlapping functions: discovery (what academics generally mean by "research"), integration (across disciplines or into larger intellectual patterns), application (responsible application of knowledge to consequential problems), and teaching (transmitting, transforming, and extending knowledge through interaction between teachers and students).

portfolio came to be seen as potentially the most effective method for accomplishing this purpose. As a result, twelve of the instructor project participants explored the idea further by constituting what became known as the AAHE Course Portfolio Working Group. Most of this group developed individual course portfolios which were eventually presented as case studies in a volume published by AAHE (Hutchings, 1998b). None of the course portfolios were in a business discipline.

Course portfolios serve three basic purposes: contribution to the field, personal growth, and rewards (Hutchings, 1998d: 47). They contribute to the field of teaching by directly connecting teaching and scholarship and by adding to the knowledge base of what teaching effectiveness means within a given course area and how to achieve it. In the view of Lee Shulman (1998), former Stanford professor and President of the Carnegie Foundation for the Advancement of Teaching, who was advisor to faculty involved in the AAHE course portfolio project:

The course portfolio is a central element in the argument that teaching and scholarship are neither antithetical nor incompatible. Indeed, my argument is that every course is inherently an investigation, an experiment, a journey motivated by purpose and beset by uncertainty. A course, therefore, in its design, enactment, and analysis, is as much an act of inquiry and invention as any other activity more traditionally called "research" or the scholarship of discovery ...

For an activity to be designated as scholarship, it should manifest at least three key characteristics: It should be public, susceptible to critical review and evaluation, and accessible for exchange and use by other members of one's scholarly community ... When we portray those ways in which teaching can become scholarship through course portfolios, therefore, we seek approaches that render teaching public, critically evaluated, and useable by others in the community. (p. 5)

The scholarship of teaching and learning is also a growing field of inquiry within various of the business disciplines. For example, in management science there is an increasing array of disciplinary outlets, a new genre of writing draws on the personal stories and learnings of prominent management professors, and the financial and moral support for scholarly work on teaching provided by schools, professional associations, and accrediting agencies has increased (Bilimoria and Fukami: 2002). Course portfolios have been developed within some business disciplines (e.g., New et al., 2000; Peer Review Project, n.d.)

but have not yet had a significant role in the scholarship of teaching and learning for the business disciplines.

In addition to contributing to the scholarship of learning and teaching, course portfolios can serve a variety of personal growth and reward purposes:

– promote individual course improvement by requiring systematic reflection and documentation that aids perception and memory (e.g., Cutler, 1998) and focusing attention on student learning (e.g., Chein, 1998; Martsolf, 1998)
– provide personal stimulation, growth, and development at various points in one's career (e.g., Cutler, 1998; Heiss, 1998; Hutchings, 1998a; Langsam, 1998)
– stimulate or aid discussion among peers about course goals, teaching practices, and student learning (e.g., Cutler, 1998; Hutchings, 1998a)
– provide information on course effectiveness to peers and/or other interested parties, including in personnel reviews (e.g., Bass, 1998; Bernstein, 1998; Cerbin, 1996; Cutler, 1998; Martsolf, 1998, Mignon, 1998; Passow, 1998). In this way they respond to those who believe "to improve business teaching on a broad front [and] to give appropriate rewards for good teaching to the many teachers who are not engaged in primary research, new techniques are needed that will give schools objective measures of expertise that are as powerful and generally respected as the peer review process" (Danos, 2004).

Defining features and relationship to other forms of scholarship

Hutchings (1998c) identified three defining features in the course portfolios prepared in the AAHE project. First, they focused on the unfolding of a single course. This provided several advantages (Huber, 1998): (a) The course is both the most common and most strategic "unit" of teaching, (b) it is "within the course that knowledge of the field intersects with knowledge about the particular students and their learning"; and (c) "courses, like research, are acts of intellectual invention, and . . . the way . . . one teaches a course enacts the way one thinks about and pursues one's field of study" (p. 32).

The second defining feature of a course portfolio is its focus on student learning and providing relevant evidence for it. Bernstein (1998) argues that the major benefit of the course portfolio, relative to the many activities that instructors can engage in to develop their teaching, lies in uncovering how effectively course goals for student learning are being met. He observes that this focus on "results" is also true for traditional academic research, where a scholar's work generally describes results and claims a relationship between the described activity and those results (p. 77).

The third defining feature of a course portfolio is its investigation into the relationship among course goals, strategies, methods, and outcomes. More than a description of what the teacher typically does, it is "an account of what happens when he or she does something deliberately and explicitly different. It is not, that is, a report of what *is* but a purposeful experiment and investigation – a process, if you will, of scholarly inquiry into what *might* be" (Hutchings, 1998c: 15). This perspective has been part of the course portfolio idea since its beginning, as indicated by Cerbin (1996), a professor of psychology who many see as the first practitioner of the approach:

Ernest Boyer's *Scholarship Reconsidered* appeared, and I was very struck by his notion of the scholarship of teaching ... thinking about teaching as scholarly inquiry began to lead me in the direction of something I had not seen anyone else doing: a portfolio that focused on the course rather than on all of one's teaching. Being a social scientist, I began to think of each course ... as a kind of laboratory – not as a controlled experiment, of course, but as a setting in which you start out with goals for student learning, then you adopt teaching practices that you think will accomplish these, and along the way you can watch and see if your practices are helping to accomplish your goals, collecting evidence about effects and impact ... [O]ne thing I now see is that the course portfolio is really like a scholarly manuscript – not a finished publication, but a manuscript, a draft, of ongoing inquiry. (1996: 52–3)

With its focus on the individual course, each of which can be viewed as an "experiment" focusing on student learning, those involved in the course portfolio movement believe that course portfolios more closely resemble the products of the scholarship of discovery than does the broader teaching portfolio. As described earlier in this chapter, the teaching portfolio is designed to provide a more comprehensive account of one's teaching practice over a longer portion of a career, and rarely shares the more detailed and defining features of the course portfolio.

Preparing the course portfolio

While the form and format of course portfolios vary widely and are currently a work in progress, some broad areas have been recommended for inclusion (Peer Review Project, n.d):

1. A statement of the content and goals of the course,
2. A plan to accomplish key objectives in student learning,
3. Evidence and assessment of student achievement toward these goals, and
4. A reflective narrative on the relation among the preceding three elements.

Table 2 identifies more specific components that would be reasonable to include within these broad areas. We have seen no estimates of the length of a course portfolio or the length of time required to develop it. Our own experience with developing a course portfolio and our reviews of those of others leads us to believe that it demands considerably more effort and time than developing a teaching portfolio.

Figure 25.2. *What to include in the course portfolio*[5]

MAJOR SECTION (sample length given on website)	DISCUSSION TOPIC
Portfolio Purpose (1 page)	• Goal(s)/objective(s) of the portfolio (1/2 page) • Personal reflections on the chosen course, describing major objectives and their attainment • Question(s) you would like readers to address when reviewing the portfolio
Course Design (3–4 pages)	• Description of course and its context • Who are students in course • Summary of course goals and learning objectives • Place of the course within department and university curricula

[5] Adapted from the Peer Review Project (n.d.) conducted by the University of Nebraska, Indiana University, Kansas State University, University of Michigan, and Texas A&M University and funded by the Fund for the Improvement of Post-Secondary Education (FIPSE).

Figure 25.2. (*contd.*)

Teaching Methods (2–5 pages)	• Teaching methods, course materials, and course activities (e.g., lectures, labs, discussions) • Evaluation mechanisms (exams, quizzes, homework, participation, etc.)
Outcomes/Student Learning (2–5 pages)	• Evidence of student learning; indicators of effectiveness • Progressive development and attainment of learning objectives
Reflections on Course (3–6 pages)	• What you have learned in developing this portfolio • Future plans for course (e.g., addressing misconceptions, problem areas)
Additional Materials	Most portfolios include a copy of the course syllabus and examples of student work. The latter should include only work upon which you offer detailed reflection. It would also normally include only those key areas (paragraphs, sections, questions, that are key to your reflections)

Criticisms

The previous criticisms of the teaching portfolio by Burns (2000) can also be directed at the course portfolio. In addition, given the focus of the course portfolio on contributing to the scholarship of teaching, the extent to which course portfolios will become more widespread depends on (1) the valuation of the scholarship of teaching by higher education in general and in individual fields, and (2) whether course portfolios come to be accepted as legitimate contributions to a scholarship of teaching.

Other criticisms we have heard include:

– scholarly attention to teaching technique may diminish the natural energy and spontaneity that many instructors believe is important to effective teaching

- following a recipe, no matter how scholarly the development of that recipe may have been, may not work from context to context or from personality to personality of instructor
- instructors may not want to "give away" the intellectual and other investments they have made in course development
- in the absence of institutional encouragement and reward, many instructors will not see the benefit to investing time and energy into scholarly work that may not be published and may not "count" toward institutional promotion.

In the current system of university instructor work and rewards, these inhibitors have limited the development of the portfolio movement including its use in the business disciplines. However, we believe this presents an opportunity for some instructors (and their professional organizations) to provide intellectual leadership in what could eventually become an established and important domain of scholarship. Perhaps one day there will be a "gallery" of peer-reviewed business course portfolios, some developed by the leading scholar-teachers in the field, available for review at the Web sites of some of our professional associations.

Current course portfolio projects and resources

A number of efforts have been made to accumulate and disseminate knowledge about the course portfolio and to contribute to the scholarship of teaching and learning. The individual course portfolios that were produced in the AAHE project are described in Hutchings (1998b). A subsequent AAHE edited volume focuses on various types of electronic portfolios and includes four course portfolios (Cambridge, 2001).

Over 175 course portfolios have been developed as a result of the Peer Review Project (n.d.) initiated by the University of Nebraska and including Indiana University, Kansas State University, University of Michigan, and Texas A&M University. Twenty of these are publicly available, including three from faculty in business and accounting.

The Carnegie Academy for the Scholarship of Teaching and Learning (CASTL) sponsors faculty research into teaching and learning though their Carnegie Scholars Fellowship Program. Thirteen course portfolio projects have been developed by Carnegie Scholars and are exhibited in Carnegie's Knowledge Media Laboratory (n.d.). These courses are in various fields including music, psychology, nursing, mathematics, education, chemistry, and history (none in business). Several course portfolios developed through this initiative are also described in Hutchings (2000).

The CASTL program also works with selected scholarly and professional societies to provide networking opportunities and an invitational small grants program. There are currently 23 registered societies, and the grant program has led to several discipline-specific course portfolio projects including two samples provided by the American Historical Association (n.d.).

Other individual course portfolios are available (after free registration) through the Portfolio Clearinghouse (n.d.) of the American Association of Higher Education or are posted at individual university sites.

Conclusion

Many instructors have reported that developing a teaching or course portfolio was a valuable and worthwhile experience. While there are no empirical studies to support a general claim, we believe that the large number of individuals reporting success indicates that portfolios can be effective when developed for appropriate purposes and using appropriate methods. Our intent in this chapter was to provide some guidance to help individual instructors make good choices.

Further reading

American Historical Association Web site: http://www.historians.org/teaching/AAHE/aahecover.html (accessed 29 January 2005).

Anstendig, L., and C.A. Knapp, "Teaching portfolios at Pace University: a culture in transition." In P. Seldin (ed.), *The Teaching Portfolio: A Practical Guide to Improved Performance and Promotion/Tenure Decisions*: 77–83. Bolton, MA: Anker, 2004.

Bass, R., "A hypertext portfolio for an experimental American Literature course." In P. Hutchings (ed.), *The Course Portfolio: How Faculty Can Examine their Teaching to Advance Practice and Improve Student Learning*, Washington, DC: American Association for Higher Education, 1998, 91–96.

Bernstein, D., 1998. "Putting the focus on student learning," In P. Hutchings (ed.), *The Course Portfolio: How Faculty Can Examine their Teaching to Advance Practice and Improve Student Learning,* Washington, DC: American Association for Higher Education, 77–83.

Bilimoria, D., and C. Fukami, "The scholarship of teaching and learning in the management sciences: disciplinary style and content." In M. T. Huber and S. P. Morreale (eds.), *Disciplinary Styles in the Scholarship of Teaching and Learning: Exploring Common Ground*, Washington, DC: American Association for Higher Education, 125–42.

Boyer, E. L., 1990. *Scholarship Reconsidered: Priorities of the Professoriate*, Princeton: Carnegie Foundation for the Advancement of Teaching.

Braskamp, L. A., and J. C. Ory, 1994. *Assessing Faculty Work: Enhancing Individual and Institutional Performance*, San Francisco: Jossey-Bass.

Burns, C. W., 2000. Teaching Portfolios: another perspective. *Academe*, 86, 1: 44–7.

Cambridge, B. L. 2001. (ed.), *Electronic Portfolios: Emerging Practices in Student, Faculty, and Institutional Learning*, Washington, DC: American Association for Higher Education.

Carnegie's Knowledge Media Laboratory Web site: http://gallery.carnegiefoundation.org/ (accessed 25 January 2005).

Cerbin, W., 1996. "Inventing a new genre: the course portfolio at the University of Wisconsin-La Crosse." In P. Hutchings (ed.), *Making Teaching Community Property: A Menu for Peer Collaboration and Peer Review*: 52–56, Washington, DC: American Association for Higher Education.

Chein, O., 1998. "A course portfolio in mathematics." In P. Hutchings (ed.), *The Course Portfolio: How Faculty Can Examine their Teaching to Advance Practice and Improve Student Learning*: 39–45, Washington, DC: American Association for Higher Education.

Cox, M. D. 2004. "Using multiple pathways to foster portfolio development at Miami University of Ohio." In P., Seldin, *The Teaching Portfolio: A Practical Guide to Improved Performance and Promotion/Tenure Decisions*: 61–70. Bolton, MA: Anker.

Cutler, W. W., III, 1998. "Writing a course portfolio for an introductory survey course in American history," In P. Hutchings (ed.), *The Course Portfolio: How Faculty Can Examine Their Teaching to Advance Practice and Improve Student Learning*: 19–24. Washington, DC: American Association for Higher Education.

Danos, P. 2004. "Finding the link: good teaching relies on research." *eNewsline*, 3 (5), St. Louis: AACSB International – the Association to Advance Collegiate Schools of Business.

Devanas, M. A. 2004. "The Teaching Portfolio at Rutgers University." In P. Seldin, *The Teaching Portfolio: A Practical Guide to Improved Performance and Promotion/Tenure Decisions*: 84–91. Bolton, MA: Anker.

Frady, M. 2004. "Developing and implementing the Teaching Portfolio at Oxford College of Emory University." In P. Seldin, *The Teaching Portfolio: A Practical Guide to Improved Performance and Promotion/Tenure Decisions*: 71–76. Bolton, MA: Anker.

Frost, P. J., and C.V. Fukami, teaching effectiveness in the organizational sciences: recognizing and enhancing the scholarship of teaching. *Academy of Management Journal*, 40: 1271–82.

Heiss, M.A. 1998. "A course portfolio for a colloquium in 20th-century American foreign relations." In P. Hutchings (ed.), *The Course Portfolio: How Faculty Can Examine their Teaching to Advance Practice and Improve Student Learning*: 35–38, Washington, DC: American Association for Higher Education.

Huber, M.T. 1998. "Why now? Course portfolios in context." In P. Hutchings (ed.), *The Course Portfolio: How Faculty Can Examine their Teaching to Advance Practice and Improve Student Learning*: 29–34, Washington, DC: American Association for Higher Education.

Hutchings, P. 1998a. A course portfolio for a creative writing course. In P. Hutchings (ed.), *The Course Portfolio: How Faculty Can Examine their Teaching to Advance Practice and Improve Student Learning*: 85–90, Washington, DC: American Association for Higher Education.

Hutchings, P. (ed). 1998b. *The Course Portfolio: How Faculty Can Examine their Teaching to Advance Practice and Improve Student Learning*: 85–90, Washington, DC: American Association for Higher Education.

Hutchings, P. 1998c. Defining features and significant functions of the course portfolio. In P. Hutchings (ed.), *The Course Portfolio: How Faculty Can Examine their Teaching to Advance Practice and Improve Student Learning*: 13–18, Washington, DC: American Association for Higher Education.

Hutchings, P. 1998d. "How to develop a course portfolio." In P. Hutchings (ed.), *The Course Portfolio: How Faculty Can Examine their Teaching to Advance Practice and Improve Student Learning*: 47–55, Washington, DC: American Association for Higher Education.

Hutchings, P. 2000. "Introduction: Approaching the scholarship of teaching and learning." In P. Hutchings (ed.), *Opening Lines: Approaches to the Scholarship of Teaching and Learning*: 1–10, Menlo Park, CA: The Carnegie Foundation for the Advancement of Teaching.

Kahn, S. 2004. "Making good work public through electronic teaching portfolios." In P. Seldin, *The Teaching Portfolio: A Practical Guide* to *Improved Performance and Promotion/Tenure Decisions* (3rd edn): 36–50, Bolton, MA: Anker.

Langsam, D. M. 1998. "A course portfolio for midcareer reflection." In P. Hutchings (ed.), *The Course Portfolio: How Faculty Can Examine their Teaching to Advance Practice and Improve Student Learning*: 57–63, Washington, DC: American Association for Higher Education.

Lim, T. 2004. The Teaching Portfolio Program at Drexel University. In P., Seldin, *The Teaching Portfolio: A Practical Guide to Improved Performance and Promotion/Tenure Decisions*: 52–60, Bolton, MA: Anker.

Martsolf, D. 1998. "A course portfolio for a graduate nursing course." In P. Hutchings (ed.), *The Course Portfolio: How Faculty Can Examine their Teaching to Advance Practice and Improve Student Learning*: 25–28, Washington, DC: American Association for Higher Education.

Mignon, C. W. 1998. "Post-tenure review: A case study of a course portfolio within a personnel file." In P. Hutchings (ed.), *The Course Portfolio: How Faculty Can Examine their Teaching to Advance Practice and Improve Student Learning*: 65–70, Washington, DC: American Association for Higher Education.

Miller, M. A. 1998. "Preface." In P. Hutchings (ed.), *The Course Portfolio: How Faculty Can Examine their Teaching to Advance Practice and Improve Student Learning*: v-vi, Washington, DC: American Association for Higher Education.

New, J. R., Clawson, J. G., and Coughlan, R.S. 2000. *The Course Portfolio: A Tool for Improving the Scholarship and Practice of OB Teaching?* Paper presented at the annual meeting of the Organizational Behavior Teaching Conference, Carrollton, Georgia.

Passow, E. 1998. "A portfolio that makes a point." In P. Hutchings (ed.), *The Course Portfolio: How Faculty Can Examine their Teaching to Advance Practice and Improve Student Learning*: 71–75, Washington, DC: American Association for Higher Education.

Peer Review Project. n.d. Retrieved January 29, 2005, from http://unl.edu/peerrev/examples.html

Portfolio Clearninghouse. n.d. Retrieved January 29, 2005 from www.aahe

Rodriquez-Farrar, H. B. n.d. The Teaching Portfolio. Last retrieved January 25, 2005, from http://www.brown.edu/Administration/Sheridan_Center/publications/teacport/html

Seldin, P. 2004. *The Teaching Portfolio: A Practical Guide to Improved Performance and Promotion/Tenure Decisions* (3rd edn). Bolton, MA: Anker.

Seldin, P. 2000. "Teaching portfolios: a positive appraisal." *Academe*, 86(1): 37–44.

Shulman, L. S. 1998. Course anatomy: The dissection and analysis of knowledge through teaching. In P. Hutchings (ed.), *The Course Portfolio: How Faculty Can Examine their Teaching to Advance Practice and Improve Student Learning:* 5–12, Washington, DC: American Association for Higher Education.

Simpson, N. J., & Layne, J. E. L. 2004. Teaching portfolios at Texas A&M University: reflections on a decade of practice. In Seldin, P., *The Teaching Portfolio: A Practical Guide to Improved Performance and Promotion/Tenure Decisions* (3rd edn): 36–50. Bolton, MA: Anker.

Wandel, T. L. 2004. Teaching portfolios at the University of Evansville. In P. Seldin, *The Teaching Portfo-lio: A Practical Guide to Improved Performance and Promotion/Tenure Decisions* (3rd edn): 36–50. Bolton, MA: Anker.

26 | *Conclusion: is this on the exam?*

MARK E. HASKINS AND
JAMES G. S. CLAWSON

A man who carries a cat by the tail learns
something he can learn in no other way.
— Mark Twain

Put me in, Coach — I'm ready to play today.
— John Fogarty

We all want to do well whatever it is that we do. We strive to do
that through preparation and "getting in the game." Whether you are
just starting out as an instructor or have been at it for a couple of
decades, there is always some aspect of the teaching craft waiting to
be explored, experimented with, and enjoyed. This book was born of
a desire to encourage and arm instructors to be committed stewards of
a sacred trust: helping others to learn. No book can comprehensively
cover the full gamut of topics embedded in that objective. We have,
however, attempted to share our insights, born of trial and error, success
and failure, and years of debate and discussion. If this book is an
encouragement to you, we are thankful for that. If this book shortens
your "trial" time and minimizes your "errors," we are thankful for
that, too.

As we think back over our combined 18 years as college students,
there are several instructors that we clearly remember as excellent at
what they did. What was it about those instructors that so engaged us,
so inspired us, and in large measure enticed us into a teaching career?
Three attributes stand out. First, they each brought their subject matter
alive — making it interesting, relevant, and understandable. Second,
they conducted themselves in and out of the classroom in a manner
that was approachable and that encouraged and invited us to join
them in a journey of discovery and learning where it was not only
okay, but valued, to ask questions and to say, "I don't know, let's go

480

find out." Last, they were superb professionals – always prepared, very fair, and they wore their well-earned respect graciously and carefully. Who among us does not want to be thought of by those sitting in our classrooms in similar ways?

Throughout this book, we have discussed issues and ideas pertaining to two sides of the same coin – learning and teaching. We have striven to provide insight into the portals for adult learning and some tried and true tools and techniques for creating contexts conducive to learning. We cannot, however, close this book without acknowledging the crucial role of an instructor's values, assumptions, beliefs, and expectations (VABEs). These, too are an important part of the mix.

VABEs

The things that people assume and believe deeply affect their behavior. This is especially true of teachers. What instructors believe about how adults learn will shape what they do in the classroom. Carl Rogers made this very clear more than 40 years ago in his brief remarks to a Harvard conference on teaching and student-centered learning. His assumptions or beliefs about how people teach and learn touched a number of well-known and credentialed teachers at the level of their core values and caused a minor firestorm of discussion.[1] Among his controversial premises were, whatever you can teach to another must be inconsequential, only learning that influences behavior has value, real learning comes from experience not from the teachings of others, and experience based learning can hardly be communicated to others. Rogers acknowledged that he was not sure himself that he believed the premises he made, however, by making them, he caused many in the room to question and debate their own assumptions about teaching and learning.

Here are some assumptions that will surely affect your approach to teaching. We invite you to consider which if any might be closer to your beliefs, and what the implications of all of them might be for how a person approaches teaching.

---

[1] Carl Rogers, "Personal Thoughts on Teaching and Learning," *On Becoming a Person: A Therapist's View of Psychotherapy* (New York: Houghton Mifflin, 1961, 1995), pp. 273–78.

Assumption	Implication for Me
Teachers speak, students listen.	
Students who can repeat concepts will use them.	
Adults learn best by being actively involved.	
Ideas are interesting in and of themselves regardless of whether a person's behavior changes or not.	
Tell them what you're going to tell them, tell them, and then tell them what you told them.	
Teaching is not "entertaining."	
Teaching is about content not packaging.	
Teaching is tertiary to research.	
Exams reflect what people "know."	
People learn by doing.	
People learn by seeing.	
People learn by hearing.	
People will respond to data and logic.	
True learning is nonemotional.	
You cannot teach anything.	
There is always a correct answer.	
Most students are clueless.	
The purpose of teaching is to pass on knowledge.	
Effective learning requires reflection time.	
Most people know (don't know) what's right for them.	
Much good learning is about discipline and repetition.	
People learn because they have to, not because they want to.	
Learning is fun (boring).	
Students should not cheat.	

These statements may or may not match your beliefs about teaching. What *are* your beliefs about teaching and learning? And what do they imply for your instruction?

My VABEs about Teaching and Learning	Implications for Me

As you review your beliefs about teaching, you may discover some implications that trouble you. We have. We think that's good. Those who profess to influence the lives of others ought to, we think, be constantly reflecting on what they think they know and how they go about sharing that with others. As Mark wrote in the preface to this book, none of us can teach in the way that others teach. Teaching, or perhaps more accurately, facilitating learning is so closely linked to a person's core values, assumptions, beliefs, and expectations about the way the world is or should be that one cannot simply imitate what others do. In the end, both teaching and learning are profoundly intimate endeavors, perhaps infinitely varied. That said, ignoring what others have learned about teaching and learning doesn't seem wise. There is much we can learn from what others have done and written about.

In closing

You are never going to be tested on the content of this book – thank goodness those days are over, right? You are going to be tested, though, every time you walk to the front of a classroom. In that special place, you are going to be pitted against your own desire to excel and the expectations of those sitting before you. During that hour or two, you have implicitly asked those in attendance to invest time with you under the assumption that the journey of discovery that you will take them on will be worth their time. As we all know, time is the one resource that once gone, can *never* be regained. We must, therefore, hold dear the time given to us by those attending our classes. To do otherwise is to cheat them of something valuable.

Thomas Jefferson, a revered former citizen of the community where we live, has a resume rivaled by no one. Indeed, among other notable accomplishments he was the third president of the United States, a vice president of the United States, the governor of Virginia, minister to France, secretary of state under George Washington, a path-breaking botanist, a well-studied linguist, a renowned architect, an indefatigable inventor, and the visionary sponsor of the Lewis and Clark expedition. He was also author of his own epitaph. He left instructions that his gravestone was to read (and it does – we have seen it with our own eyes): "Here was buried Thomas Jefferson, author of the Declaration of American Independence, of the statute of Virginia for religious freedom, and father of the University of Virginia." Clearly, many of his other accomplishments and contributions to the world could have been the foci of his epitaph. Yet he chose just those three aspects of his life to mention, and he instructed his survivors to add "not a word more." We believe he focused on these three accomplishments because he had a passion for freedom, for ideas, and for education. Our own classrooms should be about freedom, ideas, and education. As we each, in our own ways, build resumes listing books, articles, consultancies, and ever-increasing positions of responsibility, let's also strive for a worthy legacy of exercising our freedom to explore new ideas and helping others learn well.

Index